Socialism Since 1889

Dedicated to Freddy Anderson:
Poet, Dramatist and Independent Writer

Socialism Since 1889
A Biographical History

James D. Young

Barnes & Noble Books
Totowa, New Jersey

First published in the United States of America in 1988 by
Barnes & Noble Books
81 Adams Drive, Totowa, New Jersey, 07512

First published in Great Britain in 1988 by
Pinter Publishers Limited
25 Floral Street, London WC2E 9DS

ISBN 0-389-20813-2

Library of Congress Cataloging-in-Publication Data

Young, James D., 1931–
   Socialism since 1889 : a biographical history / by James D. Young.
     p. cm.
   Bibliography: p.
   Includes index.
   ISBN 0-389-20813-2
   1. Socialism—History—19th century. 2. Socialism—History—20th
century. 3. Socialists—Biography. I. Title.
HX39.Y78   1989   88-23588
335′.009—dc19   CIP

Printed in Great Britain

Contents

Acknowledgements

The vague ambition to write a history of socialism developed long before I aspired to become a University teacher. (The ambition was environmentally-engendered within my own 'totalitarian' labyrinth of socialist dissidents. As adversaries of the advocates of socialism-from-above within the divided House of Labour, we sought to spread socialist enlightenment. This forced us to go back to the sources of the crisis of international socialism in the late nineteenth century.) Then, when the organisers of an international cultural festival in Hamburg in 1985 invited me to give a lecture on the socialist-humanism of Antonio Gramsci and Rosa Luxemburg, the plan to produce *Socialism Since 1889: A Biographical History* ultimately began to crystallise. But the precise shape and form of my history of international socialism since 1889 owes a great deal to the literary sensitivity of Vanessa Couchman, my editor at Pinter Publishers. It had, however, been germinating for a long time beforehand.

Although Edwin Muir, the distinguished Scottish poet and literary figure, influenced my understanding of totalitarian 'socialism' in Eastern Europe after the Second World War, the insights he helped me to develop have been cumulative and enduring. Certainly, I feel a special intellectual debt to my friend Seymour Papert. It was he who, in 1956, introduced me to the then Samizdat books and pamphlets of C.L.R. James. Now the author of the brilliant best-seller *Mindstorms* (New York, 1980) and a world authority on computers at the Massachusetts Institute of Technology, Seymour had a profound influence on my development as a labour historian. In those days of austerity when *almost* everything in our labyrinth was subordinated to the struggle for socialism, Seymour was the most intellectual, the most critical and open-minded, and the least pretentious person that I encountered in the labour movement in London.

At a time when I was writing for obscure left-wing newspapers in Britain and America, Seymour Papert encouraged me to write about working-class life, experience and politics from the centre of my own experiences, insights and, as he put it, 'artistic vision'. In touch with Cornelius Castoriadis and the 'Socialisme ou Barbarie' group in Paris, Raya Dunayevskaya and the News and Letters group in Detroit, and C.L.R. James and the Correspondence group in London, Seymour stimulated me to read the writings of George Padmore and C.L.R. James. Although he did not belong to the same socialist group as James, he was very enthusiastic about the *Black Jacobins* (1938), *Mariners, Renegades and Castaways* (1953) and, above all, *Facing Reality* (1958). In reaching back – however tenuously, and perhaps without being conscious of what he was doing – to the 'lost world' of the socialist historiography of the Second International and the earlier world of classical Marxism, James's books provided a new generation of socialists with a beacon of enlightenment in an increasingly brutal, disoriented and bewildering world.

Before offering a formal acknowledgement to individual authors and publishers who have granted me permission to quote extracts from books on the history of socialism, I wish to emphasise that the extensive footnotes at the end of *Socialism Since 1889: A Biographical History* are an inadequate guide to the archives I have researched in Scotland, England, Holland, America, Austria and Israel. Moreover, I owe a special debt to Herbert Steiner and Barry McLoughlin, Hal Draper and Irena Gantar-Godina for translating obscure socialist documents into English. Arthur Lipow obtained rare pamphlets and provided me with hospitality in his home in London; and in New York Sam Bottone introduced me to veteran American socialists who were happy to share their memories of past events with me.

Although I did not begin to write *Socialism Since 1889: A Biographical History* until 1986, I can now locate its origins and evolution in some of the articles I published in the *Political Quarterly*, *New Politics*, *Labor History*, the *Bulletin of the Society for the Study of Labour History* and *Survey* in the 1960s. The germination of *Socialism Since 1889: A Biographical History* was assisted, however, by the generosity of Phyllis and Julius Jacobson and Daniel Leab in allowing me to develop some of my ideas on Antonio Gramsci, Rosa Luxemburg and Daniel De Leon in the pages of *New Politics* and *Labor History*. But I would not have been able to develop my ideas at all if both the Carnegie Trust for the Universities of Scotland and the British Academy had not provided me with research grants to work in the archives of the Socialist Party of America, the Socialist Labour Party and the Socialist League in Duke University, North Carolina, the Historical Society of Wisconsin, Madison, Wisconsin and the Institute of Social History, Amsterdam. Though I have not yet completed the manuscript of my biography of Daniel De Leon, I feel that this deviation will prove to be ultimately productive in the eyes of those who want to *quantify* everything.

The impetus for *Socialism Since 1889: A Biographical History* was provided by the historians that I met at Linz conferences of the ITH (historians of the international labour movement) in 1983, 1984, 1985 and 1987. In acknowledging the stimulus, encouragement and practical help that I received from such diverse historians as Hans Pelger, Ingemar Norrlid, Jürgen Rojahan, Gregory Kealey, Malcolm Sylvers, Janos Jemnitz, Susan Legene, Shlomo Avineri and Marcel van der Linden, I wish to stress that they are not responsible for my interpretation of socialist history. By publishing my papers on 'Class Consciousness, the Class Struggle and International Labour History' and 'Individualism and Individuality: A Forgotten Chapter in Socialist History, 1880–1939', the organisers of the ITH institute in Vienna, Austria, allowed the development of *a dialogue* between the historians of 'the two socialisms'.

In acknowledging the permission that C.L.R. James granted me to quote extracts from his books and articles, I want to pay tribute to his unselfish and generous scholarship. In acknowledging the permission to quote extracts from *The Fate of the Revolution: Interpretations of Soviet History* (London, 1967) and *Germany Today: A Personal Report* (London, 1985), I also wish to thank Walter Laqueur for publishing my first academic article almost a quarter of a century ago. In thanking Julius and Phyllis Jacobson for permission to quote extracts from Ivan Svitak, 'The Czech Bureaucratic Class' and Julius Jacobson, 'Socialism and the Third Camp', in *New Politics*, Vol. XI, No. 2, 1974 and in the new *New Politics*, Vol. I, No. 1, 1986, I acknowledge the stimulus and the example of the scrupulous scholarship they have provided independent socialist historians with over a long period of time.

In acknowledging the permission granted to quote extracts from the following books and articles, I wish to thank the owners of copyright in literature that helped to shape the modern world:

Boris Souvarine, *Stalin* (Secker and Warburg), Bertram D. Wolfe, *Three Who Made A Revolution* (Penguin), Julius Braunthal, *History of the International* and *In Search of the Millennium* (Victor Gollancz), Helmut Trotnow, *Karl Liebknecht: A Political Biography* (Shoe String Books), Karl W. Meyer, *Karl Liebknecht: Man Without a Country* (Washington Press), Ralph Samuel, 'Sources of Marxist History', *New Left Review* and Peter Worsley, 'Frantz Fanon and the "Lumpenproletariat"' (Merlin Press).

In offering my thanks to Lorna, Alison and David (or in my non-hierarchical socialist alphabet, Alison, David and Lorna), I acknowledge their tolerance, encouragement and critical criticism. Although the weapon of criticism is very inadequate in the often barbarous world of the late twentieth century, we are not prepared to surrender it. It is, in fact, what offers us a margin of hope in conditions where liberalism and socialism seem to be very much out of fashion.

James D. Young
Polmont, Falkirk,
Stirlingshire.
June 1988.

Introduction

You don't remember the Wobblies. You were too young. Or else not even born yet. . . . They called themselves materialist-economists but what they really were was a religion. They were workstiffs and bindlebums like you and me, but they were welded together by a vision we don't possess.

James Jones, *From Here to Eternity*

The history of modern scientific (as distinct from Utopian) socialism began in 1848 with the publication of the epoch-making *Communist Manifesto*. But although the material and cultural conditions or pre-conditions for socialism had been maturing since the late nineteenth century, authentic twentieth-century democratic socialism-from-below has suffered from a succession of cumulative tragedies and crises. Indeed, as early as 1899, Antonio Labriola, the Italian socialist philosopher, ridiculed and satirised the 'alleged *death of socialism* on account of a so-called "Crisis of Marxism"'.[1]

Nevertheless the first major crisis of international socialism began with the virtual collapse of the Second International in 1914. Despite the widespread multinational hopes and dreams of a socialist millennium inspired by the foundation of the Second International in Paris in 1889, the International was utterly destroyed in 1914. As Julius Braunthal explained: 'It fell, the first victim of the world war.'[2]

The model for this wide-ranging biographical history of world socialism between 1889 and 1986 was suggested by the brilliant and illuminating book, *Three Who Made Revolution: A Biographical History*, by Bertram D. Wolfe.[3] In interweaving three major biographical studies of Vladimir Ilyich Lenin, Leon Trotsky and Joseph Stalin, Wolfe sought to portray the origins, development and predestined failure of the Bolshevik revolution through the lives of its three leading personalities. What was unique about *Three Who Made Revolution* was its classical Marxist insistence on the role of the distinctive Russian milieu in shaping and fashioning the Bolsheviks' socialism-from-above.

Although the heyday of workers' internationalism between 1889 and the outbreak of the First World War produced many pathbreakers – thinkers, writers, artists, agitators and political leaders – the International remained Eurocentric. In those dramatic and intellectually productive two-and-a-half decades, socialism achieved a closer unity of theory and practice than it would ever attain afterwards. Because the International was predominantly Eurocentric in its geographical development and theoretical orientation, it did not produce any black leaders who were integrated into their own labour movements.

Yet although the pre-1914 International was intellectually richer and much more democratic, pluralistic and multiferious than the communist Third International founded in 1919 or the Labour and Socialist International founded in 1923, the international labour movements subsequently produced major figures. However, if the Second International was a victim of the First World War, democratic socialism-from-below was a victim of autocratic Bolshevism after 1917. From the perspective of the late twentieth century, the years 1914 and 1917 were watersheds in the historical development of world socialism.

With very old and tenacious roots in intellectual and plebeian movements throughout the world, authoritarian socialism-from-above antedated the rise of autocratic Bolshevism. Even before Bolshevism was transformed into totalitarian collectivism, it was always autocratic. In sketching in the history of 'the two souls of socialism', Hal Draper made an important distinction between democratic socialism-from-below and authoritarian socialism-from-above from 1848 onwards.[4]

Moreover, there were potential socialist dictators in Western society before the Bolsheviks seized power in Russia in 1917. In a pioneering, brilliant and perceptive study of *Authoritarian Socialism in America: Edward Bellamy and the Nationalist Movement*, Arthur Lipow[5] analyses the sources and origins of 'the anti-capitalist views and the bureaucratic socialist utopia' sketched in the novel, *Looking Backward*, by Edward Bellamy (1850–98). Despite Bellamy's exclusion from this biographical history of international socialism, he was an important representative of authoritarian attitudes and intellectual currents in nineteenth-century labour movements. He was not, however, an 'organic intellectual' who illuminated problems in the history of socialist struggles or practice.

Although Vladimir Ilyich Lenin and Georgy Plekhanov were arguably representatives of authoritarian socialism-from-above during the heyday of the Second International, this was not crystal-clear before 1917. In fact the most obvious and environmentally-conditioned aspect of the Second International was its Eurocentric world-view. With an insistent emphasis on the progressive role of colonialism in Africa and Asia in creating a potential proletariat, the Second International was not interested in encouraging the emergence of black socialism. While Sen Katayama, the Japanese socialist leader, was seen by the leaders of the International as a symbol of international workers' solidarity during the Russo-Japanese war in 1904, the European socialist leaders did not seek his opinions about the anti-imperialist attitudes of black people. The task of fostering black revolts as an aspect of the socialist struggle against imperialism was left to Lenin and the Third International.

The eighteen men and women portrayed and analysed in this biographical history of international socialism did not represent continuity in the history of the workers' movement. Any possibility of continuity was shattered by the splits and divisions induced by the outbreak of the First World War and the unpredictable workers' insurrection in Petrograd in

1917. Furthermore, although the two-and-a-half decades between 1889 and 1914 imposed a certain superficial continuity on the history of the international working-class movement, the eight men and women whose personal, intellectual and political lives belonged essentially to the milieu of pre-war socialism did not represent any sort of uniformity of theory and practice. In selecting H.M. Hyndman, Daniel De Leon, Karl Liebknecht, Jean Jaurés, James Connolly, Rosa Luxemburg, Clara Zetkin and Countess Markievicz rather than others who were formed in the milieu of the Second International, this biographical history will illuminate the diverse problems and predicaments confronting those socialist intellectuals who played crucial roles in the leadership of working-class parties – or the left-wing tendencies of such parties – in Britain, America, Germany, France and Ireland.

With the exception of Antonio Gramsci, the socialist figures whose lives were woven into the milieu of the Second International were more aware of the complexities and complications of twentieth-century socialism than most of their later European counterparts. In contrast to the unique Antonio Gramsci, who spent a large part of his adult life in fascist prisons, Hyndman, De Leon, Liebknecht, Connolly, Luxemburg, Jaurés and Zetkin squared their particular Marxist creeds with their socialist practice before the Russian revolution.

Despite a nominal commitment to atheism and the materialist conception of history, religious and sub-religious feelings, attitudes and millenarian dreams remained powerful emotional and intellectual currents in the workers' movements. Like the Wobblies, many of the rank-and-file workers in the socialist parties affiliated to the Second International had an almost religious vision of life and the future. Moreover, in depicting and characterising their own contemporary leaders as *sinners*, *saints*, *martyrs* and *fugitives*, they often used religious metaphors and symbols. Although those particular traditions and traits of *socialist individuality* were almost eradicated by the more aggressive atheism of the communist leaders of the Third International, they played a major role in the history of the Second International.

In focusing on pre-1914, transitional and internationally prominent 'communist' figures like Joseph Stalin and Mao, this biographical history of international socialism will illuminate the political and theoretical issues represented by those individuals rather than simply the very interesting lives of the individuals themselves. Although the 1920s and 1930s did not produce many outstanding independent socialist thinkers whose thought was matched by activism in mass labour movements, Claude McKay, George Padmore and C.L.R. James were evidence of the autonomous black Marxism and movements predicted and encouraged by Lenin as early as 1916.

H.M. Hyndman and Daniel De Leon were chosen because they represented the 'two souls' of socialism in the Second International before the advent of Leninism and Stalinism. Furthermore, in the religious idiom used by rank-and-file workers, Hyndman and De Leon were socialist 'sinners' as well as important socialist practitioners. They were also remarkably contrasting personalities whose formulation of their respective concepts of socialism-from-above and socialism-from-below were carefully expounded in books and pamphlets. While they had counterparts in the American and French socialists, Morris Hillquit and Jules Guesde, Hyndman and De Leon were much greater activist-theorists.

In contrast to many of the other major socialists whose lives were moulded within the milieu of the Second International, Eugene Victor Debs and John Maclean were not great thinkers. While Debs was the most important orator produced by the American socialist movement, Maclean was probably the most important popular teacher in Western Europe. Although they were important as agitators, they did not make a significant contribution to socialist thought.

De Leon, Debs, Maclean and Luxemburg believed that traditional culture could be employed by socialists to demystify social relations within capitalism. Therefore, they encouraged working-class men and women to read poetry and the classics of European literature. Furthermore, they implicitly repudiated the elitist Leninist notions of the role of the 'vanguard' Party in communicating its 'superior' wisdom to working people. This was why they were criticised posthumously in the 1920s for their alleged 'failure' to understand the role of the *'vanguard' Party* in the struggle for socialism.[6]

Before the First World War, Karl Liebknecht and James Connolly embraced the 'contradictions' locked within the Second International. In a nominally atheist milieu, they were both religious. Moreover, while Liebknecht stamped his anarchistic personality on the youth movement in Germany as a passionate anti-militarist, Connolly attracted support from such Irish nationalists as Countess Markievicz during the dramatic conflict between capital and labour in 'disturbed Dublin' in 1913. But although they were both predestined for matyrdom, the potential disaffection they had always exhibited as activist-thinkers was imprisoned by the institutional framework of the Second International.

Antonio Gramsci and Rosa Luxemburg were the two most outstanding European *individualists* and socialist-humanists who came out of the milieu of pre-1914 socialism, though in some specific ways Gramsci belonged more to the early tradition of the Third International. With a passionate belief in the socialist potential of the European and American working classes, they contributed more insights into the human condition than any of their contemporaries. Nevertheless the First World War was the *crucible* in which they deepened their insights and perfected their ideas about exploitation, alienation and human potential. In producing many essays and pamphlets, Gramsci and Luxemburg really identified with classical Marxism and democratic socialism-from-below.

Seen through the lens of the late twentieth century, Hyndman, De Leon, Liebknecht, Connolly, Luxemburg, Jaurés, Zetkin and Markievicz seem to have been surrounded by an aura of political innocence. With the exception of De Leon and Jaurés, whose deaths more or less coincided with the demise of the Second International, the intellectual development and personal fate of the others could not have been predicted exactly. Although Connolly, Markievicz, Luxemburg and Liebknecht died in the prolonged holocaust unleashed by the First World War, they at least played some part in fashioning their own fate by attempting to accelerate the revolutionary process. By contrast the victims of the Moscow Trials in the 1930s were the hapless tragedians of a new phase in the history of international socialism.

In portraying eight of the men and women whose intellectual formation occurred within the milieu of the Second International, the choice of H.M. Hyndman, Daniel De Leon, Karl Liebknecht, James Connolly, Rosa Luxemburg, Jean Jaurés, Clara Zetkin and Countess Markievicz was motivated by their limited success in integrating the unity of socialist theory and practice in their own labour movements from the perspective of the objectives that they set for themselves before the First World War. Although Keir Hardie, Frantz Mehring, Julius Martov, William Morris, Antonio Labriola, August Bebel, Eduard Bernstein, Karl Kautsky, Georgy Plekhanov, Helen Crawfurd, Dora Montefiore, Sylvia Pankhurst and Mother Jones also belonged to the rich galaxy of socialist men and women in the Second International, they do not fit into the conceptualisation behind this biographical history of world socialism. Despite their inherent importance in the history of the workers' movements, they did not in themselves *illuminate* the cumulative problems that they helped to bequeath to the late twentieth century.

While Keir Hardie and August Bebel were important workers' leaders in Britain and Germany, they and others who have been excluded from this study were brilliant educators in Britain, Germany, Italy and Russia rather than brilliant leaders (or activist-intellectuals) in autonomous working-class movements. In *Considerations on Western Marxism*, Perry Anderson insists that Labriola, Mehring, Kautsky and Plekhanov 'were concerned in different ways to systematise historical materialism as a comprehensive theory of man and nature, capable of replacing rival bourgeois disciplines and providing the workers' movement with a broad and coherent vision of the world that could be easily understood by its militants'.[7] Indeed, Antonio Labriola, though a brilliant philosopher and writer, did not join the Italian Socialist Party at all.

Moreover, while Antonio Gramsci belonged in a strictly chronological sense to the milieu of the Second International, he was an important transitional figure who straggled the Second and the Third International. In common with Sen Katayama, who also became a professional communist functionary after 1917, Clara Zetkin was a similar transitional figure. Unlike Gramsci, however, Zetkin ceased to be a critical, creative or independent socialist after the murder of Rosa Luxemburg and Karl Liebknecht in 1919.

Alone among the important transitional socialist figures who embraced the Second and the Third International, Antonio Gramsci made original and penetrating analyses of the problems confronting socialist militants after the First World War. Although he shared Rosa Luxemburg's sympathy with primitive revolt, populism, urban revolts and millenarianism,[8] he was closer to the traditions of classical Marxism and the Enlightenment than Vladimir Ilyich. So were C.L.R. James, Claude McKay and George Padmore. In 1919 Gramsci already acknowledged a 'class struggle of the coloured peoples against their white exploiters and murderers'.[9]

With the murder of Jean Jaurés in 1914, the epoch of socialist idealism, innocence and morality had come to an abrupt end. Although Jaurés had much in common with such socialist reformists and revisionists as Eduard Bernstein and Karl Kautsky, he took the socialist vision of a new society of equals much more seriously than they did. Although he was a reformist, he did not deny the existence of the class struggle. In contrast to Lenin, Jaurés sought to build alternative working-class institutions and a socialist counter-culture within capitalist societies. Unlike Lenin, he devoted an inordinate importance to the rule of law, Parliamentary institutions and the democratic process. Furthermore, although Lenin had consigned Jaurés' thought and thought-world to 'the dustbin of history' in 1917, the ideas of Jean Jaurés are exceptionally relevant to the crisis of late twentieth-century socialism.

In post-war Ireland the absence of an independent working-class movement forced Countess Markievicz into the arms of the bourgeois Nationalists; and in Germany Clara Zetkin was lost and bewildered within an inward-looking and confused workers' movement dominated by internecine warfare. If the Bolshevik revolution had created the impression that international socialism was an idea whose time had come, Western capitalism was much more resilient than Vladimir Ilyich Lenin had envisaged.

By 1920 the end of the era of feminism contributed to the dominant elitist and authoritarian world-view in the international workers' movement.[10] Despite the advent of such important black socialist intellectuals as Claude McKay, George Padmore and C.L.R. James, the history of socialism in the 1920s and 1930s was increasingly characterised by conformity, uniformity and growing totalitarianism. It was a black and bleak phase in the history of socialism.

In Ignazio Silone's book, *The School for Dictators* (London, 1939) and in Boris Souvarine's biography, *Stalin* (London, 1939), the slow strangulation of militant democratic socialism-from-below at the combined hands of fascism and 'dictatorial communism' was portrayed with passion, pessimism, perception, insight and a sense of inexorable inevitability. In using 'Marxism' as an ideology for legitimising the industrialisation of backward countries such 'socialist' dictators and potential dictators as Joseph Stalin and Mao Tse-tung repeatedly attempted to silence the voices of independent socialist dissent. Although Stalin and Mao did not really contribute to human emancipation, they played a major role in the cumulative problems and tragedies of modern socialism.

Of the eighteen men and women portrayed in this biographical history of modern socialism, Leon Trotsky was unique. It is one of the ironies of history that he succeeded in keeping faith in revolutionary socialism after the rise of Stalinism by becoming very doctrinaire. Because he was obsessed with the need for 'correct' proletarian leadership, he tried to transform classical Marxism into a new, almost heresy-hunting, orthodoxy. Nevertheless he produced more brilliant analyses of the cultural factors behind the rise of Hitler's Germany in the 1930s than anyone else; and he began to cast aside his youthful hostility to Yiddish and 'minority' languages and dialects. Unfortunately, he *reflected* rather than confronted the crisis of twentieth-century socialism. But in the dialogue that he engaged in with C.L.R. James, he contributed to the survival of the socialist idea.

The savage destruction of Austrian Marxism was a turning-point in the history of twentieth-century socialism. In 1934 the bold experiments in democratic socialism in 'Red Vienna' were drowned in workers' blood; the Austro-Marxist thinkers who had inspired those experiments were driven into exile; and it seemed as if there had been a complete and irreparable rupture between the organic unity of socialist theory and practice. In commenting on the role of fascism and Stalinism in destroying this unity of theory and practice, Perry Anderson has argued that: 'By the epoch after the Second World War, however, the distance between them was so great that it seemed virtually consubstantial with the tradition itself.'[11]

However, socialism was, as Karl Marx discovered in the nineteenth century and Antonio Labriola and C.L.R. James rediscovered independently in the twentieth century, latent in the actual day-to-day lives of ordinary working-class men and women. In isolated corners of the world a small number of independent socialist thinkers did merge their lives in workers' struggles during and after the Second World War. In recoil from doctrinaire Trotskyism, C.L.R. James began to develop independent analyses of Stalinism and advanced capitalism in the West. In characterising Russia as 'a State capitalist society', he sought to put socialism back onto the agenda by illuminating the complexity of capitalism and State capitalism in the twentieth century.

In America, in Poland and in France at the end of and after the Second World War, C.L.R. James, Leszek Kolakowski and Frantz Fanon refused to believe that socialism was an idea whose time had gone. In attempting to develop a humanistic socialism relevant to 'the terrible hell of the twentieth century', they merged their lives and existentialist thought-worlds with some of the traditions of the socialist past. But in an era of decaying colonialism and totalitarianism, Fanon and Kolakowski became socialist cartographers and travellers who lost their way on a journey out of an *Orwellian 1984*. Meanwhile other socialist thinkers throughout the world attempted to address the theoretical and practical questions posed by twentieth-century socialism's cumulative crises and tragedies.

But although Paul Sweezy, Ernest Mandel, Isaac Deutscher, Irving Howe, Milovan Djilas, Nelson Mandela, Amilcar Cabral and Michael Harrington have all made enduring contributions to later twentieth-century socialist thought and literature, the task of probing the depths of the human condition in a context of 'the air-conditioned nightmare', totalitarian collectivism and racist colonialism was left to C.L.R. James, Leszek Kolakowski and Frantz Fanon. In acknowledging the presence of fascism and totalitarian collectivism in the modern world, James at least made it very difficult for ruling elites to consign the socialist idea to the dustbin of history.

Chapter 1

The history of socialism: An overview, 1889–1939

Whereas the Second International aimed at uniting the moderate wing and the communist wing of the working-class movement, apart from the anarchist and the revolutionary syndicalist elements, the Third or Communist International represents a union of the communist elements with some of the anarchist elements of the working-class movement.

G.M. Stekloff

The Second International played a major part in fostering socialism throughout the world. The new International was engendered in 1889 by existing working-class struggles and agitations. With its demise in 1914 as a consequence of the outbreak of the First World War, socialists everywhere were compelled to confront cumulative problems and crises. But, although the break-up of the Second International contributed to the advent of the Third International, the Second International flourished during the period of socialist innocence and socialist idealism between 1889 and 1914.

By 1889 socialism was seen by many working-class men and women throughout the world as 'a new gospel of salvation'. Socialism was already compared, in the idiom of Julius Braunthal, 'with Christianity in the days of the early Church before it became established as a State religion'. The Second International existed and functioned during 'the apostolic period of socialism, the time of preaching and propagation, preceding the assumption of political power'.[1]

During the years after the Paris Commune of 1871, working-class movements in Europe and America witnessed the creation of their own sinners, saints, martyrs and fugitives. From 1889 onwards 'revolutionary songs were sung to hymn tunes – as in Edward Carpenter's much-loved anthem *England Arise* – and adopted the language of Christian martyrology as in Jim Connell's *Red Flag*'.[2] In acknowledging the role of their sinners, saints and fugitives during the apostolic years of socialist innocence, the leaders of the Second International attached most importance to the martyrs of working-class struggles.

Between 1871 and the Bolshevik revolution in 1917, socialists placed an enormous emphasis on the martyrdom of the Communards. The Paris Commune of 1871 was the most colourful episode in the history of all the working-class struggles in the nineteenth century. As Edward S. Mason put it: 'The 18th of March has taken its place among *the holy days* in the proletarian calendar and the ritual of its celebration is in the full process of development.'[3] Moreover, in the early years of the Second International, several German metalworkers told a middle-class visitor to their factory that: 'What Jesus Christ was until now someday Bebel and Liebknecht will be.'[4]

The Christian images and imagery were very apposite. It was a period of mass strikes, workers' risings, primitive rebellion and mass yearnings for the socialist millennium. In America, Europe and South Africa, the ruling classes practised a form of international solidarity against the revolutionary movements of working-class men and women as well as the militant peasantry. Emperors, kings, princes, noblemen, popes, landowners and presidents responded to the advent and growth of the Second International by waging a propaganda war – almost a noly war – against tne heretics, fugitives, saints, humanists and sinners who were attempting to turn the capitalist world upside down.

The foundation of the Second International was already foreshadowed in 1880 when the socialists in Belgium addressed an appeal to the socialists of the Old and the New World to construct a new International. A part of this historic appeal to the socialistic working-class men and women read as follows:

Poverty is universal. According to the bourgeois economists, this is an inevitable evil. We socialists know that the teaching of bourgeois economic science is persistently false. We know the causes of the evil and how to fight it. Why should we wait? The wide diffusion of our ideas: the vast movements involving territories that extend from the banks of the Tagus to the banks of the Volga, from the British Isles to the Danubian principalities – does not all this bear witness to the fact that a new 1789 is at hand, a great rising of all the people against the old order of society? Brothers, in face of this great event, it behoves you to draw instinctively together. Everywhere the old quarrels are being made up, everwhere the old discords are being resolved into harmonies, everywhere the working people are joining hands, everywhere hearts are beating in unison. In the proletariat of the Old World and the New, a spirit of concord prevails. Among the suffering and the oppressed there is increasing hatred of their oppressors, increasing distrust of their capitalistic oppressors. Do you not feel, brothers, that this is the decisive hour? The essential thing is that we should take some practical steps to revive the International Workingmen's Association. ... More loudly than ever before, raise the old war-cry: "Workers of all lands, unite".

Although Italy, Spain, Austria, Britain and Holland were not represented at the ensuing international socialist congress at Chur in October 1881, representatives of socialist groups in Germany, Denmark, Belgium, France, Switzerland, Poland, Russia, Hungary, Portugal and Buenos Ayres responded to the Belgian socialists' appeal. In assessing the significance of the work of the participants of the Chur Congress, G.M. Stekloff said: 'They admitted that the new preliminary requisites were still lacking. But within a few years of the holding of the Chur Congress the requirements were adequately fulfilled.'[5]

I

When the Second International functioned between 1889 and 1914, it was a 'seeding time' for socialism, a period of germination and growth in which the socialists attracted mass support in Europe and America. But although the Second International was really a Eurocentric movement during the last decade of the nineteenth century, it increasingly gathered minority support outside of Europe during the decade before the outbreak of the First World War. By the beginning of 1914 small socialist movements existed in China, Turkey, Chile, Uruguay, Romania, Mexico, Brazil, Persia and Peru. In a detailed factual account of the growth of the small socialist movements outside of Europe, Thomas Kirkup said: 'Only in Abyssinia, Afghanistan, and perhaps Hayti is it still possible to escape wholly from the all-pervading influence of this world-wide movement.'[6]

While many of the leaders of the Second International were hostile to organised religion and religious ideology, others were quite sympathetic. Although some German socialist newspapers portrayed the priest and the Junker sitting together in 'close and loving proximity', the Belgian socialist newspaper, *Le Peuple*, wrote with great sympathy about the activities of the socialist priest, Abbe Vral. Nevertheless some European socialist newspapers persisted in portraying workers being 'shepherded into the fold and led in closed battalions at the biding of reactionary priests'. In the fullness of time, a small minority of socialists modified their hostility to the Church. As J.H. Harley put the argument with considerable exaggeration: 'The earlier socialists saw religion only as embodied in an authoritative and often tyrannical Church. Its dogmas were medieval, not modern. It basked in "Paradise" or writhed in "Inferno" when thralls were in suffering at the Castle gates. So the legend arose in the "old socialism" that religion was other-wordly, that it cared little or nothing for the struggles and sufferings of oppressed spirits in the working world of today. The new Social Democracy has none of these haunting suspicions and fears. It holds out the friendliest of hands to Christianity'[7] Yet the Second International remained very hostile to Clericalism.

But socialists were sometimes anti-Clerical without being anti-religious. Writing in 1896 Richard T. Ely depicted the growing socialist movements throughout Europe in which the socialist propagandists expressed the enthusiasm of apostles. As he put it: 'Socialism has become a religion to many, and the devotion which it has awakened is such as nothing short of a religious force is able to rouse.'[8] At much the same time the conservative sociologist, M. Gustave Le Bon, emphasised the religious 'irrationality' of the men and women who were active in the Second International.[9]

America and Europe were seen as the strongholds of socialism on the eve of the First World War. Contemporary observers did not doubt the powerful appeal, authority and force of organised socialism before the war destroyed international working-class solidarity. In 1913 S.P. Orth acknowledged the almost religious zeal of socialists everywhere. In summing up, he said: 'Socialism has organised the largest body of human beings that the world has known. Its international organisation has but one rival for homogeneity and zeal – viz., the Church.'[10] Yet in contrast to the Church, the Second International did not receive any *benediction* from the ruling classes.

Throughout the world, where left-wing labour organisations existed, socialists were hounded, persecuted and sometimes killed. Although persecution and repressive laws were well-known in Europe, they also existed in non-European countries, too. Far from persecution and repression weakening the Second International, they actually heightened working people's awareness of exploitation and social injustice. By 1914 socialism was a formidable cultural force – at least in Europe. In glancing at the state of the international labour movement as late as 1930, S.F. Markham insisted that: 'Its opponents may laugh it to scorn, may accuse its supporters of being traitors and a hundred even less beautiful epithets, but socialism has spread to every civilised country in the world.'[11]

The period between 1880 and 1914 was, as Leszek Kolakowski put it, 'the golden age of Marxism'. Moreover, the working-class socialist movements in Austria, Russia, Poland, Italy, Spain and Belgium were 'permeated by Marxism to a greater or lesser degree.'[12] Unlike the Third International after the First World War, the Second International was not a uniform, centralised organisation. But although it was not a directive body like the Third International, it served a much greater function than being simply a clearing-house for disseminating information.

Although the International Socialist Bureau was not created until the Paris congress in 1900, the successive congresses of the Second International held in Paris, Brussels, Zurich, London, Paris, Amsterdam, Stuttgart, Copenhagen and Basle in 1889, 1891, 1893, 1896, 1900, 1904, 1907, 1910 and 1912 gave the socialist movement a new authority in working-class communities in nations throughout the world. Within the context of the period in which it functioned, it served a very important purpose in giving leadership and coherence to socialists who were scattered and sometimes isolated. This was particularly true after the formation of the International Socialist Bureau. As Lewis L. Lorwin explained: 'By means of appeals, circulars, correspondence, and public meetings, the Bureau was focusing more and more the attention of socialists everywhere on lines of common policy, and was building up habits of mind which were to make the Second International what its designers had intended it to be – the guide and arbiter in matters of international economic and social policy for the labour and socialist movement of the world.'[13]

While the German socialists were the strongest national section in the Second International, they were not very dictatorial. In fighting for socialist policies within a very unpropitious milieu, they were able to add a new moral authority to their already established intellectual stature as the leading interpreters of Marxism. Despite the weaknesses of the working-

class movements in Belgium, Switzerland and Austria, the socialist parties
in those countries were modelled on German social democracy. As James
Joll summed up: 'The parties founded on the German model in Belgium,
Switzerland and Austria were too weak to be of international importance,
though they were to contribute individual leaders to the international
movement. In Italy and Spain the situation was comparable to that in
France, but with the causes of working-class weakness even stronger;
economic backwardness and doctrinal disunity meant that as yet neither
Italian nor Spanish socialism was very important.'[14]

Far from the anti-socialist laws in various European countries suppressing working-class sympathy for socialism, they had the opposite effect.
Before the anti-socialist laws expired in Germany in 1890, the Kaiser
unwittingly contributed to the growth of socialist sympathies among working men and women in other parts of Europe. In depicting the significance
and political consequences of the Kaiser's anti-socialist laws, Samuel P.
Orth said:

Meetings were suppressed everywhere, and dismissed often for the most trival
reasons. The police were given the widest powers and exercised them in the
narrowest spirit. A hateful system of persecution, espionage, and aggravation was
established, and its victims were the classes most susceptible to disaffection.

On the unique *index expurgatorius* of the government were over a thousand
titles, including the works of the high priests of the party, the poetry of Herwegh,
the romances of von Schweitzer, the photographs of the favourite socialist saints,
over eighty newspapers and sixty foreign journals. Bales of interdicted newspapers
were smuggled in from Switzerland to feed the morose and disaffected mind of the
German working man.[15]

Although the political situation in Germany became much more complex after the expiry of the anti-socialist laws, persecution and repression
kept the German working class disaffected from the established social
order. The persecution of the socialists was at its worst, however, in Russia
and Japan. An important consequence of the Russo-Japanese war in
1904–5 was the hounding of the Russian and Japanese socialists who had
sought to develop anti-war movements. When he published a book, *A
Short History of Socialism*, in 1913, Thomas Kirkup said:

Japan has but little in common with its old enemy Russia, but one characterisitc
now belongs to these two nations alone: in Japan the holding of socialist opinions is
virtually persecuted as it has been persecuted for decades in Russia. Professor Sen
Katayama began to teach socialism and trade unionism in 1897. In 1901 a Social
Democratic Party was formed in Tokio and was promptly dissolved by the police.
Several socialist newspapers were started, but they were suppressed and their
editors imprisoned. In 1906 another attempt at organisation was made, but the
socialists assisted in a strike against the Tokio tram fares, and a dozen of them were
imprisoned and their society broken up.[16]

In 1914 Sen Katayama published an article in which he said: 'Not only are socialists hounded in Japan, the natives in Korea and Formosa are revolting sturdily against oppression. A plot of revolt was recently discovered in Formosa and 300 Formosans were arrested.'[17]

In Mexico the socialists' manuscripts expounding the new gospel of socialist revolt were seized. In Mexico and Guadalajara socialist meetings were 'dispersed by the police'; and 'capacious prisons of solid stone' were waiting to welcome the critics who dared to 'speak or write a word of opposition to the governing power'.[18] Besides, the growing power of organised labour in civilised France did not protect the militant workers from brutal ruling-class repression. As W.A. McConagha put it: During strikes or labour disturbances of any kind it was the army which was always available to cow the workers, even to shoot them down if need be, or to take their place as strike breakers.'[19]

In many European countries the socialists focused on the agitation for universal suffrage. Although this particular agitation gathered momentum in the late nineteenth century, it was still very prominent in socialists' priorities in the years before the outbreak of the war. In an article in the *International Socialist Review* in 1906, Nicholas Klein reported that: 'Demonstration after demonstration has stirred the country (Hungary) and a number of times within the past year, the windows of the House of Deputies met many a disaster from the stones thrown by the marching multitudes.' It was, therefore, anticipated that 'if the disturbances become too threatening a remarkable programme will be offered by a representative of the Crown'. But this did not, in fact, happen; and by 1913 less than four per cent of the Hungarian working class were qualified to vote, strikes were illegal, and trade unions were only tolerated as friendly societies.[20] Elsewhere the experience of other European socialists was often similar.

The ruling classes lived in fear of workers' risings; and in Paris on 1 May 1906, an anticipated workers' uprising was attributed to the teachings of the French history teacher, Gustav Herve. In Belgium in 1893 a general strike compelled the Chamber of Representatives to widen the franchise. But although universal male suffrage was granted to all male citizens of twenty-five years of age, the new electoral law was modified by granting additional votes in favour of 'property and education'. Men who possessed diplomas from the higher schools were given two additional votes. In 1895 the Clericals in the Chamber of Representatives imposed 'the teaching of religion in the communal schools'[21]; and on the eve of the war the socialists were still waging a campaign against compulsory religious education.

Side-by-side with the socialists' agitation for free, secular and *critical* education, the struggle for effective Parliamentary democracy was intensified. With the implementation of a new electoral law in Saxony in 1909, the new electorate was divided into 'four classes according to their incomes'. The system in Prussia was even less democratic, and in one precinct in Berlin in 1913 'one man paid one-third of the taxes and consequently possessed one-third of the legislative influence in that precinct'. Yet despite the fact that radical meetings could only take place in the presence of police officers down to 1914, the socialists continued to campaign for universal suffrage by demonstrating in their hundreds of thousands in cities and towns in defiance of the police.[22]

In Austria the socialists fought for universal suffrage and meaningful democratic education. In a passage of great vividness, Samuel P. Orth said: 'On November 1, 1905, a vast army of working men and women, estimated at 300,000 by the anti-socialist papers, marched under the red flag through the streets of Vienna as a protest against the existing franchise laws. They were given the right of way and walked in silence through the streets of the capital.' The simultaneous struggle for democracy in Russia – the precursor of the Bolshevik revolution – resulted in the revolutionary upheaval of 1905. In an article on 'Revolutionary Russia', the editor of the *International Socialist Review* said:

When we first heard of the great strikes in dark despotic Russia we were somewhat puzzled. Had the Goddess of discontent and revolt turned her eyes toward the land of the knout? Had liberty showed her enticing beauty to the poor oppressed people of an unfortunate land? We might well ask ourselves these questions. For we pay very little attention to Russia's inner life, when things go on in their "normal" course. But whether we know it or not, these strikes of today, those for liberty as well as for bread, are the natural result of years of hard work on the part of liberty loving men and women.[23]

What demonstrated the socialists' role in the process of radicalising the working classes was their educational and cultural work. In arguing that the socialists unwittingly contributed to the process of de-radicalisation, Peter Stearns said: 'Busy in his separate socialist society the worker could to an extent ignore the larger environment. In fact the separate socialist society helped integrate many workers into the industrial world in a variety of ways.' But the complexity of the role of socialist education in a capitalist world was sometimes seen in the workers' negative response to how the ruling classes expected them to behave.[24]

In Spain the *Casas del Puebelo* or Workers' Houses provided free lending libraries in towns and cities where public libraries did not exist. The socialists did, as Stearns says, raise the self-respect of working-class men and women. As Gerald Brenan said: 'They made it clear that members of their union had to be serious men: they could not get drunk, take bribes or go to brothels. Even bull fights were frowned on'. Because the Spanish socialist workers refused to vote in either the Parliamentary or municipal elections in conditions where the elections were a sham, Pablo Iglesias, the leader of the Spanish socialists, was, in Brenan's idiom, forced to 'fall back upon a plan of moral preparation of such of the working classes as he was able to draw over to his party. This gave the Spanish socialist movement a peculiarly severe and puritanical character'. But just as the Spanish workers refused to vote in sham elections, so they developed a truly radical counter-culture. But far from the Spanish socialists' integrating workers into the established social order, they kept them alienated from everything bourgeois. As Brenan argued with perception and accuracy: 'It was the Castilian, authoritarian spirit of the Socialist Party that made it uncongenial to the Catalan workers.'[25]

When the Second International was founded in Paris in 1889 Field Marshall von Hotzendorf, the old Emperor of Austria, said: 'Believe me, this country cannot be ruled constitutionally.' The working class did not possess any representation in the Austrian Parliament until 1895, and a relatively 'liberal' franchise was only introduced in 1907. As C.A. Macartney summed up: 'And up to the fall of the Monarchy, they were fighting a battle against a system which was always really, often avowedly, hostile.' Meanwhile, the Kaiser was working behind the scenes as well as in public speeches to defend the established social order from the socialists' critique.[26]

Despite the growth of socialist representation in the Parliaments of Europe, the ruling classes did not abandon their deep anti-socialist attitudes. In discussing the Kaiser's role in anti-socialist activity, Samuel P. Orth said:

A number of years ago he is reported to have said that the Social Democrats are a band of persons who are unworthy of their fatherland ("Eine Bande von Menschen die ihres Vaterlands nicht wurdig sind"). And more recently: "The social Democrats are a crowd of upstarts without a fatherland" ("Vaterlandslose Gesellen"). The Kaiser joined in the public rejoicing over the check that had apparently been administered to the growth of the Social Democracy by the elections of 1907, and in a speech delivered to a throng of citizens gathered for jubilation in the palace yard in Berlin, he said that the "socialists had been ridden down" ("niedergeritten"), a military figure of speech.

Moreover, the monarchs throughout Europe were backed to the limit by the Catholic Church. As C.A. Macartney put it: 'She (the Catholic Church) was the chief stay of the Monarchy, but more powerful even than that, for she has outlived it. She is the upholder of conservatism, loyalty, piety, respect and obedience, the supporter incidentally, of country against town, and Gentile against Jew.'[27]

In the dialectic of the class struggle, the dual processes of radicalisation and de-radicalisation were already crystallising by the late nineteenth century. By 1910 the socialists in Britain, Germany, Austria, France, Italy, Spain, Finland, Norway, Sweden, Denmark, Holland, Belgium and Switzerland had polled 505,690, 4, 250,000, 1,041, 948, 338,885, 40,000, 316,951, 90,000, 75,000, 98,721, 82,494, 483, 241 and 100,000 votes respectively. In those same countries the number of socialist seats held in 1910 was 5.97, 38.81, 17.06, 13.01, 8.26, 0.25, 43.000, 8.94, 21.81, 21.06, 7.00, 21.08 and 4.11.[28] In Spain the low vote for the socialists was an index to socialist workers' alienation from the established social order; and

American socialism was 'less forward than in any other democratic country' in terms of its electoral strength.[29]

Meanwhile, the growth of socialist organisations' membership and Parliamentary representation in various countries served to mask the fundamentally undemocratic character of the bourgeois social order. In any case, the nominal growth and development of Austrian socialism did not – to take only one example – integrate the working people into the Habsburg Empire. In fact the electoral reform of 1908 'took the last vestiges of independence from the non-Magyar nationalities in Hungary'. Furthermore, the electoral reform of 1908 prepared the way for the collapse of the Habsburg Empire during the First World War. In portraying the situation there before 1914, C.A. Macartney said: 'The Monarch and the Magyar nobles had thus succeeded, in an astonishingly short space of time, in turning the most loyal races of the Monarchy into the most dangerously discontented. The feeling of Yugoslav unity received a great impulse. In Serbia, Montenegro, Bosnia, Herzegovina, Dalmatia, Croatia, Southern Hungary and Solvenia the Southern Slavs rallied together to form one bloc, united by none knew what secret threads.'[30]

Moreover, the national question in the Balkan countries retarded the growth of socialism. Nevertheless socialist parties were formed in Bulgaria in 1893 and in Serbia and Rumania in 1903. As the Second International became better organised after the congresses in Paris and Amsterdam in 1900 and 1904, a new emphasis was placed on restricting admission to those political parties and groups whose activity arose from 'the fundamental principles of socialism'. But no attempt was made to impose doctrinal purity on any of the affiliated organisations; and the door was always left open to admit 'trade unions which did not take part directly in politics, but which "placed themselves on the basis of the class struggle"'.[31]

In Austria the socialists were much stronger in the German districts than elsewhere, though the reasons for this were far from obvious. Although the Austrian socialists were not, in C.A. Macartney's phrase, 'a disruptive force', they were nevertheless hated by the ruling classes.[32] But whether socialists could function openly or not, they were not really integrated into the established social order. A major reason for this was simply the ruling classes' bitter hatred of the socialist counter-culture. And this was just as true in democratic America as it was in autocratic Germany.

In challenging the dominant historiographical orthodoxy that the socialists' support for the war in 1914 was evidence of the extent to which they had been integrated into their own societies, Dick Geary has argued that: 'Exactly what the patriotism of the European working class in August 1914 tells us, apart from the fact that it was in the main patriotic, is difficult to see.'[33] Also the ruling classes had repeatedly delayed war down to August 1914 for the simple reason that they were unsure about the European workers' degree of patriotism. For example, during the tense relations between France and Germany in 1891 and again during the Morrocan crisis in 1905, the Kaiser deferred making war because of his fear of the

German socialists' disaffection. In the book *Prussian Memories* published in 1916, Poultney Bigelow said: 'Each of these sovereigns regarded Germany's greatest danger as coming not from the Rhine, much less from the Vistula, but rather from the mysterious and most disconcerting development of popular agitation which, for the want of a better name, is labelled socialism.'[34]

II

A profound, though sub-conscious and half-hidden, duality in pre-1917 European socialism was that between voluntarism and historical determinism. The contradictory commitment to voluntarism and determinism existed within the same individuals as well as within the same European socialist movements. Nevertheless a consistent theme of the European socialists was the important and indispensable role of industrialism in transforming a pre-industrial force into a modern proletariat.

There were, of course, differences as well as similarities between British and German socialists during the heyday of the Second International and these were alluded to by J. Hunter Watts in an article he wrote for *Justice*, the organ of the Social Democratic Federation:

The German socialist party has incorporated in its ranks all the forces of discontent with military feudalism as well as those of discontent with industrial feudalism or capitalism. It is no exaggeration to say that at least fifty per cent of its members became socialists after they joined the Party, whereas in this country we are still jealous of anyone who cannot utter the party shibboleths.[35]

Like Watts, the leading spokespersons of European socialism, whether revisionists or revolutionaries, shared the assumptions of Karl Marx and Frederick Engels about the indispensable role of industrialism in forging a class-conscious working class; yet, in spite of the theoretical disagreements between different European socialist leaders, a thread unifying a common anti-democratic elitism of the Hyndmans and the Kautskys was their explicit repudiation of Marx's concept that the emancipation of the working class had to be achieved by the workers themselves.[36]

Karl Kautsky, the Pope of Marxism, challenged Marx's most fundamental, democratic concept of how socialism could be accomplished when, in the early twentieth century he wrote:

Modern socialist consciousness can arise only on the basis of profound scientific knowledge. . . . The vehicles of science are not the proletariat, but the bourgeois-intelligentsia: it was out of the heads of this stratum that modern socialism originated, and it was they who communicated it to the more intellectual-developed proletarians who, in their turn introduce it into the proletarian class struggle where conditions allow that to be done. Thus socialist consciousness is something introduced into the proletarian class struggle from without, and not something that arose within it spontaneously. Accordingly, the old (Austrian) Hainfeld programme quite rightly stated that the task of the Party is to imbue the proletariat with the consciousness of its position and the consciousness of its tasks. There would be no need for this if consciousness emerged from the class struggle.[37]

This was the theoretical position of the orthodox Marxists like Karl Kautksy as well as of revisionist thinkers like Eduard Bernstein. In Contrast to this approach, socialists like Antonio Labriola and Rosa Luxemburg argued that Marxian socialism had arisen from the class struggle itself.[38]

But although many of the German socialists were more cautious and conservative than their counterparts in America, Spain or Belgium, they were always a potential threat to German capitalism. This was why the German socialists were victimised and discriminated against in circumstances where the authorities encouraged the 'socialists of the chair' to promote reformist or 'economic doctrines' with the tendencies of State socialism.[39] While 'the socialists of the chair' were actually encouraged by the Kaiser, the Marxian socialists were victimised down to 1914. As Samuel P. Orth explained: 'This silent hostility is not confined to political offices and civil services; it extends into the professions. Judges and public physicians, pastors in the State church, teachers in the public schools, professors in the great universities are included in the ban.'[40]

To argue that the socialists' educational work integrated working-class men and women into the established social order is to ignore the anti-socialist context in which socialist enlightenment was disseminated. In Italy, where only 7 per cent of the population could vote because the franchise was restricted to those who could read and write, the socialists' propaganda was inherently explosive and disruptive. Despite the Southern Italian 'condition of poverty, subjection and ignorance which was almost medieval', a minority of the peasants displayed sympathy for socialist ideas.[41] In depicting this socialist education, one historian said: 'This education is extended to adults by the press and by self-imposed studies. The eagerness with which men and women flock to lectures and night classes is a great omen. In Paris the *Ecole Socialiste* and *Universite Populaire*, in Germany and Belgium the night classes in the labour union club-house, the debates and the lecture courses, are evidence of intellectual eagerness'.

In Belgium the socialists discouraged alcoholism at the same time as they encouraged the workers' self-education. A similar trend was seen in Germany. In praising the work of the German socialists, Samuel P. Orth said: 'They take no narrow, provincial view of such questions, and set an example that might with profit be followed by parties who claim for themselves the prerogatives of culture. They are constantly working for better public educational facilities, and are especially hostile to the encroachments of the Church upon the domain of public education.'[42] In circumstances where Church and State obscurantism were powerful, the socialists sought to diffuse enlightenment. Though he was far from sympathetic to what the pre-1914 European socialists were doing, C.A. Macartney paid the Austrian socialists an indirect tribute when he said:

The textbooks and lectures are marred by hateful propaganda, which, far from enlightening a child's mind, can only acquaint him too early with bitterness and coarseness. The anti-Clerical campaign is generally vulgar and not infrequently absurd; for in their eagerness to reject what the Church approves, and vice versa, the socialists are apt to accept anything that is "modern", such as atheism, psycho-analysis, crematoriums or easy divorce, and to devote endless panegyrics to them all without, we must suspect, having learned or thought anything at all about them except that the priests dislike them.[43]

However, if the socialists in Germany were more systematically victimised than their counterparts elsewhere in Europe, the ruling classes in America, Spain and in other countries would soon follow the Kaiser's example. As a result of a strike of the printers' and typographers' union led by Pablo Iglesias in the 1880s, newspapers and printing establishments in Madrid refused to employ socialists. In Britain socialists were also victimised, though the employers' power was weakened as a result of the detemination and disaffection of large sections of organised labour.[44]

The socialists' role in Spain was not one of integrating the workers into Spanish society. The socialists there were rather a disruptive force. Although Marxian socialism was restricted mainly to the proletarian milieu of Castile, the socialists there played the role of building up a cumulative revolutionary force. Anarchism and anarcho-syndicalism were strong in Catalonia and Andalusia, while socialism caught a grip on the workers and peasants in Castile. In explaining why this development occurred at all, A. Ramos Oliveira said:

Castile had no industry and lacked a modern proletariat, the proletariat of Marxism. The workers did not work in factories but in workshops, and the employer knew them all by name. The workshop with a hundred operatives was a rarity. Castile was, then, without a bourgeoisie, and when the proletariat shouted "Down with the bourgeoisie", because they had heard the phrase on the lips of their French, English, Belgian and German comrades, they meant something quite different. They meant "Down with the landowners." ... Such was the social atmosphere of Castile at the beginning of the nineteenth century, and such it has been up to the present day. In these surroundings, there could be no place for the cold, mechanical and impersonal cruelty of capitalism. That was why Castile rejected anarchism and why the anarchist philosophers who were born in these regions went to preach their phalansterian doctrines and their nihilist hatreds in the regions where social inequality was an eruptive force and where there existed a resentful industrial proletariat.[45]

Nevertheless there was a marked increase in socialist influence throughout Spain between 1910 and 1917. In summing this up, Gerald Brenan said: 'The great mining and steel-producing centres of the north – Bilbao and the Asturias – increased their membership and began to *proselyise the south*.'[46]

Moreover, the socialists' campaigns against militarism were successful in many European countries. For not only did the socialists persuade the ruling classes to delay the war which finally erupted in August 1914, but they also attracted support for socialism by exposing the way in which the rich could buy exemption from military service. It was the success of the Spanish socialists in denouncing the war against Morocco in 1909 which led to the martyrdom of Senor Francisco Ferrer, the anti-Clerical educational rebel.

As a result of the socialists and anarchists' agitation against Spanish militarism and colonialism during 'the Red Week' or 'the revolution of July' in 1909, they were adhering to the policy laid down by the Stuttgart congress of the Second International: 'Better insurrection than war'. In a contemporaneous account of what happened, Jaime De Angulo said: 'It seems that the striking elements did not take any part in the looting of the churches and convents, but, on the contrary, prevented it wherever they could; however, such occasions are always festival days for the criminal elements of the slums and they could not be prevented from looting and pillaging.' Working-class women played the most prominent role in the anti-militarist agitations; and the women were incensed by the fact that 'the son of the bourgeois, who could afford to pay sixty pounds for exemption, need not join the army at all'.

Senor Francisco Ferrer's educational work was seen as the main cause of the workers' insurrection, though he did not play any part in 'Red Week'. In any case, he was arrested and shot in Montjuich prison. Ferrer's cold-blooded judicial murder led to mass protest meetings throughout the world. Also there were no countries where the bourgeoisie were less than happy with the socialists' ongoing educational activity; and they were even more worried by the socialists' anti-Clerical counter-culture in the urban communities.[47]

Moreover, reformist socialists in such countries as Spain, Italy and Russia often stressed the necessity for anti-militarist propaganda just as much as the anarchists and orthodox Marxists. In relating militarism to the nature of European capitalism such socialists as Rosa Luxemburg and Karl Liebknecht tried to prevent the growing socialist movements from being integrated into the capitalist system. In the best-selling *Autobiography of a Working Woman*, Adelheid Popp described how she first heard 'militarism discussed from the socialist standpoint' in her native Austria after the foundation of the Second International:

Militarism was described as an oppression of the people, and I was obliged to agree with this. War was the massacre of men, not for the defence of the frontier of one's country against a wicked savage enemy, but in the interests of dynasties, dictated by greed or land or contrived by diplomatic intrigues.[48]

Although the Second International had to confront many more complex theoretical questions than existed during the period of the First International, it was forced to debate such issues as militarism, revisionism,

Ministerialism, colonialism and the national question within a very hostile milieu. In a report to the International Socialist Bureau in 1912, Professor Roubanovich gave an account of the strength of the Russian Socialist Revolutionary Party in which he said: 'The only figures I can give you are the number of members of our party who are prisoners of the Tsar and are confined in fortresses, in prisons, and places of exile. We reckon their number at 30,000, among whom are 10,000 women.' While conditions were slightly better within the Austro-Hungarian Empire, the Austrian socialists had to function within the framework of an 'absolutist, militaristic, police State'.[49]

What was not in doubt was the consistent anti-militarist propaganda of the socialist parties affiliated to the Second International. Although the dispute over revisionism was, as Leszek Kolakowski puts it, 'the most important event in the ideological history of the Second International', it was much more than an episode in the intellectual history of socialism. Furthermore any discussion of revisionism which ignores the hostile milieu in which socialists had to function will end up fostering obscurantism and confusion.[50]

Although Eduard Bernstein was an attractive and sympathetic figure, he did not just play down the unsympathetic milieu in which the Second International was compelled to exist. He also attempted to 'revise' the very fundamental intellectual assumptions on which socialism rested. As well as calling for a revision of the Marxian theories of surplus value, the progressive pauperisation of the working class and the economic interpretation of history he also advocated political alliances with anti-socialist politicians and parties for the promotion of 'democratic reforms'. But although Karl Kautsky and other orthodox Marxists opposed Bernstein's revisionism by defending some of the basic tenets of classical Marxism, they were already accommodating themselves to capitalist society at the turn of the century.[51]

In 1899 and 1903 the party conferences of the German socialists rejected the revisionism of Eduard Bernstein. In discussing this aspect of the history of the Second International, Wolfgang Abendroth said: 'Had not the rejection of Bernstein's revisionism proved that the party had avoided the danger of adjusting to Wilhelmine military monarchism? Would the party not heed the argument advanced by Engels who in 1891 pointed out that a capitalist class society might conceivably be overcome by peaceful methods in England, France, and America, but not in Hohenzollern, Hapsburg, or Romanov Empires?' In answering his own questions, Abendorth emphasised the role of bureaucracy in the German socialist movement in reconciling the labour movement with German capitalism.[52]

But although such socialists as Rosa Luxemburg and Daniel De Leon always criticised the role of nominally Marxist organisations in forcing socialists to play a conservative role in capitalist societies, they did not see this as an irreversable trend. Though he insists that Eduard Bernstein and Karl Kautsky played a conservative role in European socialism before 1914, because 'they no longer lived for, but also off the working-class movement', Abendroth ignores the fact that Rosa Luxemburg and Karl Liebknecht also lived off the labour movement.

Moreover, the problem of Ministerialism in France led most of the socialist parties affiliated to the Second International to confront the problem of whether socialists could legitimately enter bourgeois governments without abandoning their commitment to fundamental social and economic change. But before the revisionists were defeated by the Left at the Amsterdam congress in 1904, the infamous Dreyfus case brought the forces of the Left into bitter conflict with French capitalism. Although the French socialists were not 'agreed among themselves about their attitude to the Dreyfus case', Jean Jaurés' defence of an obscure army officer, who was the victim of injustice and anti-Semitism, not only strengthened socialism. It also exposed the role of the French army and Catholic institutions in attempting to impose obscurantism and backward-looking authoritarianism on the French people.[53]

In Britain and America, too, the socialist oganisations and groups were far from integrated into their own capitalist societies. In Britain a combination of disparate agitations including the 'labour unrest', the suffragette agitation and the Irish question shook the established social order to its very foundations. Although the revisionists were strong in America, the militant socialists who were led by Eugene V. Debs and Mother Jones shook the complacency of American democracy. Certainly, American socialism was largely, if not predominantly foreign, partly because it was brought over by immigrants and partly because so large a proportion of the lower grades of labour was composed of immigrants or their immediate descendants'.[54] However, if socialism in America had been originally 'an immigrant sensibility', the immigrants' strength of 'collective self-identification' gave American socialism a dimension of deep disaffection before the First World War.[55]

Within a very hostile milieu in which even the most conservative workers could be radicalised as well as de-radicalised, even the workers in democratic America moved to the Left before the collapse of the Second International. In examining this development, the American historian, David Montgomery, focused on 'the transformation of workers' consciousness after 1909. In the mass strikes documented by Montgomery, both immigrant and indigenous workers refused to allow their class consciousness to atrophy despite the democratic framework of American capitalism.[56]

Although the Second International always protested against the European imperialists' atrocities against colonial peoples, they nevertheless regarded colonialism as a progressive historical development. In setting out European socialist attitudes towards the colonial question, Victor Kiernan said: 'They (Marx and Engels) may be said to have left a loophole for an indulgent attitude to colonialism, because in their eyes, although colonial rule was bad the old feudal stagnation it broke was worse still. A rude, painful jerking awakening of the other continents by European technology might indeed be called their version of the "civilising" mission that Europe credited itself with.' It was only in 1928 that the socialist International adopted a new programme calling 'explicitly for self-government and independence'.[57]

Nevertheless, during the years before the First World War, the Second International was committed to the emancipation of the whole of mankind. Although they hoped to overturn European capitalism and then emancipate the colonial peoples, most socialists, whether revisionists or revolutionaries, nevertheless conceived of colonialism as a progressive force. But the main emphasis of all socialists was on the liberating effects of emancipation from capitalism. As Julius Braunthal observed: 'In the days before the 1914 war Austrian socialists, and even the leaders of the socialist movement, could without embarrassment speak of "our holy cause" and "our holy struggle", because every socialist still believed that he stood for something sacred.'[58]

The biggest theoretical question facing the socialists before the collapse of the Second International was the national question, the question of questions. In an unsympathetic and inaccurate account of the socialists' attitude to 'nationalism and internationalism', Lewis L. Lorwin wrote:

But the socialists were also in favour of large States, and they never faced the issue squarely as to the best method of reconciling the claims of small nationalities with those of large political organisations. The failure to face this issue caused much bitterness among the socialist and trade union groups of the smaller nationalities in such countries as Austria and Russia. In the economic sphere as well, with regard to migration and colonialism, the Second International showed a dual character. While it made efforts to reconcile countries of emigration and immigration, colonising nations with colonial countries, it recognised the lines of division between "aliens" and natives, "backward" and advanced races, and acquiesced in exclusivist and exploitative and colonial policies.[59]

In making similar points with the emphasis on Rosa Luxemburg's 'dogmatism' on the question of the principle of national self-determination, Kolakowski is also guilty of depicting the history of the Second International as a *history of ideas* without attempting to reconstruct the milieu in which socialists had to function between 1889 and 1914.[60]

In the first place, the Second International was not a totalitarian organisation. It did not impose doctrinal uniformity on its members; and the diverse theoretical contribution of European socialists was environmentally engendered within a context of free and open debate. The reason why the Austrian socialists developed the idea of cultural autonomy within a multinational State was a consequence of the distinctive milieu in which they found themselves. And Rosa Luxemburg's ideas on nationalism and internationalism were, as we will see, more complicated than many historians have been willing to admit.

The context in which the Austrian socialists worked and agitated before 1914 was very hostile and authoritarian. As Oscar Jaszi, a historian who was not a socialist, put it: 'If the army could be called the military

bodyguard of the Hapsburgs and the Catholic church its spiritual bodyguard, then, the bureaucracy played the role of an official and police
bodyguard. In the atmosphere of the *ancien regime* so full of feudal
intrigue, treasons, and local interests, it was not an easy task to establish
such a reliable bureaucracy and, therefore, the dynasty as a matter of fact
employed by preference foreigners, very often adventurers, who sought for
bread and glory in the Imperial service.' The Austrian socialists responded
to the concrete – and indeed unique – problems they faced in relation to
the national question with courage, open-mindedness and imagination. As
Jaszi put it: 'The national problems of the monarchy greatly aroused the
interests of the party because its leaders realised perfectly the danger which
menaced the unity and efficiency of the labour movement in consequence
of the national differentiation of the proletarian masses. . . . In their theory
the interests of the proletariat were in harmony with the well-understood
interests of the State, because the socialist considered the elimination or at
least the mitigation of national struggles as a paramount condition for
social and cultural progress.'[61]

Moreover, the Austrian socialists' ideas, though not typical of the
socialist thought developed within the Second International in relation to
the national question, were characterised by profoundly democratic conceptions of the rights of national minorities. In the book, *Austro-Marxism*,
Tom Bottomore and Patrick Goode observed that 'Austro-Marxism suffered oblivion' after the First World War. It was, moreover, rendered
impotent and irrelevant by the advent of Bolshevism in 1917. Yet the
Austrian socialists developed original ideas on how to cope with the
national question in the specific circumstances of the Austro-Hungarian
Empire. As far back as 1899 the Austrian socialists' programme asserted
that the national question could be solved only 'in a strictly democratic
community, based on universal, equal, and direct suffrage in which all the
feudal privileges in the State and in the provinces are eliminated'. In
summing up the significance of this programme, Oscar Jaszi said: 'It
attacks equally the bureaucratic centralised State and the feudal autonomy
of the crownlands and designates the democratic "Confederation of
Nationalities" as the State ideal of the Austrian working-classes. Instead of
the old nation on a territorial basis, a new nation should be constituted as a
purely cultural association. It acknowledges emphatically the right of all
nationalities for cultural self-expression and admonishes the workers of
Austria that "the peoples can only achieve progress in their culture
through a firm solidarity with each other and not in petty strife against each
other.'[62]

Despite the Austro-Marxists' role in defending the democratic heritage
of classical pre-1914 socialism, they had criticism and abuse heaped upon
them during and after the First World War. They were not only savaged by
Lenin and Trotsky. They were also denounced and imprisoned by the
Austrian fascists later on. Opponents of the Hapsburgs – and their fascist
successors – the Austrian socialists had opposed such revisionists as

Eduard Bernstein with principled fortitude and creative imagination. Yet when Bernstein had declared that 'the socialist movement was everything and the goal nothing', he was not abandoning the ideal of a classless society. Like Sidney Webb and the Fabians, Bernstein came to believe that socialism would grow and evolve out of the existing capitalist system without revolution, serious conflict or class struggle. This was the real tragedy of early twentieth-century European socialism.

Before the First World War most socialists were very sensitive to the rights of minorities. This arose from their profoundly democratic conception of how they thought social, cultural, economic and intellectual life ought to be organised. The socialists' sensitivity to the plight of oppressed nationalities was seen in Rosa Luxemburg's writings and speeches at the congresses of the Second International in 1893 and 1896.

In opposing 'the Germanisation of Polish life' in speeches and writings between 1893 and 1900, Rosa Luxemburg defended the language and the culture of the Polish people. In the pamphlet, *In Defence of Nationality*, Luxemburg said:

The Prussian government has launched yet another attack on the Polish people. A recent decree of the Prussian Minister of Education, Studt, does away with the remnant of school instruction in the Polish language . . .

What are the aims in all this? Obviously to create such a situation that the Polish language and national feeling disappear, and that the Poles should forget their birthright and become Prussian Germans: the children should forget their parents' tongue, the grandchildren should not remember that their grandparents lived on Polish soil.

Moreover, the Polish aristocracy, the magnates, factory owners, bankers and coalowners were identifying with the Prussian government and those who wanted to deprive the Polish working class of their nationality. In those concrete circumstances, the Polish working people required to 'fall in behind the flag of Social Democracy' in order to 'find protection for their economic well-being, their family life, civil rights and mother tongue'.[63]

In defending nationality (as distinct from bourgeois nationalism), Rosa Luxemburg testified to the Second International's profoundly democratic dimension of Marxian socialism. Furthermore, the advent of 'freedom of conscience' during the bourgeois revolution was one of 'the great conquests of civilisation'.[64] In envisaging socialism as an extension of the conquests achieved by the bourgeois revolution, Daniel De Leon predicted that socialism would bring 'a new code of morals'. Yet De Leon and most of the major socialist thinkers in the pre-1914 years rejected workerism altogether.[65]

Far from endorsing the sort of post-1917 workerism of Vladimar I. Lenin, Daniel De Leon and other Second International socialists insisted on making distinctions between the reactionary and progressive functions policemen required to perform in class-torn capitalist societies. As De Leon put it: 'But the policemen have other duties besides protecting the capitalists class in the possession of its stolen property. They have to stand on the streets, and prevent blockades, and answer questions, and similar duties.'[66] In rejecting the elitist notion of the role of the 'great man' in manipulating the historical process, most socialist intellectuals emphasised the creativity of ordinary working-class men and women. In speaking for the dominant tradition of international socialism, Georgy Plekhanov asserted that 'the kingdom of reason' only begins to 'approach us with seven league boots when the "crowd" itself become the hero of the historical action.'[67]

In the fullness of very accelerated time, the profoundly democratic traditions of the Second International were strangled. The war unleashed in 1914 engendered totalitarian fascism and authoritarian socialism-from-above. Although he was very aware of the complex background to what had happened in 1914, Julius Braunthal wrote with great perspicacity in 1945 when he said: 'In fact, it was the increasing antagonism of the Great Powers which produced the disaster of the First World War; and it was the attempt to restore the capitalist system after the war which produced a series of most devastating economic crises from which fascism and the Second World War emerged. For fascism – whether in its German, Italian, Japanese or Spanish garb – is fundamentally the most accentuated expression of nationalistic and imperialistic tendencies imminent in the capitalist system.'[68]

III

In the midst of the world-wide de-stabilisation engendered by the Bolshevik revolution of 1917 – 'the ten days that shook the world' – the critique of Leninism developed by such scattered and relatively isolated socialists as Rosa Luxemburg and Eugene V. Debs was almost eradicated from human memory by the Russian communists' very powerful hegemony. As a torch of liberty and a harbinger of human liberation, the Bolshevik revolution stimulated the collective imagination, unleashed the pent-up energy and heightened the dream-like millennial expectations of millions of working men and women throughout the world.

With the advent of the Bolshevik revolution, Vladimir I. Lenin and the Bolshevik Party automatically gained an extraordinary hegemony over working-class movements and socialist parties. When the old socialist parties met in March 1919 at a conference in Berne, with the aim of reconstituting the old, 'Second' International, the Bolsheviks felt that they had to split the Western labour movement by setting up the Comintern or Third International.[69]

The Third International was founded in circumstances of unprecedented revolutionary optimism. The collapse of the Second International destroyed, in the idiom of George Lichtheim, 'the precarious balance between "reformist" and "revolutionary" strands within the European labour movement.'[70] What was much worse was that the Third International was founded on the Leninists' illusion of the imminence of revolution on a world scale.

In arguing for the imminence of world revolution, Vladimir I. Lenin observed that only a tiny upper crust of 'aristocratic' workers stood between Western capitalism and the world revolution. When he defended the whole Leninist heritage as late as 1939, Leon Trotsky asserted that 'The relative decline of the masses' standard of living has been superseded by an absolute decline.'[71] Like Lenin, Trotsky continued to insist that the 'aristocracy of labour' in the West was the final bulwark against the international socialist revolution. This was really a fundamental revision of Marx's own attitude to the 'labour aristocracy'. As G.M. Stekloff explained:

Furthermore, Marx was well aware that there was only one way of preventing the working-class aristocracy from deserting the workers' movement, of compelling "the favoured labour caste" to serve the general interest of the proletariat. This was by the creation of a stable mass organisation embracing the majority of the working class; an organisation that would rally them and enlighten them, would deliver them from the influence of bourgeois ideology and from all inclination towards sectionalism.[72]

A major tragedy of international socialism after 1917 was the Russian communists' hegemony over Western labour movements. In explaining the practical significance of this hegemony, Bertram D. Wolfe said: 'The gulf between Lenin's small conspiratorial underground party of professional revolutionary intellectuals and the great, democratically (and sometimes bureaucratically) run mass parties and trade unions of the West was so deep that he could not understand the psychology of the West European leaders.' Moreover, in discussing the reservations that Leo Jogiches, Karl Liebknecht and Rosa Luxemburg expressed about Leninism's applicability in the West, Wolfe speculated that: 'Particularly Rosa Luxemburg felt that the battle to win the minds and hearts of the million-headed membership of the socialist and labour movements of Germany and Europe had barely begun. Had these experienced leaders lived, and entered the Comintern on their conditions, they would perhaps have cured it of its fatally one-sided Russianism.'[73]

Although the early years of Russian communism saw the growth of literature and art as well as scope for libertarian experiments in mass education, the interference of the Third International within the former Austro-Hungarian Empire was much less progressive. The birth of Hungarian communism in 1919 took place in very unfavourable circumstances. As the Hapsburg monarchy in 1918 became 'a concept void of any sense', the government of 'Mr Hussarek made an official declaration that the aim of the Emperor and his cabinet was to rebuild the monarchy on a confederative basis.' By then it was too late, and the First World War culminated in the dissolution of the Hapsburg monarchy.[74] Writing in

1919, Henry De Man observed that: 'There is Bolshevism, which believes in the establishment of socialism through the dictatorship of force; and there is democratic socialism, which conceived socialism as the outcome of the freely expressed will of a majority.'[75]

Although it was not understood or appreciated at the time, the Communist International set out from the beginning to split the forces of Western socialism. A flamboyant announcement issued on 1 May 1919 read: 'The dulcet jingling of the bells of the Second International may soon be drowned by the tocsin of the Communist International. The north wind of Russia will soon sweep away the political horizon of Western Europe clear of the spiritual fog-banks of the social patriots.'[76] In Hungary communism was, according to the anti-communist historian, Oscar Jaszi, seen at its best and simultaneously at its worst. As he put it: 'Unquestionably there was a certain greatness, and a consolation for much else, in the seriousness and the enthusiasm with which the proletarian dictatorship took in hand the things of the spirit.' Yet this did not prevent Jaszi from emphasising that: 'The new State made it a physical impossibility for anything but communist thought to find expression, except with the gracious consent of the State. Every printing works, every publishing house, every ream of paper, every instrument of dissemination had passed into the hands of the State.'

But the short-lived 'communist' experiment in Hungary was soon replaced with a fascist regime. By 1919 totalitarian fascism was in the saddle. Not content with 'the complete suppression of popular liberties', the Horthy system not only murdered political opponents. It also gave 'statutory recognition' to 'class differences' and restored the big estate system. In a book published in 1924 Oscar Jaszi said:

In excuse of its horrors, the statement is often heard that the White Terror really only continued the method of the Red. I have no desire whatever to palliate the brutalities and atrocities of the proletarian dictatorship; its harshness is not to be denied, even if its terrorists operated more with insults and threats than with actual deeds. But the tremendous difference between the Red and White Terror is beyond all question. During the counter-revolution the decreased spread of the Terror was compensated by increased brutality and by an entirely different and psychological and moral quality. The Terrorist actions of the Reds usually revealed the primitive cruelty of coarse and ignorant men; the Whites worked out a cold and refined system of vengeance and reprisal, which they applied with the cruelty of scoundrels masquerading as gentlemen.[77]

In Austria, where the Marxian socialists under the leadership of Otto Bauer refused to impose a dictatorship of the proletariat, democratic socialism began to make real progress in the sphere of municipal administration and State education. Despite the fact that Vladimir I. Lenin and Leon Trotsky denounced the Austro-Marxists as 'yellow' socialists, the Austrians created 'Red Vienna' as a beacon of socialist light and enlightenment in the heart of Europe.

Instead of attempting to create proletarian dictatorship in Austria at the end of the First World War, the Austrian socialists extended, reinforced and democratised the Parliamentary system. As Otto Bauer explained later on: 'The workers and soldiers could have established the dictatorship of the proletariat any day. There was nothing to hinder them. Only their own intelligence, which told them that the Red Terror under existing international conditions would inevitably be followed by a White Terror, could preserve them from this temptation.'

Although the Austrian socialists were restricted in what they could do – for example, until the serious political crisis of 1927, they were hemmed in by coalition governments of the right-wing parties – the democratisation of social, economic and political life 'afforded a new field of activity for the newly-released mass energy'. While Clericalism opposed the abolition of compulsory religious education, the Revolution liberated the educational system. As Otto Bauer explained:

The children have no longer to learn by heart what the teacher recites to them. From their own observation, their own activities, and their own work they have to master the various branches of science. The curriculum is no longer determined by a logical pattern, but by the experience of the children. There are no longer separate hours of instruction for languages, arithmetic, or writing. The children look around them on educational walks, and instruction is based upon what has been seen during the walks.[78]

What the far-sighted Austrian socialists achieved in the heart of Europe was real, authentic socialist experiments in the sphere of municipal government, education and health. But elsewhere in Europe, the forces of fascism were gaining in strength and audacity. Although Adolf Hitler did not come to power in Germany until 1933, the 'majority socialists' prepared the way for Nazism long beforehand. During the political conflict within Germany towards the end of the First World War, Edwyn Bevan described the tensions within the divided socialist movement: 'In two of the debates the extreme irritation of the old Party against the Government at this juncture was made manifest. When General Groner had presided over the War Department, which administered the Auxiliary Service Law, the relations between the "majority socialists" and the War Office, in the working of the Auxiliary Service Law, had been remarkably friendly. As we saw, there was at one time even a tendency in "majority socialist" circles to exalt the military authorities above the civil.'

The year 1918 was a turning-point in the history of European socialism. In *The Tragedy of European Labour*, Adolf Sturmthal wrote: 'The aftermath of November 9, 1918, found the German socialist leader, Friedrich Ebert, installed in the Chancellory in Berlin. In Vienna, Emperor Charles discussed the terms of his abdication with the leaders of the Austrian Social Democrats.'[79] But although the German revolution was allegedly a political rather than a social revolution, Maxwell H.H. Macartney admitted that

Ebert retained 'the permanent officials at the Foreign Office' as well as 'the vast horde of bureaucrats' within the State machine. But because Friedrich Ebert and Gustav Noske, a 'majority socialist', who was brought into the government in 1918, did not have the authentic socialist commitment of the Austrian socialists, they prepared the way for German fascism. In outlining the circumstances leading to the murder of Karl Liebknecht and Rosa Luxemburg, Julius Braunthal said:

But Noske, like Ebert, regarded the radical, highly excited working class as the gravest menace to democracy, and thought he could better rely on the loyalty of the former officers than on that of the workers. In fact he even doubted the loyalty of those officers who supported the Republic. . . . Thus he called into action the Free Corps commanded by counter-revolutionary officers.[80]

The Free Corps gave Adolf Hitler generous assistance in the 1920s and early 1930s.

Although he was very critical of the Bolsheviks' divisive role in German working-class politics, Heinrich Strobel, the independent socialist historian, blamed Gustav Noske for the resurrection of German militarism after the war. As he put it: 'The officer caste, from which the sceptre, wielded for centuries had been wrested on 9 November, had been raised again by Noske to sovereign power and unbounded influence.' From 9 November onwards, the German socialist government tolerated militarism and 'the governing bureaucracy.' Yet despite sharp criticisms of the role of the extreme Left, Strobel put most of the blame on the extreme Right. As he explained: 'The feeble attitude adopted by the "right socialists", and the little courage they exhibited for the safeguarding of the Revolution, is chiefly ascribed to the policy which they had pursued since the outbreak of the war. After observing the social truce for four years, and practising the policy of the most unprincipled opportunism, after regarding as the highest wisdom their shabby transactions with the bourgeois parties and with militarism, they could not suddenly find themselves at home with the policy of the class struggle and proletarian independence.'

Moreover, Friedrich Ebert and Gustav Noske were accomplices with the German militarists and counter-revolutionaries in the murder of socialists and radicals. As Heinrich Strobel put it: 'According to a careful examination, out of 318 political murders committed by the Right during the Revolution, only one was punished with 31 years and 3 months imprisonment and lifelong detention in a fortress, whereas during the same time 16 political murders committed by the Left were punished with 8 death sentences, 239 years of imprisonment, and one sentence of lifelong servitude.'[81]

The same murderous obscurantism and anti-humanism were seen in Italy after the First World War. With the decay and disintegration of the Italian socialist organisations in 1921, the fascists' big advance sprang from the landowners' hatred of the agitation for the re-distribution of land. As

A. Rossi put it: 'In 1919 Mussolini had thought that the *fasci* could only flourish in the towns. But towards the end of 1920 the landowners "discovered" fascism, took it up and left their mark on it.'[82] Yet very few socialists grasped the international significance of the victory of Italian fascism before the early 1930s.

Just as the bourgeois-democratic revolution in Germany was born out of a naval rebellion, workers' risings and the abdication of Wilhelm II, so did the fascist counter-revolution in Italy develop out of the workers' factory occupations in Turin. As the class struggle in Europe, America and the Third World countries reached a new intensity of passion and hatred, the ruling classes – or sections of the ruling classes – frequently denounced democratic socialism, liberalism, Bolshevism and democratic conceptions of how life ought to be organised and structured.

When Benito Mussolini came to power in Italy in 1922, he soon displayed a bitter hatred of the democratic heritage of the West. The Italian fascists' hatred of the Left was displayed most dramatically in Turin in 1922. As George Seldes explained: 'On December 17, 1922, occurred the massacre of Turin. On that day and the next several hundred anti-fascists were beaten and at least a score murdered. Several more succumbed later. When, on the first day of the massacre, the fascist headquarters in Turin was informed by journalists that only fourteen of the men listed for execution had been found dead, the reply was that "The Po will deliver up the remaining bodies".'

From 1922 onwards Benito Mussolini imposed a fascist programme on 'a people whose majority was still frankly anti-fascist'. In justifying the abolition of the press, Mussolini said: 'I abolished the subversive press whose only function was to inflame the minds of men.' In the Italian universities, academic freedom was also abolished. In a vivid description of the Italian universities under fascism, George Seldes wrote:

For the new academicians Mussolini established a new uniform consisting of a three-cornered hat reminiscent of the war of 1812, a coat similar to that worn by officers of the coloured branch of the Knights of Pythias, with frogs, epaulets, and gold braid, and trousers like those worn by the Louisina Zouaves in the Civil War, but in the colour of the French spahis; polo boots, spurs, and side-arms. The Academy was instructed to combat every foreign influence in art, notably American motion picture films, German architecture, and French literary style. No artistic work was to receive approval unless 100 per cent Italian style and inspiration.[83]

Yet despite the internecine strife within the Italian – and indeed the international – Left, the forces of democratic socialism refused to be silenced. By creating an underground movement the democratic Left in Italy fought back against totalitarian 'socialism'.

In 1926 Parliamentary government in Italy was abandoned. From then on the fascists in various parts of Europe made attempts to seize power. In Austria a street riot in Red Vienna in 1927 in which ninety workers were shot dead by the police led to the fascists' seizure of power in 1934. In sketching in the background to what happened in 1927, Adolf Sturmthal said:

With a socialist ruled capital city and a violently anti-socialist federal government, Austria lived in a state of perpetual stalemate and tension. Despite the socialists' flexible tactics, a clash between the clerical and anti-socialist countryside and the Labour Party, powerfully entrenched in Vienna, had become almost inevitable. The street riots of July 15, 1927, were the climax of a long revolution.

During the revolutionary post-war period, Austrian labour had taken advantage of the favourable international situation to wrest concessions from the middle-class parties.[84]

By 1934 the Austrian fascists' seizure of power was 'inevitable' and the socialists' heroic resistance was doomed.

The Nazis' overthrow of the Weimar Republic spelt the death of the democratic socialist experiment in Austria. The communists and the Third International had actually assisted the Nazis to come to power in Germany by deliberately splitting and dividing the workers' movement. The communists' pursuit of the policy of 'class against class' had been quite disastrous. In discussing the communists' role in the destruction of the German labour movement before Joseph Stalin began to seek co-operation with the new Nazi government in 1933, Julius Braunthal said:

The real root of the tragedy of German socialism was this split. It was the cause of the grotesque ideological distortion – that twisting of Marxism under which workers' civic rights were denounced as capitalist fetters, the defence of democracy "unmasked" as Social Democratic conceit, and Social Democracy itself attacked as the enemy of the working class. . . . If only the thirteen millions, who had constantly supported the two socialist parties in the elections from the birth of the German Republic up to the last vote before Hitler seized power, had been a united army, a genuine workers' alliance, a real band of brothers, the reactionaries, even if they had dared to raise their head, could certainly not have triumphed over the workers without a struggle.[85]

With Hitler's conquest of power in Germany, the focus of the international class struggle shifted to Austria.

Under the brilliant and far-sighted leadership of Otto Bauer, the Austrian socialists had moved to the Left during the First World War. As C.A. Macartney put it:

Moreover, the old, detested political system was crumbling. The leader of the left wing, Otto Bauer, saw rightly who were the men of the future and threw in his lot with them; his nationalities programme had already brought him near them. In 1917 he laid before his party a declaration demanding autonomy for the nations of Austria. For the rest, the programme of his party was that of the Independent socialists in Germany, pacifist, revolutionary, a long step forward beyond the old tenets of his party. It contained an express warning against any such insistence on reforms as should seem to countenance the existing state of affairs. Revolution was in the air.[86]

Contrary to what Leon Trotsky and the Trotskyists said during and long after the First World War, Otto Bauer was not a Friedrich Ebert or a Karl Kautsky.

Yet despite all the evidence to the contrary the communists and the Trotskyists in 1934 blamed Otto Bauer and the Austrian socialist leaders for the fascists' success in seizing power. In attacking the Austrian socialists – 'the elite section of the Second International' – the American Trotskyists insisted that 'The dead victims of the Vienna bombardment must not galvanise and refurbish the Second International'. Furthermore, in their obsessive identification of the Vienna Commune of 1933–34 with 'the rotten history of the Austro-Marxists' during the First World War, the Trotskyists asserted that the 'catchword of the "Commune of Vienna" was to be rejected.'[87]

Notwithstanding the communists and the Trotskyists' criticisms of the Austrian socialists as 'pacifists', 'traitors' to socialism, etc. in the 1920s, Julius Deutsch organised the socialists' own armed militia – the Republican Schutzbund – to prevent the fascist Heimwehr troops and 'royalist "Front-fighters"' from overthrowing Parliamentary government. But although the Austrian socialist workers did not use their arms until 1934, they had kept their weapons 'stowed away in hiding places for fifteen years.' In a bitter depiction of the Austrian fascists' onslaught, Otto Bauer said: 'all the workers' societies are dissolved. The young workers' athletic associations, the great workers' travel association Die Naturfreunde ("Friends of Nature"), which drew tens of thousands of workers away from the public house to higher forms of enjoyment, the Workers' Temperance League, which saved thousands of working-class people from the dangers of alcoholism and thereby brought honour and happiness to thousands of families – everything, absolutely everything that the labour movement, at the cost of enormous sacrifice, had contributed to the culture of the masses is wiped out.'[88]

With bitter honesty, Otto Bauer admitted unreservedly that the Austrian socialists' experiment had ended in failure at the hands of fascist thugs. In reviewing the history of Western socialism between 1918 and 1934, he said: 'We in Austria tried to tread a path midway between the Italo-Hungarian and German extremes – and we, too, have been defeated. The causes of the defeat of the working class clearly lie deeper than in the tactics of its parties or than in this or that tactical mistake.' The secret of the ruling classes' success in using fascism as a weapon to destroy organised labour lay in 'the balance of class forces.' For a considerable time to come, the Right would be 'triumphant' in many parts of the world.[89]

The Dollfuss dictatorship in Austria demonstrated its hatred of the most democratic socialism existing anywhere by destroying and wiping out the great monument to socialist enterprise in Vienna – the 'Karl Marx hof' containing 1,318 working-class flats. In a carefully documented book, *Fallen Bastions*, G.E.R. Gedye depicted what happened after the Austrian socialists had been drowned in blood:

Mrs Grundy and Mr Pecksniff received a free hand and used it. Before even the bodies of the men and women killed in the February bombardments had been buried, Dollfuss had installed priests and mission chapels in the buildings, shell-scarred by his artillery, which had been built by men and women inhabited by men and women who for more than a generation had been fervent anti-Clericals. In all directions the priests acquired power to interfere with the private life of the citizens. . . . Birth-control clinics, where the socialists had provided free instruction for working-women, to enable them to limit their families in accordance with their prospects of supporting them, were, of course, closed down overnight. The slot-machines in men's public conveniences which had so enormously decreased venereal disease by making preventives procurable with privacy at every hour of the day and night were promptly screwed down.[90]

Yet the defeat of the Left where it had some political power in the early 1930s was not in vain. In paying tribute to the Austrian socialists and the Spanish coal miners' struggles within the wider international context of Stalinist totalitarianism, Max Eastman said: 'When "yellow" socialists manned the barricades in defence of the democracy they believed in, and "reds" abandoned the armed revolution they believed in at a shout from the dictator (Stalin), it became easier for those whose hearts had been with the "reds" to think with their minds about the two beliefs.'[91]

IV

From the late 1920s until the outbreak of the Second World War, democratic socialists and democratic socialist movements were confronted with the twin evils of fascism and Stalinism. The year 1930 was a turning-point in the rise of international fascism as a formidable anti-socialist force in Europe and beyond. As G.E.R. Gedye put it: 'In the spring of 1930 Benito Mussolini, unencumbered by his declaration that "Fascism is not an article of export", began to supply money for the arming of reaction in Austria.'

By 1933 Benito Mussolini and Adolf Hitler were co-operating quite openly with the ruling classes' attacks on independent socialist movements in many countries. As George Seldes explained: 'We have already seen Mussolini ordering the press to play up Hitlerite victories; in 1933 the reward was close co-operation between the two fascist regimes.' Moreover, the Nazis played a decisive role in securing the fascists' victory in Spain between 1936 and 1939. As Denis Smyth summed up: 'It was the Italo-German transportation of Franco's army of Africa over the Straits of Gilbraltar from Spanish Morocco to metropolitan Spain, during the period late July to September 1936, that rescued geographically dispersed military insurgents against the Republic from isolation and piecemeal defeat.'[92]

In an eye-witness account of what was happening in Spain under the Russian-inspired Popular Front, Edward Conze said: 'The class struggle takes place in Spain in a ruthless and almost undisguised form. On the one side the workers. Their main weapon is the strike. On the other side the landowners, the capitalists, the Church, the army and the police. Their chief weapon is the bullet.' In summing up the situation in Europe, he said: 'Many "Lefts" in Britain believe that in France the millennium is round the corner. What is round the corner is fascism, the inevitable consequence of disappointment with the socialists.'[93] The prophecy was soon to be fulfilled – indeed, only too soon. For in abandoning the class struggle in Spain and France in the interests of a Popular Front to defend 'socialism' in Russia, communist parties throughout the world began to reinforce the *status quo* everywhere as a conscious 'socialist' policy.

Chapter 2

H.M. Hyndman and Daniel De Leon: Socialist sinners

The direst poverty, the grossest injustice, the most revolting brutality do not, of themselves, engender revolution. They have very frequently occasioned wide-spread revolts of an alarming kind, accompanied by hideous atrocities, on the side of the oppressed as well as of the oppressors.

H.M. Hyndman

In order to safely judge men, their race, their language and the literature of their country should be known. He who is not versed in these three sources of information will not, unless he be a reckless mind, venture upon a positive estimate.

Daniel De Leon

Socialist sinners and saints existed side-by-side with socialist martyrs and fugitives in the combined demonology and revolutionary eschatology of the Second International. There were Popes in the labour movement, too – for example, Karl Kautsky, the 'Pope of Marxism' and Daniel De Leon, the 'New York Pope.' However, in contrast to the socialists' self-created sinners and saints, the socialists' martyrs and fugitives before 1917 were created by ruling-class brutality, judicial murder and naked repression. In so far as myths and mythology have always played a crucial role in ongoing class struggles, the long list of socialist martyrs – the Chicago martyrs (1887), Alfred Linnell (1888), Francisco Ferrer (1909) – was used as a weapon against capitalism.

Although Henry Mayers Hyndman (1842–1921) and Daniel De Leon (1852–1914) were the sinners of the international socialist movement, Eugene V. Debs, John Maclean and Rosa Luxemburg were the saints and Leon Trotsky and C.L.R. James were, in later times, the fugitives, there were often elements of martyrdom, fugitivism, sinfulness, saintliness and heresy woven into the day-to-day lives of the same major – and minor – figures of the Second, Third and Fourth Internationals. After the First World War a prominent place in the Marxian Decalogue was occupied by the socialist martyrs, James Connolly and Karl Liebknecht.

Within a nominally Marxist working-class movement before 1917, there was a distinctive and discernible substratum of religious and para-millenial beliefs. As Raphael Samuel puts it: 'Communism began life as a para-religious movement, and it is no accident that its first credos – the statements of faith required for membership of the secret workers' societies of the 1840s – were framed in the form of catechisms, as indeed was the *Communist Manifesto* in the original draft Marx and Engels prepared for the Communist League. The association remained strong in the later nineteenth century phase of the socialist movement, despite the adoption, under the influence of Marx and Engels, of a philosophic materialism. Indeed, Dietzgen, one of the most influential of the propagators of the new materialist creed, and as a self-educated working man one of the most representative, explicitly rejected atheism in favour of a species of revolutionary pantheism, with God descending from heaven unto earth "not as in the days of old in the flame of religion and in the spell of wonder, but in reason and reality". In the period of the Second International it may be seen not only in the substratum of millenial or para-millenial beliefs – as in the frequent references to "the Day" – but also in such syncretic manifestations as the "God-building wing" of revolutionary social democracy in Russia – a movement to which Gorky, Lunacharsky and Bogdanov subscribed – and the Labour Churches (and Socialist Sunday Schools) in Britain.'[1] This substratum of revolutionary Christianity was not, moreover, restricted to symbolism.

By the 1870s Karl Marx himself was less ready to use militant atheistic language. In making this point, Lewis S. Feuer argued that: 'When Marx's wife and an elder daughter attended the services of Charles Bradlaugh of the National Secular Society, Marx was displeased. "He had a dislike of secularism", said Eleanor Marx. He told them that if they wanted to satisfy their metaphysical needs, they should read the Jewish prophets. The old Marx had come to recognise metaphysical needs in human beings.'[2] Nevertheless orthodox and some semi-orthodox Marxists have never been happy about the existence of the substratum of religious feelings in the labour movement.

In speaking of the greater sensitivity of 'the old Marx' to the importance of religious feelings, Lewis S. Feuer was formulating heretical perceptions often ignored by the more orthodox socialists after 1917. In contrast to Victor Serge's startling revelation that Leon Trotsky 'surprised the Dewey Commission (in Mexico in 1937) with his theory about the birth of a new religion on the morrow of the coming revolutions, when mankind would have time to rest after the struggles which would have ushered in a new future',[3] most socialist scholars did not subsequently acknowledge this important aspect of Trotsky's political thought towards the end of his life.[4]

I

The left-wing political parties affiliated to the Second – and indeed the Third – International were full of colourful characters, men and women, treasurers and thinkers, sinners and saints, martyrs and fugitives. H.M. Hyndman and Daniel De Leon, though sharing some political characteristics and attitudes, were prominent and quite different types of socialist sinners rather than socialist saints. They were both exceptionally controversial figures, often inspiring obsequious devotion from some (a small minority) and undying hatred from others (a majority) within working-class movements in Britain and America. Though they were both socialist journalists, writers and propagandists, only De Leon could be described as a major socialist thinker.

Daniel De Leon died when he was sixty-two years of age; H.M. Hyndman when he was almost eighty years of age. In contrast to Hyndman (a man who used the prosaic language of bourgeois *rationalism*), De Leon used a precise and colourful Marxist language born out of his early training as a lawyer and University teacher. While Hyndman spoke prosaically about 'the evolution of revolution' and 'the inevitability of socialism', De Leon spoke poetically about 'the beautiful language of the Bible', 'the greater glory of the God Capital' and 'The heart, which, pregnant with celestial fire, gives birth to a poem that thrills the mind with lofty emotion'.

Before the emergence of an uncompromising atheistic Leninism in the international labour movement, socialist sinners and saints were perceived and categorised by ordinary workers as well as by rank-and-file socialists. Although they belonged to different sides of what Hal Draper has characterised as 'the *two souls* of *socialism*', both Hyndman and De Leon were widely regarded and characterised as socialist sinners on account of their shared and uncompromising sectarianism. In contrast to socialists' post-humous perception and presentation of Rosa Luxemburg, John Maclean and Eugene V. Debs as the saints of international socialism, De Leon and Hyndman were already categorised as socialist sinners before, though especially after, their deaths in 1914 and 1921. This was partly because De Leon and Hyndman identified with elitist minorities within minority anti-capitalist working-class movements.

As major figures in pre-First World War socialism, Hyndman and De Leon were both very autocratic in temperament. While Hyndman engendered deep loyalty and devotion amongst such intellectuals in the Social Democratic Federation (SDF) as Ernest Belford Bax, Dan Irving, Jack Williams, Herbert Burrows and Harry Quelch, De Leon sometimes evoked the simplistic admiration of ordinary men and women.

When W.J. Ghent contributed a sketch of Daniel De Leon to the *Dictionary of American Biography*, he said: 'In 1895 he led a seceding faction from the Knights of Labour and founded the Socialist Trade and Labour Alliance, and in the following year obtained its endorsement by the national convention of the Socialist Labour Party. An opposing faction, friendly to the old unions, now began to make headway, and charging De Leon with being a "doctrinaire" and a "dictator", gradually won to its side the greater part of the membership. In July 1899, failing to oust De Leon from his place, this faction withdrew and formed a new organisation, which ultimately became the Socialist Party of America.[6] Yet despite De Leon's sectarianism and divisive policies, he sometimes inspired ordinary rank-and-file workers by his role in strikes and other struggles. In a private letter sent to De Leon after his participation in the Pullman railway strike in 1895, an unlettered worker said:

I agreed with Brother Adams of the Ohio United Mineworkers' you are one of the very true labor leader. The best tribute that I can give you and seen the most of the workings of you during the strike is that "All the gold that could be got in the City Hall of Chicago" could not sway you one iota from your purpose for you to benefit the condition of the Proletarian. Your worst enemy cannot say anything against your character as a labor leader.[7]

In a clear, concise and brief depiction of H.M. Hyndman's importance in the history of British socialism, Stanley Pierson says: 'Hyndman's leadership of the Social Democratic Federation was marred by a somewhat autocratic temperament and policies in which political opportunism and dogmatic theory were curiously blended. Hence the series of defections and schisms that marked the development of the Federation. Some, most notably William Morris, departed because they believed that the socialist vision was being hopelessly compromised; others because Hyndman failed to see the practical importance of the trade unions and other working-class organisations.' De Leon also made many enemies in the labour movement by articulating 'a strong antagonistic attitude toward the existing trade unions and characterising their leaders as "Labour fakers".' By 1895 he abandoned the traditional Marxist policy of 'boring' (or working) within the existing trade unions and proceeded to set up 'dual' (or socialist) trade unions to oppose the Knights of Labour and the American Federation of Labour.[8] Unlike Hyndman, however, he did not deny the crucial role of working-class struggles in the battle for socialism.

A common motivation behind the passionate and unyielding sectarianism of H.M. Hyndman and Daniel De Leon was an unshakable belief in the need for socialism. Of legendary significance during their own lifetimes, their very real sectarianism was exaggerated by communist historiography after 1917.[9] In contrast to Hyndman (a socialist intellectual who did not participate in many working-class struggles), De Leon always identified with ongoing class struggles and the potential creativity of working men and women.

While Hyndman was always consistently hostile to trade unions *per se*, De Leon participated in some of the major activities of American trade unions from the Knights of Labour to the Industrial Workers of the World. Although they were both intellectuals and prolific writers, De Leon made a much more *serious and enduring* contribution to *socialist theory* than Hyndman. Yet despite their shared sectarian attitudes towards existing labour movements, Hyndman and De Leon conceptualised the role of the working class in history in profoundly different ways.

At the heart of the differences in the political orientation of the two men was the distinction Hal Draper, the American historian, has made between 'the two souls of socialism': democratic revolutionary socialism based on a mass working-class movement, struggling from below for the extension of democracy, versus the many varieties of socialism-from-above.[10] Hyndman and the dominant leadership of the SDF identified with the authoritarian concept of socialism-from-above from 1881 onwards, while De Leon and the American Socialist Labour Party (SLP) always argued for democratic socialism-from-below.

The central feature of the Hyndman/De Leon contribution to socialist politics was their divisive sectarian attitudes towards authentic working-class movements. While the most striking thing about H.M. Hyndman was the synchronisation between his theoretical orientation as an advocate of socialism-from-above and his political practice, the most visible aspect of De Leon's role as theoretician and activist was the dichotomy between his constant advocacy of democratic socialism-from-below and an elitist, sectarian practice. Though both men played a largely negative role in practical socialist politics, De Leon at least bequeathed a legacy of coherent and penetrating Marxist thought to posterity.

The member of a wealthy family, educated at the University of Cambridge and a stockbroker, H.M. Hyndman began to dabble in cricket, company promotion and journalism in the 1870s. The turning-point in his life came in 1880 when he discovered and read a French edition of volume one of Karl Marx's book, *Capital*. Autocratic in temperament and authoritarian in outlook and behaviour, he passionately believed in socialism-from-above. Nevertheless, he did make enormous sacrifices for the socialist cause as he understood it. As H.W. Lee put it in *Social-Democracy in Britain*:

The close of 1886 was the beginning of very bad times for the Hyndmans. Hyndman had come of a wealthy family, and was certainly to be classed among the well-to-do when he began his career as a socialist with the founding of the Democratic Federation in 1881 . . . and for the socialist movement he lived and worked until he passed away at the end of 1921, nearly eighty years of age. . . . A moderate fortune may quickly disappear without being squandered, if little or no attention is paid to it by its possessor or anyone on his behalf, and Hyndman's socialist activities no doubt prevented certain expectations he may have had from maturing.[11]

But the most interesting aspect of the quality of Hyndman's socialism was its authoritarian, anti-working-class *elitism*.

From his arrival on the British political scene in 1881, when he played a leading role in founding the Democratic Federation (re-named the SDF in 1883), until his death in 1921, H.M. Hyndman always scoffed at and ridiculed the British working class. In 1900, for example, he wrote: 'I have often thanked my stars or my forebears that I was not born a working man. Very likely if I had been I should have grown up just such another as the majority of my "intelligent" working men countrymen around me.'[12]

Moreover, when he published the autobiographical volume, *The Record of an Adventurous Life* in 1911, he described a meeting with Georges Clemenceau, the French bourgeois politician, a few years previously: 'I especially remember two things about that luncheon. Clemenceau would not have it that anything really valuable could come out of the English proletariat. They were incapable of any high ideals for their own class. "In short", he said, "la classe ouvriere en Angleterre est une classe bourgeoisie"; and so far, I am compelled to admit, with the deepest regret, this caustic appreciation of my toiling countrymen is in the main correct.'[13] In a second autobiographical volume, *Further Reminiscences*, published in 1912, Hyndman made it plain that the key role in any future revolutionary struggles would, in his view, be played by 'the educated' classes. As he put it: 'In really stirring times her (the Countess of Warwick's) qualities will manifest themselves more conspicuously than it is possible they should in the transition period we are now passing through. The various currents which at present divert even the most enthusiastic from their direct course will then be absorbed in the one great stream. Aristocrats had, to a large extent, led in the great bourgeois uprising in France at the end of the eighteenth century. The *educated middle class* will, apparently, play the same part in *the vast social revolution* which is manifestly *preparing* all over the civilised world. But here, in Great Britain, there will, I venture to predict, be at least one aristocratic figure in the van of the great struggle on the side of the people, and that will be the Countess of Warwick.'[14]

Hyndman was an advocate of socialism-from-above, not below. He actually repudiated socialism-from-below; and, when he published *The Evolution of Revolution* in 1920, he gave chapter twenty six of his massive book the typical title, 'Useless Revolts against Capital.' Furthermore, in an extremely gloomy, pessimistic and a-historic assessment of British working-class activity over several centuries, he concluded thus:

So true is it that all history up to the present time has to be rewritten, and all the terrible facts of the past of the human race revealed in their true proportion, before we can hope to master the truth about the long martyrdom of man, from the break-up of the gentile and communal period, onwards, to the forms of private property production and exchange. In all this, for the most part, ethic has no say; human sympathy plays little or no part. For the mass of the people it is ever the same. Each generation in turn enters upon its mournful heritage of suffering, and passes on its burden of never-ending sorrow to the next, and the next, and the next.[15]

Although he sometimes spoke and wrote about 'the limits of historical determinism', he was convinced of the *inevitability* of socialism.

Despite ever-recurring frustrations and disappointments about the socialists' progress in Britain, Hyndman agitated for socialism-from-above from 1881 until 1921. In distancing himself from the fundamental thesis of Karl Marx and Frederick Engels that 'the emancipation of the working class must be brought about by the working classes themselves', he wrote ridiculing working-class men and women as conscious agents of the history-making process. Also the SDF was permeated with Hyndman's ideas about working people from the top to the bottom, though some prominent members such as John Maclean remained sympathetic to the concept of socialism-from-below.[16]

The leading figures in the SDF, whether middle class or working class, were usually steeped in the tradition of authoritarian socialism-from-above. Therefore elitist, anti-working attitudes were scattered throughout their theoretical writings as well as in their speeches and articles in *Justice*, the newspaper of the SDF. Although he was frequently optimistic about the prospects of socialist revolution during significant *moments* of social upheaval, Hyndman never trusted the workers' ability to enact social transformation. As E.P. Thompson argues: 'Andreas Scheu thought (an interesting suggestion) that Hyndman had been influenced by the mode of Dr Kenealy's Titchborne Claimant agitation: "Edward Carpenter saw Hyndman as living in imminent expectation of revolution, when the SDF would resolve itself into a committee of Public Safety, and . . . it would be for him as chairman of that body to guide the ship of State into the calm haven of socialism".'[17] Moreover, Thompson adds that 'the self-isolating consistency with which Hyndman for forty years, "disapproved" of nearly all *popular phenomena* which eluded his own control' was the most distinguished feature of his prolonged activity in British politics.[18]

In a blistering critique of the leaders of German social democracy written in 1877, Marx and Engels could have had H.M. Hyndman, Ernest Belford Bax and Harry Quelch in mind when they observed:

On the foundation of the (First) International, we expressly formulated the battle cry: the liberation of the working class must be the work of the working class itself. We consequently cannot go hand-in-hand with people who openly declare that the workers are too uneducated to liberate themselves, and must be liberated from above at the hands of the philanthropic big and petty bourgeois.[19]

This formulation caught and fixed the spirit of the essentially *democratic soul* of classical Marxism.

Yet Hyndman and the dominant figures in the leadership of the SDF represented the *authoritarian soul* of socialism-from-above in the British labour movement. In locating the SDF precisely in this tradition, Ernest Belford Bax wrote: 'Socialism did not signify everything *by* the people, but everything *for* the people.' In depicting this elitism in the SDF, Stuart Macintyre insists that: 'The air of gloomy antagonism to the bone-headed working man was extremely prevalent among the pre-war Marxists and emerges with particular clarity in Harry Quelch's own sub-Dickensian short stories about working-class life which were collected in his *Literary Remains* (1914).'[20]

What was central to the strategy of the dominant leadership of the SDF was the constant and unchanging assumption that capitalism contained the seeds of its own destruction. In an uncompromising, though very elitist, portrayal of the orientation of the SDF, Ernest Belford Bax wrote:

The majority, therefore, under a capitalist system will necessarily for the most part vote for the maintenance of that system under one guise or another, not because they love it, but out of sheer ignorance and stupidity. It is only by the *active minority* from out of the *stagnant* inert mass that the revolution will be accomplished. It is to this socialist minority that individuals, acting during the revolutionary period, are alone accountable.[21]

Although there were elitist and authoritarian socialists in the Socialist League, the Independent Labour Party and the infant Labour Party after 1900, the SDF was unique in so far as the authoritarian socialism-from-above orientation of Hyndman, Bax and Quelch dominated the SDF's whole political strategy in relation to the rest of the labour movement into the 1920s.

Instead of learning from their own practice that sectarianism was divisive and counter-productive – or instead of accentuating the positive developments in working-class politics – Hyndman used Marxist theory, in the idiom of E.P. Thompson, 'less as a guide to action than a rationalisation after the event.' In summing up Hyndman's weaknesses as a socialist leader, Thompson says: 'It is my opinion that the greatest of Hyndman's blunders was to remain unextinguished for so long. Whatever his intentions – in which disinterestedness and vanity were oddly compounded – his personal and theoretical influence was disastrous. Had the SDF merged with the ILP in 1893 or remained in the Labour Representation Committee a sturdy socialist party might possibly have come out at the other end. As it was the SDF became a kind of transit camp – Eduard Bernstein suggested that "well over *a hundred thousand*" passed through it.'[22]

II

Nevertheless many British socialists believed in the ultimate collapse of West European capitalism,[23] and, in 1889, J. Hunter Watts predicted that the existing social and economic system 'would die of self-immolat(ion)'.[24] There was, however, a working class hostility to socialist ideas. This led Harry Quelch to argue that the British workers were 'most backward in contrast to elsewhere in Europe.'[25] Such pessimism, together with the importance they already attached to 'bourgeois' science and raising the general cultural level of the working classes, increasingly led certain socialists into an elitist posture.

Appalled by the illiteracy and ignorance of the working classes and profoundly convinced of the utility of science and education, H.M. Hyndman wrote: 'Nowhere more than in England do we need the help of the class which has absorbed all the higher education.'[26] Then, in an editorial entitled 'Ignorance and Education', *Justice* put the case for more and better education and criticised those Establishment elements who were opposed to educating the working classes: 'No doubt they think that if the "lower orders" were educated they would not be such subservient slaves as they are today. Well, we are inclined to agree with them, and it is precisely the reason why we want better education.'[27] This commitment to raise the cultural level of the workers was quite compatible with the elitist outlook of many socialists. Working class cadres in the SDF were just as elitist as their middle class counterparts and were, in their own estimation, culturally superior.

A decisive circumstance in deepening H.M. Hyndman's initial elitism and hostility to working people was the SDF's complete isolation from the mainstream of working class social life.[28] From 1883, when the SDF became committed to socialist principles,[29] down to 1921 the members of the SDF adopted an elitist position which was out of alignment with Marx's fundamental thesis that the workers had to emancipate themselves. The members of the SDF broadly identified with some aspects of Marxism; but they also separated themselves from some of the basic assumptions Marx expounded about the complex relationship between politics, education and economics. Hyndman wrote: 'That, as Marx said, the emancipation of the workers must be brought about by the workers themselves is true in the sense that we cannot have socialism without socialists. But a slave class cannot be freed by the slaves themselves. The leadership, the initiative, the teaching, the organisation, must come from those who are born into a different position, and are trained to use their faculties in early life.'[30]

For Hyndman and the SDF the relationship between the innate laws of history which would ultimately create the supreme revolutionary moment and the political role of their cadres was complementary and not dichotomous.[31] Democracy and authoritarianism, like voluntarism and determinism, existed within the same individuals. In 1885 the British working classes were being gradually 'stampede(d) towards socialism' and 'a compact minority' of revolutionary socialists were waiting to 'take advantage of some opportune accident that will surely come.'[32] From this perspective 'the bourgeois intelligentsia' and 'the more intellectual-developed proletarians' had an indispensable role to play in creating a class-conscious working class.[33] In the face of formidable difficulties and apparent mass working-class apathy, if not hostility, to elitist socialists, the social democrats held firmly to the concept of the vital role their compact minority would play in making the socialist revolution when the time arrived for decisive action. As working class hostility towards élitist socialism was intensified, the SDF persisted for nearly four decades in prosecuting their original approaches to the working classes.[34]

Everything that socialists valued most – knowledge, learning, culture and dignified protest – was sometimes ignored and dismissed by many unorganised working-class men and women. For example, an unlettered worker in Glasgow, who wrote to the secretary of the Socialist League in London in 1886, mentioned in passing that socialism, though discussed by working people, was often 'a butt for ridicule.'[35] When asked what would happen to the workers under socialism, a rather didactic, though idealistic, member of the SDF who was lecturing to his fellow artisans on the need for a socialist society, replied. 'When we get socialism there won't be any people like us, we shall all be civilised.'[36] Alongside what was only a slightly repressed hatred of the working class as it actually existed, socialists in the SDF soon discovered a strong, if not always acknowledged, identity with the 'educated elements' of the middle class. Then a growth of middle class sympathy for some socialist ideas in the 1890s[37] made many British socialists increasingly sensitive to the possibility of the riotous unemployed and striking workers alienating middle-class 'public opinion.'

Moreover, if the working classes were 'cussed'[38] and indifferent to their atrocious conditions and fate, this could not be said of the leaders of the middle classes. The latter were fighting for improved working-class social conditions and were displaying sympathy for socialism as they understood it. Since patience was a cardinal virtue in the individual cadres who made up the compact minority,[39] their resolution was of prime importance. As early as 1888 their commitment to wait for the 'opportune accident' that would destroy capitalism had been stiffened by their belief that socialist ideas had 'permeated the thought of the age.'[40] But in a society where the working classes were seemingly so indifferent to the things the social democrats regarded as important, and where trade unionism and socialism were often associated in the 'popular mind'[41] with incendiarism and bloody revolution, the SDF considered it necessary to project a collective image of responsible, if not actually licensed, protest and revolt.

The unending defections and schisms in the SDF were provoked by Hyndman's dictatorial opportunism, anti-democratic hostility to the women's movement, hostility to spontaneous working-class struggles and a lust for power and high political office. Born out of a profound antipathy towards the struggles of ordinary people, he was always drawn to the so-called 'high and mighty' such as Georges Clemenceau, the Countess of Warwick and Lady Dorothy Nevill. In opposing the agitations of such women as Eleanor Marx and Dora Montefiore, Hyndman and the dominant leadership of the SDF in the mid-1890s attracted the criticism of De Leon and the American SLP.

Ernest Belford Max was the strongest critic of the agitation for women's rights, and he always argued that women were actually 'enslaving men.'[42] In an editorial in *Justice* entitled 'The Cult of Abstractions', the SDF criticised the agitation for women's rights in the name of socialist 'principle.'[43] By the late 1890s the SDF's hostility to the agitation for women's rights and general opportunism including their support for 'Alexandre Millerand and two other French socialists' who, in 1900, joined the bourgeois government of Waldeck-Rousseau provoked a massive resistance.[44] This gave birth to the 'impossibilist revolt' in the SDF and the foundation of the British SLP.

Although Daniel De Leon's writings inspired the 'impossibilist revolt' in the SDF, Hyndman had surprisingly little to say about him in his two volumes of autobiography. He was much more interested in the Countess of Warwick than in the Marxist critics of 'reformism'. With the development of the 'impossibilist revolt' and the total disaffection of the Scottish branches, the SDF became what it had been at its inception – a small sectarian group of elitist, authoritarian middle-class socialists. But De Leon and the De Leonites were, and remained, a thorn in Hyndman's smug bourgeois posture.

In presenting the views of the Scottish 'impossibilists' in 1901, William Gee wrote: 'The comrades pick up this journal (*The People*) and read articles breathing the militant revolutionary spirit which stirs and invigorates them; they read remorseless denunciations of all "efforts" at compromise and belabour fiercely (most fiercely) all progressive opponents. Then they pick up *Justice* and read, for instance, a note regretting the death of a man like Hammill, who was a most inveterate opponent of the SDF'.[45] Arthur Keep, who had lived in London, and De Leon attacked Hyndman and the SDF in the pages of *Justice* and *The People*; and men like John E. Ellam responded by sending private letters to De Leon in which they objected to the 'strictures and criticisms of English socialism.'[46] When he judged and evaluated the 'impossibilist revolt' much later, H.W. Lee said:

His (De Leon's) was the SLP doctrine, which became so mischievous here for a while – the notion that the working classes were "an unconscious revolutionary mass" kept back from revolutionary action by "freaks and fakirs" of labour leaders, when all who were doing their best to "educate, agitate and organise" them knew only too well that if the majority of the working classes were "unconscious", they certainly were not "revolutionary."[47]

Because the 'impossibilist revolt' was initiated and supported by working-class members of the SDF, it was particularly obnoxious to H.M. Hyndman. Yet despite disappointment and frustration with the 'progress of socialism', he did not give up. By 1905 the Countess of Warwick had convinced him that he would soon be 'the first Socialist Prime Minister' in Britain. In a private letter to an American socialist, Hyndman wrote:

Her idea is that, within two years, I, *moi qui vous parle*, shall "have the ball at my feet". That seems to me incredible. But things are moving, and Lady Warwick would not have joined the SDF, the most advanced and irreconcilable body in Great Britain, without careful consideration of possibilities.[48]

Moreover, at the conclusion of his chapter on Syndicalism and the women's agitation, Chuchichi Tsuzuki, Hyndman's biographer, says: 'There were thus many forms of serious social unrest in the period immediately preceding the European war. Hyndman disapproved of them all.'[49] Although he was not quite so reactionary as Bax, he was, as Tsuzuki puts it, 'of the opinion that women who advocated women's emancipation as "a sex question ought to be sent to an island by themselves".'[50]

For almost four decades the SDF criticised the trade unions, and some historians have normally explained their overall criticisms of working men and women in terms of their 'sectarianism' instead of seeing their 'socialist' criticism as part of a conscious and carefully worked out socialism-from-above conception of politics. In a brilliant essay on 'The Marxism of the

Social Democratic Federation', the late Henry Collins traced the SDF's hostility to the trade unions back to Lassalle's concept of 'the iron law of wages';[51] but the SDF mainly opposed trade unions because they allegedly created 'inharmonious interests' within the working class[52] and simultaneously alienated 'public opinion' by conducting strikes.[53]

Moreover, the Lib–Labs, for all their faults from a socialist point of view, were much less elitist than Hyndman, Bax, Quelch or Irving. In 1896 the President of the Falkirk Trades Council might have bemoaned their failure to establish a branch of the Women's Protective and Provident League because they had begun 'too low down the social scale';[54] but they had voiced their disappointment with as much human sympathy as the president of the Aberdeen Trades Council had done a few years earlier. In supporting a strike of labourers, who had little experience of trade union organisation, he had told the artisans that: 'He trusted they would forget that they were masons, joiners, and so many different sections of tradesmen, but that they would keep in mind that they were all workmen and therefore had an interest in the general cause of labour, and in whatever tended to all advancement and elevation of the workmen.'[55] Such sentiments, for all their implicit elitism, were much more likely to strike cords in the developing social consciousness of many workers who were still being forced into factories by the de-population of long-established rural communities than the anti-working-class comments in *Justice* and in SDF pamphlets.[56]

Furthermore, newcomers to industrial life, who were often bawdy, rumbustious and unruly, were not going to be attracted by the self-conscious, self-righteous elitist socialists in the SDF who were *lecturing* them on what were essentially middle-class values. At a time when Saturday night drunkenness was commonplace in many British working-class communities, one of Hyndman's friends wrote: 'Socialism is not to be won by riots, but by the steady combined movement of an educated social democracy.'[57] An additional sign of the SDF's intense commitment to *law and order* beyond their concern not to alienate British 'public opinion' was seen in their criticism of the spontaneous working-class food riots in Italy in 1898, because they were 'individualistic' and not an expression of educated social democracy.[58]

The SDF's socialism was the socialism of H.M. Hyndman or socialism from the top down. Consequently, he identified with the right-wing elements in the international labour movement from 1881 until 1921. In commenting on Hyndman's opposition to militant trade unionism during the years before the First World War, Andfe Tridon said: 'While the British socialists have not as yet pronounced against the Syndicalists as definite a sentence of excommunication as the Americans, the executive committee of the British Socialist Party has felt called upon to define its attitude by means of a manifesto. . . . The manifesto ends by appealing to all members not to let themselves be forced into committing errors by the appeal of the direct actionists in the present critical period.'[59] But although Hyndman always frowned upon agitation from below, he never lost faith in the possibility of socialism-from-above. In 1917, when G.V. Plekhanov invited him to visit Russia, he informed an American socialist, G.E. Russell about his reasons for staying at home:

There is a general feeling that, under all the circumstances, I ought to go to Petrograd and Moscow. In fact, some of the papers are pressing me to do so, and the War Cabinet would be glad for me to go. But I am not at all convinced that British influence in Russia would gain by further efforts. . . . Moreover, we may have a revolution here, as I have said, before we expect it, and then I ought to be present.[60]

III

Born on 14 December 1852, in the Dutch colony of Curacao, Daniel De Leon was the son of a Dutch army surgeon. Educated in Germany and the Netherlands in the 1860s, he took up residence in the United States of America in 1872. A distinguished student at Columbia Law School, he subsequently joined Columbia's political science faculty. His university teaching career began in 1883 and was self-terminated in 1889.

De Leon's radicalisation came abruptly and unexpectedly. It was triggered by a strike of tramway workers in New York City in 1886. Out of this metamorphosis, he was to emerge as a militant pro-labour sympathiser. When he joined the SLP in 1890, the nascent American labour movement was faced with almost insurmountable problems and difficulties. Inward-looking and anti-intellectual, the American labour movement to some extent shared British labour's obsessive preoccupation with the agitation for land reform.

De Leon's pro-labour sympathies led him, in the late 1880s, to middle class radicalism rather than socialism; and his experience and disappointments in the protest movements of Henry George and Edward Bellamy stimulated a new interest in the writings of Marx and Engels. His socialism was, therefore, born out of pro-labour sympathies and his frustrated experience in middle-class radical movements.

A dedicated socialist, a brilliant orator, lecturer, journalist, translater and agitator, De Leon exerted an enormous influence on the American labour movement between his conversion to Marxism in 1890 and his death in 1914. As a militant intellectual who was a consistent advocate of socialism-from-below, he was very sectarian during the decade of the 1890s. Caught up in the class struggle in 1886 – or as he put it in 1902, 'It is now sixteen years since a "cat's paw" of the labour movement drew me within its whirl'[61] – he never abandoned the sceptical iconoclasm of the formative years he spent in the labour movement prior to his conversion to Marxism.

In two seminal essays on Daniel De Leon's role in American socialism, L. Glen Seretan and James Stevenson have portrayed the so-called 'American Lenin' as being (1) 'flexible' in regard to the internal affairs of the SLP and (2) responsive to the views of the rank-and-file with whom he carried on a lively dialectical debate.[62] De Leon's *major* contribution to *socialist thought* was, moreover, dwarfed by the reputation he acquired in the 1890s as *the* sectarian sinner of American socialism *par excellence*, though he tried to make amends after 1900. By then, however, it was too late.

In 1895 De Leon persuaded the SLP to abandon the traditional socialist strategy of 'boring from within' the existing trade unions. Appalled and outraged by the reformist mentality of the leaders of the orthodox trade unions, the SLP now launched the Socialist Trade and Labour Alliance (STLA) as a rival to the Knights of Labour and the American Federation of Labour. Being quite obsessive about the need for ideological purity within the STLA, De Leon soon crushed a rank-and-file revolt led by Ernest Bohm and Thomas J. Morgan. Moreover, after De Leon's purge was repudiated in 1896 and the STLA removed him from power within the movement, he still managed to reverse the convention's democratic decision and placed one of his more malleable SLP members in a position of power.[63]

Although De Leon adopted greater flexibility towards other socialists in the labour movement from the foundation of the Industrial Workers of the World (IWW) in 1905 onwards, the new hostility he engendered amongst such anarchistic leaders of the IWW as William Trautman and Vincent St. John did nothing to enhance his credibility in the wider labour movement. Though he was much more flexible during the phase between 1905 and 1908, it did not save him from explusion from the IWW or the posthumous calumny of his enemies.[64] By 1908 the anarchist elements in the IWW needed a socialist sinner – or devil – who could be blamed for their lack of success in fostering the class struggle, and they found their man in De Leon. As the American historian, Melvyn Dubofsky puts it: 'They found their devil in Daniel De Leon; indeed, if he had not existed, they would have had to invent him.'[65]

Equally opposed to anti-intellectualism and the glorification of the proletarian status *per se*, De Leon took part in the labour movement as a *bona fide* trade unionist, and his experience, observations and reflections led him to conclude that most intellectuals drifted into the socialist movement to 'shine' and 'gather coppers'. Moreover, since higher education was only made possible by the excessive toil and hard work of the proletariat, middle-class intellectuals owed to the working class 'whatever advantages of education' they enjoyed.

In contrast to V.I. Lenin, Karl Kautsky and H.M. Hyndman, De Leon was fundamentally opposed to the existence of financially privileged intellectuals within the labour movement. When Louis Boudin applied for admission to the IWW, De Leon opposed the application and depicted lawyers as intellectual-exploiters or 'parasites upon those who draw interest'. His objection to Boudin's membership of the IWW was not a reflection of workerist anti-intellectualism, but part of an overall critique of the role of intellectuals in the labour movement.[66]

Unlike H.M. Hyndman – a man who dabbled in stockbroking and other entrepreneurial activities – De Leon refused to play the role of the entrepreneur. As L. Glen Seretan explains: 'De Leon refused to accept any remuneration for his writings, translations, and lectures and declined offers to write on socialism for commercial publications, because he could not abide personally profiting from his political work.'[67] Because he distrusted the alleged socialist commitment to many intellectuals in the labour movement in Europe and America, he sought to convince rank-and-file workers of the importance and accuracy of his analysis of the intellectuals' proper role in the struggle for socialism by living simply and unostentatiously.

A man of his own time and culture, De Leon placed an enormous importance on the historic achievements of the bourgeoisie in creating Parliamentary democracy, rudimentry mass education and the free and critical thought of the eighteenth-century Enlightenment. Far from being self-effacing or totally immersed in either the socialist movement or the American proletariat, it is difficult to think of a comparable militant intellectual in the international socialist movement who was more conscious of his own personality.[68] A well-defined consciousness of his own personality and intellectual gifts, together with an unshakeable belief in the socialist dream, reinforced De Leon's fearless critique of the shortcomings of the labour movement.

As De Leon belonged to the same socialism-from-below tradition as Antonio Labriola and Rosa Luxemburg, he attacked elitism in every shape and form. Opposed to the arguments of H.M. Hyndman that socialist theory must be evolved by intellectuals outside the working-class movement and injected into it, De Leon nevertheless fought for recognition of the indispensable role of the socialist intellectuals in helping to formulate Marxist theory. However, socialist intellectuals' contribution to socialist theory could only be authentic and effective in so far as they articulated the actual experience of working people engaged in struggle against capitalism. As this, in turn, meant that socialist intellectuals required to play a role in the day-to-day struggles of the working class, there could not be any scope in the labour movement for intellectuals as a privileged caste who were immune from party discipline.[69]

Moreover, as the first era of modern American class conflict began in 1885,[70] De Leon's appointment as a lecturer in law in an elite university in New York in 1883 placed him in a position where he could not ignore the eruption of struggles between rapacious employers and striking workers. If 'social being determines social consciousnss' as Marx argued in the 1840s, it is clear that the way individuals see themselves is an important part of their social being. As a man who had a strong social conscience, outstanding intelligence, unusual perception and high principles, De Leon's own mental conflicts, inner sufferings and search for an identity almost certainly gave him a *predisposition* to side with socialism when he found himself confronted with an inescapable choice.[71]

In a very profound sense De Leon anticipated many of the insights, perceptions and concepts of the Italian socialist thinker, Antonio Gramsci; and, though he was an avowed Marxist thinker and agitator, De Leon's distinctive socialist outlook and mental universe were not shared by many of the socialist leaders in the Second International. A thinker who always stressed the need to accentuate the dynamic of the class struggle, he implicitly repudiated the dominant orthodoxy of G.V. Plekhanov that 'being conscious of the absolute inevitability of a given phenomenon can only increase the energy of a man who sympathises with it and who regards himself as one of the forces which called it into being.'[72] Instead of ceding socialism to the automatic laws of history, De Leon asserted that:

The Socialist Republic is no predetermined inevitable development. The Socialist Republic depends, not upon material conditions only: it depends upon these – plus clearness of vision to assist the evolutionary process. Nor was the agency of the intellect more needful at any previous stage of social evolution in the class struggle to the extent that it is needful at this, the culminating one of all.[73]

As someone who, like Gramsci later on, made a conscious choice to become a socialist, De Leon repudiated the elitist notion that the working class would only come to socialist consciousness as a result of material deprivation.

If the bitter class conflict of the 1880s had done little to eradicate the problem of the paucity of socialist literature, the absence of a systematic body of Marxist doctrine provided De Leon with the stimulus to work out original analyses of a whole host of problems facing the American labour movement. As most of the works of Marx and Engels were still unavailable, the circumstances were propitious for De Leon to develop his ability to 'expound Marxist doctrine in the language of the marketplace.'[74] However, if what can often be seen with the benefit of hindsight as the crucial role of particular individuals in particular struggles testifies to the importance of the role of the individual in history, there can be no doubt of the importance of the interaction of the objective conditions within America and De Leon's distinctive personality in stimulating the growth of a native Marxism.

Nevertheless, heresy-hunters determined to judge De Leon 'guilty' of deviations from the strict letter of Marxist doctrine would not have too much difficulty in finding evidence. Even so, he was much more faithful to the critical, radical and *revolutionary spirit* of classical Marxism than many of the other socialist intellectuals of his generation. Like Marx, he refused to 'see reality in "the superficial semblance of things".' As he also shared Marx's conviction that 'the truth lay below the level of immediate perception' and required to be rescued by 'well-informed men with a gift for theorising and philosophical reflection or seized by the intuition of great artists',[75] he sought to 'teach the workers, to enlighten them on the great issues and of the great historic drama in which most of them (were) still unconscious actors.'[76]

Since the role of mystification in the day-to-day social life of capitalist society was such a dominant motif in the thought of Marx and Engels, it is not really surprising that De Leon devoted so much attention to the relationship between the role of mystification and working-class consciousness. Like Marx, De Leon also believed that, in S.S. Prawer's phrase, 'dreary words are meant to lull to sleep, to hide a praxis that goes on in the darkness or behind the scene, to conceal actions and motives never avowed in public.'[77] But while a highly developed awareness of the role of mystification engendered by the newspaper press, imaginative literature, the churches and the educational institutions of capitalist society led socialist intellectuals like Kautsky and Hyndman to portray working men and women as ignorant, servile, docile and uncultured, De Leon's conception of the 'vanguard' party of socialism rested on the assumption that the working class was capable of making a new civilisation. As his profoundly democratic and anti-elitist view of the working class was central to his interpretation of Marxism, it is worth quoting what he told a meeting of striking workers in New Bedford, Massachusetts in 1896:

Three years ago I was in your midst during another strike. The superficial observer who looks back to your attitude during that strike, who looks back to the strikes that preceded that one, who now turns his eyes to your attitude in the present strike, and who discovers substantially no difference between your attitude now and then might say, 'Why, it is a waste of time to speak to such men; they will eternally fight the same hopeless battle; the battle to establish "safe relations" with the capitalist class, with the same hopeless weapon: the "pure and simple" organisation of labour'. But the socialist does not take that view. There is one thing about your conduct that enlists for and entitles you to the warm sympathy of the socialist, and that is that, despite your persistent errors in fundamental principles, in aims and methods, despite the illusions you are chasing after, despite the increasing poverty and culminating failures that press upon you, despite all that you preserve manhood enough not to submit to oppression, but rise in *the rebellion* that is implied in a strike. The attitude of workingmen engaged in a *bona fida* strike is an inspiring one. It is an earnest that slavery will not prevail. The slave alone who will not rise against his master, who will meekly bend his back to the lash and turn his cheek to him who plucks his beard – that slave alone is hopeless. But the slave who, as you of New Bedford, persists, despite failures and poverty, in rebelling, there is always hope for.[78]

In contrast to those socialists – for example, H.M. Hyndman and Karl Kautsky – who regarded the working class as 'a dumb driven herd', the major architect of American socialism asserted again and again that 'Pantomines, double sense and mummery may answer the purpose of a movement in which the proletariat acts only the role of dumb driven beasts of burden.'[79] Nevertheless, De Leon spent the whole of his life from his conversion to Marxism in 1890 to his death in 1914 urging the international working classes of the need for *'vanguard'* socialist parties. As James A. Stevenson puts it: 'Long before the Bolshevik party was formed, De Leon's work, *Reform or Revolution*, defined the nature of the revolutionary vanguard party and served with his other writings as the inspiration for the "impossibilist" revolt against the amorphous (British) Social Democratic Federation.'[80] Moreover, as the critical, iconoclastic, revolutionary spirit of Marxism permeated every aspect of De Leon's writings and interventions in strikes and debates, it needs to be emphasised that his unyielding advocacy of the need for a disciplined 'vanguard' socialist party complemented and reinforced the agitation for socialism-from-below. In *Two Pages from Roman History*, De Leon summed up the role of an authentic socialist party in tearing away 'the veil of hypocrisy with which the capitalist class' sought to conceal its 'deeds of mayhem and murder' and the task of the advocates of socialism-from-below when he said: 'Other revolutions could succeed with loose organisation and imperfect information. In the first place, they were otherwise ballasted; in the second, being grounded on the slavery of some class, a dumb driven herd of an army could fit in their social architecture. Otherwise with the proletariat. It needs information for ballast as for sails, and its organisation must be marked with intelligent co-operation. The proletarian army of emancipation cannot consist of a dumb driven herd.'[81]

Against the background of the intense class conflict of the late 1880s Daniel De Leon was convinced that the American working class was, in Stephen Cohen's phrase, 'in the process of becoming a conscious mass of conscious personalities.'[82] Though De Leon frequently deviated from the strict letter of Marxist orthodoxy, he was much closer to its critical, iconoclastic and revolutionary spirit than Kautsky, Hyndman or Plekhanov. Yet he did not assume that working people were only motivated to protest against the injustices engendered by capitalism by some direct material stimulus. Just as he repudiated the notion that the working classes were the victims of a game of behavouristic chess, so he did not hesitate to blame the leaders of the British Social Democratic Federation for the extreme poverty and degradation of the working class. In contrast to Karl Kautsky who lambasted the British workers for being 'dumb' and spiritless',[83] De Leon put the blame on the leaders of British socialism such as Hyndman and Bax:

It is not capitalism that must alone bear the blame for the degraded condition in which the British workers are to be found. The British socialists are themselves to blame, and theirs is the main blame.[84]

In an interesting, analytical study of *Daniel De Leon: The Relationship of the Socialist Labour Party and European Marxism, 1900–1914*, James Stevenson argues that 'another omission which seriously hampered the practical acceptance of his doctrine was the idea that the social revolution required no transitional period such as the "dictatorship" of the proletariat".'[85] However, while it could be argued that De Leon's assessment and analysis of the problem of the transition to socialism was naive and inadequate, he did not ignore the problem.

As one of the seminal thinkers of his generation of titanic socialist figures, De Leon's conception of socialism rested on a profound faith in the ability of the Anglo-American working classes to undertake the socialist reconstruction of society. An undying confidence in the ability of working men and women to make new social relationships was inseparable from De Leon's condemnation of the elitist socialism-from-above prescriptions of State socialism. This is aptly summed up in Frank Bugden's autobiography where he says: 'What gave all believers faith in De Leon's interpretation of Marxist theory was that it showed a way ahead unobstructed by a "dictatorship of the proletariat". The loyal Engles' attempt to gild that bitter pill had made it no easier to swallow, whereas De Leon's interpretation made of democracy the ally of revolution.'[86] Since De Leon believed that the main problem facing the existing socialist parties was the one of mystification, he did not gloss over the question of the 'transition to socialism.'[87]

Besides, as De Leon did not believe that working-class culture was inimical to the development of socialist sentiments on a large scale, he could conceive of the growth of a mass movement for socialism-from-below provided the 'vanguard' socialist parties took advantage of the opportunities afforded to them by existing democratic structures. Capitalist cultural 'supremacy' was certainly a formidable problem, and in the American SLP's report to the Zurich International Socialist Congress in 1893 De Leon directed attention to the problem of the mystification of social relationships within capitalist society.

The difficulties that surround the work of enlightened propaganda are increased by a school system of automatic thinking, that disables the mind from going to the bottom of things, thus preventing it from comprehending the causes of the recognised evils, and keeping it from undertaking any systematic changes in public life; this school system prompts our people to stick fast to existing conditions, or at best to resort to spasmodic and planless experiments, which naturally run speedily into the ground, leaving nothing but shattered hopes behind.

This was, moreover, *the* problem which had to be overcome before the socialist reconstruction of society could be undertaken. Once the problem of capitalist cultural 'supremacy' had been overcome, the working classes would already have taken the most important step in beginning to solve the problem of the transition to socialism. As De Leon put it in 1901: 'The overthrow of the government you must aim at must be to the end of using governmental power to perfect the revolution that must have preceded your conquest of public powers. The *initial revolution must be accomplished in your minds*. You must have divorced yourselves from the habits of thought that have been used to your enslavement; you must have come to an understanding that you are the sole producers of all wealth.'[88]

But if the existence of a mass socialist consciousness was a basic pre-condition for solving the problems of the transition to socialism before the conquest of State power, the complexities of De Leon's thought born out of a collective experience in the class struggle led him to conceive of socialist education as a dialectical phenomenon. As he told a mass meeting of working men and women after the witch-hunt of members of the SLP following the assassination of the American President, William McKinley: 'You cannot move faster than the masses move with you in this twentieth century. Aye, even in Russia the masses have a good deal to say. In some countries they are active forces, in other countries, passive forces: but forces, social forces, they have become all the same.'[89]

It was, moreover, a recognition of the peculiarities of American capitalism and the distinctive obstacles inhibiting socialism which led De Leon to observe that 'The natives' old illusions regarding material prospects draw the bulk of the immigrants into their vortex.'[90] But just as he saw mystification and capitalist cultural 'supremacy' as a contradictory, double-edged phenomenon, so he also argued that 'the backwardness of the socialist movement in America (was) on the surface only.'[91] However, as De Leon's optimism about mass socialist consciousness did not in 'these days of electric rapidity' need '*five hundred years* to shape the proletariat of the land into another world-fagot', he theoretically solved the problems inherent in the transition to socialism without surrendering the gains attained by bourgeois Parliamentary democracy when he summed up thus: 'As in biology the same elements when submitted to different temperature and atmospheric pressure will produce different substances, so in sociology. The Socialist Republic will not leap into existence out of the existent social loom, as a yard of calico is turned out by a Northrop loom. Nor will its only possible architect, the working class – that is, the wage earners, or wage slaves, the modern proletariat – figure in the process moved mechanically. In other words, the world's theatre of social evolution is not a Punch and Judy box, nor are the actors on the world's stage manikins operated with wires.'[92]

Since De Leon argued that '*revolutionists* ripen fast' in situations where effective 'vanguard' socialist parties could accentuate 'the awakening socialist sentiments' of working men and women,[93] he was aware that violence could not be ruled out during the transition to socialism. But just as the SLP 'decline(d) to be responsible for the life of a single human being sacrificed upon the alter of facuity',[94] so did De Leon argue that the socialist revolution was not 'ripe enough to triumph' by means of a general strike unless it could first triumph by means of securing a mass socialist vote at the polls.[95] Furthermore, as he assumed a mass socialist consciousness as a necessary pre-condition for the social revolution, he spelt out what differentiated previous social revolutions from the new socialist civilisation.

In none of these other uprisings did the masses count; in all of them a minority class alone was interested, struck the keynote and furnished the music – with the masses only as deluded camp-followers. It is otherwise with the approaching Social Revolution. It is of the people, if it is anything.[96]

IV

H.M. Hyndman's deep emotional attachment to the concept of socialism-from-above dictated and shaped his world-view including his support for militarism. Unlike Daniel De Leon whose shared sectarianism also played a counter-productive role in working-class movements struggling for socialism, he left no intellectual legacy of value to democratic socialists in the late twentieth century. Yet despite De Leon's often ferocious sectarian attitudes in the 1890s, he always opposed racism and imperialism throughout the world. By contrast, Hyndman often articulated anti-Semitic prejudices and sometimes adopted pro-imperialist stances towards other countries.

In 1896 when the Irish Socialist Republic Party published a manifesto supporting the agitation for Irish independence, Hyndman argued that 'talk of winning complete separation from all connection with the British Empire sounds a bit out of place in a socialist manifesto'. Against Hyndman's constant and consistent ambiguity towards British imperialism, De Leon characterised 'the British flag with its Three Crosses quartered' as a symbol of the violent 'annexation of Scotland and Ireland to England.'[97] After the outbreak of the South African war towards the end of the nineteenth century, Hyndman said: 'I do not believe we are acting worse than the other European powers would have acted under the circumstances.[98]

At the very heart of De Leon's conception of socialism-from-below was the assumption that working men and women were capable of making history and governing their own lives. In applying the principle of socialism-from-below to other countries as well as America, he wrote about the Russian revolution of 1905 as follows:

At any rate the start has been given. The "white man's burden" was suddenly assumed by the yellow man of Nippon. "Backward" Japan in the Far East gave a kick westward; that set Russia agoing. Is Russia, in turn, to transmit the kick further West, and each successive nation rising to their feet stamping out their special varieties of Czarism?[99]

In sharp contrast to Hyndman's narrow English nationalism, De Leon was always interested in the latent militancy of oppressed peoples in underdeveloped countries as well as in the potentialities of the *proletariat* in the metropolitan countries.

Although Hyndman shared De Leon's interest in the writings of Eugene Sue, he did not really transcend the prosaic attitudes and language of the English bourgeoisie. While he planned to 'write a utopian romance in the vein of Edward Bellamy's *Looking Backward* or Morris's *News from Nowhere*, and this was to be entitled *The Life to Come*: only a prefatory section, however, was completed before his death.'[100] Unlike De Leon's proclivity for communicating in the 'vulgar' tongue and in 'the idiom of the working man',[101] the centrality of socialism-from-above within Hyndman's world-view compelled him to 'write down' and 'talk above' the heads of working men and women.

Means and ends were inseparable. The authoritarian and democratic souls of socialism dictated the distinctive languages used by H.M. Hyndman and Daniel De Leon. By comparison with De Leon, Hyndman made no real contribution to socialist literature. As a self-avowed elitist, Hyndman could not derive any strength or stimulus from ordinary men and women in working-class movements. Yet despite his sectarian attitudes towards reformist trade unions, *some* of De Leon's attitudes were democratic. Without being unaware or uncritical of his many sins and weakensses as a socialist practitioner, John Carstairs Matheson, the Scottish socialist, identified what was of enduring value in De Leon's life when he wrote:

To the consternation of the old school, De Leon proved that simplicity and directness of appeal do not involve a sacrifice of consistency and soundness, but that these qualities go hand in hand. He had earned for himself a place in the Pantheon of Labour's mighty dead, if for no other reason than his masterly lucidity as a expounder of socialism.[102]

Chapter 3

James Connolly and Karl Liebknecht: Socialist martyrs

It is true that the romantically attractive and unblemished image of the days of Debs and Jack London can never return. Socialists can never again be the "golden boys" of history that they were in pre-World War I years, idealism unscathed, overwhelmingly persuasive to men and women of goodwill, with every moral credit in the column, and nothing shameful to answer for.

Harry Braverman

The list of our martyrs is as long as the life of the working class. Fortunate were those among them who fell fighting the open class enemy, fell in the midst of battle with their comrades beside them. Most terrible of all is to die alone at the stiletto point of those who call themselves socialists or communists, as Karl Liebknecht and Rosa Luxemburg died, as our comrades are dying in the execution chambers of Siberian exile.

Felix Morrow

Out of the protracted and bitter struggle for socialism, the creation of martyrs was inevitable. With the exception of Jean Jaurés, who fell as a victim of war hysteria in 1914, most of the modern socialist martyrs – for example, the Chicago Martyrs (1887), Alfred Linnell (1888), Francisco Ferrer (1909) and Sacco and Vanzetti (1928) – were the victims of uncomplicated ruling-class repression or simple vindictiveness. Furthermore, the First World War did not only split and ensure the demise of the Second International; it also engendered murderous schisms in labour movements throughout the world.

James Connolly (1868–1916) and Karl Liebknecht (1871–1919) were not seen as clear-cut, unambiguous socialist martyrs at the time of their deaths. Although Leon Trotsky singled out John Maclean, the Scottish socialist, for special praise when he published an article on the Dublin rebellion in 1916, he did not even mention James Connolly. He was much more interested in stressing Sir Roger Casement's 'outworn hopes' of a 'national revolution' in Ireland. Yet in 1919 Trotsky depicted Karl Liebknecht as a socialist martyr who belonged 'not to a nation but to the Communist International.'[1]

Moreover, although the 'heroes' of the 'Dublin barricades' required, in Trotsky's opinion, to be defended against the criticism of Georges Plekhanov, the Irish workers' revolt against 'militarism and imperialism' was fought 'under an out-of-date flag'. Therefore the omission of the name of James Connolly in an article in which John Maclean was cited could not have been accidental. In Lenin's article on 'The Irish Rebellion of 1916', Connolly's name was again omitted. For Lenin it was 'the misfortune of the Irish that they rose prematurely, before the European revolt of the proletariat had had time to mature'. While supporting the workers' revolt in Dublin in 1916, Trotsky and Lenin could not support – still less portray as a socialist martyr – a working-class leader who fought under an outmoded nationalist flag.[2]

By 1919 the communist Third International did not have any difficulty in claiming Karl Liebknecht as a socialist martyr, though he acted independently of the German communist leaders. As Leon Trotsky put it: 'Karl Liebknecht represented the genuine and finished embodiment of an intransigent revolutionary. In the last days and months of his life there have been created around his name innumerable legends: senselessly vicious ones in the bourgeois press, heroic ones on the lips of the working masses.'[3] At the same time, H.M. Hyndman the pro-war English socialist leader, claimed Karl Liebknecht as a genuine socialist martyr who was most certainly not a Bolshevik. In summing up, he said:

There is nothing whatever to show that either of our friends and comrades (Karl Liebknecht and Rosa Luxemburg) of old time shared in the hideous cult of Moloch, of which Trotsky, Lenin, Tchicherine, Litvinoff and their followers are the high priests. Far from that, both were high-minded and humane Social-Democrats with an anarchist strain in them. The Bolsheviks were traitors and murderers in German pay from the start. But that does not by any means imply that everyone who takes part in a forcible movement against capitalism is a Bolshevik.[4]

Of the two major socialist martyrs created by the events unleashed by the First World War, James Connolly was much more of an enigma than Karl Liebknecht. Though there were enigmatical elements in the lives of both men, the spartan Connolly was the sphinx at the end of the columns celebrating Labour's martyred dead. In any case, contradictions abounded. While Liebknecht's martyrdom had been anticipated in the international labour movement long before 1919, Connolly's martyrdom had not been foreseen at all. Unlike Lenin and Trotsky, H.M. Hyndman did not approve of the Easter rebellion in Dublin. But in depicting the death of James Connolly, he wrote an essay illuminating why Connolly could not be acknowledged or shared by a unified community of the Left as a socialist martyr. He concluded as follows:

Much more than a reverence for Ireland's history and language, and an eager desire to control their country's destiny at any cost, was needed to give such a revolution-ary effort any chance of success against the overwhelming forces on the other side. ... Though Connolly had long gone out of our own movement, he did thoroughly good service while he was with us, and was unquestionably an honest, determined and capable enthusiast with brains. ... There can be no sadder criticism of our society of today than that fine, able fellows should have seen so little hope for their class and their country that they deliberately threw themselves away on this mad endeavour; and that the *national soldiers* of the same social stratum as themselves should feel impelled to shoot them down as men afflicted with criminal insanity.[5]

By 1919 it was crystal-clear that the gulf separating the Bolsheviks from the independent Left throughout the world was quite unbridgeable. Although James Connolly and Karl Liebknecht perceived and portrayed themselves as Marxian socialists, they did not see the world through the same Bolshevik lens as Lenin and (after 1917) Trotsky. Being sceptical of narrow materialist interpretations of history, Connolly and Liebknecht did not accept a prefigurative form of Bolshevik morality. While Connolly's socialism was always suffused with Catholicism,[6] Liebknecht's socialist-humanism owed more to the European Enlightenment than 'the world of socialist theory.'[7]

In identifying the enigmatical elements in James Connolly's develop-ment as a socialist martyr, Owen Dudley Edwards says that he was 'a devoutly spiritual materialist, a Marxist Catholic and a nationalist inter-nationalist.'[8] Similarly, in depicting the hitherto hidden enigmatical strands in Liebknecht's personality, Helmut Trotnow said: 'Although Liebknecht can be regarded as a determinist as far as the goal of human development is concerned, as a humanist and follower of the Enlightenment, he was convinced of the good in man.' In sharp contrast to this diverse world of Western socialism stood the more uniform world of Leon Trotsky and the Bolshevik intelligentsia for whom a-moral materialism was often a static force reinforcing the existing social order. As Isaac Deutscher put it:

Trotsky, however, does not invoke the innate goodness or rationality of man, nor does he believe in any automatic perfectability of human society. . . . He is all too well aware of the somber impasses into which men had driven themselves so many times, of the vicious circles within which rising and declining civilisations had moved, of the countless generations, faceless and nameless to us, that had lived in unredeemable slavery and of the huge, immeasurable mass of cruelty and suffering man has inflicted on man.[9]

But Connolly's passionate nationalist hatred of English imperialism was just as powerful a force for historical change as Lenin's hatred of Tsarism.

James Connolly was not, however, immediately seen as a hero or socialist martyr. By 1916 he was more of a nationalist than a socialist, and it was not until 1919 that the communists in Britain depicted him as a socialist martyr. He was, in a phrase he used about Karl Liebknecht in 1914, 'a martyr for conscience sake' but he was not in any unambiguous sense a socialist martyr.

Already a potential socialist martyr in 1914, Karl Liebknecht's martyr-dom in 1919 was also problematic and questionable. Furthermore, it has been suggested that his actual 'martyrdom' was a product of his own political expediency rather than conscience. In any case, the enigmatical threads of the cloaks with which Connolly and Liebknecht shrouded themselves were woven within the democratic cottage-industry of the Second International.

Just as there were two James Connollys, so there were two Karl Liebknechts. While the enigmatical strands – or double-identity – of Connolly's political personality were begot in 'Little Ireland', Edinburgh, Liebknecht's double-identity as a German and international socialist crystallised within the family milieu of his famous fugitive father, Wilhelm Liebknecht. In capturing the essence of Connolly's enigmatic personality, Austen Morgan says: 'There was but one Connolly, but he drew on the separate traditions of Second International Marxism and Irish nationalism. Hence two Connollys can be detected in his work in the unrelated and incompatible paradigms of class and nation.'[10] Similarly, Karl W. Meyer, the American historian, insisted that Liebknecht 'wanted Russian Bolshevism, not German socialism.'[11] Although he would not have accepted Meyer's depiction of Liebknecht as an advocate of Russian rather than German socialism, Leon Trotsky conveyed a similar image when he said:

Distinctive even in his appearance, especially his thick lips and dark curly hair which made him look like a "foreigner" although he was a pure German, Liebknecht always remained half a stranger in the house of German Social-Democracy with its inner sense of measure and perennial readiness to compromise.[12]

I

James Connolly was born in Edinburgh in 1868. He began to work in 1878, when he was ten years of age, enlisted in the British army four years later, and discharged himself in 1889. An activist in the Scottish labour movement between 1889 and 1896, scholars and historians are at odds with each other over the question of when he first became an Irish nationalist. His stark and soul-destroying poverty and deprivation in 'proletarian' Edinburgh were mitigated by the experience of living in a cohesive community of Irish immigrants.

Although the terrible poverty of Connolly's upbringing and early life almost certainly contributed to his alienation from capitalist society, the Scottish sectarian prejudice he must have been subjected to during his formative years gave him an Irish nationalist disposition. In sketching in the background of Connolly's early life, C. Desmond Greaves says:

Anti-Irish feeling, with a sectarian tinge, had much in common with anti-Semitism. Two lives were lost when the tents of provision sellers at Musselburgh races were searched for Irishmen after a minor dispute. On another occasion local labourers invaded the Cowgate area and assaulted every Irishman they could find, wrecking the shops of second-hand clothes sellers, and smashing the doors and windows of Irish houses.

The effect was to drive the Irish close together in the ghetto of "Little Ireland" and to increase the overcrowding of its teeming warrens. To some extent class-consciousness was postponed.[13]

In discussing James Connolly's 'socialist beginnings', Carl Reeve and Ann Barton say: 'Murtagh Lyng, friend and associate of Connolly as a young man, said "Connolly was dragged up like most proletarian boys", though he was, nevertheless, "well educated" as the result of the different circumstances under which he lived. He developed "a deep hatred of those institutions which have weighed so heavily on the working class".' It was, in fact, Connolly's intense hatred of existing bourgeois institutions which ultimately led him on the road to Easter Week, 1916, not any prefigurative Leninism.[14]

Hatred was a powerful motive in the radical politics of James Connolly from the late nineteenth century onwards. Although C. Desmond Greaves does not discuss hatred as a motive-force of Connolly's politics, he sketches in some of the ingredients that probably went into the making of the so-called Irish Lenin's profound sense of disaffection from the established social order. In the first place, Connolly developed slight bow-leggedness as a result of rickets. Secondly, while he was still a boy, he experienced a breakdown in health. At the same time, he imbibed the nationalist passions of the Irish immigrants. As C. Desmond Greaves puts it: 'Whatever the precise foundation for the family tradition that Connolly was taught Irish nationalism by a Fenian uncle who enlisted under the name of MacBride and retained it after settling in Edinburgh, in these days he could scarcely have escaped it. The jailing of the Land League leaders in 1881 was followed by a manifesto calling for a general withholding of rent.'[15]

Yet despite C. Desmond Greaves authoritative biography, Connolly remains an enigma. P. Berresford Ellis speculates that he probably developed 'his Irish nationalist consciousness' while he belonged to the King's Liverpool Regiment.[16] Since Connolly spent most of his army service in Ireland, he could not have escaped the influence of Irish nationalism. Nevertheless, Bernard Ransom argues that his 'definite ethnic consciousness' should not be confused 'with Irish nationalism as an intellectual/spiritual commitment'. In attempting to locate the growth of Connolly's Irish nationalism *after* he went to Dublin in 1896, Ransom argues that:

Indeed, his total detachment from the emigre Irish nationalist cause in his Edinburgh years is indicated by his municipal campaigns in 1894 and 1895, when his avowed socialist candidacies were advanced in "Little Ireland" in the teeth of virulent opposition from the local caucus of the Irish National League.[17]

In searching for the sources of James Connolly's profound hatred of the established social order, it is not possible to ignore the interaction of ethnic consciousness, Irish nationalism and a *vague* radicalism among the immigrants in Edinburgh and elsewhere in industrial Scotland. Although some of them came to the Scottish working-class movement before and some of them after Connolly's conversion to socialism in 1889, he was only one of a small army of Irish immigrants who helped to create Scottish radicalism in the late nineteenth century. The innumerable Irish-Catholic immigrants who played a major role in the Scottish labour movement included R. Chisholm Robertson, Hugh Murin, John L. Mahon, J. Shaw Maxwell, John Leslie, John Wheatley, Pete Curran, Andew McCowie and Patrick Mac-Gill, the novelist.[18]

In using a remarkably accurate phrase 'Irishmen as Scottish socialists', H.W. Lee and E. Archbold went on to say that 'some of the best comrades in the socialist movement in Scotland were Irishmen'.[19] But although they often developed a sort of dual-identity as Irishmen and Scots, they owed their basic loyalty to the objectives of socialism.

While John Leslie converted James Connolly to socialism in 1889, Leslie remained an anti-nationalist Marxian socialist until his death in 1921.[20] R. Chisholm Robertson, the Scottish miners' leader and first secretary of the Independent Labour Party, was also a passionate Irish nationalist and socialist in the 1880s and 1890s.[21] A practising Catholic and prominent member of the Irish National League, he was often at loggerheads with the leaders of Irish nationalism in Scotland over their refusal to muster the Irish-Catholic vote for the evolving Labour Party.[22]

Seen in the much wider context of the radicalisation of the Irish immigrants in Slammanan, Broxburn, the Lanarkshire coalfields and Edinburgh, it is simply wrong to assert that James Connolly was not an Irish nationalist before he went to Dublin as an organiser for the Dublin Socialist Club in July 1896. When he wrote to Keir Hardie from an address in Edinburgh in July 1894, Connolly described himself 'as an Irishman who had always taken a keen interest in the advanced movements in Ireland'. Then he went on to advise Hardie: 'Now if you were to visit Dublin and address a good meeting there, putting it strong and straight, without reference to either of the Irish parties, but *rebellious*, *anti-monarchical* and outspoken on the fleecings of both landlord and capitalist, and the hypocrisy of both parties for a finale.'[23] But in contrast to John Leslie, John L. Mahon, R. Chisholm Robertson or any of the other Irish immigrants in Scotland, Connolly was already much more alienated from British imperialism.

The combination of the absorption of Fenian attitudes within his family during his formative years with persistent poverty toughened James Connolly's revolutionary sentiments and convictions. By 1896 it became virtually impossible for the Connolly family to exist in Edinburgh and arrangements were made for them to emigrate to Chile. A last minute attempt was made to find an alternative, and John Leslie wrote in *Justice*: 'Connolly is, I have said, an unskilled labourer, a life-long abstainer, sound in mind and limb. . . . Married, with a young family, and as his necessities are therefore very great, so he may be had cheap.'[24] The upshot was that the Dublin Socialist Club gave him a job as a full-time organiser.

As early as 1896 James Connolly corresponded with and developed connections with the De Leonite Socialist Labour Party in New York. Despite the De Leonites notorious reputation for doctrinaire sectarianism, they were particularly sympathetic towards Connolly's strange brand of Irish-Marxism. In a letter that he sent to Henry Kuhn, the secretary of the Socialist Labour Party in May 1896, Connolly said: 'We recognise the enormous importance of being duly represented among our countrymen in America, and we also hope you will perceive how much it would help you, to assist the socialist movement in Ireland. Irishmen are largely influenced by sentiment and tradition, and therefore a word from what they affectionately term the "auld sod" will far outweigh any amount of reasoning applied to American issues only. Show them that socialism has a definite message from Ireland and you awaken their sympathy immediately.[25] However, what the American De Leonites really appreciated in Connolly was the obvious strength of his revolutionary convictions. Yet in reading Connolly's late nineteenth-century letters to other socialists, it is difficult to disentangle his revolutionary, non-partisan but all-embracing Irish nationalism from his very partisan Second International Marxism.

Although the almost schizophrenic quality in his simultaneous attachment to the Second International and disaffection from the established social order was often hidden from Connolly's contemporaries, it sometimes came to the surface long before the outbreak of the First World War. Ethnic and religious tensions existed in the Scottish socialist movement itself and not just among unorganised men and women. In promoting Patrick MacGill's first socialist book in the pages of *Forward*, the Scottish socialist newspaper, John Maclean articulated strong anti-Catholic remarks. Even Maclean, the least sectarian of the Presbyterian' socialists, was, in Harry McShane's phrase, 'opposed to the Catholic Church in a Calvinist way as well as in a Marxist way.'[26] This was the background against which Connolly sometimes expressed resentment when socialists like Maclean criticised the Catholic Church.[27]

In reconstructing the context of the Scottish socialist movement at that time, Ralph Samuel says: 'Scottish socialism in this period seems to have been particularly militant in its atheism, and for many of those who came to it – whether through the Independent Labour Party, the Social Democratic Federation or the Socialist Labour Party – religion and the Church were "the big enemy".'[28] What was interesting about this conflict inside Scottish socialism was Tom Bell's account of it many years later. He described his encounter with Connolly during their shared agitation for the Socialist Labour Party in Scotland in 1903:

I remember challenging him one day, after a meeting at Falkirk Cross when the question was hotly debated by some Orangemen who were in the crowd, and asking him how he could reconcile being a Catholic and an exponent of the materialist conception of history. His reply was that in Dublin the children who go to Catholic schools invariably turn out to be rebels but if they are brought up in the Presbyterian Church they turn out to be howling jingoes. To me this was not a convincing argument, but it was left at that.

In a later version of the same story, Bell said that the Connolly who denounced the Catholic Church also stressed his own Catholicism. Furthermore, Connolly 'related stories of workers in the Irish Socialist Republican Party going to mass of a morning and delivering the *Irish Worker* at houses on the road.'[29] The most obvious aspect of Connolly's life before he went to work for the Socialist Labour Party in America in 1903 was the depth of his disaffection from the British Lion.

The context in which James Connolly functioned as a socialist organiser in Dublin between 1896 and 1903 was a very difficult one. The Irish working class was divided between the majority who supported Irish nationalism and the minority who supported Ulster unionism. Connolly's attempts to develop a powerful socialist counter-culture were vitiated by his failure to address the question of the divisions within the Irish working class.

The poverty which circumscribed Connolly's life in those years had a profound influence on his specific socialist world-view. In 1896 one young Irish nationalist was simultaneously disturbed and fascinated by Connolly's socialism. Indeed, Connolly told Ernest Milligan that: 'Politics are based on the stomach, and economic causes have moulded history.'[30] But Connolly's socialist counter-culture was much less 'economistic' than John Maclean's[31] though it was deeply nationalistic. In contrast to John Maclean's preoccupation with Marxian economics. Connolly was interested in Irish Gaelic, imaginative literature and the theatre.

In other countries prominent socialists were absorbed into the hierarchies of their own socialist organisations with the result that their revolutionary convictions were sometimes dulled. This did not happen to James Connolly. A combination of stark and crushing poverty and a 'social being' of collective social experience of working within an anti-imperialist nationalist culture kept him very hostile to the established social order.

Connolly's social being was inseparable from Irish nationalism. In approving of the rise of the Irish nationalist movement as the catalyst in Connolly's later martyrdom, Oscar Williams, an American Trotskyist, traced the antecedents of the Irish rebellion back to the cultural and literary revival in late nineteenth-century Ireland. The Gaelic League played a progressive and decisive role in this development. In summing up, Williams said:

The theatre, especially the Abbey Theatre of Dublin, also played an important role. Choosing the subject matter of their plays from the daily life of the oppressed people, these playwrights and actors became an instrument in the fight for national independence. Far from an abstract art in an ivory tower, the plays of the Abbey Theatre, through touring companies and hundreds of amateur groups, succeeded in reaching wide sections of the people in the urban and rural areas.

Some of these artists and intellectuals took leading roles in the political and social struggles and were to pay with their lives for their devotion to the fight.[32]

This was, moreover, the milieu in which Connolly lived and breathed before he went to work in America, in 1903, as a socialist agitator and teacher.

James Connolly toured central Scotland on behalf of the 'impossibilist' branches of the Social Democratic Federation (SDF) in Falkirk, Glasgow and Edinburgh. In the process of breaking away from the SDF to form the Socialist Labour Party, a letter that Connolly sent to John Carstairs Matheson on 8 April was important for two reasons. In the first place, it revealed Connolly's intense hatred of his poverty. This was clearly one of the ingredients in his ongoing disaffection. Secondly, it was one of the earliest indications of the so-called 'Irish Lenin's' close friendship with the most disaffected of the revolutionary socialists in Scotland's industrial heartlands. As Connolly wrote to Matheson: 'I am wearying for my Scotch tour to commence. It is the centrepiece of my plans for the whole year as I intend to go to America in the autumn and bring my family out after me. . . . In any case I consider that the party here has no longer that exclusive demand on my life which led me in the past to sacrifice my children's welfare for years in order to build it up.'[33]

Arriving in America in the autumn of 1903, James Connolly lived there until 1910. In those hectic, intense and dramatical years, he worked and quarrelled with Daniel De Leon and the Socialist Labour Party. Then he joined the Socialist Party of America and the infamous Industrial Workers of the World. Although Connolly produced *Labour in Irish History*, *Socialism Made Easy* and *Labour, Nationality and Religion* during his sojourn in America, he did not free himself from the bitter-sweet taste of poverty. As Carl Reeve and Ann Barton observe: 'He was dogged by poverty most of his life in the United States, often barely managing to feed his family.'[34] In contrast to Daniel De Leon, however, he did not accept his grinding, oppressive poverty at all philosophically.

During his years in America, Connolly always sought to reach the Irish-Catholic workers with his unique message of socialism-cum-nationalism. When he published a collection of his verse and songs in New York in 1907, he contributed a preface in which he said:

No revolutionary movement is complete without its poetical expression. If such a movement has caught hold of the imagination of the masses, they will seek a vent in song for the aspirations, the fears and hopes, the loves and hatreds engendered by the struggle. Until the movement is marked by the joyous, defiant, singing of revolutionary songs, it lacks one of the most distinct marks of a few, and not the faith of the multitude.[35]

In quarrelling with De Leon over Marxian socialists' attitudes to the Catholic Church, Connolly also argued with De Leon over sexual questions, 'free love', and the nature of socialist revolution as well as religion.

Connolly was, of course portrayed as the ideal prefigurative Bolshevik leader in Irish history – at least by a later generation of Trotskyists. As early as 1936 Maurice Ahearn, an American Trotskyist, suggested parallels between the arguments presented in Trotsky's *Permanent Revolution* and Connolly's *Erin's Hope, the End and the Means*. In making a case against the Stalinists, he said that Connolly, too, was guilty of 'skipping stages' in the struggle for socialist revolution.[36]

Furthermore, Albert Gates, the American Trotskyist, subsequently argued that 'internationalist, though he (Connolly) was, the problem of the Irish revolution' remained paramount in his preoccupations. Far from regarding Connolly's work in the Socialist Labour Party, the Socialist Party of America or the Industrial Workers of the World as being important in the history of American socialism, Gates insisted that:

There is a great similarity in the conduct of Connolly during his stay in the United States and that of the Bolsheviks in exile. While he carried on a literary and speaking campaign to advance the socialist movement and industrial unionism in America, his real interest was Ireland and the development of the Irish revolution. As a matter of fact, Connolly never once regarded his migration to the United States as anything permanent. And when the labour movement in Ireland began to manifest a new restlessness, when new forces made their appearance, when the objective situation became more tense, his return to Ireland was only a matter of days.[37]

In 1913 the major employers in Dublin combined forces in a sustained attempt to crush the Irish Transport and General Workers' Union. This world-famous struggle between the forces of capital and labour had a profound influence on James Connolly's martyrdom in 1916. In the first place, it gave rise to the emergence of the Irish Citizen Army.[38] Secondly, the failure of the labour movement in Scotland, England and Wales to respond to what was happening in Dublin deepened Connolly's disillusionment with the British labour movement. As Desmond Ryan put it:

The subsequent failure of the British labour movement to back the Dublin workers by industrial action sadly disillusioned him . . .

A powerful internationalist and Industrial Unionist note dominated all his speeches. . . . As one reads, the memory returns to recall vividly the stolid yet fiery apostle of the Labour evangel, ever idealist and human, never losing sight of the stars as he battled in the mire of mean streets, nor in the arid debating rooms of socialist sectarians, nor yet in capitalists' offices for the welfare of the class he loved, the vision of the future commonwealth shining above many a weary and dreary struggle.[39]

But although the bitter conflict in 'disturbed Dublin' played a major part in the making of Connolly's martyrdom, there was something almost 'predestined' about the forces transforming both Connolly and Liebknecht into 'socialist' martyrs of world stature.

II

Once the First World War broke out in 1914, it was quite clear that James Connolly and Karl Liebknecht might seek martrydom as a means of promoting and advancing the socialist cause. While Connolly's constant and unmitigated poverty and ethnic alienation gave him a strong disposition to become a martyr, the motivation behind Liebknecht's martyrdom was, though predictable, very complex.

Karl Liebknecht was born on 13 August 1871, the same year in which his father, Wilhelm, was arrested on the charge of high treason. It was a very difficult time for the Liebknechts, though Karl's mother was a committed socialist in her own right. In touching on the formative influences in Karl's early life, Walter Weyl said:

His mother was wont to say that she bequeathed to her son all the sorrow that was hers during that period, all the courage and all the strength which she had to summon to her aid to live through those days; and with her bequest went all the sorrow for the sufferings of humanity, and all the courage and all the strength to battle for the cause of the people, which were back of the father's trial.[40]

This experience in itself gave a clue to at least one of the strands in Karl Liebknecht's psychological motivation in going to the absolute limit of socialist revolt in 1919.

Though such German socialists as Wilhelm Liebknecht and August Bebel did not function in quite so oppressive an atmosphere as their Russian counterparts, Prussian Germany was a very repressive, dictatorial and illiberal society. By comparison with Russia or Germany, Britain was a relatively liberal and democratic society. Nevertheless, the German exiles in Britain, like Karl Marx and Frederick Engels, were hostile to capitalist societies throughout Europe. In leaving an insightful account of the lives of the Marxian socialists in London in the mid-nineteenth century, Wilhelm Liebknecht said: 'In our "civilised" society with its perpetual state of war one cannot always tell the truth. . . . But even if it is often inadvisable to say the truth, it is not always necessary to say an untruth.'[41] Such an intense, embattled atmosphere of *socialist fugitivism* contributed more than a mite to the forging of Karl Liebknecht's revolutionary psychology.

In fact Karl Liebknecht's character and personality were formed within a very intellectual-cum-revolutionary socialist milieu. In summing this up, Helmut Trotnow says: 'He must have been aware of the second wave of persecution, which began in 1878 with the introduction of legislation to "combat the efforts of social democracy which threaten the community". After all, he was ten years old when in 1881 the "Lesser State of the Siege" was imposed on Leipzig, where the Liebknechts lived in No. 11 Braustrasse. Wilhelm Liebknecht was forced to leave the family home in order to continue his political work; and although he found lodgings in nearby Borsdorf, he lived apart from his family which included, in addition to Theodor and Karl, Otto (born in 1876), Wilhelm (born 1877), and Kurt (born 1879).'[42] Yet despite Karl's alienation from Prussian Germany, he developed, as Karl W. Meyer put it, 'an anti-materialist philosophy of life'. Furthermore, he 'memorised parts of Faust and took a deep interest in humanistic studies and classical art.'[43]

Nevertheless when Karl Liebknecht went to the University of Leipzig in 1881, he decided to study law and political economy 'in order to defend Marxism'. Yet although he was better off than James Connolly, he was not sheltered from the reality of Prussian capitalism. In describing this and other important aspects of Liebknecht's life as a young socialist, Karl W. Meyer said:

Because his father's income was small, it was only with the party's help that he was able to carry out his studies. . . . In 1893 and 1894 his professional pursuits were interrupted when he and his older brother, Theodor, served with the Imperial Pioneer Guards in Potsdam. Here in the uniform of the Emperor, he learned about the militarism which he learned to despise. After passing his law examination, he accepted a post as junior barrister in the Westphalian region of Arnsberg and Paderborn. His mystic soul found some compatibility with the native Catholic region. He drew himself to the proud Westphalian peasants, the Volkstum, who like his kind struggled for an existence.[44]

Like James Connolly, he was drawn to Catholicism in Germany because of its almost innate spirit of disaffection.

Although the younger Liebknecht was much less puritanical than James Connolly, he shared Connolly's ability to reconcile Marxism and Catholicism. As Karl W. Meyer says: 'Although he could carry a "good cargo of drink and eat a hearty meal", he was usually satisfied with much less. He once confided that he lost all religious faith; but if he should become a believer again, he would "go the whole hog and become a Catholic". Only two classes of people were sympathetic with the workers: socialists and priests.'[45] So although Connolly and Liebknecht were not unusual in their sympathy for Catholicism – or a reconciliation between Catholicism and Marxism – they did not say this in any of their public pronouncements. In this, they were very like many inarticulate rank-and-file socialists.

While there was something intangibly spiritual about Karl Liebknecht's Marxian socialism, this did not detract from the intensity of his disaffection from German militarism or the monarchy in Prusso-Germany. What fitted – or rather 'predestined' him for the role of the socialist martyr – was the depth of his disaffection. He shared this quality with James Connolly, though Liebknecht was never completely outside of the established social order in Germany before 1914.

Karl Liebknecht was most certainly an outsider, an outcast. In making this point, Helmut Trotnow says: 'However, as he grew older, and his father was officially outlawed, Karl was drawn more and more into the web of persecution. That he was an outcast from society was first revealed to him during his school days. At the gymnasium especially he met children from the middle and upper classes who excommunicated him because of his name.'[46] Yet he was never so isolated as James Connolly had been long before the First World War.

While he was always on the Left of the Social Democratic Party – the socialist party of Imperial Germany – he unquestionably felt a strong sense of loyalty towards it. In explaining why Rosa Luxemburg, Franz Mehring, Karl Liebknecht and others found it difficult to break with the Social Democratic Party, Carl E. Schorske says:

To grasp the magnitude of the decision to go into open opposition, we must understand that the party was almost life itself to these individuals. The party had given him that psychological security, that ethical satisfaction which they had not found in society as a whole. . . . No matter how advanced had been the radicals' disillusionment with the party's course before the war, it had not brought them to the point of breaking the powerful emotional ties which bound them to the party.[47]

Moreover, during the Social Democratic Party's debate on discipline at the annual conference in 1910, Liebknecht said: 'I have, so to speak, grown up in the life of the party . . . I imbibed it (discipline) with my mother's milk and it rang in my ears from my earliest childhood from my father's lips. One thing is necessary: discipline.'[48]

In sketching in some of the major aspects of Liebknecht's life before 1914, Karl W. Meyer said:

In 1898 he advanced to the position of accessor and moved to Berlin as a lawyer. In 1900 his father died; and in the same year he entered into his first marriage. Ten years later his wife, by whom he had three children, died. In 1912 he married the woman who became his second wife, a Russian by birth and a graduate of the University of Heidelberg. There were no children by his second marriage.[49]

In 1902 he was elected to the city council of Berlin; and in 1908 he was elected to the Prussian House of Deputies. Then in 1912 he won a seat in the Reichstag in the so-called Kaiser's constituency. The fact that his ultimate martyrdom was not altogether preordained can be deduced from what Liebknecht told the crowds flooding the streets of Berlin in 1907 at the time of his trial for high treason: 'Do not fall for the idea that has already been expressed in bourgeois newspapers that I am a party martyr. There can be no talk of that.'[50] It is difficult to conceive of James Connolly or Eugene V. Debs repudiating the notion that they were, in similar circumstances, socialist martyrs.

Although some of Karl Liebknecht's biographers have exaggerated the *degree* of his unorthodoxy as a Marxist thinker, he most certainly did not adhere to the concept of economic determinism. He was motivated by the humanism of the European Enlightenment – a humanism imbibed from the classics and his father's idealism – rather than Marxian economics. In identifying some of the enigmatical strands in his thought, Helmut Trotnow says:

Liebknecht's hesitation in following his father's political footsteps was not at all surprising; from his earliest childhood he had experienced the way in which political activity affected family life. This was not altered in the least by the fact that he had seen not only how his father was outlawed by the state but also how the proletariat venerated him as a labour leader. At the 1904 party conference, for example, he reported one such positive experience: "During the socialist law, sometime in the mid-1880s, my father in exile in Borsdorf, was visited by a delegation of rural labourers. They opened up their hearts to him about their appalling situation and asked him if he would put in a good word for them with the Kaiser to get it improved."

After he became a Marxist and activist in the labour movement, he told Julius Motteler: 'I hope to emulate a little the most valuable example of my father by ceaseless activity and unending powerful and inspiring unselfless- ness; this is going to be my worship of the ancestors, in which I am deeply engrossed at the moment and in which I want to be engrossed deeply.'[51]

As a left-wing socialist Liebknecht had the deep sensitiveness, the artistic nature, the burning militancy and the self-sacrifice of a James Connolly or a Eugene V. Debs. Unlike Leon Trotsky, he believed in the innate goodness of humankind; and he did not emphasise the 'immeasurable mass of cruelty and suffering man had inflicted on man'. In discussing the article that he published in 1902 on 'The New Method' in which he criticised the ideas of the right-wing 'revisionists' in the Social Democratic Party, Hel- mut Trotnow concludes that: 'In his capacity as a politician he too wished to make sure that circumstances did not lead to the pauperisation of the proletariat.'[52]

But Karl Liebknecht's greatness before the First World War resided in his work in the German socialist youth movement as an advocate of anti-militarism. When he published his world-famous book, *Militarism and Anti-Militarism*, in 1907, he was soon punished by being sent to jail for an extended period. After deliberating for a mere half hour, the court passed the following sentence on Liebknecht:

The accused is found guilty of having set on foot a treasonable undertaking and is condemned to incarceration in a fortress for eighteen months. The costs of the prosecution are to be paid by the accused. All copies of the work *Militarism and Anti-Militarism* which has been put under the ban, in the possession of the author, printer, publisher, wholesale booksellers and booksellers, as well as the publicly exposed copies of this work, or those offered for sale, as well as the plates and forms for their production, are to be destroyed.[53]

As *Militarism and Anti-Militarism* was being destroyed in Germany, it was almost simultaneously being translated and published in other languages throughout the world.

Far from being silenced by his incarceration in a Prussian jail, Karl Liebknecht devoted most of his attention between 1907 and 1909 to the question of exposing the role of German militarism in corrupting the labour movement as well as the wider society. In a series of thorough and extended analyses of Prusso-German militarism, he focused on militarism as a 'state within the state' or perhaps even 'a state above the state'. In denouncing the influence of militarism on working-class men, Liebknecht identified the indoctrination of young workers into accepting a 'childish, distorted view of ths world geared to the needs of militarism'. He also objected to the fact that civil servants, members of the judiciary and educators were 'almost without exception' subject to military discipline.

When he discussed the enigma of Liebknecht's character, Carl E. Schorske described him as 'mercurial'. Similarly, in a more sympathetic sketch of Liebknecht than he produced in his book, *In Defence of Marxism*, Leon Trotsky said: 'Liebknecht was not a theoretician. He was a man of direct action. Impulsive and passionate by nature, he possessed an exceptional political intuition, a fine awareness of the masses and of the situation (in 1919) and finally an unrivalled courage and revolutionary initiative.'[54] Towards the end of his own life, Trotsky was somewhat less laudatory when he wrote:

Max Shachtman on the other hand argues that Liebknecht left a posthumous work against dialectical materialism which he had written in prison. Many ideas enter a person's mind while in prison which cannot be checked by association with other people. Liebknecht, whom nobody, least of all himself, considered a theoretician, became a symbol of heroism in the world labour movement.[55]

But although Liebknecht repeatedly tried to finish his important theoretical work, *Studies on the Laws of Motion of Social Development*, in later years, he never found the time to complete it.

Though he was more of a theoretician than Leon Trotsky would admit, he was not a major thinker of the same calibre as Rosa Luxemburg or Daniel De Leon. Yet he persisted in working on his important theoretical study. *Studies on the Laws of Motion* was begun during Liebknecht's first spell in jail in 1907; and in 1917 he wrote to his wife from another jail: 'I am not getting anywhere in my main work. The basis was there a long time ago in the first draft – but in a chaotic form. Now I have to put it in order, arrange it, and extend it.' Yet in the years before the outbreak of the First World War he criticised 'the passive politics' of the leadership of the Social Democratic Party. Furthermore, in the unfinished *Studies on the Laws of Motion of Social Development*, he insisted that 'mistakes, erroneous action' were better than 'weakness of will and inaction.'[56]

III

At the beginning of the First World War, James Connolly made it plain that he regarded 'atonement' and 'martyrdom' as weapons in the socialist struggle. In an article that he published in *Forward*, the Scottish socialist newspaper, in August 1914, he said:

As I am writing this the news appears in the press that Dr Karl Liebknecht has been shot in Germany for refusing to accept military service in the war. The news is unconfirmed, and will, I trust, be found later to be untrue, but I proposed to take it this week as a text for my article.

Supposing, then, that it was true, what would be the socialist attitude toward the martyrdom of our beloved comrade? There would be little hesitation in avowing that all socialists would endorse his act, and look upon his death as a martyrdom for our cause.

In urging socialists to be ready to die for 'the holiest of causes – the sanctity of the human soul, the practical brotherhood of the human race' – he was a very un-Leninist revolutionary.[57]

Unlike James Connolly, Liebknecht was not, in 1914, on the extreme Left. A member of the International Socialist Bureau of the Second International, he did not 'go much beyond the point of view of the majority of the Executive' in proposing how to deal with the problem of the war. Indeed, Liebknecht disagreed with the extreme Left's attitude to the war question. In summing this up, Georges Haupt said:

The extreme Left to which Lensch, Radek, and Pannekock belonged saw imperialism as a "necessity immanent in the further development of capitalism", the "ultimate and highest stage" in which the armaments race was an inevitable, economically necessary phenomenon.

Yet Liebknecht, as Haupt said, 'saw disarmament and understanding between nations as an opportunity to preserve peace.'[58]

Like Eugene V. Debs, John Maclean and many other socialists throughout the world in 1914, Karl Liebknecht felt an inner conflict between his deep revolutionary convictions and his loyalty to the socialist party to which he belonged. He voted for the war credits in the German Parliament on 4 August 1914, out of loyalty to the Social Democratic Party. It was his failure to bring about a reversal of the Social Democratic Party's policy which pushed him further and further to the extreme Left.

In an eloquent comment dealing with the collapse of the Second International in the face of the tragedy of the First World War, Julius Braunthal said: 'Every socialist party in the belligerent countries was afflicted by a *tragic sense of guilt* arising from the decision to combine, come what may, with the ruling classes in an alliance against the national foe – the "enemy" whose camp included fellow-workers and fraternal parties with whom, until the outbreak, they had been joined in solidarity.'[59] But the guilt was suffered much more deeply by individual socialists than by socialist parties. With their artisitc natures and boundless militancy, Connolly and Liebknecht felt this guilt much more deeply than the more orthodox opponents of capitalist militarism. And yet their guilt led them along quite divergent paths.

With the outbreak of the war, James Connolly was determined to challenge the *status quo* in Ireland. In discussing Connolly's attitudes in August 1914, Ryan said:

Our view of Connolly's mind, during these early 1914 days, grows more and more clear, as we study his writings, often excellent polemics, always vigorous, and often illuminative of the trend of the stirring times.

In reply to a question at a gathering of the Irish volunteer officers where he lectured on street fighting, Connolly said, "how do I know so much of military and revolutionary matters?" Then laughingly: "You forget that my business is Revolution".[60]

The Irish nationalist note was, however, very strong in his speeches – at least in Ireland. Writing in the *Irish Worker* on 15 August 1914, he said: 'Alas! that I should live to see it. North, south, east and west, the Irish volunteers are marching and parading with the Union Jack in front of them, the bands playing "God Save the King", and their aristocratic officers making loyalist speeches.'[61]

When he addressed the May Day demonstration in Glasgow in 1915, however, he struck a much more internationalist note. Since this was the last meeting that he addressed outside of Ireland before he was executed by the British authorities, Tom Bell's account of it is important. As Bell put it:

Connolly attacked the imperialist war in the interests of "royal freebooters and cosmopolitan thieves". He declared, "War waged by the oppressed nationalities against the oppressors, and the class war of the proletariat against capital . . . is *par excellence* the swiftest, safest, the most peaceful form of constructive work the socialist can engage in".

Connolly attacked the Redmondities of the Irish Parliamentary Party for their chauvinism, and recruiting of Irishmen into the British army. He lashed the Republicans for *their pan-Germanism*, for their blatant campaign in favour of the German War Lord".[62]

The duality – or enigmatical elements in Connolly's political personality – could be seen very clearly in 1914, though it was cloaked in internationalist socialist rhetoric.

Writing in the American periodical, the *International Socialist Review*, in March 1915, Connolly argued for civil war as an alternative to the capitalists' war in Europe. The outbreak of the war ought to have been, in his view, 'the signal for rebellion'.[63] In this approach, he did not differ too much from Karl Liebknecht. Although it was not obvious at the time, Connolly was already beginning to move in a nationalist direction.

In replying to an invitation from Arthur MacManus to address an anti-conscription meeting, Connolly said he was too busy to visit Glasgow in November 1915. In asking MacManus to convey his regrets to his friends in Glasgow, he wrote:

Tell them that we in Ireland will not have conscription, let the law say what it likes . . . we know . . . that no force in their possession can decide for us where we will fight. That remains for us to decide, and we have no intention of shedding our blood abroad for our masters. Rather we will elect to shed it, if need be, for the conquest of our freedom at home.[64]

Then on Easter Monday, 1916, Connolly marched to battle against the hated British foe. At the time, a sympathetic Irish observer said: 'Things are desperate, indeed, when this anti-militarist, this humanitarian, this internationalist leads us into this.'[65]

The Left in Scotland – a country in which James Connolly was well known to most of the prominent activists in the labour movement – were puzzled by the so-called 'Irish Lenin's, role in the Dublin revolt. Writing much later, T.A. Jackson said: 'The unofficial (Glasgow) left-wing frankly could not understand how a socialist like Connolly, could have got mixed up in a nationalist rising.'[66] With the benefit of hindsight and uncorroborated oral testimony, H.W. Lee insisted that: 'There are those who knew Connolly better than I did, and who are convinced that he was not a consenting party to the Easter outbreak of 1916.'[67] W.P. Ryan, who was a more reliable and authoritative witness, argued that he was 'determined upon eventual revolt, and said so repeatedly.'[68]

Although James Connolly initially wanted a socialist revolt in Ireland in 1914, he could not muster the necessary left-wing forces for such bold, revolutionary upheaval. In acknowledging this, he made no secret of his intention to sabotage the European imperialists' war efforts. When John Leslie published 'James Connolly: An Appreciation' in *Justice*, he said:

In the most recent conversation I had with him, one could note a growing Irishness which, while it might not mean a narrowing of vision, yet showed plainly that if he had influenced Sinn Fein, the influence had been mutual and reciprocal, and that Sinn Fein had made its mark on him; but that does not explain everything. I will venture my own opinion for what it is worth. I have reason to believe that Connolly did not place a very high estimate upon the Labour or socialist movement here. Knowing the man, I say it is possible that, despairing of effective assistance from that quarter, and indeed believing that it would act as a drag upon his efforts to form an Irish Socialist Party, he determined at all costs to identify or to indissolubly link the cause of Irish labour with the most extreme Irish nationalism, and to seal the bond of union with his blood if necessary.[69]

Unlike Connolly, Karl Liebknecht did not support nationalist struggles during the First World War.

Indeed, in 1916 Liebknecht displayed distinct hostility towards the socialists' identification with any sort of *realpolitik*. He was not a James Connolly at that point, although the communists would later try to link the Bolsheviks, the Spartacists and the Dublin rebels. An anti-imperialist, an uncompromising opponent of militarism and a critic of realpolitik, he implicitly criticised and repudiated Connolly's role in the Easter rising. In addressing a letter to the Royal Court in Berlin in May 1916, he criticised the German authorities for their 'planned seduction of the Ukranians, Georgian, Baltic, Polish, Irish, Mohammedan, and other prisoners of war in the German prisoners' camps, to act as traitors to their countries by taking up arms or acting as spies on behalf of the Central Powers; the Under Secretary of State, Zimmerman's agreement of December 1914 with Sir Roger Casement about the formation, equipment, and training of the "Irish Brigade" composed of British prisoners of war in German prisoners' camps; and attempts by threats of internment to force civilians of enemy nations residing in Germany into treasonable war service against their country, etc.'[70] Despite the divergent attitudes of Connolly and Liebknecht towards realpolitik in 1916, the socialist martydom anticipated by Connolly and Liebknecht towards realpolitik in 1916, the socialist martyrdom anticipated by Connolly was not so easily come by.

If martyrdom was always potentially latent in Karl Liebknecht's life, the drama leading to his murder in 1919 began in February 1915. The decisive factor in the making of his martyrdom was the Bolsheviks' triumph in 1917. In an attempt to gag a major critic of German militarism at the beginning of 1915, he was drafted into the army as a construction labourer. As a Deputy in the Reichstag, he could 'leave the war area and intervene directly in the labour movement's activities' when the German Parliament was in session. He took advantage of his Parliamentary privileges to assist the organisation of anti-war left-wing socialists throughout Germany. The new group, Spartacus, was led by Liebknecht, Franz Mehring, Rosa Luxemburg and Clara Zetkin.

In a brilliant speech that Karl Liebknecht gave in the Prussian Assembly in March 1916, he displayed a passionate commitment to the agitation for a democratic educational system. In arguing that the educational system could not be 'separated from social conditions', he accused the authorities of trying to 'make the pathway to higher education an act of grace, whereas in reality it is an original human right'. While he stressed the importance of what the socialists were saying in opposition to the 'endeavours' of the ruling class to 'mask the reality of things', he went on to say:

Classical education of today is only a parody on real classic education. Classics surely do not consist in driving home languages and some other knowledge of facts, but their essence is the spirit of humanism, the spirit of independence, of clear vision, of criticism, of everything which is felt to be harmful.

Liebknecht's speech on education in Germany was important for many reasons. In the first place, it showed that he was a product of – and supporter of – the European Enlightenment. Secondly, it refuted the oft-repeated assertion that he was not a theoretician. And finally, it demonstrated that he had a very good turn of phrase as well as a good style. In one paragraph of great eloquence, he said:

The new method of teaching history is a sign of barbarism, a sign of the fight to death being fought by the educational ideal of the bourgeoisie. I spoke before about the poem of Schiller in which it is said: "Only a miracle can carry you into the beautiful wonderland". To the proletariat, for the unsaved souls, this word cannot be applied. No miracle and no blessing from above can bring the proletariat into the wonderland, in which all the treasures and magnificence of the human soul are to be found. And when Dante's world-epic speaks about those unsaved souls who live without hope and longing, that is also not true of the proletariat. It does not live without hope, but full of confidence.[71]

The Spartacists' conception of education was a profoundly democratic one; and in the midst of their other agitations the Spartacists did not overlook the importance of education.

Under the dynamic leadership of Karl Liebknecht, the Spartacist organisation issued a number of 'underground' leaflets including Liebknecht's famous leaflet, 'The Main Enemy is at Home'. It opened with the stirring words:

The senseless slogan, "Hold out to the end" is bankrupt and only leads deeper into the genocidal maelstrom. The task of the hour for socialists is the international proletarian class struggle against international imperialist slaughter.[72]

By the middle of March 1916, the left-wing socialists in Germany actually proceeded to re-organise themselves. In summing this up, Paul Frolich said: 'Delegations were present from most of the industrial areas – from Berlin, Saxony, Thuringia, Central Germany, Frankfurt, Wurttemberg, Bavaria and Upper Silesia. Above all, the Socialist Youth, which had held a secret conference in Jena in Easter 1916, stood overwhelmingly behind *Spartakus*.'[73]

This was the backdrop against which Karl Liebknecht and Rosa Luxemburg agitated for peace. As a result of the Spartacists' agitations in the factories in Berlin in March and April 1916, 10,000 workers gathered in Potsdamer Platz on 1 May to demand an end to the war. Paul Frolich described what happened before Liebknecht was arrested, and then imprisoned:

Karl Liebknecht, in uniform, and Rosa Luxemburg were in the midst of the demonstrators and greeted with cheers from all sides. Liebknecht's voice then rang out: "Down with the war! Down with the government'. The police immediately rushed at him and tore him out of the crowd. Trying to shield him, Rosa flung herself in the way, but was roughly thrust aside. Indignation rose among the masses, and an attempt was made to free Karl, but it was ridden down by mounted police.[74]

But there were already profound political differences between Liebknecht and Luxemburg about the role of the socialist Left and the working class in the ongoing struggle.

Liebknecht was a man of the European Enlightenment. In the letters that he sent to his sons in 1916, he stressed the importance of education and enlightenment. As Karl W. Meyer put it: 'He urged them to make the most of their schooling, while reminding them of the millions of others whose financial plight made learning unavailable. Diligence in school would have its later rewards. He advised them to cultivate self-confidence, to aim with diligence and all the given talents; but self-confidence should not develop into self-complacency and egotism. Books would become their best friends, he counselled his lads, if they sat with them for hours at a time.'[76] In the family letters that he sent to his wife and children in 1915 and 1916 there were hints that he was already looking half-way to posterity.

Then in October 1918, Karl Liebknecht was freed from jail and 'welcomed in triumph by the Berlin workers'. Emancipated by the German bourgeois-democratic revolution, he proceeded to make an all-out attempt at a Bolshevik-type revolution. In organising the Spartacist uprising in January 1919 without the approval of Rosa Luxemburg, the KPD (or Communist Party of Germany), he most certainly departed from his own earlier and more democratic positions.[77] The Liebknecht who, in 1916, implicitly repudiated James Connolly's political behaviour in co-operating with Sir Roger Casement now became a practitioner of *realpolitik*. As Karl W. Meyer puts it:

Liebknecht contracted a secret treaty with the Bolsheviks in 1918, which specified that "a Russian army would take the offensive to support a Spartacist uprising in Berlin". In return for this support, Liebknecht promised to establish a German Red Army of 50,000 men after defeating the Ebert government. This agreement must have spurred Liebknecht on to commit his January folly against the advice of Luxemburg.[78]

IV

For the majority of the leaders of the Social Democratic Party of Germany the Revolution had come to an end on 10 November 1918 with the abdication of the Kaiser and the foundation of a nominally democratic state. In a non-partisan description of their objectives, Julius Braunthal said: 'They regarded it as their duty to create a Parliamentary state with guarantees for freedom, crowned by a Parliament which should incorporate the Republic's will and serve as an instrument for achieving socialism.'[79] In following the example of the Bolsheviks, Liebknecht wanted to turn the political revolution into a social revolution. But although both James Connolly and Karl Liebknecht possessed some of the necessary qualities for the making of martyrs, the Bolsheviks and their sympathisers outside Russia were slow to claim the so-called 'Irish Lenin'.

Moreover, in 1916 there was great dubiety about James Connolly's status as a socialist martyr. Louis B. Boudin, who was 'one of the fathers of the left-wing of American socialism', wrote an article on 'The Irish Tragedy' of 1916 in which he concluded:

Revolutionary movements, like true faith, thrive on the blood of martyrs. But in order to have that effect no suspicion of its having been spilt in the service of Baal must attach to it. Like the blood of the sacrifical lamb it must be pure, and innocent of all contaminating influence. The real and surpassing tragedy of the recent Irish revolt lies in the fact that its greatest sacrifices were not made on the alter of Irish

Freedom – that is, not in a manner that could now or hereafter rebound to the advancement of that cause. The guilt of the Unholy Alliance with German Militarism and Imperialism will rest upon it forever, and prevent the blood of its martyrs from ever bearing the holy fruit of freedom.[80]

Although many socialist newspapers protested against Connolly's execution on humanitarian grounds, not one socialist newspaper anywhere claimed him as a *socialist martyr*.

The communists did not claim James Connolly as one of their own until 1919. In doing so, they identified Bolshevism, extreme Irish nationalism and Connolly with a common anti-British imperialism.[81] As Selma Sigerson put it: 'The masses turned to nationalism with a new meaning, which will yet assure them a place inside Bolshevik Russia and Spartacist Germany in the true International, and if James Connolly had lived the expression of that meaning would never have been minimised.'[82] In contrast to Karl Liebknecht however, Connolly's revolutionary self-sacrifice was particularly attractive to the Trotskyists in the 1930s. Connolly was seen as an advocate and practitioner of the 'permanent revolution'.

A few months after the murder of Karl Liebknecht, the Bolsheviks and those who were sympathetic to Bolshevism claimed him as a socialist martyr. On 1 May 1919, William Paul, a British communist, published a very long article in *The Socialist* on 'Karl Liebknecht: The Man and His Work'. In his biography of *Karl Liebknecht: Man without a Country*, Karl W. Meyer makes out a very credible case suggesting that Liebknecht sought martyrdom when he addressed the May Day demonstration in Berlin in 1916:

Evidence points to the martyr's role as certainly a worthwhile alternative goal in the event he failed to incite rebellion, if not the real tactical goal, which Liebknecht had in mind. In this role he could satisfy his strong sense of duty for which he had a fanatical respect. What appeared to many people to be his light-mindedness could have been in reality a calculated plan carried out with considerable success. His imprisonment aroused more agitation than any previous act of resistance, and the government unwittingly played into his hands.[83]

In praising Liebknecht as a prefigurative Leninist, William Paul said: 'Many people have been impressed with the courage and determination of Liebknecht. They have also noticed a close resemblance between his tactics and those formulated by Lenin.' Moreover, a particularly impressive feature of Liebknecht's activity before the outbreak of the First World War was his attack on German imperialism.[84]

In the fullness of time, the Stalinist revisionists in the 1930s – the Stalinist revisionists without Lenin – would once again revise their own revisionism. Joseph Stalin denounced Rosa Luxemburg for what must surely have been her 'posthumous' Trotskyism; and Karl Liebknecht became an easy target for such British heresy-hunters as Emile Burns. With the enormous condescension of Stalinist posterity, Burns said:

As we have seen, Liebknecht was weak in much of his theory; he did not fully understand the relation between militarism and imperialism; for a long time he hardly passed beyond hand to mouth radicalism.[85]

In a more objective critique of Liebknecht's weaknesses, Karl W. Meyer said: 'This unreal approach to practical problems, however, was characteristic of Liebknecht. His vivid imagination and ultra-idealism relegated practical considerations to the background in his make-up.'[86]

After the rise and fall of the Second International the qualities which socialism needed most – for example, vivid imagination and ultra-idealism – were lost in the mists of *realpolitik*; and the utilitarianism attacked by James Connolly and Karl Liebknecht have increasingly dominated the historiography of the international labour movement. But the socialists who could speak, as Liebknecht did, about 'walking through the forest of the spirits which have not sinned' were far too imaginative, creative and egalitarian to allow European imperialism to stifle their dreams of a New Society of Equals.

Chapter 4

Antonio Gramsci and Rosa Luxemburg: Individualists and socialist-humanists

Can one 'explain' what Mozart's music is? Can one 'explain' the magic of life to someone who cannot perceive it from the smallest everyday things or, better, who does not carry it in himself?

Rosa Luxemburg

For us small movements can appear great because we relate them to those others which we alone feel, because we are living them. . . . We feel ourselves to be the molecules of a world in gestation, we feel this great tide rising up slowly but inexorably, the solid cohesion of the infinitude of drops composing it; we feel that in this awareness the International is truly alive.

Antonio Gramsci

Being profoundly aware of the innate humanism of authentic democratic socialist philosophy, Antonio Gramsci (1891–1937) and Rosa Luxemburg (1871–1919) were powerful, critical, iconoclastic and very individualistic figures within the world socialist movement. Born in 1871, the year of the Paris Commune, Luxemburg was raised in a wealthy cosmopolitan Jewish family in the Polish city of Zamose. By contrast, Gramsci was reared in a displaced lower middle-class family in Ales, Sardinia, exactly twenty years later, in 1891.

Rosa Luxemburg died when she was forty-eight years of age. Antonio Gramsci died when he was forty-six years of age. Both died in truly tragic circumstances, though their brilliant writings diffused enlightenment throughout the world long after their deaths. But, although they both ultimately gained posthumous and immortal fame in the late-twentieth century, the differences and the similarities in their contribution to socialist literature and thought have increasingly gathered intellectual significance as a result of the re-emergence of militarism, mass unemployment, racism and resurgent fascism.

Moreover, although they were great writers and socialist-activists, Gramsci and Luxemburg were, above all, great *individualists*. But because the history and concepts of authentic individualism and individuality are now in the 1980s being increasingly appropriated by conservatives and ultra-conservatives, an account of their lives will illuminate just how much real individualism and individuality were embodied in the lives of some of the pioneers of modern socialism.

The social and intellectual world occupied by Rosa Luxemburg and Antonio Gramsci – the world of the eighteenth-century European Enlightenment – was extremely class-conscious, unimaginably hierarchical and profoundly undemocratic. In the late eighteenth century, for example, the great English writer, Samuel Johnson told James Boswell that: 'You are to consider that it is our duty to maintain the subordination of civil society; and when there is a gross or shameful deviation from rank, it should be punished so as to deter others from the same perversion.'[1] Then in the mid-nineteenth century Thomas Carlyle the Scottish historian, attacked Chartist working men and women in Britain for challenging the 'natural' hierarchy in the world. As he put it: 'Recognised or not, a man has his superiors, a regular hierarchy above him, extending up, degree above degree, to Heaven itself and God the maker, who made his world not for anarchy but for rule and order.'[2]

In rejecting the traditional hierarchical principles which were antithetical to the possibility of the development of working-class individuality, Rosa Luxemburg and Antonio Gramsci deepened the classical Marxist critique of bourgeois individualism as expounded by Samual Johnson, James Boswell, Thomas Carlyle, W.H. Malloch and other British champions of capitalist 'freedom'. In a brilliant description of the abstract *Individual* of bourgeois ideology, Royden Harrison says: 'Sexless, classless, nationless he/she is the all-important nothing of middle-class wisdom.'[3]

In spelling out the major difference between bourgeois individualism and socialism, the Shorter Oxford English Dictionary defined individualism as 'Self-centred feeling or conduct as a principle'. But, although Antonio Gramsci and Rosa Luxemburg rejected that particular view of individualism, they were nevertheless profound and aggressive individualists. Because an individualist society was conceived of as a society characterised by privatisation and atomistic social relations, the bourgeois and socialists conceptions of individualism were inherently incompatible. As Ellen Meiksins Woods observes: 'There is a specific meaning to the fact that "individualism" and "socialism" are opposed to each other and that for liberal individualism it is a logical absurdity, a contradiction in terms, to speak of socialist individualism – an individualism based on the view that the individual self-realisation and development of all men can be achieved only through socialism, while capitalist individualism militates against fully realised individuality for all.'[4]

In portraying the lives and socialist-humanism of Antonio Gramsci and Rosa Luxemburg, it will become clear that contemporary socialists are the inheritors of a rich, democratic and progressive culture. In the light of the present-day tendency to portray the history of socialism as the history of heresy-hunting anti-democrats, it is important to recall the European context in which socialists struggled to initiate democratic reforms from below. It was, after all, a context in which the German Kaiser wrote to the Chancellor von Bülow at the time of the Morrocan crisis in 1905:

I cannot dispense with a single man at a moment when the Social Democracy preaches insurrection. We have first to shoot and behead the socialists and to render them innocuous – if necessary by a massacre – and then let's have war. But not before and not *a tempo*.

I

The year 1917 was a crucial and world-shattering *moment* in the history of modern socialism. If the Bolshevik revolution weakened the existing structure of international capitalism, and if the ensuing class struggles played a role in the rise of fascism, Rosa Luxemburg and Antonio Gramsci met the crossroads-crisis for the actuality of bourgeois individualism and the potentiality of socialist individuality with passion, curiosity and imagination.

Major intellectual figures in the democratic socialist movement in Germany and Italy, and destined unpredictably to be the victims of proto-fascism and actual fascism, they gave more sustained thought to the questions of humankind's role in the universe, imaginative literature, literary criticism, individualism and the characteristics of the democratic personality and individuality than any other socialist intellectuals before or after 1917. While there were inevitably character, generational and personality differences between Rosa Luxemburg and Antonio Gramsci, they had much in common in terms of their early experience.

Both Luxemburg and Gramsci suffered from physical deformities which developed during their childhoods; and they were already in early life predisposed to identify and sympathise with the weak, the vulnerable and the exploited. As they were simultaneously gregarious and yet detached from their fellows in their youth, they only succeeded in becoming critically 'integrated' into their own societies after they became socialist-humanist activists. Despite the differences in their ages and personalities, they both developed some of their deepest insights into the dialectical relationship between their own societies and the theoretical problem of individuality when they were incarcerated in dictators' jails.

The First World War and its immediate aftermath played a pivotal role in stimulating the seminal works produced by Rosa Luxemburg and Antonio Gramsci. Although the most substantial body of Luxemburg's literary and theoretical work was already behind her in 1914, and although Gramsci's immortal prison notebooks were not written until the years between 1929 and 1937, the years between 1914 and 1919 were very productive years in their lives. A really significant aspect of the years between the war and 1919, when Luxemburg was murdered by ultra-right wing army officers, was that the war stimulated their rich literary productivity, creativity and insights into individualism and the barbarism latent in modern societies. While Luxemburg perfected, sharpened and added to her earlier cumulative thought and reflections about the relationship between capitalist civilisation and 'the invading socialist society', Gramsci mapped out the theoretical questions – questions stimulated by the coalescence of his earlier personal life and experiences in the working-class movement in Turin – he would attempt to answer in Mussolini's jails.

Like the other outstanding socialist intellectuals in working-class movements throughout the world, Luxemburg and Gramsci were deeply aware of their formidable intelligence, literary and analytical gifts and highly developed insights into the workings of the historical process. In this specific sense, they were – and were conscious of being – members of an *avant-garde*, cultural and political movement dedicated to the overthrow of capitalism. Far from adopting an elitist disdain towards 'the masses', they devoted their adult lives to the task of encouraging the exploited, the weak and the vulnerable to make their own history.

Since they both developed a very high sense of self-esteem, consciousness of their own distinct individuality and intense emotional identification with struggling humankind, they were utterly out of sympathy with the many socialists who wanted to obliterate or deny the theoretical problems of reconciling their own individuality with the 'vanguard's' dedication to the politics of the 'mass struggle'. Because they were aware of the indispensable role of *avant-garde* intellectuals within the working-class movements, they gave their gifts unstintingly to the struggle to prevent the emergence of the leader–saviour–supermen of nineteenth-century bourgeois philosophy. In opposition to Thomas Carlyle's concept of 'Heroes and Hero Worship', they offered the ideal of mass democratic struggle against alienation, exploitation, injustice and oppression in which 'the masses' would become *conscious personalities* proud of their *individuality*.

The uniqueness of the Luxemburg/Gramsci contribution to socialist theory and culture was that they gave more attention to the relationship between their own intense individuality and the exploited working people than any other socialist intellectuals. With rich inner lives born out of frequent personal unhappiness and misery, they always related their own unhappiness to the problems of suffering, struggling humankind. Although they usually tackled the concepts of 'genius', individualism versus individuality and socialist humanism in private letters or asides, the profundity of their thought exposed the shallowness of Samual Johnson, James Boswell, Thomas Carlyle and W.H. Malloch.

In shining through and colouring everything that they wrote for the socialist movement, the socialist–humanism of Rosa Luxemburg and Antonio Gramsci was the real thing – the authentic voice of the tradition of socialism-from-below because it reflected their inner lives. In contrast to Karl Kautsky,[5] H.M. Hyndman,[6] Victor Berger or Morris Hillquit, Luxemburg and Gramsci never made elitist, condescending remarks about working-class men or women. Moreover, although they were no saints and could lash out at their enemies with sharp and wounding invective, they always refused to express disappointment over the alleged 'cowardice' or 'weakness' of the working classes.

In campaigning for the abolition of the death penalty in 1918, Rosa Luxemburg wrote:

Unrelenting revolutionary activity coupled with boundless humanity – that alone is the real life-giving force of socialism. A world must be overturned, but every tear that has flowed and might have been wiped away is an indictment; and every man hurrying to perform a great deed who steps on even a worm out of unfeeling carelessness commits a crime.[7]

Far from this statement representing the sort of socialist-humanist lyric beloved by the 'neutral' liberal Academy, she was giving voice to the thoughts which dominated her inner life.

In a prolonged, stormy, unhappy and yet creative realtionship with her lover, Leo Jogiches, Luxemburg wrote letters worthy of a Dante or a Goethe. On one occasion she was appalled by the letters he was sending to her: 'When I open your letters and see six pages covered with debates about the Polish Socialist Party, and not a single word about . . . ordinary life, I feel faint'. Then in very private letters expressing her most intimate thoughts about individualism and individuality, she said:

The two of us constantly "live" an inner life. It means we keep changing and growing and this creates an inner dissociation, an imbalance, a disharmony between some parts of our souls and others. . . . But in order not to lose the overall sense of our existence that I belief a life committed outward, constructive action, creative work, one needs the control of another human being. That human being must be close, understanding and yet separate from the "I" that seeks harmony.

In other letters to her 'comrade and lover', she defended her potential as a great socialist writer and yet attacked the bourgeois concept of 'genius' and the *Individual*. In forecasting the path-breaking essays that she had yet to write, she observed that:

Something is moving inside me and wants to come out. It's something intellectual, something I must write. Don't worry, it's not poetry again or fiction. No, my treasure, it's in my brain that I feel something . . .
    It's the form of my writing that no longer satisfies me. In my "soul" a totally new, original form is ripening that ignores all rules and conventions. It breaks them by the power of ideas and strong convictions. I want to affect people like a clap of thunder, to inflame their minds not by speechifying but with the breadth of my vision, the strength of my conviction, and the power of my expression.

Yet she always attacked the bourgeois concept of 'genius' and self-centred feelings and behaviour, particularly when they were seen in the lives of so-called 'socialists'. Thus in a letter to Leo Jogiches, she said:

I, for one, follow the principle that people's primary concern is to support themselves and their children or parents, and only then should they think of becoming great scholars. Besides – *sind' Rosen, nun sie werden bluhen* (if they're roses, they'll bloom). No genuine talent ever flourished because it devoted all its time to self-development.[8]

The Rosa Luxemburg who expressed her most intimate thoughts about the relationship between the collective working-class movement and individuality was a whole, integral socialist personality. It was because she was a whole person that she could inform her close friends Robert and Mathilde Seidel about the reasons for the terrible dullness and unimaginative uniformity of articles in socialist newspapers:

Do you know what disturbs me? I'm not satisfied with the way in which people in the party usually write articles. They are all so conventional, so wooden, so cut-and-dry . . . I believe that the cause lies in the fact that when people write, they forget for the most part to dig deep into themselves and to feel the whole import and truth of what they are writing. I believe that every time, every day, in every article you must live through the things again, you must feel your way through it, and then fresh words – coming from the heart and going to the heart – would occur to express the old familiar thing. But you get so used to a truth that you rattle off the deepest and greatest things as if they were the "Our Father". I firmly intend, when I write, never to forget to be enthusiastic about what I write and to commune with myself.[9]

But although most of these comments were written in private letters before the outbreak of the First World War, the subsequent letters written in prison are full of insights into human frailty and vanity.

Like Rosa Luxemburg, Antonio Gramsci attained his profoundly democratic outlook out of the long struggle he fought against the emotional problems and isolation created by his physical deformity. Yet both Luxemburg and Gramsci were confronted with additional problems before they developed into profound thinkers and activists. While Luxemburg was a woman and a Jewess, Gramsci was a very poor middle-class Sardinian from the 'backward' peasant economy of Southern Italy. Utilising the great stimulus obtained from their early isolation and inwardness and sensitive to the suffering of others, they responded to the socialist challenge of their own times with passion, stubborn determinism and hope.

As early as 1915 Antonio Gramsci acknowledged the role of the socialist idea in creating his individuality as well as integrating his life with the struggles of the Italian working class. In a letter to his family he wrote:

I should never have detached myself so far from life in the way I did. I've lived right out of this world for a couple of years: it was like a long dream. I allowed all the links which bound me to the world of men to snap off, one by one. I lived entirely by my brain, and not at all by the heart . . . not only as far as you were concerned. It was as if the whole of humanity had ceased to exist for me, and I was a wolf alone in its den.[10]

The conversion to socialism was the turning-point in his life. He threw himself into the life around him; and he contributed to the socialist press with verve, originality and total commitment.

Like Rosa Luxemburg, he was always aware of his own intense individuality. But, although he merged his individuality within the Italian and international working-class movements, he never abandoned the 'critical criticism' which led him into socialism. Once committed, he merged himself in the struggles of his time – even in Mussolini's prisons – and used his complete immersion in the labour movement to develop his insights, literary genius and individuality. In a pamphlet published in 1917 on *The City of the Future*, he aggressively expressed his conception of individualism and socialist individuality:

Indifference is a powerful force in history. It operates passively but effectively. . . . Events mature in the shadows, a few hands accountable to no one weave the web of collective living, and the "masses" know nothing of what happens because they don't mind . . . I am a partisan, I do mind. I feel beating within me the virile awareness of my own side – the life of that city of the future has already begun to build . . . I am alive, I take sides. Hence I detest whoever does not, I hate indifference.[11]

In plunging into the ongoing class struggles during the First World War, Gramsci denounced the fatalism and the economic determinism represented by Italian socialism and the Second International. An outstanding contribution to the critique of Social Darwinian inevitability, the article he produced in 1917 describing the Bolshevik revolution as 'The revolution against *Das Capital*' was motivated by the deeply-held belief that Marx was not 'a Messiah who left a string of parables laden with categorical imperatives'.[12]

A major socialist intellectual whose intense sense of his own individuality stimulated him to predict that the success of socialism would ultimately depend on its ability to create 'a faith which would influence every aspect of the life of its adherents',[13] Gramsci was a profoundly creative, democratic and, above all, independent and sometimes lonely figure. Sharing the same sense of loneliness at various phases in his life as Luxemburg did in hers, and sometimes exhibiting the same 'common touch' with humankind as Eugene Victor Debs, the American socialist, he was a fighter as well as a witness to *the tragedy* of many aspects of *twentieth-century socialism*.

Although Gramsci's physical life was not snuffed out until the late 1930s, there was a profound sense in which Gramsci, in common with other potential intellectual giants of socialist internationalism, was cut off from militant working people by the coalescence of the combined forces of fascism and Stalinism. Also he shared a common fate with Luxemburg in the sense that many of his great writings and critiques of the established social order and 'Marxist' dogmas were suppressed, bowdlerised or concealed.

While some of Gramsci's writings are more abstract and complex than the writings of Luxemburg, a profound commitment to democracy and humanism permeated everything that they wrote. In a letter written to his brother from inside a fascist jail, Gramsci said: 'To obtain that (a democratic outlook) something has to take place inside you, you have to try and improve your mind, and feel inside you that it is necessary for all your fellows to reach the level you have reached, regardless of whether you reach your goal or not. You must lend them a hand, reach down to them if necessary, and raise them up to yourself. A democratic mind must set the highest standards for the human "personality", because, when there is no respect for that, there is no real idea of democracy'.[14]

Without feigning a false humility and reconciling their superior education and *avant-garde* role as socialist intellectuals with a profound democratic praxis, Luxemburg and Gramsci saw militant working-class men and women as the real 'saviours' of civilisation. An important difference of temperament and generation resulted in Luxemburg confronting the outbreak of·the First World War with a much greater sense of tragic foreboding than Gramsci did. In *The Janius Pamphlet* published anonymously in 1915, Luxemburg observed that:

Another such war, and the hope of socialism will be buried under the ruins of imperialistic barbarism. That is more than the ruthless destruction of Liege and of the Rheims Cathedral. That is a blow, not only against the capitalist civilisation of the past, but against socialist civilisation of the future, a deadly blow against the force that carries the future of mankind in its womb, that alone can rescue the precious treasures of the past over into a better state of society. Here capitalism reveals its death's head, here it betrays that it has sacrificed its historic right of existence, that its rule is no longer compatible with the progress of humanity.[15]

If Rosa Luxemburg was sometimes less optimistic than Antonio Gramsci, she never lost faith in the crucial role of the *avant-garde* socialist intellectuals and working-class activists. Basically optimistic and unwilling to yield before the aggressive forces of capitalist barbarism, she wrote to Mathilde Wurm from prison in Germany in 1917:

Your arguments against my motto: 'Here I stand – I can do no other' amounts to saying: that's all very fine and good, but people are too cowardly or too weak for such heroism; *ergo* we must adapt our tactics to their weaknesses according to the principle: *chi va piano, va sano* (slowly but surely). What a narrow view of history, my dear lamkin! There is nothing more changeable than human psychology. Especially since the psyche of the masses always harbours – like Thalatta, the eternal sea – all sorts of latent possibilities: deadly calm and raging storm, the basest cowardliness and the wildest heroism. The masses are always what they must be, what the given historical conditions make of them, and they are always on the brink of becoming totally different from what they seem to be.[16]

At approximately the same time, Gramsci placed more emphasis than Luxemburg on the socialists' *avant-garde* role in developing both revolutionary and cultural activity amongst working-class men and women:

Man is above all mind, consciousness – that is, he is a product of history, not of nature. There is no other way of explaining why socialism has not come into existence already, although there have always been exploiters and exploited and selfish consumers of wealth. Man has only been able to acquire a sense of his worth bit by bit, in one sector of society after another. ... This means that every revolution has been preceded by an immense labour of social criticism, of cultural penetration and diffusion.[17]

As anti-socialist concepts of genius, bourgeois individualism and the 'Great Man' theory of history are again disappearing from Western labour movements with the emergence of a new working-class praxis, and as militant men and women are again engaging in mass struggles against social injustice, inequality, poverty and mass unemployment, the now widely available writings of Rosa Luxemburg and Antonio Gramsci beckon the forces of socialist humanism, democracy and anti-militarism to move forward.

Moreover, if the forces which beckoned humankind forward after 1917 suffered as many setbacks as they experienced historic advances, the seeds of capitalist barbarism and regression were already present within the international working-class movement itself before the First World War. Yet despite the agonising scenes witnessed by Luxemburg, and Gramsci and many others after 1917, the Bolshevik revolution put the fate of humankind on to a still extant auction-block marked with a large question mark: 'Socialism or barbarism?'

II

Although Gramsci and Luxemburg frequently experienced spells of personal misery and unhappiness, Luxemburg never suffered from the deep human misery which ran like a hiatus hernia throughout the whole of Gramsci's life. Though they both enjoyed supreme moments of happiness, elation and deep fulfilment, it was Luxemburg who attached the most importance to human happiness, as Stephen E. Bronner explains: 'Luxemburg's concern for happiness is part of her *joie de vivre*, and it marks the way in which she experienced literature, thus, she could agree with her beloved Korolenko's simple statement: "Happiness is salubrious and elevating to the soul. And I always believe, you know, that man is rather obliged to be happy".'[18]

Being the son of a lower-middle class family in peasant Sardinia, Gramsci was much closer to human suffering than Luxemburg. While Gramsci's and Luxemburg's perceptions of human suffering and cruelty were shaped by the distinctive societies in which they developed and grew up, the major factor in shaping their unique approaches to socialism was their distictive *class backgrounds*. This was even more important than the different national cultures inherited by them.

As the product of a wealthy cosmopolitan bourgeois background in Poland, Luxemburg imbibed the most advanced *internationalist* thought, art and culture of the Enlightenment before she was converted to socialism. Consequently, she not only rejected the *avant-garde* culture and art of the Futurists and the Expressionists, but she also remained more of an orthodox Marxist than Gramsci. Therefore, it took the brutality and barbarism unleashed by the First World War to open her eyes to the truth of Voltaire's portrayal of human vice and depravity in eighteenth-century France. At the beginning of 1918, she wrote to Sonja Liebknecht announcing her re-evaluation of Voltaire's book, *Candide*, in the light of the new experiences opened up by the First World War. In a letter from the women's prison in Breslau, Luxemburg confessed: '*Candide* is such an exquisite edition that I could not bring myself to cut the leaves of the book. I read it with the leaves uncut; it was quite easy since it is bound in half sheets. Before the war, I would have thought that this wicked compilation of all human misery a caricature. Now it strikes me as altogether realistic . . .',[19]

The formative influence of Rosa Luxemburg's cosmopolitan Jewish background probably played an important role in 'determining' both her attitudes towards nationalism in general and the Jewish people in particular. Yet in rejecting even 'the most civilised brand' of nationalism,[20] she did not reject the importance of nationality, as Paul Frolich explains: 'In 1900 Rosa Luxemburg issued a pamphlet entitled *In Defence of Nationality*, vigorously inciting resistance to the official attempts to Germanise Prussian Poland. This resulted in proceedings against her on a charge of having insulted the Prussian Minister of Culture. The "crime" was atoned with a fine of 100 marks.'[21]

In asserting that 'the famous Jewish socialist organisation – the Bund – held no attraction and her concerns always transcended nationality',[22] Stephen Bronner is not, as we have seen, altogether accurate in dismissing Luxemburg's interest in nationality if not nationalism. Yet she was strangely indifferent to her Jewishness. This stood out in contrast to Gramsci's deep and constant emotional attachment to the commonalty in Sardinia.

Nevertheless, although later generations of socialists would be much more sensitive towards the Jewish question than Rosa Luxemburg or Daniel De Leon seem to have been, Luxemburg rejected any *special* sympathy for the Jews in the Ghetto out of a profound, if somewhat abstract, socialist internationalism. In a letter sent from prison in 1917 to her close friend, Mathilde Wurm, she said: 'What do you want with this particular suffering of the Jews? The poor victims of the rubber plantations in Putumayo, the Negroes in Africa with whose bodies the Europeans play a game of catch, are just as near to me. Do you not remember the words written on the work of the German General Staff about Trotha's campaign in the Kalahari desert? "And the death-rattles, the mad cries of those dying of thirst, faded away into the sublime silence of eternity". Oh, this "sublime silence of eternity" in which so many screams have faded away unheard. It rings within me so strongly that I have no special corner of my heart reserved for the Ghetto: I am at home wherever in the world there are clouds, birds and human tears . . .'.[23] Yet unlike De Leon with whom she had much in common, she did not deny her Jewishness.

By contrast, Antonio Gramsci was very sensitive to the cruelty and suffering he had seen in his native Sardinia. In sketching in Gramsci's awareness of cruelty in the human depths of Sardinia, John M. Cammett says:

Gramsci later remembered relations between adults and children in Sardinia as being generally brutal. On day, as a boy, he accompanied a woman of Ghilarza to a junkyard outside the town, In the corner of the place was a kind of pigsty, about four feet high and without windows. The woman unlocked the door and was greeted by a kind of animal yelping . . .
    The cruelty, both to children and old people, came chiefly from what Gramsci called the 'middle generation', the generation between twenty and fifty. Many people of this age emigrated. Those who remained to scratch out a living became bitter and self-centred and too often vented their bitterness on their children and their unproductive elderly relatives. Gramsci felt that he had been a victim of this treatment.[24]

With fewer illusions about the inherent barbarity of capitalist society than Luxemburg even before the outbreak of the First World War, Gramsci was correspondingly more savage in his denunciation of the established social order. Occupying a more marginal role in Italian society than Luxemburg occupied within the ranks of German Social Democracy, Gramsci was much more receptive to the new, the bold and the innovative ideas of the Expressionists and the Futurists. Glancing back to the revolutionary avant-garde movements in art, culture and the theatre before the First World War, in 1921 Gramsci wrote: 'The Futurists had a clear and well-defined conception that our age, the age of industry, of the great working-class city, of intense and tumultuous life, had to have new forms of art, of philosophy, of social habits, of language . . .'.[25]

Being even more inconoclastic than Luxemburg, Gramsci refused to embrace the superficially sophisticated and abstract 'internationalism' characteristic of so many socialists in the Second International. Though he anticipated and then fought nationalistic fascism, he did not cast off his emotional attachment to Sardinia. As James Joll explains: 'Gramsci's roots in Sardinia were deep, not only because of his early experience of the poverty and social injustice in the island but because he had come to respect the indigenous folk culture of a backward community.'[26]

Because he belonged to such a background, Gramsci was always preoccupied with the theoretical problems implicit in attempting to reconcile the Southern or national question with both Italian socialism and workers' internationalism. In commenting on Gramsci's attitude to the national question, Giuseppe Fiori says:

So Gramsci became a socialist without burying his own past. While his socialist viewpoint made him aware of the ambiguity, limits and weaknesses of certain forms assumed by the Sardinian protest movement, so his Sardinian background made him quite naturally conscious of the ideological defects in a working-class movement inclined to see the Mezzogiorno as 'a ball and chain' obstructing civilized progress. Socialism brought him new answers to the questions posed by his early experience; but, as a Sardinian, he refused to separate the rural problem from the problem of the socialist revolution.[27]

Both before and after the outbreak of the First World War, Gramsci and Luxemburg shared a passionate interest in imaginative literature. Out of the same curiosity about life which led them to become socialists, they both frequently drew character-sketches of the men and women they encountered in social and political life. But the war most certainly deepened their insights into human weaknesses, foibles, vanity and cowardice. Writing to Luisa Kautsky in 1917 about her husband's character, Luxemburg exposed and lampooned his 'comfortable fatalistic optimism'. And for good measure, she added the comment: 'That's why I hate your revered "spouse".'[28] Then in a letter to Mathilde Wurm, she analysed a number of prominent German socialist leaders in character-sketches consisting of a few sharp sentences and concluded: 'When I think of your heroes, a creepy feeling comes over me.'[29]

With the combined gifts of the novelist and the psychologist, Gramsci also probed the weaknesses of individuals on whom the fate of many human beings seemed to depend. Like Luxemburg, he could be simultaneously critical, generous, open-minded and receptive to the unsuspected potential for progressive change and growth within specific individuals. Nevertheless, in a conversational character-sketch of the Italian adventurer, Umberto Cao, in 1925, a year before Cao went over to fascism, Gramsci told Velio Spano: 'That man never believed in anything but himself.'[30] Yet Gramsci and Luxemburg were hostile to the historical determinism and economic reductionism which would become such a prominent feature of 'Marxism' in the years between the two world wars.

The anti-determinist dimension of Gramsci's Marxism found eloquent expression in his famous article welcoming the Bolshevik revolution entitled 'The Revolution against *Das Capital*'. It was the same hostility towards deterministic forms of Marxism which led him, in 1921, to attempt to organise armed resistance to Italian fascism by making contact with 'the Fiuman legionaries'.[31] But although he was never a devotee of historical determinism, Gramsci, like Luxemburg, derived a confidence – a confidence often bordering on a qualified certainty – about his ability as a Marxist activist to interpret and even predict the potentialities, the possibilities and contradictory social, economic and political trends within existing society.

Because Luxemburg was so anti-determinist, she did not hesitate to lambast such close, personal friends as Emanuel and Mathilde Wurm for their lack of courage in opposing capitalistic militarism once the war had broken out. In stressing the importance of personal courage and example in the struggle for a new socialist society, she spoke out with a sharp objective, though not really hostile, frankness:

In your melancholy view, I have been complaining that you people are not marching up to the cannon's mouth. "Not marching" is a good one! You people do not march; you do not even walk; you creep. It is not simply a difference of degree, but rather of kind. On the whole, you people are a different zoological species than I am and your grousing, peevish, cowardly and half-hearted nature has never been as alien, as hateful to me, as now. . . . For you people, the simple words of honest and upright men have not been spoken: "Here I stand, I can't do otherwise; God help me". Luckily, world history, up until this point, has not been made by people like yourselves. Otherwise, we would not have had a Reformation and we probably would still be living in the *ancien regime*.[32]

Though Gramsci's hostility towards historical determinism is often 'explained' away in terms of his so-called 'Crocean idealism', Luxemburg, a more orthodox Marxist, also rejected the attractions and emotional security provided by a belief in historical determinism. Indeed, both Gramsci and Luxemburg attached an inordinate importance to subjective factors in the struggle for socialism. In summing up this particular aspect of Luxemburg's thought, Lelio Basso says: 'But whereas Marx at that time (that is, when he wrote the *18th Brumaire*) placed the emphasis on pre-existing circumstances, that is to say on what is objectively given which weighs "like an incubus on the brain of the living", Rosa Luxemburg emphasises the subjective factor, that is to say, men's actions. So we are here in no way dealing with a mechanistic and deterministic interpretation of Marxism.'[33] In an undated letter sent from prison to her friend Marta Rosenbaum, she set out her credo and relationship with classical Marxism when she said:

Human will must be spurred on to the utmost, and our job is to struggle consciously with all our might. But what I mean is: now, where everything seems so absolutely hopeless, the success of this conscious influence on the masses depends on the elemental, deeply hidden coiled springs of history. . . . Above all, never forget: we are tied to historical laws of development and these never break down, even when they do not exactly follow the plan we have laid.[34]

III

But in a bureaucratised world daily sinking into the most appalling and wretched barbarism and inhumanity, Gramsci and Luxemburg will always be remembered for their profound individualism and socialist-humanism. In Gramsci's deep and touching concern for his mentally-ill wife in far-off Moscow, he depicted the enormous pressures exerted by complex modern societies on the weak and the vulnerable:

The most important point seems to be this: that a psychoanalytic cure can be helpful only to those elements which romantic literature used to call the "insulted and injured" . . . those individuals who are caught up between the iron contrasts of modern life . . . people in short who fail to overcome warring contrasts of this nature and are incapable of arriving at a new moral serenity and tranquility; i.e. an equilibrium between the impulse of the will and the ends which the individual can reach. The situation becomes dramatic at certain definite moments in history and in certain environments; when the environment is superheated to extreme tension, and gigantic collective forces are unleashed which press hard on single individuals. . . . Such situations become disastrous for exceptionally refined and sensitive temperaments . . . I believe therefore that a person of culture, an active element in society (as Giulia certainly is . . .) is and must be his own best psychoanalyst.[35]

In writing to Sonja Liebknecht from the confinement of the dictators' cell in 1917, Luxemburg also revealed the *existentialist* humanism of a socialist personality when she wrote:

The other day a lorry came laden with sacks, so overladen indeed that the buffaloes were unable to drag it across the threshold of the gate. The soldier-driver, a brute of a fellow, belaboured the poor beasts so savagely with the butt end of his whip that the wardress at the gate, indignant at the sight, asked him if he had no compassion for animals. "No more than anyone has compassion for us men", he answered with an evil smile, and redoubled his blows . . .
   I stood in front of the team; the beast looked at me; the tears welled from my own eyes. The suffering of a dearly loved brother could hardly have moved me more profoundly than I was moved by my impotence in face of this mute agony.[36]

Although such expressions of helplessness very occasionally crept into the letters of Gramsci and Luxemburg, they usually emphasised that man *could* become 'the master of his own fate'. This was particularly evident in the specific way they conceived of the coming of socialism as a creative, democratic act from below rather than from above. Writing on this topic in 1916, Gramsci said: 'This means that every revolution is preceded by an intense labour of criticism, of cultural penetration, of permeation of ideas among men who first resist them and who think only about how to resolve, from day to day and from hour to hour, their personal and economic problems, without uniting with others who find themselves in a similar situation.'[37] In a similar, though not identical, picture of the socialist revolution, Luxemburg said:

In popular revolutions it is not the party committee under the all-powerful and brilliant leader or the little circle calling itself a fighting organisation which counts, but only the broad masses shedding their blood. The "socialists" may imagine that the masses of the working people must be trained under their orders for the armed struggles, but, in reality, in every revolution it is the masses themselves who find the means of struggle best suited to the given conditions.[38]

But the summation of Gramsci/Luxemburg approach to the struggle for socialism was expressed by Rosa Luxemburg with crystal-clarity in a prison-letter to Sonja Liebknecht:

Sonyusha, you are feeling embittered because of my long imprisonment. You ask: "How can human beings dare to decide the fate of their fellows? What is the meaning of it all?" You won't mind – I could not help laughing as I read. . . . My dear little bird, the whole history of civilisation (which according to a modest estimate extends through some twenty thousand years) is grounded upon "human beings deciding the fate of their own fellows"; the practice is deeply rooted in the material conditions of existence. . . . Your query is not a reasonable one to make concerning the totality of life and its forms. Why are there blue-tits in the world? I really don't know, but I am glad that there are, and it is sweet to me when a hasty "zeezeebey" sounds suddenly beyond the wall.[39]

Moreover, the Gramsci/Luxemburg critique of capitalism is still valid and relevant in the late-twentieth century, though their fundamental ideas on education, socialist-humanism and the re-distribution of wealth have not yet been implemented anywhere in the world. Because of this, the defenders of the established social order are all too often inclined to depict Antonio Gramsci and Rosa Luxemburg as an interesting, if intelligent and creative, collective curio of history. In short, as historical failures.

To those who are inclined to dismiss the Gramsci/Luxemburg contribution to the uncertain fate and future of humankind, perhaps the defenders of Antonio and Rosa may retort by quoting what E.H. Carr says in his book, *What Is History?*:

Pregant failures are not unknown in history, History recognises what I may call "delayed achievement"; the apparent failures of today may turn out to have made a vital contribution to the achievement of tomorrow – prophets born before their time.[40]

Chapter 5

Jean Jaurés and Vladimir I. Lenin: The ambiguous 'saints'

I know that in my estimate of Jean Jaurés' intellectual integrity I probably differ from many a comrade of the admirable Parti Socialiste de France. But men in a hand-to-hand struggle with another cannot always do him exact justice. It is impossible to have our pound of flesh without the corresponding drops of blood. Jaurés has been an unqualified nuisance in the socialist movement of the world at large, of France in particular. He must be removed – with all the tenderness that is possible, but with all the harshness that may be necessary. Yet he is a man of convictions and noble purpose.

Daniel De Leon

The fact that all his (Lenin's) powers and energies are concentrated upon one thing makes it easy for him to appear extraordinary in the eyes of the masses and become a leader, in the same way that those who really concentrate on God become saints and those who live only for money become millionaires.

Ignazio Silone

Although Jean Jaurés was regarded by the fundamentalists in labour movements in Western Europe and America as a troublesome reformist, the most uncompromising radical critics of reformist socialism also depicted Jaurés as something of a saint. While Daniel De Leon insisted that Jaurés had 'been an unqualified nuisance in the socialist movement of the world at large', he acknowledged the *saintly* aspect of man's character.[1]

With much greater generosity towards reformist socialists than Daniel De Leon was usually prepared to display, Leon Trotsky wrote of Jean Jaurés as follows: 'His spiritual profile corresponded fully to his physical build: elegance and grace as qualities in themselves were foreign to him; yet inborn in his speeches and actions was that higher beauty which distinguishes the manifestations of a self-confident creative force.' Jaurés's saintliness was seldom recognised by the most orthodox Marxists. As Trotsky put it:

Paul Lafargue, a Marxist and an ideological opponent of Jaurés, called him a human devil. This devilish power – as a matter of fact it was a genuinely devine power – everyone, both his friends and his enemies, sensed in him.[2]

In contrast to Jean Jaurés, the reformist saint, Vladimir I. Lenin was originally regarded within the Second International as an intransigent, intolerant revolutionary. The world's revolutionaries saw Lenin as a devout, though ambiguous, trouble-maker – perhaps a socialist saint. Yet even in the late nineteenth century some socialists regarded him as a devilish figure. In *Reminiscences of Lenin*, Clara Zetkin wrote:

It was in 1907 at the World Congress of the Second International at Stuttgart when Rosa Luxemburg, who possessed an artist's eye for the characteristic, pointed Lenin out to me with the remark: "Take a good look at him. That is Lenin. Look at the self-willed, stubborn head. A real Russian peasant's head with a few faintly Asiatic lines. That man will try to overturn mountains. Perhaps he will be crushed by them. But he will never yield".

When Maxim Gorky first encountered Lenin at the Congress of the Russian Social Democratic Labour Party in London in 1907, he was shocked to discover the extent to which the reformist socialists regarded Vladimir Ilyitch as a revolutionary trouble-maker. The Mensheviks saw him as an all too human – a very unsaintly – socialist activist. As Gorky summed up: 'The fury of these disputes at once chilled my enthusiasm, and not so much because I felt how sharply the Party was divided into reformers and revolutionaries – I had realised that in 1903 – but because of the hostile attitude of the reformers to Lenin'.[3]

Although leading socialists in the Second International, whether reformists or revolutionaries, often depicted Jaurés as a man surrounded by a *saintly glow*, Lenin was only seen as a saint between his death in 1924 and 1956. In speaking about the 'saintly' Lenin, Tamara Deutscher said: 'When, after 1956, the "cult of the personality" began to be deprecated in Moscow, Lenin's figure assumed a human shape anew: he was no longer the *Byzantine saint* to be invoked ritualistically by the faithful at every possible opportunity.'[4]

In identifying the four ingredients which sometimes go into the making of great men, J. Hampden Jackson located all four of them in the rural upbringing of Jean Jaurés. As he put it: 'There is no recipe for the breeding of great men, but certain ingredients recur with a frequency astonishing even to the psychologists. So often there is a feckless father, a religious dominant mother, an eminent soldier (or sailor, or priest) not too far back in the family, and a small-town or rural background.' Born on 3 September 1859, in the small provincial town of Castres, Jaurés spent his formative years on a farm in the Tarn. This formative experience made it 'impossible for the grown man ever to neglect or to over-simplify the land question or to sentimentalise the peasant life'. A brilliant pupil, whose talent was detected by an Inspector of Education from Paris when he was only sixteen years of age, he seemed destined for an academic career.[5]

An historian, a Parliamentarian, a genius, advocate of the need for a democratic army, a critic of imperialism, Jaurés, the great Frenchman and citizen of ths world, was assassinated, in 1914, on the eve of the First World War. As J. Hampden Jackson says. 'It was as if Lenin had died in Zimmerwald or Masaryk in London. He was never in power, never even a minister in a capitalist cabinet. The party which he had spent twenty years in building up went to pieces after his death'.[6] But he did not suffer so badly as Vladimir I. Lenin. Transformed into a mummy and icon after his death in 1924 within a context of evolving totalitarianism, Lenin endured a totally unpredictable fate.

While both Jean Jaurés and Vladmir I. Lenin made an inordinate number of enemies, the life and works of Jaurés were neglected after his death. But much worse than the neglect foisted upon Jaurés by an ungrateful and insensitive posterity, Lenin suffered the fate of being deified and rendered 'harmless' by Stalinist totalitarianism. To destroy all memory of the democratic heritage of the Second International before its collapse in 1914, Stalinist scholars ensured that the elementary facts of Lenin's biography in Tsarist Russia would be hidden in obscurity and mystery. As Bertram D. Wolfe put it:

Nowadays, he is (in the 1940s) habitually treated as if he were born a Bolshevik, and as if his father had been a revolutionist before him. The persistence of such a legend in his official biographies is illuminating. In a land where hereditary status is ingrained in the very texture of life, where one's right to schooling was denied under the old regime if one were "the son of a cook", and was later to be denied under the new regime if one were "the son of a kulak", such legends are more than an attempt to evade the problem of tracing the development of their subject's views. Moreover, the current cult of the infallibility of the leader and the *apostolic* succession requires him to have sprung, ideologically fully armed, from the womb, as the Greek Goddess of wisdom from the forehead of Zeus.[7]

A man of great simplicity and modesty, Vladimir I. Lenin's intransigent disaffection from the Tsarist social order was environmentally conditioned. It was rooted in Russian absolutism and the unique traditions of the nineteenth-century intelligentsia. Although he was born into a solid respectable and bourgeois family at Simbirsk – a backward, desolate and provincial capital on the banks of the Volga – on 22 April 1870, Lenin did not possess many of the ingredients for greatness identified by J. Hampden Jackson. In focusing on the extent to which Lenin's *revolutionary* socialism was begot by Tsarism, Wolfe says:

All the reminiscences of brothers and sisters and family friends, as in Lenin's own occasional references to his childhood, there is nothing to accord with the fashionable "psychological" explanations of the careers of the world's great rebels, nothing to document the formula of mother or father fixation, no unhappy family life, maladjusted childhood, no traces of a sense of inferiority due to failure at school or in childish competitive sports, no sign of queerness or abnormality. True, the hanging of his brother, Alexander, for an attempt on the life of the Tsar when Vladimir was only sixteen, was an event to put iron into his soul, but that only moves the question a little further back: what made brother Alexander into a plotter and a rebel? We shall have to look elsewhere than to the maladjustments of a miserable childhood for the motive forces that drove him to hate feudal barbarism and despotism and to choose revolution as a way of life.[8]

Jean Jaurés was a much more tolerant man than Vladimir I. Lenin. This was reflected in their basically different attitudes to life as well as politics. With a liking for good booze, Jaurés 'had a healthy appetite and was a Frenchman interested in good food'. He disliked narrow utilitarianism in politics; and he disliked puritanism except perhaps in relation to sexual questions. By contrast, Lenin was 'extremely frugal and disliked drinking, smoking, and overeating'. Furthermore, their distinctive traits of character were seen in what they thought about – and how they behaved in relation to – money.[9]

In sketching in and suggesting the existence of a harmonious coalescence between Jaurés's democratic outlook and his attitude to money, J. Hampden Jackson says:

He travelled second-class, standing outside on the platform. The conductors, who knew him, would pick up the newspapers which fell from his over-loaded and often torn pockets and laugh when he discovered that he had not enough *sous* to pay the fare. This pennilessness, incidentally, was the habit of a lifetime; in his Ecole Normale days a fellow-undergraduate had noted: "Jaurés is absolutely ignorant of the value of money; he lived as happy as a king without a penny in his pocket and often had not enough to take an omnibus. . .". He died worth under £400.

With a fundamentally different attitude towards the political process and functioning as a professional conspirator, Lenin attached an inordinate importance to money. As Stefan T. Possony put it:

Completely uninterested in earning money for his personal comfort, he was extraordinarily adept at raising funds, if often by illegal and criminal means. Money was an instrument of the political struggle, wholly unconnected with morality – and the single-minded Lenin knew how to spend effectively the money he had, whether to finance propaganda, procure arms, or to buy votes and souls. His ability to obtain funds and his skill in using them are among the key conditions of his success.[10]

Being much closer to the dominant democratic outlook of such socialists within the Second International as Eugene V. Debs, Rosa Luxemburg or Karl Liebknecht, Jaurés was impatient with doctrinal purity and intellectual intolerance of the sort displayed by De Leon and Lenin. In 1906 Jaurés wrote an article expounding his own conception of the function of the socialist party: 'It is true that I have not much taste for disputes within the Party. We have such an enormous task to fulfil, such an incessant struggle to wage against adversaries of every type, that these quarrels about tactics and methods within the Party weary me. I am convinced that there is a place in the Party for every type of temperament and for every type of activity, and that we would all get in each other's way less if we were to work more.' This puralistic approach to socialist politics was anathema to Lenin. In his pamphlet, *One Step Forward, Two Steps Back*, Lenin said: 'A free and open struggle. Opinions have been stated. The shades have been made clear. The groups have taken shape. Hands have been raised. A decision has been taken. A stage has been passed. Forward! That's the stuff for me! That's life!'[11] Just as there were two conceptions of socialism, so there were two conceptions of the role of the 'vanguard Party' in the struggle for the Society of Equals.

It was the repressive conditions in Tsarist Russia which were at least partly responsible for engendering Vladimir I. Lenin's unique conception of the 'vanguard Party' as a party of 'professional revolutionaries'. Before 1917 Lenin's conception of the vanguard role of the Bolshevik Party was not incompatible with democratic attitudes. One of Lenin's most critical, informed and scholarly biographers, Bertram D. Wolfe, said: 'For Lenin in those days, was a convinced democrat, and the problem of political freedom concerned him deeply. Not only in those days, but until he seized power in 1917.' But although Jaurés shared the pre-1917 Lenin's democratic socialist objectives, he rejected the arguments of the sectarians like De Leon, Jules Guesde and Lenin who advocated doctrinal purity and the expulsion of socialists who were less than Simon-pure.[12]

With a predilection for doctrinal intransigence, heresy-hunting and expulsions, Lenin's interpretation of the classical Marxist view of the role of the 'vanguard Party' in the struggle for socialism might be justified within the peculiar conditions prevailing in Tsarist Russia. But Lenin was equally contemptuous of parliamentary democracy in Western Europe before 1917. The retrospective criticism that Lenin's wife, Nadezhda Krupskaya, explained in *Memories of Lenin*, was revealing:

By attending French election meetings, we got a clear insight into what elections mean in a "democratic republic". To an outside observer, the thing seemed simply astonishing. That is why Illyich was so fond of the revolutionary music-hall singers who poured ridicule on the election campaign.[13]

I

Seen through the lens of the late-twentieth century, Jean Jaurés was a much more attractive figure than Vladimir I. Lenin. To such a sympathetic, critical and perceptive democratic socialist as Max Beer, Lenin and Jaurés were, as late as 1933, the two socialists he bracketed together in a new Hallway of Fame. In summing up, he said:

Of all the men I had the good fortune to come across, Lenin and Jaurés impressed me most. Both had their roots deep down in the soil of their native land, while their minds were immersed in the ideas, and inspired by the acts, of the revolutionary upheavals of their forefathers. Man makes history, but history also makes man.

Yet in contrast to Jaurés, Lenin almost always displayed autocratic traits long before the Bolshevik revolution.[14]

When Maxim Gorky discussed Lenin's role in the Bolshevik revolution, he readily admitted that Russian socialism was somewhat authoritarian. As he put it: 'The duty of the true-hearted leaders of the people is super-humanly difficult. A leader who is not in some degree a tyrant, is impossible. More people, probably, were killed under Lenin that under Thomas Munzer; but without this, resistance to the revolution of which Lenin was the leader would have been more widely and more powerfully organised. In addition to this we must take into account the fact that with the development of civilisation the value of human life manifestly depreciates, a fact which is clearly proved by the growth in contemporary Europe of the technique of annihilating people, and the taste for doing so.' Yet despite his profound admiration for Vladimir I. Lenin, Max Beer also acknowledged the authoritarianism in Lenin's socialism. In tracing Lenin's authoritarian socialism back to the traditions of the nineteenth-century Russian intelligentsia, Beer summed up thus:

A Socialist Peter the Great, though living and studying for years in Central and Western Europe and admiring much of what he found there, his heart and his spirit were always dwelling in his Russian land, in the midst of its workers and peasants, and in the records of its revolutionary martyrs from the time of the Dekabrists (1826) to that of the last fighters of the Narodnaya Volya, among whom was his martyred brother Alexander (1887), whose pseudonym was "Lenin". They all bequeathed to him much that went to the making of Bolshevism.[15]

Despite the profound differences in their distinctive socialist outlooks, Jaurés and Lenin saw themselves as representing an *avant-garde* without any attachments to traditionalism. Yet within the personalities and lives of Jean Jaurés and Vladimir I. Lenin, the new, the innovative and the revolutionary world-view of nineteenth-century socialism co-existed with some traditional attitudes and values. Although Jaurés spent a lot of time at home, he did not do any of the domestic chores. While Mme Jaurés did 'the dusting and airing of which the house stood so peculiarly in need, Jaurés would gather up his correspondence and make his way upstairs to the tiny study'. While Jaurés had two children, Lenin and Krupskaya remained childless.[16]

Although Lenin's marital relationship with Krupskaya was democratic in some ways, it was quite traditional in others. In a very favourable portrait of Lenin, Max Beer wrote: 'Lenin and his wife lived an austere life, in total abstinence from smoking and alcohol and all those articles of food which in a working-class family would be called luxuries. They did their housework by themselves and alternated weekly in the work; one week he swept the room and kitchen, made the beds, prepared the food, and the next week it was her turn to care for the house. She helped him in his literary work, made researches in the British Museum, and copied his manuscripts.' Yet Lenin was much more of a traditionalist in relation to the 'woman question' than Eugene V. Debs or Karl Liebknecht.[17]

Perhaps because Jaurés had less understanding of 'the depths of human perfidy' than Lenin, he was more tolerant of religion and the many dimensions of the human condition. In the sphere of religion, Jaurés, the *ambiguous* socialist saint, developed a more complex analysis of the significance of religion than Lenin ever did. Moreover, the concept of a vanguard Party of professional revolutionaries was alien to his specific world-outlook. In capturing some aspects of Jaurés's distinctive socialist attitudes, J. Hampden Jackson said:

He could never conceive of the Universe as anything but a unity: God could not exist without man, nor man without God; good and evil are but different aspects of the same thing. ... He could never be convinced that men were essentially unequal: "There are not some men who are philosophers and others who are not. Every man carried in him the philosopher and the common man ... when the philosopher despises the common man, he despises himself and when the common man laughs at the philosopher he laughs at himself".[18]

An idealist in philosophy, he was nevertheless an *unorthodox 'Marxist'*.

In contrast to Jaurés, Lenin always argued that 'in the hands of the bourgeosie' religion was 'a means of diverting the masses from the class struggle' and for stultifying workers' minds. In discussing the continuity of Lenin's hostility to religion, Nadezhda Krupskaya said:

Even as a boy of fifteen, Ilyich understood the pernicious character of religion. He then ceased to wear a cross and stopped going to church. In those days this was not so simple a matter as now.

Lenin was of the opinion that the more subtle religions, those that were free from obvious absurdities and externally slavish forms, were *more pernicious* than the rest. Such religions, he thought, were likely to exercise greater influence on people. He regarded God-creating (attempts to create new religions and new faiths) as of this class.[19]

But although Jaurés and Lenin were atheists and opponents of clericalism, they did not quite transcend traditional attitudes towards sex and sexual questions. For Jaurés 'free love' was simply a caricature of marriage; and he argued that 'the pseudo-revolutionary solution of divorce' penalised the woman in capitalist societies. Yet he questioned and criticised some of the most traditional ideas about sexual behaviour. As one of his biographers put it: 'But if the example and teaching of Jaurés were opposed to all sexual bohemianism, they were equally opposed to the narrow puritanism which is the opposite pitfall of those who call themselves revolutionaries.'[20]

An orthodox Marxist in some fundamental matters of economics and culture, Lenin was puritanical and pedantic in sexual matters. Although he shared the classical Marxists' dislike of 'bourgeois marriage' and property laws, he was less libertarian than Jaurés. Indeed, in the early 1920s, he criticised Clara Zetkin's behaviour in encouraging working-class women to discuss questions of sexual liberation. He condemned Zetkin for participating in discussions on sexual questions at a time when 'the first country of proletarian dictatorship' was 'surrounded by the counter-revolutionaries of the whole world'. Moreover, he criticised the new forms of sexual behaviour amongst communists in Bolshevik Russia. As he put it: 'The changed attitude of the young people to questions of sexual life is, of course, based on a "principle" and a theory. Many of them call their attitude "revolutionary" and "communistic". And they honestly believe that it is so. That does not impress us old people. Although I am nothing but a gloomy ascetic, the so-called "new sexual life" of the youth – and sometimes of the old – often seems to me to be purely bourgeois, an extension of bourgeois brothels'.[21]

A major attraction of Lenin's socialism in the West after 1917 was its simplistic emphasis on a primitive one-dimensional assault on world capitalism. In anticipating the more subtle analysis of modern capitalism developed by the New Left in the 1960s, Jaurés was more sensitive to the social, cultural and intellectual strengths of capitalism.

Jean Jaurés's socialism was not, however, simply complex. It was also comprehensive, all-embracing and many-sided. In a major biography, *The Life of Jean Jaurés*, Harvey Goldberg captures and conveys something of the great Frenchman's complexity as a practitioner of modern socialism. By 1892 Jaurés had made the transition from radicalism to socialism. As Harvey Goldberg puts it:

In a very special sense, therefore, his socialism was religious. Certainly, Jaurés had rejected formal theology and broken forever with Catholicism. Christianity, he charged, had become a pseudo-religion, its institutions oppressive, its charity hypocritical, its doctrine a mass of lies and myths. But in socialism, in the harmony and unity of mankind, Jaurés foresaw a genuine religion, the triumph of man's moral aspirations and the deepest expression of his love . . .

But Jaurés' socialism was equally materialistic. Unlike the absolute idealists, he accepted the material universe and its shaping influence. The economic transformation of society, the internal development of capitalism, as Marx had described it, determined the direction of history and presaged the triumph of socialism.[22]

But the many-sided generosity of Jaurés's socialism was matched by its openness and innate attachment to democracy.

Although both Jaurés and Lenin submerged their individual personalities in the socialist movements of France and Russia, they were nevertheless great individualists. While the writings of both men were remarkably free from personal reminiscences, the differences in their distinctive approaches to life were enormous. For example, Jaurés seems to have been much more aware of the tragedy inherent in the human condition than Lenin ever came within reach of understanding. In contrast to Lenin's much more fundamentally Promethian approach to life, Jaurés always sought co-operation with the latent forces of progress in all social classes. In summing up Jaurés's basic attitude to politics, Harvey Goldberg said: 'Sensitive though he was to the deep sorrows of life, Jaurés welcomed the challenge of living. So, if the world of public affairs was often discouraging, it was also the world of good and noble actions.'[23]

In ridiculing the Frenchman's response to Rosa Luxemburg's 'scathing Phillippic' against him at the Amsterdam Congress of the Second International in 1904, Daniel De Leon mocked Jaurés with sustained invective: 'And yet, within a few minutes, you will see the citizen Rosa Luxemburg translating me into German; you will see how there can be useful co-operation despite conflict.' Unlike Lenin and De Leon, who often sought to create doctrinal purity through expulsions and decrees, Jaurés always worked for unity within the socialist movement. As Margaret Pease put it:

In his philosophy Life was a whole, and the course of history a real development, so that he did not believe in cataclysms, and socialism became to him simply a necessary result of all that had gone before. So, too, we find him always seeking the point of contact, even with those opposed to him in many things, for he believed in contact, in comprehension of others, even in submitting to them at times.[24]

But Jean Jaurés was, above all, a socialist – not a liberal reformer with a saintly glow. As Harvey Goldberg argued: 'Others, like Eduard Bernstein and the socialist revisionists, content with reforms under capitalism, would later proclaim that the movement was everything and the end nothing. Jaurés would never join them. If his method was peaceful and evolutionary, his goal was revolutionary'. But although there were very few personal reminiscences in Jaurés's letters or writings after he was converted to socialism, there was an unbroken continuity – a unity – in his life and work. His socialism sprang from 'an acute and unexpressed affection for people and from an intense sensitiveness to what religious writers would call the Godhead, and Jaurés the humanity, in every man.'[25]

Unlike Lenin, Jaurés saw the need for socialist-humanism in the daily lives of working-class men and women. In identifying the symbiotic relationship between idealism and materialism in industrial societies, Jaurés wrote: 'The humanity that socialism seeks to arouse is in no sense fictitious, but an actual humanity, a humanity that is part of nature. Hence socialism is the greatest and most efficacious moral force that has yet appeared in the world.' By contrast, Lenin regarded all talk of socialism as 'a moral force' as a digression from the ongoing class struggle.[26]

Being unsure about whether he should present Lenin as a saint or a sinner in the 1920s, Maxim Gorky focused on the world bourgeoisie's 'nakedly and repellently manifest hatred' for *the* architect of the October revolution. Just as there were obvious continuities in the life and thought of Jaurés, so the continuity of the thought and attitudes of the nineteenth-century Russian intelligentsia found expression in Lenin. Far away and spiritually distant from the intellectual thought-world of the Western socialist, Lenin sought, in Maxim Gorky's idiom, to overcome his 'organic "social idealism" for the sake of the triumph of the socialist cause' he was serving before and after 1917. Gorky's brilliant pen-portrait of the embattled, internal fugitive during the early years after the Bolshevik revolution deserves to be quoted at length:

One evening in Moscow, in E.P. Preskovskaya's flat, Lenin was listening to a sonata by Beethoven being played by Isaiah Dobrowein, and said: 'I know nothing which is greater than the Appassionata; I would like to listen to it every day. It is marvellous superhuman music. I always think with pride – perhaps it is naive of me – what marvellous things human beings can do!'

Then screwing up his eyes and smiling, he added, rather sadly: "But I can't listen to music too often. It affects your nerves, make you want to say stupid, nice things, and stroke the heads of people who could create such beauty while living in this vile hell. And now you must not stroke any one's head – you might get your hand bitten off. You have to hit them on the head, without any mercy, although our ideal is not to use force against anyone. H'm, h'm, our duty is infernally hard".[27]

Despite the brilliance of Vladimir I. Lenin's scholarship, Marxist analyses and prolific writings during his prolonged exile in Central and Western Europe, he did not really understand the labour movements outside of Tsarist – or, indeed, outside of Soviet – Russia. Although Maxim Gorky spoke movingly of Lenin's 'clear-sighted directness of vision', Gorky's reminiscences were far too eulogistic to reveal the full extent of Lenin's conspiratorial interpretation of the way ruling classes were functioning in most of Europe. In quoting an example of Lenin's conspiratorial thinking about the sources of the ruling-class domination of the Capri fishermen in Italy in 1911, Gorky said:

He asked in detail about the life of the Capri fishermen, about their earnings, the influence of the priests, their schools. I could not but be surprised at the range of his interests.

When a priest was pointed out to him, the son of a poor peasant, he immediately asked for information as to how often the peasants sent their children to the seminaries, and whether the children returned to their own villages as priests.

"You understand? If this is not an isolated case, it means that it is the policy of the Vatican – an artful policy".[28]

Nevertheless Lenin's attitudes towards the labour movements in Western Europe, while often naive and simplistic, were constantly changing, though not in substance, before the triumph of Bolshevism in 1917. In describing Lenin in London in 1902, Nadezhda Krupskaya said:

He searched the papers for advertisement of working-class meetings in out-of-the-way districts, where there was no ostentation, no leaders, but merely workers from the bench – as we now term them . . . Ilyich would listen attentively and afterwards joyfully exclaim: "Socialism is simply oozing from them. The speaker talks rot, and a worker gets up and immediately, taking the bull by the horns, himself lays bare the essence of capitalist society". Ilyich always placed his hope on the rank-and-file British workman who, in spite of everything, preserved his class instinct. People travelling to England generally notice merely the labour aristocracy who have been corrupted by the bourgeoisie and themselves become petty bourgeois. Ilyich, of course, studied also this upper stratum and the concrete forms which this bourgeois influence assumed. But while not forgetting for one moment the significance of this fact, he also endeavoured to feel the pulse of the motive forces of England's future Revolution.

At approximately the same time, Lenin and Krupskaya condemned the German socialists in Munich for not *defying* the Prussian authorities. As Krupskaya put it: 'That year the German social democrats were permitted for the first time to organise a procession, on condition that they did not form crowds in the town, but arranged the celebrations in the countryside. . . . This May-day celebration did not at all resemble a demonstration of working-class triumph throughout the world.' In contrast to Jean Jaurés, the 'saintly' reformer who favoured peaceful methods for revolutionary ends, Lenin wanted bloody insurrection in Western Europe as well as in Tsarist Russia.[29]

When he went to live in Switzerland in 1908, Lenin appeared to revise some of his analyses of the nature of Parliamentary democracy in capitalist countries. But rather than appreciating the need for more subtle tactics in the ongoing battle of ideas, he seems to have opted for a more intransigent and uncompromising insurrectionary approach to the political struggle. As Nadezhda Krupskaya put it:

The fight for a democratic republic was a point in our programme at that time. Ilyich now realised with particular clarity that a bourgeois democratic republic was perhaps a more subtle instrument than Tsarism, but nevertheless an instrument for enslaving the toiling masses. In a democratic republic the authorities do all in their power to imbue the whole of social life with the bourgeois spirit.

It seems to me that had Ilyich not lived through the 1905 revolution and the second period of exile, he would not have been able to write his book, *State and Revolution*.[30]

II

Elected to the Chamber of Deputies in 1886 three years after he had been given a lectureship at the University of Toulouse, Jean Jaurés with a few brief interruptions remained a member of Parliament until his murder in 1914. A consistent and unrelenting critic of imperialism and militarism from the 1890s onwards, he was the only major socialist thinker in the Second International who systematically attempted to develop reformist methods of socialist struggle for revolutionary ends. As Jaurés's commitment to socialism deepened, he developed new insights into the nature of modern capitalism. In making this point, Harvey Goldberg said:

His (Marx's) disciples in the Second International, lacking his intellectual depth, converted his full-blooded philosophy into a mechanistic determinism, which did justice neither to his humanism nor to his historical insight. Jaurés, who was no man's disciple, nonetheless became Marx's spiritual *confrere*.[31]

Parliamentary democracy in France was in its infancy. This context shaped Jaurés's growing awareness that unequal economic power in a society undergoing industrialisation dictated the objective need for socialism. As one historian argued: 'In Spain and Italy democracy was almost a farce during these years; but even in France, employers and landed aristocrats could apply strong pressure on poor workers and peasants so that elections might be anything but free.'[32] With Jaurés's deepening understanding of Marxian socialism, he became more rather than less determined to extend democracy within the framework of French capitalism.

This was seen in Jaurés's response to the Dreyfus affair in 1898. During this 'dark hour for the soldiers of "truth and justice"', Emile Zola published his famous letter 'J'accuse (I accuse) in defence of Captain Dreyfus, a Jewish army officer, who was framed on a charge of espionage. In alliance with the Catholic Church, Monarchist and anti-Semitic elements, the most *extreme* right-wing forces in France used the Dreyfus affair as a pretext for the sustained attack on the foundations of the Republic. Matthew Josephson described the ensuing tumultous turmoil:

Mobs paraded the streets, manifesting. Zola was burnt in effigy and hurled into the Seine. The *Libre Parole* called fearlessly for the sacking of his house, for his assassination. The rest of the press demanded variously his trial, his incarceration, his execution. He had "insulted the army" – so he had – the government, the whole nation.

The constant turmoil which had gripped Paris for two months was not comparable to the vast uproar that arose now. A few days, and there were bloody uprisings in Algiers, where anti-Semitism had made brilliant progress. . . . There was sacking of Jewish quarters in many towns throughout France. There was indescribable disorder in the House of Deputies (14 January 1898), Jaurés being the centre of the storm.[33]

Although Jaurés was much closer in spirit to Emile Zola than to Jules Guesde, he was much less concerned than most of the left-wing socialist Deputies about losing his seat in Parliament. Jaurés's championship of Dreyfus was also important in stimulating and strengthening support for socialism among working-class men and women throughout France. Yet the most orthodox advocates of 'Marxism' refused to participate in the Dreyfus agitation launched by Emile Zola and Jaurés. When Zola, the outstanding novelist and practitioner of realism in literature, gave an interesting interview to Max Beer, he said:

I am not a socialist, still less a leader in socialist thought. I believe with one of our clearest intellects, Ernest Renan, that science and education will lift the mountains of poverty and prejudice from the shoulders of mankind, but I sincerely wish to have all socialists as my friends. You see, only Jaurés and his friends are supporting me; the Geusdists are standing aloof; some of them have been behaving badly. They do not see that I am not fighting for a rich *bourgeois*, but for liberty, and for the free development of our great and noble France against a conspiracy of mighty foes – militarism and the Catholic Church allied to the remnants of the old feudal aristocracy. My fight is a continuation in the direct line of the French revolution.[34]

In sharp contrast to Lenin's conscious decision to suppress compassion and 'social idealism', Jaurés made such human qualities as pity and suffering weapons in the socialists' struggle for justice and dignity. When he addressed himself to the question of what the Dreyfusards had to do with socialism, Jaurés said:

If Dreyfus has been condemned contrary to all law, condemned falsely, what an absurdity to count him among the privileged class! No: he is no longer an officer of that Army which, by a criminal error, has degraded him. He no longer belongs to those ruling classes which by the cowardice of their ambition hesitate to re-restablish legality and truth on his behalf. He is merely an example of human suffering in its most poignant form. He is a living witness to military lies, to political cowardice, and to the crimes of the authorities. Surely we can, without departing from our principles or going back on the class war, listen to the dictates of pity. For all our revolutionary struggle, we can keep some sense of human compassion.[35]

In the short run, Jaurés's militant reformism led to an alliance with some of the bourgeois radicals like Alexandre Millerand.

But the alliance that Jaurés forged with Millerand was soon to be broken. As a result of the conflict between right and left in the Second International, it was destined to be short-lived. With Millerand's entry into the Waldeck-Rousseau government – he was the first European socialist to sit in a 'bourgeois cabinet' – the alliance formed during the Dreyfus affair between the bourgeois radicals and the reformist socialists soon fell apart.

Jean Jaurés was, however, a reformist socialist – not a saintly bourgeois reformer. Although he distanced himself from the Marxism being popular-ised by Rosa Luxemburg and Karl Liebknecht, Jaurés did not, as some sectarian socialists predicted, abandon the labour movement. While he continued to argue for what might be described as a sort of militant reformist socialism within the Second International, he had a profound respect for solidarity among socialists. As Val Lorwin put it: 'Jaurés, greatest of the French socialists, defended Millerand's action. But – in one of the few real manifestations of international socialist discipline – Jaurés and his followers bowed to the condemnation of "Millerandism" by the Socialist (or Second) International in 1904'.[36]

From 1892 onwards, Jaurés's socialism was concrete and authentic. In 1889 when he was making the transition from Jacobinism to socialism, he accused the reactionary industrialists in France of using corruption as well as their economic power to win elections. But although he was always more of a scholar or academic than Lenin, he refused to live in an ivory tower.

Also the often dramatic self-activity of the French working class played an important role in the growth of his involvement in political struggles and socialist thinking. As Harold Weinstein explained: 'In 1892 the strike of the workers at Carmaux against the political pressures of the Marquis De Solages occasioned the assertion by Jaurés that the merging of reaction and capitalism was a menace to universal suffrage and the Republic'.[37]

Yet despite Jaurés's firm commitment to Parliamentary democracy, he did not neglect the battle of ideas. During the years between 1898 and 1902 when he did not sit in Parliament, he wrote four books on the great French revolution from a socialist point of view. This was part of a series on the history of France written as an attempt to develop a socialist world-view among ordinary men and women. In justifying and promoting this vast enterprise, he wrote: 'When a new class arises and affirms its strength, it attempts not only to prepare the future but to understand and interpret the past according to the new light of its consciousness.' The ambitious plan to develop nothing less than a socialist counter-culture included 'an encyclopedia which would pave the way to the *socialist revolution* of the twentieth century, an encyclopedia to be supplemented by a people's university, a people's theatre and a people's press'.[38]

Anticipating some of Antonio Gramsci's conceptions of how socialism would come in Western Europe, Jean Jaurés was incapable of conceiving of socialism as a latent potentiality without the intervention of what he called 'revolutionary majorities'. Unlike Lenin, he did not believe that socialism could ever be imposed on the working classes. Because he was steeped in the revolutionary culture and traditions of the French revolution, he did not think that socialism could gain political power before it triumphed intellectually.

After the triumph of Bolshevism in Russia, Lenin told Clara Zetkin: '*Illiteracy* was *compatible* with the *struggle* for the seizure of *power*, with the necessity to destroy the old state apparatus'.[39] But long before his death in 1914, Jaurés was irritated by such elitist attitudes in the socialist movement at large. It was very annoying to Jaurés that Jules Guesde 'not content with advocating the method of propaganda as the only work for socialists, and the catastrophic revolution as the *daystar* of their *hope*, should also criticise with such bitterness each attempt to ameliorate the lot of the workers as it came within sight and was discussed in Parliament, although he (Guesde) was not opposed to the use of the vote'. From Jaurés's perspective, socialism required a minimum of material well-being, literacy, education, democracy and enlightenment.[40]

Therefore, Jaurés dismissed the orthodox Marxist argument that working-class emancipation would develop out of 'absolute destitution'. In this respect, Jaurés was at one with the German revisionist, Eduard Bernstein. In her biography of Jean Jaurés, Margaret Pease explained why he rejected the theory of increasing misery as an essential part of the road of socialism: 'If it were so the socialists at the beginning of the twentieth century would have cause to feel hopeless indeed. For to Jaurés the "one undoubted fact which transends all others" is the growth in numbers, in solidarity, in the self-consciousness of the workers. They have gained the vote, they are organised in trade unions, and in co-operative societies, they have shorter hours and better pay, they are immensely better educated and have more weight than ever before. Many of them now have an ideal of a new social order founded on a different principle altogether from the present one'. In his insistence that the latent possibility of socialism was rooted in an open-ended and open-minded methodology – not dogma – he wrote:

The future, gentlemen, is not in the recipes of parties.
The future is not in a machine to be turned out at will.
The future is built up gradually by those who have a point of view and a method.[41]

Unlike Lenin, who in 1917, was determined to impose socialism on the Russian people, Jaurés consistently opposed such an approach. When he published a collection of essays, *Studies in Socialism*, in 1906, he asserted that 'the socialist revolution will not be accomplished by the action, or the sudden stroke of a bold minority'. In discussing the crucial need for a socialist mandate, he wrote: 'Those great social changes that are called revolutions cannot, or rather can no longer be accomplished by a minority. A revolutionary minority, no matter how intelligent and energetic, is not enough, in modern societies at least, to bring about a revolution. The co-operation and adhesion of a majority, and an immense majority, are needed'.[42]

Indeed, a mass socialist consciousness was a basic pre-condition for socialism in the twentieth century. Just as the Reformation, the Renaissance and the French revolution of 1789 had 'filled the people with a consciousness of their rights', so socialism would require to develop its own mass counter-culture before it could conceive of gaining political power.[43] Yet despite Jaurés arguably un-Marxist attitude to the capitalist state, he was really – in the absence of a more colourful phrase – a revolutionary reformist. His revolutionary programme for transforming the existing capitalist state into a more democratic one was seen in 1910 when he presented a Bill in the French Parliament on Army Reorganisation.

At the same time, Jaurés published a book on *Democracy and Military Service* in which he presented detailed plans for a democratic army within the existing capitalist system. In addressing the problem of an anti-working-class militarism, he suggested that the army should be democratised by ensuring that the officers should come from and represent 'all social classes'. While he proposed that a third of all army officers should come from the working class, he displayed an awareness of the problem of how individuals could be absorbed into the French military establishment when he said:

Let these boys, supported partly by the workmen's societies and partly by the nation, be sent to the higher schools and to the University for their degree in military science; then there will be a visible bond between these young men and the permanent Labour organisations of the country. These officers, while they rise, will feel that they are not leaving the great working class from which they sprang.[44]

Jaurés had developed his plans for a democratic army as a result of his experiences during the campaign to defend Captain Dreyfus. Although the quarrel that he was involved in over socialist reformism initially interrupted his preoccupation with the need for a democratic army, he kept coming back to it during the years before his murder. But because of the criticisms levelled at him by the left-wing Marxian socialists in the Second International, Jaurés's role in raising critical questions about the authenticity of the German socialists' alleged radicalism has been glossed over.

The split in the Second International over the controversial issue of reform versus revolution resulted in such essentially bourgeois politicians as Millerand, Briand and Viviani deserting the French labour movement to join right-wing parties and gain high office in 'bourgeois cabinets'. The conflict between Jean Jaurés and Daniel De Leon actually obscured other more important political conflicts at the Amsterdam Congress of the Second International. The bitter clash between Jaurés and August Bebel ten years before the outbreak of the First World War was very revealing. In prolonged conversations with Max Beer, Jaurés discovered how hollow and superficial the commitment to socialism of most German social democrats really was in the years before the beginning of the European blood-bath. But in a speech full of bitter invective, Jaurés told the delegates at Amsterdam what he thought of German 'socialism' at a time when Lenin still believed in its profound authenticity:

What pressed so heavily upon the socialist-labour movement of the world, he exclaimed prophetically, was not French reformism and the so-called watering down of the revolutionary principles of our faith; it was the deplorable inactivity, the political inefficiency, of Germany social democracy, our teachers in theory and organisation, which paralysed our international movement. . . . How did they think to attain to their objective? Through the Reichstag? Quite an impossible assumption, and there was no evidence whatever that they were training the masses to resist, and manfully to resist, the fatal policy of their government.[45]

What was particularly interesting about Bebel's reply to Jaurés was its intense and aggressive nationalistic tone. In his nationalistic arrogance, Bebel was already prefiguring the *majority socialists'* response to their fellow socialists in Belgium a few months after the outbreak of the First World War. In responding to Jaurés's critique of their 'softness' towards German absolutism, Bebel insisted that the French Republic deserved to be condemned by socialists everywhere. As he summed up: 'No social insurance, no Labour legislation, no honest income-tax, but indirect tax burdens laid upon the workman's food, and the employment of the military to suppress strikes and shoot down the strike leaders! Where, then, was the celebrated influence of French socialism? The Frenchmen were proud of their Republican institutions. Were they won by the French people? No! They owed the French Republic to Bismarck. "Give me a constitutional monarchy like the English, and I will make you a present of a Republic like that of France".'

Unlike the majority socialists in Germany, Jean Jaurés had always campaigned against imperialism and expansionist aspirations. Although August Bebel was not a Gustav Noske, he had, in Rosa Luxemburg's view, encouraged conservatism with a small c in the German labour movement. In any case the tragic imperialistic postures of the majority socialists were revealed in September 1914, when Noske, a member of the Reichstag, and Franz Koster, the editor of the *Hamburgh Echo*, visited the socialists at the Maison du Peuple in Brussels. As Emile Royer explained in a book, *German Socialists and Belgium*, published in 1915:

Noske and Koster could not understand why the Belgian socialists, as well as other people, had opposed the German entrance into Belgium, inasmuch as the Belgians would have been liberally compensated for all the losses they might have suffered, and would in addition have received the benefit of universal suffrage and of insurance – laws which they had not been able to obtain from their own Government. These Prussian socialists made no mention of the electoral system of "three classes", which crushes them in their own country, nor of the political impotence of the Reichstag. But when something was said to them about Belgium's respect for international treaties and about her honour which she was defending, Koster replied that this was mere "ideologie bourgeoisie", and that, as historic materialism taught that the development of the proletariat was closely bound up with the development and economic prosperity of the nation, German socialists were bound to side with the Government, which was defending the very existence of the country against the attacks of England, France and Russian despotism.[46]

This very representative German chauvinism would not, if he had lived, have surprised Jaurés.

But would the survival of Jean Jaurés have made any difference to the post-war history of European socialism? In addressing the difficult question of whether Jaurés, if he had lived, would have rallied to the cause of national defence against Germany as Jules Guesde did, the English labour historian, G.D.H. Cole said the answer was probably 'yes'. Yet Cole added that Jaurés would probably 'have shown greater wisdom' than Guesde in 'working for a negotiated peace'.[47]

Although Jaurés was much more pessimistic about the human condition than Vladimir I. Lenin, he was also more open-minded and responsive to new circumstances. While Lenin wanted, as Maxim Gorky reported, 'to spread among the masses all the old revolutionary literature here and in Europe', Jaurés became more pessimistic about imaginative literature. At the same time as he lauded the work of Ibsen and Hauptman, he criticised them for 'never fully understanding the course of history'. Furthermore, in contrast to Lenin, who never succeeded, in Bertram Wolfe's phrase, 'in handing down to his disciples' his respect for the creative freedom of the artist', Jaurés did inspire some socialists after the First World War with his democratic conception of the efficacy of a socialist counter-culture within capitalist societies.[48]

III

With the advent of Stalinism, the question of Vladimir I. Lenin's role in engendering totalitarian 'socialism' was raised again and again in Western labour movements. When Max Eastman, the American socialist, published his book, *Stalin's Russia and the Crisis of Socialism*, in 1940, he insisted on the *dominance* of the *libertarian* motive in Lenin's life and work. Saddened and disillusioned by the monstrous totalitarianism which was masquerading under 'socialist' rhetoric, he said: 'Lenin will perhaps stand out, when the commotion about his ideas subsides, as the greatest rebel in history. His major passion was to set men free.' In summing up, he quoted what Lenin said in the spring and summer of 1917:

> Do not allow the police to be re-established.
> Do not allow the re-establishment of the all-powerful officialdom which is in reality not subject to recall and belongs to the class of landowners and capitalists.
> Do not allow the re-establishment of a standing army separated from the people, serving as a perpetual incentive for various attempts to crush liberty and to revive the monarchy. Teach the people, down to the lowest strata, the art of administration, not through books but through actual practice to be begun immediately and everywhere, through the utilisation of the experience of the masses. Democracy from below, democracy without an officialdom, without police, without a standing army; discharge of social duty by a militia comprising a universally armed people – this will insure the kind of freedom which no Tsars, no pompous generals, no capitalists can take away.[49]

Although it is not obvious that Lenin practised such libertarian democracy between 1917 and his death in 1924, the evidence supporting Max Eastman's description of his libertarian *motives* was formidable. Furthermore, Lenin's detailed plans for a libertarian socialist revolution as outlined in his pamphlet, *State and Revolution*, did indeed owe much to the Russian revolution of 1905. What Isaac Deutscher depicted as the 'flowering of plebeian freedom, with the Soviet and the socialist parties working in the open', though soon to be 'nipped', had a lasting impression on Lenin's thinking about the nature of socialist societies.[50]

While a series of complex questions about Lenin's alleged un-idealist opportunism and obsession with power have dominated Western historiography since 1917, Walter Laqueur, a very critical and well-informed analyst of the Russian revolution, addressed such questions as Lenin's involvement with the German general staff of the Prussian army:

What is the political importance of these revelations? Very limited indeed. The sums of money involved were fairly small; the fact that Lenin accepted them did not make him a German agent. There were no strings attached. Lenin did not undertake to pursue a policy other than his own. The "sealed compartment" admittedly changed the course of history. Had the Germans not permitted Lenin to reach Petrograd there would have been no revolution. The Germans wanted to use Lenin to weaken the Russian war effort; Lenin used the Germans for his own, very different, purposes. There is no doubt who got the better bargain out of this deal.[51]

Moreover, there was absolutely no doubt about the world-shattering significance of the Bolshevik revolution of 1917. In a contemporaneous account of the Russian revolution – an account full of white-hot passion, invective and enthusiasm – Arthur Ransome wrote:

Of course, no one who was able, as we were able, to watch the men of the revolution at close quarters could believe for a moment that they were the mere paid agents of the very power which more than all others represented the stronghold they had set out to destroy. We had the knowledge of the injustice being done to these men to urge us in their defence. But there was more in it than that. There was the feeling, from which we could never escape, of the creative effort of the revolution. There was the thing that distinguishes the creative from other artists, the living, vivifying expression of something hitherto hidden in the consciousness of humanity.[52]

In an equally enthusiastic and contemporaneous account, *My Reminiscences of the Russian Revolution*, M. Philips Price did at least acknowledge the crucial importance of the intelligentsia and peasantry in overthrowing Tsarism and making the *proletarian* revolution:

But the Marxian school among the Russian intellectuals was only the outcome of developments in other social layers. It did not make, it only guided, the Revolution. Without the mass movement from below, it would have become like a stream wasting in a sandy desert. Here we come to the second of the great influences on the events of the last three years in Russia – the influence of the material environment in which the Russian masses found themselves on the eve of the great Revolution. I have already described how the relics of an agrarian feudalism, which had not been swept away by the middle-class revolutions in Europe at the end of the eighteenth century, weighed up till the summer of 1917, when they were forcibly removed from below, weighed most heavily upon the Russian peasants.[53]

Despite the later emergence of totalitarianism, the October revolution was a vast popular upheaval. In bursting through the bonds of Tsarist tyranny, the Russian working class, though numerically small and circumscribed by a large, and often conservative peasantry, articulated its long-repressed socialist sympathies. With passion, insight, perceptive observation, and the red-hot prose of a prose-poet, John Reed described the advent of the October revolution:

All around them (the ruling class) great Russia was in travail, bearing a new world. The servants one used to treat like animals and pay next to nothing, were getting independent . . . But more than that. In the new Russia every man and woman could vote; there were working-class newspapers, saying new and startling things; there were the Soviets; and there were the unions. The izvoshtchiki (cab-drivers) had a union; they were also represented in the Petrograd Soviet. The waiters and hotel-servants were organised, and refused tips. On the walls of restaurants they put up signs which read, "No tips taken here –" or, "Just because a man has to make his living waiting on a table is no reason to insult him by offering him a tip!"

Moreover, in acknowledging that 'The thirst for education, so long thwarted, burst with the Revolution into a frenzy of expression', he added: 'Russia absorbed reading matter like hot sand drinks water, insatiable. And it was not the fables, falsified history, diluted religion, and the *cheap fiction* that *corrupts* – but social and economic theories, philosophy, the works of Tolstoy, Gogol, and Gorky'.[54]

But although the October revolution was a profound expression of socialism-from-below, Lenin and the Bolsheviks made sure that the workers' primitive rebellion would soon be transformed into socialism-from-above. Towards the end of 1917, Vladimir I. Lenin told the delegates to the Peasants' Congress in Petrograd that: 'If socialism can only be realised when the intellectual development of all the people permits it, then we shall not see socialism for at least three hundred years. The socialist political party – this is the vanguard of the working class; it must not allow itself to be halted by the lack of education of the mass average, but it must lead the masses, using the Soviets as organs of revolutionary initiative'.[55]

The latent authoritarian traits in Lenin's socialism were evident long before the October revolution. An inherent part of the cultural baggage of the nineteenth-century Russian intelligentsia, authoritarian socialism-from-above was waiting to ambush the workers' creative revolution from below. In the important book, *Encounters With Lenin*, Nikolay Valentinov described Lenin's authoritarian attitudes towards working people as early as 1903. As Valentinov explained:

But it was not this that struck me while I listened to him. I was far more impressed by the point about smacking the boy who damages his desk, and about the need for coercive and repressive measures to ensure the safety of Lenin's chalets – which had to be understood in a wider sense, of course. I remember that I was in complete agreement with Lenin about the need for timely chastisement; Krupskaya, however, reproachfully shook her head. Krupskaya was not the only one to disagree with "Ilyich" in this matter. It can be said that no one in the Party would have thought in those days that socialists might resort to "chastisement" of the masses and the repressive measures against them. Everybody was all for punitive measures, even savage ones, but not against the "people", only as a concomitant of the revolution. . . . As far as influencing the masses was concerned, they thought exclusively in terms of moral education, persuasion, and appeals to reason, conscience, and self-interest. I felt that in this important respect Lenin's views diverged considerably from the sentimental idea of political "pedagogy" advocated by all other socialists.[56]

Moreover, Lenin's approach to politics was frighteningly utilitarian. Leon Trotsky implicitly acknowledged this when he said: 'His works as a scholar mean *only* a preparation for action'.[57] In fact, Lenin was always much less objective and detached from the day-to-day political struggle than Jean Jaurés. In her funeral oration, Krupskaya said: 'He did not come to Marx as a man in love with books. He came as a man searching for answers to the pressing questions that tormented him. And he found the answers. And he took them to the workers'.[58]

In his book, *Moscow Under Lenin* – a subconsciously un-democratic title – Alfred Rosmer emphasised the libertarian aspects of Russian life in the early years after the Bolshevik revolution. In sketching in the very real libertarian aspects of Bolshevism, he said: 'On an obelisk standing at the entrance to the Kremlin gardens were inscribed the names of the precursors of communism, of the champions of the working class. What struck me was the "eclectism" with which the names are chosen. The "Utopians" were all there, and, more surprisingly, Plekhanov too. Violent polemics and harsh controversies had in no way prevented the recognition of the contributing of doctrinal opponents to the cause of human emancipation'.[59] In making the point about the libertarian aspects of the educational system before the rise of Stalinism, Anna Louise Strong explained that 'even textbooks on mathematics are rewritten, to conform to the new mode of teaching'. In summing up this point, she said:

Is there a communist mathematics, I asked in amazement. They explained patiently. Their idea is modelled more on the Dewey ideas of education than on anything else we know in America. Every book by Dewey is grabbed and translated into Russia for consultation. Then they make their own additions.[60]

Perhaps no one captured the complex, contradictory, libertarian-cum-authoritarian elements in Vladimir I. Lenin's personality better than Ignazio Silone, the Italian socialist novelist: 'Whenever he came into the hall, the atmosphere changed, became electric. It was a physical, almost a palpable phenomenon. . . . But to see him, to speak with him face-to-face – to observe his cutting, disdainful judgments, his ability to synthesize, the peremptory tone of his decisions – created impressions of a very different kind that overrode any suggestion of mysticism'.[61] But although the roots of Lenin's utilitarian authoritarianism were present when he abandoned the possibility of becoming a great classical scholar to search, in Isaac Deutscher's phrase', 'for roads to revolution', they did not strangle the latent fruit of socialism-from-below until after 1917.[62]

Although socialism under Lenin was initially democratic, Vladimir I. Lenin usually articulated the intolerant authoritarianism of the Russian intelligentsia. The intellectual intolerance so alien to the Western socialism represented by Rosa Luxemburg, Karl Liebknecht, Antonio Gramsci and Otto Bauer was seen in Lenin's comment to Clara Zetkin about the growth of modern psycho-analysis: 'The extension of Freudian hypotheses seems "educated", even scientific, but it is ignorant, bungling. Freudian theory is the modern fashion. I distrust the sexual theories of the articles, dissertations, pamphlets, etc, in short, of that particular kind of literature which flourishes luxuriantly in the dirty soil of bourgeois society'.[63] Moreover, when M. Philips Price published *My Reminiscences of the Russian Revolution* in 1920, he said: 'And it is not without interest to know that there are those in Russia today who say that education and historical research are one of the most powerful instruments of the ruling class to secure their spiritual hegemony over the toiling masses'.[64] While these intellectual attitudes did not grow in the dirty soil of bourgeois society, they would soon flourish within the soil of Stalinist totalitarianism.

What was equally serious was the pernicious impact of Leninism on labour movements in Europe and America after 1917. Although Alfred Rosmer claimed that Vladimir I. Lenin 'had a rare grasp of the labour movement in the West', the surviving evidence would suggest that he did not understand it at all. Moreover, there was an almost schizophrenic quality about Lenin's analyses of Western labour movements long before the Bolshevik revolution as well as afterwards.[65]

In 1903 Lenin told Nikolay Valentinov that: 'Our workers in Kiev and Rostov who showed that amazing solidarity and their readiness to use even the most extreme forms of struggle, are in a sense very much more socialist than the British workers. The same could be said about America. There is no revolutionary spirit in America, though the objective prerequisites for socialism are even greater there than in Britain. To forget the subjective factor, the character and revolutionary spirit of the workers' movement in a particular country and to take into account only the objective economic factor would mean to "vulgarise" Marxism'.[66] By 1919 Lenin had become much more optimistic about the American and British workers. With incredible naivete, he told Arthur Ransome that the proletarian revolution was now on the agenda in Britain. As Ransome explained:

He asked whether Sidney Webb was consciously working in the interests of the capitalists, and when I said I was quite sure that he was not, he said, "Then he has more industry than brains. He certainly has great knowledge".

He was entirely convinced that England was on the eve of revolution, and pooh-poohed my objections. "Three months ago I thought it would end in all the world having to fight the centre of reaction in England. But I do not think so now. Things have gone further there than in France, if the news as to the extent of the strikes is true.[67]

Being very adept at misreading the political situation in Western Europe immediately after the October revolution, Lenin saw the release of Karl Leibknecht from prison in October 1918 as the beginning of the world revolution. As he put it: 'The release from prison of the representative of the revolutionary workers of Germany is the sign of the new epoch, an epoch of triumphant socialism, which is opening out now both for Germany and the whole world'.[68]

For Lenin in those years the revolutionary working classes in the West were being held back from proletarian revolution by such intellectuals as Sidney Webb, Karl Kautsky and the economically privileged 'aristocracy of labour'. As Edward Mason explained: 'The Communists are inclined to explain the principles of Kautsky and the Second International as an outcome of the separation of the proletariat into a "higher" and a "lower" class. The "higher" class adopted bourgeois political forms: the old ideas of proletariat, etc, passed into discard and a reform policy took its place'.[69] By characterising the Western labour movements in this way and by setting out to create 'the vanguard Party of a new type' in America and Western Europe, the Leninists contributed to the process of weakening the international labour movement over the seven decades after 1917.

IV

While Jean Jaurés spent his last few months struggling to maintain world peace, Vladimir I. Lenin fought in 1923–24 to restore workers' democracy in Soviet Russia. In his valuable study of the French labour movement, Val Lorwin said: 'French socialists, led by Jaurés, had for years tried in vain to persuade the Second International to endorse ·the international general strike as one answer to the threat of war'.[70] Jaurés failed: and he was murdered by a fanatic for trying to save humankind from the maelstrom we are still trapped in today.

Within the context of late twentieth-century capitalism a growing minority of left-wing historians and scholars, though a minority within a 'socialist' minority, are increasingly focusing their attention on the tragic defeats and struggles of Jaurés and Lenin at the end of their lives rather than on their so-called victories. Writing about Jaurés, Harvey Goldberg said: 'Yet peace, the greatest of those causes, died with him. Even as men eulogised Jaurés and praised his purposes, they rallied, almost without exception, to the standards of war'.[71]

In complaining that 'the Bolshevik revolution altered everything' in the French labour movement after 1917, Marcel Sembat, a gifted European socialist, said: 'I believe I may venture to say that after the war the French Socialist Party, left to itself, would have resumed Jaurés's tradition'.[72] The fact that it did not contributed to the cumulative crisis of socialism in the late twentieth century. Moreover, the ambiguity surrounding the 'saintly' lives of Jaurés and Lenin during their active political lives survived long after their deaths.

While the death of Jaurés occurred just before the holocaust of the First World War and did nothing to further the militant pacifism he devoted his life to, the death of Lenin, the militant atheist, gave the impetus to a 'sudden outpouring of religious emotion' on the part of the Russian workers and peasant.[73] Although both men died during moments of defeat for the ideals of libertarian socialism, the cumulative crisis of late twenteith-century socialism has created a new interest in the lives of Jaurés and Lenin. A pacifist and socialist-humanist, Jaurés's ideas are coming back into fashion as the crisis of international capitalism deepens and creates ever more horrors. And there has been a similar interest in what Lenin really stood for at the end of his life. Without concealing Lenin's dictatorial policies, Marcel Liebman insists that:

Lenin's greatness lies not so much in his victories as in the way that his life ended, in almost desperate struggle. It is the fight that he put up under the conditions of his final illness that proves how genuine was his concern for democracy.[74]

Chapter 6

Joseph Stalin and Mao Tse-tung: The dictators

Democratic socialism in its various forms, in the name of legitimate defence against fascism, is almost everywhere allowing itself to be led, circumvented and compromised by dictatorial communism. The death agony of socialist hope in the world thus opens up an immeasurable ideological crisis.

Boris Souvarine

If China has gone the way of Stalinist totalitarianism, it is because faced with the implacable hostility of United States imperialism, and even more poverty-stricken than the Russia of the October revolution, it has had no choice but to follow the pattern of its Russian ally.

C.L.R. James

An unavoidable consequence of their status as dictators in two of the largest totalitarian countries in the world, some of the biographical facts of the lives of Joseph Stalin (1879–1953) and Mao Tse-tung (1893–1976) were, and are, shrouded in obscurity. Although there were significant differences in the lives of Stalin and Mao as major figures in left-wing politics, the similarities in the history of the two 'socialist' dictators were more important than any differences. With a great deal in common, both Stalin and Mao were unique among the major figures in the history of modern socialism. Yet despite their bloody niche in socialist history, there was some doubt about whether they had ever been socialists at all.[1]

While Joseph Stalin and Mao Tse-tung were to dominate much of twentieth-century socialism, they were separated in a chronological sense by the epoch-making Bolshevik revolution. After all, Stalin was a Bolshevik organiser for well over a decade before the Russian revolution, while Mao did not become a political figure until after 'the ten days that shook the world'. Because Russia was, in Royden Harrison's view, no longer a workers' state by 1921, Marxism in Russia and China was inevitably turned into an ideology. In disagreeing with E.P. Thompson's emphasis on the role of Marxism in reinforcing Stalinism, Harrison says that 'I think Marxism has more importance in relation to Stalinism as a critical device than as a supportive prop'. As he sums up:

That Marxism as method can be made to deliver conclusions about Marxism as ideology – where ideology is conceived in the strictly Marxist sense of "Necessarily false consciousness" – is, so far as I am aware, an original proposal. I do not believe that it is to be found in Preobrazhenski or Trotsky, Carr or Deutscher, Gerschenkron or Marcuse, Wittfogel or Nove – despite the fact that all of them may be more or less helpful in suggesting the need for it.[2]

By this reasoning Stalin's early socialism was somewhat counterfeit and Mao's socialism was non-existent.

Far from being illegitimate, inauthentic or false, the socialism of Joseph Stalin and Mao Tse-tung was rooted in the history and environmental circumstances of twentieth-century Russia and China. With long historical roots in the traditions of Utopian socialism, the dream of authoritarian socialism-from-above had already existed since medieval times. In outlining and analysing 'the two souls of socialism' in the history of labour movements, Hal Draper explained why Stalinist socialism gained legitimacy in the twentieth century:

One is the assumption that statification equals socialism – that is, the increasing state intervention in society and economy is *per se* "socialistic". The other is the assumption, sometimes equally unspoken but at other times explicit, that at least one way of instituting "socialism" is to impose it – either on an entirely unwilling population by force or, less crudely, on a people who are too "ignorant" to accept the "socialism" that an elite kindly wishes to hand down to them and who have to be re-educated so as to be fit to receive that which is granted by the beneficient Guardian.[3]

Stalin and Mao saw themselves as such Guardians.

I

Not every socialist was motivated by a hatred of oppression or a love of humankind. As the cumulative crisis of socialism deepened in the late 1930s, socialists themselves were forced by material circumstances to look critically at the different and conflicting sources of socialist motivation within labour movements. With the bitter hindsight of a libertarian socialist, Max Eastman divided socialists and their motivations into three groups. As he put it:

First, the rebels against tyranny and oppression, in whose motivation the concept of human freedom formed the axis; second, those yearning with a mixture of religious mysticism and animal gregariousness for human solidarity – the united-brotherhood pattern; third, those anxious about efficiency and intelligent organisation – a cerebral anxiety capable of rising in times of crisis to a veritable passion for a plan.[4]

Although these distinctions sometimes overlapped in the lives of the major figures portrayed in this study of the history of socialism, both the seekers after 'the united-brotherhood' and the advocates of 'efficiency and intelligent organisation' were at best luke-warm about plebeian revolts and uprisings.

The socialism of H.M. Hyndman, Daniel De Leon, Eugene V. Debs, John Maclean, James Connolly, Karl Liebknecht, Antonio Gramsci, Rosa

Luxemburg, Jean Jaurés, Vladimir Lenin, Claude McKay, George Padmore, Leon Trotsky and C.L.R. James was environmentally-conditioned. So was the socialism of Joseph Stalin and Mao Tse-tung. The inescapable fact that Stalin – and more particularly Mao – bequeathed much less information to posterity about their formative and early lives was largely a reflection of the environmental circumstances of the Asiatic despotism in which their personalities were formed. Indeed, the extreme paucity of information about Mao's life was a reflection of the even greater degree of Asiatic despotism in China than in Russia.

Although the socialism of Joseph Stalin was alien to the comparatively democratic traditions and outlook of many of the socialists in the Second International, it was shaped by the distinctive milieu in which it crystallised. With innumerable pseudonyms later on, Joseph Djugashvili, the son of an Armenian peasant, was born in Gori, Georgia, in 1879. In emphasising the importance of environmental factors in the making of Stalin's socialism, Boris Souvarine said: 'The barbarity of the Tsarist regime engendered cruel methods of opposing it. In the shadow of Russo-Asiatic despotism the inevitable revolutionary conflagration is preluded by the glare of explosions'.[5]

In the late-nineteenth century Stalin's milieu was unique by comparison with the environments from which most of the major socialist figures had emerged. The unique milieu to which Stalin belonged left a deep imprint on his socialism. Then in 1890 the eleven-year old Stalin entered a theological school in Tiflis. This was where he acquired his Marxism. In explaining why Stalin acquired his socialism in a religious school, Leon Trotsky said: 'In the Caucasus the Theological Seminary became the principal hearth of Marxist infection simply because there was no university at Tiflis. In backward, non-industrial districts, like Georgia, Marxism was accepted in a particularly abstract, not to say scholastic form'.[6]

In contrast to Georgy Plekhanov, Vladimir I. Lenin, Claude McKay, George Padmore or C.L.R. James, Stalin was not exposed to the ideas of classical Marxism. As Boris Souvarine put it: 'Young Stalin certainly could not imbibe new ideas or be subjected to European influence in this medieval agglomeration of Western Asia with its manifold religious and national superstitions in a backward society, with a continuous infiltration of nomads; nor in the administrative and military quarters where the Tsarist bureaucracy was housed in buildings European in style. But he entered a new sphere in the Seminary where, in the course of his clerical studies, he came for the first time into contact with the spirit of revolt'.[7] But although Stalin was full of resentments against the rich and privileged, he was not motivated by any desire for democratic socialism-from-below. Yet no one would have suggested that his socialism was illegitimate.

And yet Joseph Stalin, whose consciousness was limited rather than false, was seen within the Russian Social Democratic Party as a useful socialist. When he examined Stalin's role in Tiflis before the Russian revolution of 1905, Boris Souvarine said:

Nevertheless some of his weaknesses even served his purpose in his original environment. To be understood by Georgian and Tartar peasants, even if they donned the workman's blouse, recently emancipated serfs or sons of serfs, inaccessible to abstract ideas and ground down by poverty, what they needed was simple, rather coarse speech, appealing to the immediate interest and suited to the mentality of the race and to local circumstances. Railwaymen, tobacco workers, shoemakers and navvies understood him. But he took no part in theoretical discussion, important at that time for the future of Social-Democracy and for the direction of the movement. There is not a trace of him to be found in this sphere, for he left none.[8]

In page after page of his well-documented biography of Joseph Stalin, Leon Trotsky portrayed the man's insatiable capacity for intrigue and conspiracy. What Trotsky glossed over, however, was the historical fact that Stalin was far from exceptional in this respect – at least among the Bolsheviks.

But although Stalin's environmentally-engendered socialism was authentic, if intellectually circumscribed, it possessed a marked continuity before and after the Bolshevik revolution. It was, moreover, made up of many complex strands. When he discussed the characteristics of this socialism, Boris Souvarine said:

The first is a "will to power" disproportionate to the will to know, almost attenuating the Nietzchean conception of the end of man to material and practical requirements, ignoring the various forms of intellectual activity, analysis and synthesis and aesthetic appreciation, serving the instinctive rebelliousness of a man who had never been reconciled to his environment (the spirit of revolt not always finding expression in the conception of a loftier humanity or a rational organisation of society). The second characteristic is a narrow realism, efficacious within strict limits – a temper of mind inherited from his peasant ancestors. The third is a religious education overlaid with a travesty of Marxism consisting of elementary formulae learned by heart like a catechism, and lastly Oriental dexterity in intrigue, unscrupulousness, lack of sensitiveness in personal relations, and scorn of men and human life. Koba, more and more a professional revolutionary, felt himself to be hard and cold as the steel from which he adopted his name.[9]

Unlike Lenin or Trotsky in his lack of a sophisticated Marxist understanding of the world around him, Stalin was quite typical of a certain type of Bolshevik socialist in Russia and Poland.

In contrast to Joseph Stalin, Mao Tse-tung had a passion for education and learning. Although Mao's father forced him to abandon the primary school at Shaosham, in his native province of Hunan, when he was thirteen years old to work on the land, he continued to read novels and political works. Despite opposition from his father, he soon enrolled at the higher primary school in nearby Hsiang Hsiang hsien. Then in 1911 he entered the middle school in Changsha, where he remained for six months.

When he reconstructed a social picture of his years in Changsha much later, he spoke of his enthusiasm for socialism in 1911. However, the first

article that he published in 1917 'contained scarcely a trace of radical
ideas'. Also at this same time, he wrote to ask his parents for tuition money
to allow him to qualify as 'a jurist and mandarin'. A few years later, Mao
attended the foundation conference of the Chinese Communist Party.

Despite the paucity of information about Mao Tse-tung's early life, he
was in many ways a remarkably similar type to Joseph Stalin. Though he
appears to have had a much better, if unorthodox, education than Stalin,
Mao was not really a major Marxist thinker of the stature of Georgy
Plekhanov or Vladimir I. Lenin. When he gave Edgar Snow, the American
journalist, an oral account of his autobiography in 1938, Mao was just as
reticent about his early life as Stalin had been about his life. Edgar Snow
explained:

I was beginning to think it was hopeless to expect him (Mao) to give me such
details: he obviously considered the individual of very little importance. Like other
Reds I met he tended to talk only about committees, organisations, armies,
resolutions, battles, tactics, "measures" and so on, but seldom in terms of personal
experience. For a while I thought this reluctance to expand on subjective matters,
or even the exploits of their comrades as individuals, might derive from modesty, or
a fear or suspicion of me, or a consciousness of the price so many of these men had
on their heads. Later on I discovered that this was not the case as was the fact that
most of them actually did not remember these personal details.[10]

Yet despite the general similarities in the socialism of Stalin and Mao,
they were not simply carbon copies of each other. Notwithstanding the
military and Bolshevik political metaphors that Mao used to describe his
early life and upbringing when he spoke to Edgar Snow, Mao had, in 1938,
been agitating for women's rights for two decades.[11] By contrast, Stalin was
always a traditionalist – a patriarch – in relation to the 'woman question'.
But Mao's progressiveness in this respect should not be exaggerated.

Mao's views on women were influenced by the bourgeois nationalism of
Sun Yat-sen and the Kuomintang under the influence of the Bolshevik
revolution. Moreover, the seventeen-year old Mao did not feel any real
sympathy for the rebellious peasants in Shaoshan. In exposing the false-
hoods of Mao's official biographers, Stuart Schram says: 'During the
famine of 1910 the poor villagers of Shaoshan demanded grain from their
more fortunate neighbours, but Mao's father continued to export it to the
city as usual; the hungry villagers had then seized one of his shipments, and
he had been furious. "I did not sympathise with him", declared Mao. "At
the same time I thought the villagers method was wrong also".'[12]

Indeed, Mao did not, according to his own autobiographical account,
become a socialist until 1920. As he told Edgar Snow: 'During my second
visit to Peking I had read much about the events in Russia, and had eagerly
sought out what little communist literature was then available in Chinese.
Three books especially deeply carved my mind, and built up in me a faith in
Marxism, from which, once I had accepted it as the correct interpretation
of history, I did not afterwards waver. These books were the *Communist*

Manifesto, translated by Chen Wang-tao and the first Marxist book ever published in Chinese; *Class Struggle* by Kautsky; and a *History of Socialism* by Kirkup. By the summer of 1920 I had become in theory and to some extent in action, a Marxist, and from this time on I considered myself a Marxist'.[13] If Mao's socialism was strange and complex, it was certainly no less alien to the democratic traditions of the Second International than the socialism of Joseph Stalin.

What was of crucial importance about Boris Souvarine's pioneering biography of the first major 'socialist' dictator was that it placed Stalin firmly in the context of the history of Bolshevism. However, Stalin's marginal role in the history of the Second International should not be allowed to obscure the fact that he represented a significant trend in Bolshevik socialism well before 1917. In identifying this unique trend in international socialism, Souvarine said: 'Moreover, the life of this rebel illustrates the specific characteristics of revolutionary action in Russia; no other Party affiliated to the Second International could have produced this type of rebel. Comparison of this "professional revolutionary" of the Leninist school with any other European Social-Democrat, any representative of English labour or trade unionism or of trade unionism in the Latin countries shows how violent is the contrast created by social environment and historical circumstances. It is true that we are dealing here with an Armenian from Georgia, but one could find the same type of men in St Petersburg and in Moscow, in Poland and in the Urals.' To round off this picture of the Stalinist trend within pre-1917 Bolshevism, Souvarine emphasised the Stalinist Bolsheviks' many 'contradictions'. As he put it: 'Full of kindness in their relations as between comrades, they could be ferocious if they thought the interests of the Party were at stake'.[14]

Yet Joseph Stalin was not seen at a conference of the Russian Social Democratic Party until it met in Stockholm in 1906. As Walter Held observed: 'Stalin appears at the congress under the name of Ivanovitch as the Bolshevik delegate from the Tiflis district. His appearance itself is more than pathetic. His intervention in the agrarian question the Menshevik Dan disposes of in two sentences. Both of his other utterances on the question of the Russian revolution (where he loses himself in the dilemma: either bourgeois or proletarian revolution) and the participation in the Duma elections receive no notice whatever'. With an obviously deep psychological need for intrigue, he was expelled from the Tiflis organisation in 1901 for 'spreading an incredible slander'. Arrested and then freed, Stalin was restored to a leadership position among the Bolsheviks in Tiflis.[15]

Once again arrested in 1913, Stalin was in the Siberian steppes when the First World War broke out. Moreover, when he came to power in the 1920s, he made sure that everything he wrote between 1913 and 1917 was destroyed. In summing up Stalin's significance for Bolshevism from 1917 onwards, Leon Trotsky said:

Stalin was never a leader of the masses and according to his nature could not be; he is the chief of the bureaucratic chiefs, their embodiment and apothesis.[16]

But although Trotsky emphasised the continuity of narrow nationalism and self-interest in Stalin's make-up, he tended to ignore the fact that other Bolsheviks shared the same traits long before 1917.

Although Joseph Stalin did not come into his own as a dictator until after Lenin's death, the ideas and programmes he articulated with a growing confidence were at least partly the product of the Bolshevik world-outlook. By 1920, when Mao Tse-tung identified with Marxism once and for all, the authenticity of the 'actually existing socialism' in Russia was beginning to be questioned by socialists throughout the world. In the following year the suppression of the Kronstadt revolt deepened some Western European socialists' fears about what was happening in Russia. Then in October 1924, Stalin announced the new policy of the representatives of 'bureaucratic collectivism' – socialism in one country in place of world revolution. To make matters more complicated, however, the dream of world revolution was not abandoned altogether.

Leon Trotsky and the orthodox Trotskyists did not like Boris Souvarine's biography of Stalin for two major reasons. In the first place, it was not just a biography of Stalin. It was a biography within the context of a critical survey of Bolshevism. Secondly, Souvarine argued that Stalin was the leader of a *new class* within a new social system of bureaucratic collectivism. In delineating the transition from 'the working-class bureaucracy in Russia between 1917 and 1923 and the later bureaucracy of the new class, Max Shachtman – a veteran socialist who rejected the orthodox Trotskyist analysis – said:

Who could more easily lead in the destruction of Bolshevism and the Bolsheviks in the very name of Bolshevism – an old monarchist or Menshevik or an old Bolshevik? Who could more lightly undo the basic achievement of the revolution – the establishment of the working masses as the ruling class – than one who felt organically alien to the masses, who saw in them nothing more than an instrument for the revolutionary "committee men" whom he regarded as the only safe repository of what he understood by socialism.

At the same time as Shachtman asserted that Stalin still saw himself as a socialist, he insisted that it was hard to say 'with what degree of *consciousness* on his part or theirs' the new bureaucracy in Stalinist Russia 'quite consciously, in all probability, identified its role with the role of the bureaucracy in bourgeois society'.[17]

But in 1919 Stalinism was inconceivable. Meanwhile, the foundation conference of the Chinese Communist Party – a conference in which Mao Tse-tung played a role – was held in Shanghai in 1921; and in 1922 Joseph Stalin was appointed the general secretary of the Bolshevik Party. Before Mao became the leader of the Chinese Communists Party in 1935, it was lead by Chen Tu-hsiu. In a quite laudatory and uncritical comment contrasting Mao with the superior Chen, Isaac Deutscher said: 'Even a literary comparison of the writings of Mao and Chen Tu-hsiu, whose language was closer to that of European, especially the Russian, Marxists of the pre-Stalin era reveals a significant difference'.[18] But Chen had a 'marked aversion to the phrase "the dictatorship of the proletariat"'. As Han Suyin argued: 'For a long time Mao Tse-tung thought Chen Tu-hsiu an outstanding revolutionary. Chen was to be the first, but not the last, of Mao's disappointing experiences with "bourgeois radicals", revolutionaries and friends he would look up to and trust, and find to be unscrupulous opportunists'.[19]

Moreover, the Westernised Chen Tu-hsiu, who led the Chinese Communist Party between 1921 and 1927, did not like workers' strikes, demonstrations or peasant uprisings. As Han Suyin said: 'Chen's fear of violence was an atavistic panic, a class reaction, backed by long centuries of elitism, of the almost ineradicable superiority of scholars above manual labourers'.[20] What Chen wanted more than anything else was the modernisation of China – a powerful source of motivation for Chinese 'socialism' in the early 1920s.

This new consciousness of the need for modernisation was created by the Bolshevik revolution. As Anna Louise Strong put it: 'No wonder the Russian revolution stirred these people. Students in Peking were ravenous for Russia; Chinese merchants coquetted with Moscow against the imperialisms of the West. Great mass movements of peasants and workers were rising in South China'.[21] By 1919 hundreds of thousands of the Chinese were in revolt. In the shadow of the October revolution in Russia, Marxism came to China.

II

While socialist consciousness was at the centre of the dynamic of the Bolshevik revolution, the Chinese revolution of 1926–27 was motivated by nationalism and nationalist consciousness. In his book, *The Chinese Puzzle*, Arthur Ransome, who had previously published a sympathetic and influential book and articles on the Russian revolution, did not see any evidence of socialist consciousness in the Chinese revolution. In depicting the Chinese revolution as a bourgeois one, he said:

It was only as an afterthought that they (the Kuomintang and Dr Sun Yat-sen) realised the need for active support from the labouring masses. No other hypothesis will explain the unanimity between North and South in the struggle. The universities of the North are, in the eyes of the militarists, "hotbeds of revolution" no less than those of the South. It is a difficult thing for an educated Chinese (outside the limited class whose interests are bound up with those of their foreign employers) who does not proclaim in any company in which he feels safe that his sympathies are with the Kuomintang.

For what the revolutionaries in China were 'revolting against' was feudalism (i.e. the domination by war-lords) and imperialism – 'the use by any other nation of its political and military ascendancy for subjecting to its economic encroachment a foreign country, or territory or race' aimed at impeding China's economic development.[22]

Far from a mass socialist consciousness existing in the Chinese revolution in 1926–27, the consciousness of the tiny minority of socialists was primitive, diffuse and ethereal. In her autobiography, *I Change Worlds*, Anna Louise Strong, the America communist journalist and sociologist, described the working-class militants that she encountered in Canton in 1927. Again and again she emphasised the responses of the Chinese working-class women who told her: 'We are part of the world revolution'. But Strong was too honest to ignore the primitive character of the socialist consciousness of Chinese working people. In depicting the 'leaders of Chinese Labour' in another book, *China's Millions*, she said:

So mild and revolutionary were the demands of Tang Shou I, who had spent all his life in the mines from the days of Emperor Kwangsu, and into whose mind ideas of socialism or syndicalism had hardly entered. An honest miner in a backward land, all he asked of life was peace and steady employment at a very modest wage, and the right to organise a union. Yet under the conditions existing in China, those modest demands made him part of the Revolution, together with the more conscious agitators and organisers of Canton and Shanghai. In pursuit of his desire for food he and his fellow workers had taken control of the mines and opened them. They had dug coal and sold it in Hankow. They had armed themselves and fought as soldiers. They had made Hunan known throughout the world as the "reddest" province of China.[23]

This was the environment in which Mao's socialist consciousness crystallised and developed.

In the light of the bitter quarrel between Joseph Stalin and Leon Trotsky about the sociological nature of the Chinese revolution of 1926–27, it is important to emphasise that the Kuomintang – or bourgeois nationalist movement – was much more powerful and relevant than the Chinese communists. With vividness and factual accuracy, Arthur Ransome, who was writing in early 1927 just before Chiang Kai Shek slaughtered many working-class militants in Shanghai and Canton, said:

It is wrong to say that the labour movement is dominated by the Chinese communists. It is true that such communists as there are naturally gravitate towards the labour unions, but in the first place there are very few of them; in the second, they are subject to the Kuomintang, having themselves decided that during the present period Kuomintang directives shall be binding upon them; in the third, they are under no illusions as to the proximity of a Bolshevik revolution in China. What Lenin said is for them a revealed truth, and Lenin looked forward to a time when China should have many Shanghais of her own, and saw as a preliminary stage of the way to Bolshevism in China "a colossal development of capitalism".[24]

However, in contrast to objective observers like Arthur Ransome, the official voices of the communist Third International saw socialism as a realistic possibility in China in the 1920s.

With facile but confident optimism, Earl Browder, the American communist leader, asserted that it was no longer 'a debatable question as to whether China shall be developed as a capitalist country or whether it shall now proceed upon the road to socialism'. In contrast to 'the workers of technically more advanced countries', who had been 'misled by the traitors of Social-Democracy', the Chinese workers had now 'set their feet firmly' on the road to socialism.[25] Although there were only four million workers in China in the 1920s – or one per cent of the total population – most communists in the Third International believed that socialism was on the agenda.

In considering the complex analyses of the Chinese revolution developed by Arthur Ransome, Anna Louise Strong, C.L.R. James and Harold Isaacs in the inter-war period, a very confused and confusing picture emerges. Although Adolphe Joffe, a high-ranking Soviet diplomat, met Sun Yat-sen in January 1923, when they issued a joint statement saying that the political task in China was not the establishment of socialism but 'the achievement of national union and national independence', the Third International had not really abandoned the dream of creating socialism in China within the foreseeable future. But in contrast to Ransome, who observed that the Russian communists taught Sun Yat-sen and other bourgeois nationalists to 'rely on classes rather than individuals', Strong – at least in the 1920s – James and Isaacs were somewhat myopic about the strength and socialist consciousness of the Chinese working class.

In arguing that a bourgeois-democratic regime was impossible in China in the 1920s and 1930s, C.L.R. James concluded that the 'revolution would conquer as the dictatorship of the proletariat or not at all'. With more than a touch of melodrama, Harold Isaac wrote: 'The day the congress (of the Kuomintang) opened Lenin died, a historical coincidence that did not lack its own irony, for the Soviet Union and the Communist International he had helped create were abandoning in China the idea of irreconcilable proletarian independence that was Lenin's richest legacy'. Yet Anna Louise Strong, who attended the fourth annual congress of the All China Federation of Labour in Hankow in 1927, reported that M.N. Roy, the Indian representative of the Third International, struck the dominant note of the congress when he said:

This congress will decide not only how to secure the immediate interests of the workers represented, but how they may lead the Nationalist revolution, in which you have played in the past an important role, but are now called upon to play a decisive role. The outcome of the Chinese revolution will decide the fate of the world revolution in the present epoch of humanity.[26]

The communists' consciousness was multi-dimensional and ecumenical rather than false. It was stimulated by the man who initially influenced Mao Tse-tung – Chen Tu-hsiu. Moreover, much of the very real social progress made in China during the revolution of 1926–27 was due to the Russian communists' influence on the Nationalist government in Hankow.

This was when the question of the emancipation of women was first put on the political agenda. In an intelligent and well-documented account of what was happening in China, H. Owen Chapman said that 'a careful study of the facts on the spot at Hankow' gave 'overwhelming proof' of the influence of the Russian communists in the Chinese Nationalist government.

Without acknowledging the full extent of the Russian communists' influence on the bourgeois nationalists in China in relation to the emancipation of women, H. Owen Chapman did emphasise that the Nationalist government's 'greatest and most permanent achievement' was the promotion of the women's movement. Yet the mediating influence of Chen Tu-hsiu and, to a lesser extent, Mao Tse-tung in this process should not be underestimated. But in demonstrating that the Chinese nationalists were responsible for organising trade unions and labour movements, Chapman made it plain they were making it difficult for a genuinely independent workers' movement to emerge then or in the future. Indeed, the rank-and-file workers were denied the opportunity of administrating or playing any independent role in their own trade unions. Writing in 1928, Chapman predicted that 'the expulsion of the communists from Hankow should make it easy for Chiang Kai Shek to co-operate with the Nationalist government of the future, whether its seat be eventually at Hankow or Naking'.[27]

In those years Joseph Stalin and Mao Tse-tung already wanted a revolution-from-above in China. By contrast, Leon Trotsky wanted a proletarian revolution from below. But in the light of the enormous importance that most socialists had always attached to the role of consciousness in the struggle for a New Society of Equals, it is particularly interesting to read Trotsky's repudiation of C.L.R. James's assertion that 'Stalin sabotaged the Chinese revolution'. For the embattled Trotsky in 1939, Stalin and the hated Stalinist bureaucracy in 1927 did not just want a bourgeois–democratic revolution. They were also 'anxious', in Trotsky's view, 'for the success' of the socialist revolution in China.[28]

Moreover, although socialist consciousness in China in the 1920s was primitive and ethereal, it was nevertheless real and aggressive. The young Mao Tse-tung occupied an intellectual world in which some sort of socialist world-view was built into the infant and immature labour movement. After the traumatic defeat of the Chinese working class in the general massacre at the hands of the right-wing bourgeois nationalists under Chiang Kai Shek, Mao increasingly turned his attention to the peasantry as the agency of the coming revolution. However, in 1922 the Chinese Community Party attached great importance to the infant labour movement, strikes and trade unions in the industrial cities. This was the crucial context in which Mao's socialist consciousness was formed. In contrast to Joseph Stalin, who wanted revolution from above in China in which the revolution would be 'for the peasants', Mao was already emphasising the need for 'revolution by the peasants' rather than by the urban workers'.[29]

With a fierce determination to eradicate the 'scourge of communism' in 1930, Chiang Kai-shek 'summoned the governors of Jupei, Hunan, and Kiangsi to Lushan to plan his first major campaign against the communists' in co-operation with other Chinese army leaders. By now Chiang was the chief war-lord in China. Chiang's unending offensives against the communists led Mao Tse-tung to initiate the Long March – one of the most famous and heroic episodes in human history. Between 1934 and 1935 the Chinese Red Army marched from Juichin to Wuchichen. Then in January 1935 the famous Tsunyi conference of the Chinese Communist Party took place, and it signalised the fact that Mao was already in the process of becoming a significant dictator. In discussing this important development, Jerome Ch'en said: 'Thus for the first time Mao became the supreme leader of the CCP. Apart from being a personal triumph, his election to such an important post represented a victory of the rural Soviet over the urban Party centre, of a man who had spent all his life among the peasants and the lower orders of society over those who were well-versed in doctrines, Eastern and Western'.[30]

Although very real tensions and latent conflicts existed between Joseph Stalin and Mao Tse-tung between 1935 and 1949, the Chinese communists openly sided with Stalin and the Stalinists in those years. Yet Mao's Stalinism was intermingled with a fierce independence, too. In 1936 Mao told Edgar Snow that: 'Although the Communist Party of China is a member of the Comintern, still this in no sense means that Soviet China is ruled by Moscow or the Comintern. ... We are not fighting for an emancipated China to turn the country over to Moscow'.[31] Nevertheless in their public statements in the world's communist press and magazines, the Chinese expressed their solidarity with Stalin and the Third International. For example, in 1936 Chen Ming Chu, a founder of the 19th (Route) army, argued that the aims of the All-People's Front in China were 'similar to those of the Popular Front in many European countries today'.[32] By 1938, when the Kuomintang had given Chiang Kai-Shek 'dictatorial power in the Party', the Chinese communists were arguing that some of the independent army leaders could 'claim that their anti-Japanese attitude is of older date than his'. They also complained that 'Chiang Kai-Shek, although accepting military co-operation with the communist troops and allowing the Communist Party a legal existence, has so far not given them positions of power'.[33] But despite what Leon Trotsky said to the contrary, Mao's attitudes of realpolitik were engendered by Lenin's original encouragement of the coming nationalist revolutions in Asia.

By 1935 Mao Tse-tung was gradually establishing himself as a major dictator in China. While this was happening in China, Joseph Stalin was betraying the libertarian *rationale of Leninism*. With the acceptance of the first Five Year Plan and the New Economic Policy in the late 1920s, forced industrialisation was intended to impose socialism from above on a 'backward' country within the context of socialism in one country. Thus in one of the most decisive actions that Stalin undertook in the inter-war years, the existing egalitarianism in Russian education was destroyed in 1935 by the announcement of the new 'Decree on Academic Reform'.[34] Totalitarianism under the guise of democratic Marxism was assuming monstrous proportions.

In examining the countless crimes and atrocities in Stalin's Russia in the 1920s and 1930s, Boris Souvarine said: 'Confronted with the massacres ordered by Stalin in cold blood, and with the internecine feuds of the Bolsheviks, one is led to draw a parallel with the Russia of the sixteenth century and the reign of Ivan the Terrible'. What was equally disturbing was the thought-control being developed throughout Russian society. In summing this up and stressing the similarities with what was happening in the fascist countries, Souvarine said: 'The publications of the Marx–Engels Institute were proscribed and destroyed, even before the burnings took place in Germany'.[35] In Stalin's Russia socialism-from-above had come of age, though it would be just as barbarous and inhuman in its senility in the early 1950s.

In the years between the triumph of 'socialism in one country' and the victory of the Chinese revolution in 1949, Russian and Chinese communism shared a number of characteristics. In the first place, nationalism was a powerful force within their shared conception of the ingredients needed for socialism-from-above. Secondly, they had not experienced any involvement in the practice of democratic socialism. Although the lack of democracy in Russia after 1917 was well-documented by such careful and brilliant socialist scholars as Victor Serge, Harold Isaacs, C.L.R. James and others, Mao did not attract the attention of independent socialist scholars at all. By the time that Mao attracted the attention of biographers in the West, he had his life and times chronicled by either the advocates of the Cold War or the partisan advocates of Maoism.

And yet Chinese communism before and after the rise of Mao Tse-tung had always been profoundly un-democratic. In 1938 Mao told Edgar Snow that Ch'en Tu-hsiu had been 'the complete dictator of the Chinese Communist Party'.[36] Moreover, Li Li-san, a Hunanese student who had returned from a sojourn in Paris, was, in Snow's words, 'the nearest to a Trotsky that China produced'. But this militant socialist was soon sent to Moscow for corrective 'education', because of the hard-Left attitudes he had expressed. In advocating militant tactics and in expressing Chinese nationalist views, he was much less acceptable to the Russians than Mao. As Edgar Snow said a decade before the final triumph of the Chinese revolution: 'Perhaps his greatest "sin", in Moscow's eyes, was that in 1930 he held China to be the "centre" of the world revolution, thus denying that role to the Soviet Union'.[37]

By 1935 Harold Isaacs, who was now working with the Trotskyist movement in Peiping and New York, acknowledged that 'the Stalinist hope for the capture of the Chinese cities' by the communist peasants was at least a possibility. Furthermore, he emphasised that 'every peasant advance' was improving the opportunities for reviving the labour movement in the cities.[38] This was, however, the period of the 'popular front'; and Anna Louise Strong focused on the 'moderate' approach of Mao and the Chinese communists. As she put it:

The relation of the communists toward these growing hopes of democracy becomes at once clearer when it is known that at no time in their existence as a Party have they ever tried to establish immediate communism, or assumed that this could be done. They regard the full liberation of the Chinese people as a long, complex process, involving factors not only in China but on a world scale. For this reason they are members in good standing of the Communist International.[39]

III

The period between 1938 and 1945 was characterised by the war of resistance against the Japanese occupation of China. From their base in the Yenan, the Chinese communists upset Chiang Kai-Shek by the scale of their military successes in those years. In discussing the communists' military victories, Roger Howard said: 'The most impressive of these, whose tactics and aims it is not at all certain Mao approved, was planned by Chu Teh and Peng Teh-huai. Known as the Hundred Regiments' Offensive, it inflicted severe damage on the Japanese in five northern provinces from August to December 1940'. Chiang's government in Chungking saw this victory as a serious threat to the Kuomintang as well as the Japanese. Although Chiang's Kuomintang and the Communist Party had formed a 'united front', by 1941 Mao became increasingly aware that he would need to depend on his own military forces in the Chinese people's opposition to the Japanese.[40]

China was divided during the Second World War into three parts: the part occupied by the Japanese, the part dominated by Chiang Kai-Shek and the part ruled by the communists' own government in Yenan. However, totalitarianism ruled throughout China. Although virtually nothing was known about 'the activity of the proletariat in Chiang Kai-Shek's China, mass resentment against 'the profiteers on the market' could not be stifled or concealed. By 1944 the resentment against 'the wealthy classes' was gathering momentum.[41]

Moreover, although Rita Stone and the independent 'Trotskyists' grouped around Max Shachtman's American Workers' Party were already attacking Mao Tse-tung's compromise policy towards the capitalists and the landed gentry, they were simultaneously full of enthusiasm for what Mao was allegedly doing in the sphere of socialist education. In locating socialist consciousness at the heart of the dynamic of social change in China, Stone wrote:

Today the peasants are being given invaluable training for the social revolution. They have learned that bona fide national defence depends on them and that there is a political meaning to their instinctive rebellion. .... They have seen a popular army in the process of development and become part of it, acquiring the consciousness that the sword belongs to the community. Into the backward North here have migrated thousands of peasants and intellectuals from the South, where they have lived in closer contact with the modern world. Moreover, the Chinese masses in communist-controlled China have been indoctrinated with an international outlook. The Soviet districts regarded themselves as part of the world proletariat. The course of the civil war and the conquest of Abyssinia were followed with intense interest. In view of this background, it is possible to credit the report of a split in the Chinese Communist Party over the dissolution of the Comintern.

The training in the technique of social revolution is constantly on the verge of overflowing into practice. No modern revolution has been able to linger for long at the bourgeois-democratic stage. It has either moved forward under the impulsion of the masses or succumbed to bourgeois dictatorship. Hence the mutual hostility of the China of Chiang Kai-Shek and the China that is communist led. Ideas and techniques cannot be limited by geographical boundaries, nor hemmed in by mass armies made up of peasants.

What was incredible was that this 'socialist' consciouness was being stimulated by the hated Stalinist bureaucrats.[42] However, Rita Stone's optimism about the role she expected the Chinese masses to play 'in the world revolutionary upsurge after the Second World War was based on the rising wave of strikes among industrial workers in Shanghai during 1939–40 and the role of the Italian workers in overthrowing Mussolini.[43]

It was ironical that the Trotskyists and the communists in the West were much less optimistic about the possibility of a popular revolution in China than the independent Left. In a long article dealing with the crimes of the Stalinists in China from 1926 onwards, Li Fu-jen, a Chinese Trotskyist who was living in America, argued that 'nothing less than a socialist revolution of the proletariat united with the poor peasantry and all other layers of the exploited and oppressed' would be sufficient for the emancipation of China. But he predicted that the Stalinists would do everything they could to 'stifle, sidetrack and abort every moment in that direction'.[44] Towards the end of the war, when the Dean of Canterbury, the British communist clergyman, asked whether China would 'move left or right', he concluded that 'the signs' were not reassuring.[45]

Although Mao's successful revolution in 1949 did not owe much to Joseph Stalin – the first major 'socialist' dictator in the world – the Chinese communists paid lip-service to Stalin at the same time as they proclaimed their independence. When Chen Pai-ta, a prominent Chinese theoretician, contributed an article to the British Marxist magazine, the *Labour Monthly*, in 1944, he emphasised the complete independence of Mao and the Chinese communists. In one passage, he wrote:

Now let us say something about the communists. The thought of the Chinese nation is the thought of Mao Tse-tung – i.e., Sinoised Marxism–Leninism. As far as the theory of Marxism-Leninism is concerned, the Chinese communists not only have the same ideology as the Russian communists but also as the communists of the various nations of the world. However, scientific Marxism–Leninism demands that the communists of every nation work out their political programme and decide their policies according to their own national conditions, and rely on their own people for self-salvation. The Chinese Communist Party works according to this principle. It has created all kinds of progressive forces, entirely through its own efforts, without dependence on any "foreign country". Not an item of ammunition was given it by foreign countries, nor has it ever relied on foreign funds to carry on its fight. It determines its own strategy, and is "self-resuscitating".[46]

This was the context in which Mao later rejected Stalin's advice to seek a *modus vivendi* with Chiang Kai-Shek rather than attempt an 'uprising in China'.[47]

Long before Joseph Stalin died, and particularly after the Yalta agreement between the Big Three world powers, a strong latent conflict between Russia and China was the inevitable result of 'socialism in one country'. It was this Stalinist doctrine which was responsible for great Russian chauvinism, the 'purges', the 'show trials', the thought-control and the vast, irrational 'system' of totalitarian tyranny. The doctrine of socialism in one country also engendered an imperialistic *mentalité* in Russia culminating in the advent of 'Stalin's Satellites in Europe'.

The Yalta agreement between Stalin, Churchill and Roosevelt in February 1945 allowed Stalin to create the 'People's Democracies' in Eastern Europe in the wake of the Second World War. In establishing Satellite states, the communists were able to liquidate all independent socialist movements in Czechoslovakia, Rumania, East Germany, Poland, Hungary and Bulgaria. But the dissolution of the Third International in 1943 marked the real beginning of the disintegration of Stalinism in those countries where it held power, though the crunch came in 1953 with the death of Stalin. As Bertram D. Wolfe summed up:

Somehow, Stalin held the flawed edifice together by his machine-made prestige and his wide-ranging terror, until his death. The interregnum before a more or less authoritative successor emerged in Russia, and the shocking revelations of the "de-Stalinisation" and "rehabilitation", campaigns, revealed how strong the national centrifugal forces of revolt against exclusive Russian domination had gone: uprising in Hungary, in Prague, in East Berlin, near revolt in Poland; the widening Sino-Soviet conflict where diverging national interests mingled with ideological charges of heresy, revisionism, and betrayal.[48]

Even before Mao Tse-tung became the dictator of China in 1949, Stalin behaved like a Tsar when he met Churchill and Roosevelt at Yalta four years earlier. For not only did he sign a secret treaty committing the Russians to work solely with Chiang Kai-Shek's regime and 'not to aid his enemies (presumably Mao Tse-tung)', but Stalin also claimed the control of the Chinese Eastern Railway. Although Soviet Russia relinquished her 'imperialist rights in China' after the Bolshevik revolution, Stalin's doctrine of socialism in one country compelled him to behave as an imperialist in relation to China.[49]

It was a major tragedy in the history of socialism – and one of the many contributory factors in the cumulative crisis of late-twentieth-century socialism – that the independent Left in the West after the Second World War began to depict Stalin as a dictator and Mao as a socialist liberator. Because of the civil war in Russia between 1921 and the death of Stalin in 1953 resulting in constant attempts to eradicate all independent thought, the name of Joseph Stalin was anathema outside the diminishing circles of Stalinists in America and Western Europe. Yet despite the knowledge possessed by such independent socialist scholars as Rita Stone and C.L.R. James concerning Mao's suppression of the Chinese workers' self-activity and the general totalitarianism of Chinese society, they did not hesitate to heap lavish praise on Mao Tse-tung.

By 1958 the otherwise libertarian C.L.R. James was praising Mao and 'his fellow revolutionists' for building 'a party and an army in strict relation to their objective environment and the need of self-preservation'. Then he insisted that: 'Their resistance to the attempt of Chiang Kai-Shek to exterminate them is one of the great epics of revolutionary struggle. They were sustained by peasant support of the most heroic bravery and endurance. The "long march" of 6,000 miles from the South to the North of China takes its place among the greatest actions in history and is unsurpassed in the military history of the twentieth century.' While emphasising that 'the genuine mass revolution, the twentieth century uprising of the people' in China had yet to occur, the Chinese would not need 'forty years to begin the process of de-totalitarianism'.[50]

Although the two dictators – Joseph Stalin and Mao Tse-tung – could not have existed without nationalistic totalitarianism in their own countries, Stalinism and Maoism reflected quite distinctive environments, traditions and history. Moreover, Stalinism was in the years after the Second World War much more obviously anti-humanistic and irrational than Maoism. And yet Stalinism retained considerable appeal to authoritarian left-wing intellectuals in the West after Stalin's death. In discussing the atmosphere in left-wing socialist circles in Israel in the late-1940s and early-1950s, Moshe Lewin said:

Somewhat later we got the trials, notably in Hungary and Prague, that were part of the Cold War strategy from the East European and Soviet side. Acts of brutality and of defiance of common sense, those trials finally split my party (Mapam) and had a deeply anti-socialist effect. . . . Without the ideology of mythical "enemies of the people" Stalinism would not have been what it was. If it did not look for a tool for devouring people, it would have been different.[51]

This was the backdrop against which many socialists on the independent Left in the West looked to the Third World countries for tangible signs of 'progress' in the struggle to eradicate imperialism.

It was axiomatic that nationalist movements in the Third World, and particularly in China, had been – and were – 'progressive' if they gained liberation from right-wing dictators or foreign imperialism. What was implicit in such analyses was the assumption that totalitarian regimes of 'the "Left"' were progressive if they destroyed feudalism. By encouraging such facile thinking, a small army of socialists created immense confusion about the nature of socialism and socialist objectives. Consequently, C.L.R. James, who had previously been critical of Maoism, contributed to the new confusion by identifying Vladimir I. Lenin, George Padmore, Mahatma Ghandhi and Mao Tse-tung as the great left-wing liberators of the common people in the twentieth century.[52]

Both before and after he came to power in 1949, Mao Tse-tung's policy towards the Chinese working class was hostile and dictatorial. In setting out to create a socialist revolution by using the peasantry instead of the working class, he was revising Marxism much more fundamentally than Eduard Bernstein had attempted to do. But the unique sort of revisionism undertaken by Mao before 1949 was to shape what happened in China afterwards. As Ygael Gluckstein argued, in 1957, before Maoism became popular with the New Left:

The urban working class did not play any role at all in Mao's rise to power. This fact greatly influenced the initial trends in Peking's labour policy. The kernel of Mao's strategy was to rely on the peasantry as the bearer of the revolution.[53]

Moreover, Mao's policy after 1949 was to attempt to build socialism in China from above by means of employing forced labour. Although the Left in Western Europe and America was much more tolerant of 'forced labour' in China than in Russia, this was at least partly the consequence of the Leninist perception of the innate progressiveness of nationalism and rapid industrialisation in 'backward' countries. Even so, by the 1950s the Maoists were justifying forced labour in nakedly Stalinist language as representing 'the vanguard of socialist production in the countryside'.[54]

By then, too, thought-control, police control of the whole population, purges against 'counter-revolutionaries' and the cult of the Leader were commonplace in Mao's China. Far from signalising any attempt to end the domination of people by other people, Chinese socialism-from-above was indoctrinating a vast population into an apparent acceptance of totalitarianism. Nevertheless totalitarian Maoism could not stifle the independence of the growing Chinese working class; and this was seen, though on a smaller scale than elsewhere, in the workers' strikes which erupted in the wake of the Hungarian revolution.

IV

By 1949 totalitarian Stalinism and totalitarian Maoism were triumphant in Eastern Europe and China. Although totalitarian communism was in some specific ways a conscious expression of socialism-from-above (or an anti-working-class ideology of bureaucratic collectivism), Joseph Stalin and Mao Tse-tung nevertheless saw themselves, projected themselves and were widely accepted as the dictatorial leaders of the progressive forces in the world at large. From a democratic socialist perspective, the most important theoretical question was no longer whether Stalin and Mao were really socialists but whether they represented 'progress'.

Within the world-outlook of Stalin and Mao, socialism-from-above had become a conscious ideology. It was the ideology of bureaucratic socialists whose political power resided in totalitarian collectivist economic systems. This was seen in their constant revision of Marxism and in a variety of anti-Marxist statements. In reflecting their own distinctive socialist world-outlook Stalin and Mao tried to turn Marxism on its head by attaching much more importance to military power than they saw in the power of ideas. In almost casual comments, they expressed the *mentalité* of those who were emotionally and spiritually caught up in the philosophy of socialism-from-above. When Stalin asked, 'How many battalions does the Pope have?' and when Mao insisted that 'political power grows out of the barrel of a gun', they were turning Marxism upside down.

For Karl Marx and Frederick Engels socialism would depend on 'the alteration of man on a mass scale' and the creation of a mass socialist consciousness. In an almost prefigurative critique of the way the Stalinists and the Maoists conceived of the role of the 'hero' and the 'crowd' in the struggle for socialism, Georgy Plekhanov wrote:

So long as there exist "heroes" who imagine that it is sufficient for them to enlighten their own heads to be able to lead the crowd wherever they please, and to mould it like clay, into anything that comes into their heads, the kingdom of reason remains a pretty phrase or a noble dream. It begins to approach us with seven-league boots only when the "crowd" become the hero of historical action, and when in it, in that colourless "crowd", there develops the appropriate consciousness of self.[55]

When he sent a famous letter to Margaret Harkness towards the end of his life discussing the function of the socialist novel, Engels also insisted on the importance of discouraging notions of the leader–saviour in labour movements.[56]

Although totalitarian socialism-from-above in Stalinist Russia, Eastern Europe and Maoist China made unending attacks on independent socialist movements under the guise of fighting for democracy, the Stalinists were at least partly aware of what they were doing. While the classical socialism of the Second International had rejected the *mentalité* of the leader–saviour, Joseph Stalin had revived such elitist notions and ideas on Lenin's death. Then in 1938 Joseph Freeman, the American Stalinist and literary figure, defended the role of the 'hero' in manipulating the 'crowd' in history. He wrote about Stalin as others would later write about Mao:

The unequal development of individuals has raised a Stalin, Djerdjinsky, Chicherin or Bukharin to that leadership which every social group requires whenever such men showed a greater capacity than the average for understanding and *manipulating* the *mechanics* of history.[57]

In an important book, *Stalin's Satellites in Europe*, published in 1952, Ygael Gluckstein documented the rise of Stalin as the Leader of totalitarian communism. As he put it: 'The leader cult in the Russian empire takes the most extreme, Byzantine forms. Cities and towns are called after Stalin. . . . Since 1937 many more have been added in Russia itself and in the "People's Democracies". His name figures everywhere, even in the national anthem; he is not mentioned unless the most extravagant praise accompanies his name; he is called "our father", "our infallible one", "our sun", "our soul". But the practitioners of socialism-from-above – or bureaucratic collectivism – were very aware of the dynamic role that socialist consciousness could play in the process of industrialisation and modernisation. In this connection, Royden Harrison said: 'Moshe Levine has described to me how, in the 1930s, (Russian) workers who were chained to their benches nevertheless were persuaded that they were contributing to a world-historical event big with eventual liberation'.[58]

But although the 'authoritarians of the "Left"' (a phrase I have borrowed from Lewis Coser and Irving Howe) used socialist ideas and concepts to justify the imposition of socialism-from-above, the dictators were not objectively making any progress towards socialism. In making this point Lewis Coser and Irving Howe observed that totalitarian methods and progress towards socialism were absolutely incompatible. As they put it:

Few of the social-cultural advantages which industrialisation has traditionally brought to the West have yet appeared in Stalinist Russia. It is easy enough to say that industrialisation prepares the ground for democracy, but to say this is to view the relationship of economy to politics abstractly rather than to examine the concrete ways in which Russian industrialisation has been purchased at a catastrophic cost to human consciousness. Historically, the early phrases of industrialisation in the West were accompanied by a sharp and, in the main, open social struggle. From this process of social struggle rather than as an automatic corollary of industrialisation, the great democratic triumphs which we associate with the nineteenth century were won. They came not simply because England was being industrialised; they came because the industrialisation was accompanied by a rich social history in which a vast growth of human awareness took place.[59]

A similar process – a process in which there was no vast growth of human awareness – was seen in China, though Maoism as the cult of the Leader in a hereditary despotic country began before Mao became the dictator of the whole of China in 1949. Thus when he discussed the parallels between Stalinism and Maoism, Isaac Deutscher said: 'If Stalinism was the amalgam of Marxism with the savage barbarism of the old Russia, Maoism may be considered as an amalgam of Leninism with China's primitive patriarchalism and ancestral cults'.[60] But the cult of the Leader was already very powerful in Chinese communism in the 1920s before Mao's rise to dominance. By 1944 a selection of popular dance songs included the following song:

The East is red, the sun rises;
China has produced a Mao Tse-tung.
He plans a way of life for the people;
He is the people's great saving star.[61]

Yet the immediate precedent for the emergence of the cult of the Leader – of the Man-God – in China owed a great deal to Russian communism.

In the light of the controversy about exactly when 'communism' really began to degenerate into totalitarianism, the role of the Third International in legitimising the cult of the dictator in China was exceptionally interesting. As Ygael Gluckstein has observed:

The 1924 Kuomintang Constitution (written by Borodin, Moscow's Supreme Adviser in China) made Sun Yat-sen President of the Party for life; stated that "members should follow the direction of the President"; that the President should have the power to veto resolutions of the National Congress; and that his voice should be decisive in the General Executive Committee, which was the highest authority between Congresses.

When Sun Yat-sen died in 1925, he was – with the approval of Joseph Stalin and the Third International – 'embalmed, like one of the ancient Pharaohs, and kept in a magnificent marble mausoleum, rivalling the tombs of China's greatest emperors'. In emphasising the similarities between Stalinism and Maoism, Gluckstein unsurprisingly insists that China was 'an archetype of totalitarianism long before the term was coined'.[62]

Yet in the midst of Stalinist and Maoist totalitarianism, a minority of working-class men and women, middle-class intellectuals and plebeians in Russia, Eastern Europe and China developed one of the indispensable ingredients for any real progress towards democratic socialism – class consciousness. In a vivid description of what he experienced in Russia in the early 1940s, Moshe Lewin said: 'When I worked in the Urals, workers knew who they were and that it was the *nachalstvo*, the bosses, who had the power and the privileges. How many times did I hear from fellow workers that the *nachalstvo* take care of themselves but very little of "our kind"? The engineers and administrators had their own restaurant in the factory, and they came out of it clearly having eaten quite enough'.[63] A similar class-conscious opposition was discernible in China, too.

By 1958 a small, though independent, left-wing socialist current was beginning to develop in Mao's totalitarian China. A woman refugee from China subsequently told Raya Dunayevskaya about the process which led to her disillusionment with socialism-from-above: 'I don't think the Hungarian revolution was in the consciousness of the masses. There were

dissatisfactions with conditions in China. Many, especially the older ones –
at least at first it was the older ones – felt that after seven years of strict
military rule it was time to relax the control. I had also heard that in
Yu-men there was a strike of some oil workers'.[64] Then some of the
workers' discontent and opposition got caught up in the Cultural Revolution.

Joseph Stalin and Mao Tse-tung – the two dictators who dominated
much of twentieth-century 'socialism' or bureaucratic collectivism in much
of the world – unwittingly contributed to the emergence of a genuine
independent Left. While Stalin died a few years before a new Left of
independent socialists appeared in America and Western Europe, he
contributed to an appropriate consciousness of self among working-class
rebels, middle-class intellectuals and plebeians throughout the world.
Although only a small minority emancipated themselves from the chains of
totalitarianism, this demonstrated that the word totalitarianism now
required to be used around heavy inverted commas.

While Stalinism was increasingly called into question in the 1960s and
1970s as an agency of socialism, Mao – at least until his death in 1976 used
'the Great Leap Forward' and the 'Cultural Revolution' – to prevent, in
Royden Harrison's idiom, 'Marxism from degenerating into the ideology of
a deferred Industrial Revolution'. In assessing Mao's initiatives between
1966 and 1969, Michel Oksenberg insisted that the attempt by Mao to
promote 'a revolution from above' had ended in failure.[65] This was
self-evident to those who believed in socialism-from-below. Gods had
failed and men and women had lived in 'dark times' – the age of socialist
innocence had ended for ever.

But it was a major paradox – an irony – of history that dictatorial
Stalinism and Maoism transformed what Boris Souvarine described in
1939 as 'the death agony of socialist hope' among working people into its
opposite – a philosophy of resurrection and redemption. Despite the
enormous cost in human suffering and bloodshed, democratic socialism
was back on the agenda as a critique of totalitarian socialism-from-above.

Chapter 7

Claude McKay and George Padmore: The black heretics

It was not until my last year in school (1921) that it occurred to me that these black people, these voteless masses, were in any way concerned with the socialism I professed or that they had any role to play in the great social revolution which in those days seemed imminent. . . . The African was on a different plane, hardly human, part of the scene as were dogs and trees and, more remotely, cows. I had no special feelings about him, not interest nor hate nor love. He just did not come into the social picture. So completely had I accepted the traditional attitudes of the time.

Edward Roux

He moved a little the arm he's thought broken, it was not, only clotted with bruises, the dryness had left his throat, he lay still with a strange mist boiling, blinding his eyes, not Ewan Tavendale at all any more but lost and be-bloodied in a hundred broken and tortured bodies all over the world, in Scotland, in England, in the torment-pits of the Polish Ukraine, a livid, twisted thing in the prisons where they tortured the Naking communists, a Negro boy in an Alabama cell while they thrust the razors into his flesh with a lingering cruelty and care.

Lewis Grassic Gibbon

Profoundly aware of the racism of the European and American Left, Claude McKay (1890–1948) and George Padmore (1902–59) were powerful, critical, iconoclastic, individualistic and heretical figures within the international labour movement. Claude McKay, the young Jamaican poet, novelist, journalist and black socialist, came to prominence in 1919 in the wake of the serious 'race riots' in America and Britain; and Malcolm Ivan Meredith Nurse, the young Trinidadian agitator, writer, journalist, historian and black socialist, later known as George Padmore, became a prominent member of the American Communist Party in the late 1920s.

Claude McKay died when he was fifty-eight years of age; George Padmore when he was fifty-seven. Both died in circumstances of defeat and disillusionment, though their brilliant writings continue to diffuse critical awareness throughout African and Afro-American communities. But, although they both ultimately gained posthumous and immortal fame in the late-twentieth century, the similarities in their distinctive and very heretical contribution to socialist thought and literature are now bursting through the Eurocentric dominance of left-wing thought and political practice.

A tiny number of black socialists had played a role in the European and American labour movements before the Russian revolution of 1917 gave

Vladimir Lenin's ideas on colonialism and anti-colonialism a new authority among left-wing thinkers and activists in the world at large. Unlike Claude McKay or George Padmore, however, they did not question or challenge the Eurocentric bias of labour movements throughout the world. Although Daniel De Leon already envisaged an independent role for the anti-imperialist struggles of black workers and peasants in 1905, he could not conceive of them developing a distinctly socialist consciousness without industrialisation.

Claude McKay and George Padmore came on the labour scene at a particular conjunction in the history of socialism. Edward Roux, the son of a disciple of Daniel De Leon, described how the white socialists in South Africa ignored the question of the black workers before and after 1917: 'My father and his socialist friends were glib with their talk of the workers. But by the workers they meant the white workers and did not at all consider that in South Africa the majority of the workers were black. Later this attitude of my father's was to make a deep rift between us'.[1]

But although they challenged the Eurocentric bias of international socialism during the two decades between 1919 and 1939, Claude McKay, George Padmore and the other black heretics did not succeed in eradicating it. In discussing this conflict within international socialism, Shlomo Avineri said:

One of the problems which non-European socialists face – and I'm reading quite a lot of the Arab Marxist material – is that within non-European culture some of the statements which look to Europeans as understandable, look to non-Europeans extremely offensive. We have to take that into account. When you have a situation in which it is a fact that Marx supported America against Mexico, and viewed the annexation of Mexico as a great progress for civilisation, in which Engels supported the French occupation of Algeria, and I am quoting, he said, "The occupation of Algeria is a great step in the progress of civilisation".[2]

This was, of course, the intellectual background and foreground against which the colonial views of the Second International crystallised, developed and hardened.

Although the Second International always opposed the exploitation of the 'backward' peoples in the colonial and semi-colonial world, it did not believe in self-government for the people in the African colonies. As Julius Braunthal put it: 'Only in 1928 did the International adopt, at its Brussels Congress, a new and more concrete colonial programme calling explicitly for self-government and independence'.[3] Most socialists, however, still saw capitalist colonialism as a progressive historical development.

Because the European and American socialists saw the Africans as a 'backward' and 'primitive' people who required to be 'educated' for self-government, they inevitably expressed overtly racist evaluations and expectations of the African peasants and embryonic working classes. However, this did not always prevent them from encouraging the very few exceptional black socialists that they encountered before the First World

War. Indeed, the first black socialist to write for a British periodical was F. Colebrook, though nothing is known about him except the articles he contributed to *Justice*, the organ of the Social Democratic Federation, in the early 1900s.[4] In America W.E.B. Du Bois, the distinguished black scholar and advocate of Afro-American rights, was soon elected to the editorial board of the Marxist theoretical magazine, the *New Review*. But rare and very unusual as they were black socialists in Europe and America played an obscure and *subordinate* role in the growing socialist movements.

Before the world-shattering Bolshevik revolution, international socialism was predominantly *Eurocentric*. Black workers were regarded as being simply irrelevant to the struggle for socialism. Writing in 1913, Thomas Kirkup said: 'On this summer Sunday whilst I am writing, literally thousands, probably tens of thousands of meetings, lectures, excursions, concerts, services, are being held for the promotion of socialism. In every industrial city in Europe, in America, in Australasia, in most cities even in Asia and Africa, the economic gospel will be preached today, sometimes in large crowded halls by the best-known statesmen of the land, sometimes to little groups of ignorant artisans by some half-educated youth only less ignorant than the rest'.[5] But white socialists in such African cities as Johannesburg did not recognise the black peasantry or working class.

With the sole exception of Vladimir Lenin, no other major thinker in the ranks of the socialist movement anywhere approved of nationalist revolts in Africa before the Bolshevik revolution. In an interesting, though unhistoric, critique of Rosa Luxemburg, Raya Dunayevskaya says:

Although Rosa Luxemburg described concretely how the war between the Boers and the English was fought "on the backs of the Negroes", she did not draw any conclusions about the black Africans being a revolutionary force. That revolutionary role was reserved for the proletariat alone. . . . As we saw, during the 1910–11 debate with Karl Kautsky, Luxemburg's revolutionary opposition to German imperialism's barbarism against the Hereros was limited to seeing them as suffering rather than revolutionary humanity. Yet both the Maji revolt in East Africa and the Zula rebellion in South Africa had erupted in those privotal years, 1905–06 – although they were known, no doubt, to few others than the imperialists engaged in putting them down.[6]

The revolts and uprisings of the African peoples were not really so unknown to socialists in Europe. Moreover, Luxemburg's lack of solidarity (as distinct from sympathy) with the revolts of the black Africans was rooted in the dominant Eurocentric conception of the socialist struggle.

The outbreak of the First World War did not weaken Rosa Luxemburg's abhorence of nationalism and nationalist wars. As Max Beer explained:

Luxemburg was strongly of the opinion that in the imperialist period of history there was not room for nationalist struggles; she regarded all nationalist struggles as an anachronism; she believed all the talk about self-determination of the nations was rather retrogressive, and that it was particularly dangerous for the proletarian revolution to get involved in nationalist conflicts. Lenin opposed her, being convinced that the struggle for national independence, particularly in Asia, would play an important role in the universal social revolution. Reviewing a pamphlet written by Luxemburg in 1916 and published in 1916 under the pseudonym of "Junius", Lenin declared: "Nationalist wars against imperialism are not only possible and probable, but inevitable, and must be regarded as progressive and revolutionary.[7]

But Lenin's new and novel ideas about the role of the colonial world in the struggle for world socialism did not filter through to a minority of European and American socialists until 1919.

I

In all of his major writings, whether imaginative or sociological, between 1919 and 1946, Claude McKay was very conscious of being a black man. As a response to the brutal race riots in America in 1919, he published the militant poem, 'If We Must Die', in Max Eastman's *The Liberator*. In an important study, *Claude McKay*, published in 1976, James R. Giles says that when the poem 'appeared in Max Eastman's magazine in 1919, Afro-American literature acquired a prophetic new voice'. Moreover, the poem, 'If We Must Die', seemed to white ruling-class America, as Giles put it, 'a piece of demagogic heresy that demanded investigation'.[8] Moreover, white socialists in Europe and America also regarded McKay – and Padmore – as socialist heretics.

Race riots were not only serious in American cities in 1919. They also 'exploded' in cities throughout Britain in the same year. Although racist theories and doctrines enjoyed their greatest popularity in the British universities, scientific circles and among the intelligentsia between 1883 and 1914, working-class racism and overt hostility to blacks did not 'explode' until 1919. This new and overt racism resulted in black men and women being attacked physically in their homes as well as in the streets. It also led to the introduction of a 'colour bar' in hotels and restaurants in England, Wales and Scotland.[9]

This was the immediate backdrop against which E.D. Morel published his infamous article in the British socialist newspaper, the *Daily Herald*, on the 'Black Scourge in Europe: Sexual Horrors Let Loose by France on the Rhine'. When Germany violated the Versailles Treaty by allowing its troops to occupy the de-militarised Ruhr in the spring of 1920, France retaliated by sending in French troops including regiments of African colonials. Now in London, where he was to remain until the beginning of 1921, Claude McKay sent a reply to George Lansbury, the editor of the *Daily Herald*.

But George Lansbury refused to publish McKay's letter 'A Black Man Replies' on the grounds that it was too long. Then McKay sent it to Sylvia

Pankhurst. She immediately published it in her small communist weekly, the *Worker's Dreadnought*. McKay was also invited to and decided to join Pankhurst's small editorial staff as a full-time journalist. As a member of the *Worker's' Dreadnought* editorial staff throughout most of 1920, McKay contributed a series of articles from the perspective of a man who was a *black* heretic. But he came to hate the racism that he encountered in England amongst every strata of the population. In summing up the significance of Claude McKay's brief sojourn in Britain, Wayne F. Cooper says: 'In a real sense McKay completed in London the political self-education he had begun in the United States. At the International Club in East Road Shoreditch, he heard a wide range of British and European left-wing speakers and was impelled for the first time to read the works of Karl Marx. On the personal side, he experienced during his stay an extreme disillusionment with England and Englishmen in general.'

On the Left of the British labour movement, Claude McKay was a Leninist who did not like many of the leading Anglo-American socialists. What had upset him most, however, was the racism amongst a variety of British socialists, though he liked and admired some rank-and-file militants among the white workers he encountered. As a black socialist, poet and novelist with the temperament of a natural heretic, he developed a delicate sensitivity towards signs of class-consciousness among working people without any reference to their colour. Furthermore, McKay's experiences in New York and London at the end of the First World War made him very aware of black workers' race-consciousness, too.

But Claude McKay's sympathy for race-consciousness as a progressive historical force both antedated his conversion to socialism in 1919 and survived his growing disillusionment with Stalinism from the early 1930s onwards. The unexpected racism that he encountered in England played an undying role in shaping his political thought and attitudes. As Wayne F. Cooper put it:

As a young man in Jamaica he had embraced British culture as his own and had idolised its great men of letters. Once in the United States, of course, he had acquired a broader, soberer view of the world. But he had, nevertheless, gone to England with some of his old schoolboy enthusiasm still intact. After all, as a "black Briton", was he not at last going home? Once among the English, however, McKay quickly discovered that the kinship he felt for them was not reciprocated. On the contrary, he found all classes and shades of political opinion imbued with frank, scarcely conscious assumptions of racial superiority, as well as with an amazing ignorance of the psychological effects European imperialist rule had had upon the colonised peoples of the world.[10]

The consequence was that McKay became even more heretical and critical of the 'socialism' of the European and American socialists.

In contrast to George Padmore, whose socialist heresy consisted almost solely of a sympathy for race-consciousness and black nationalism, Claude McKay's socialist heresy was much more comprehensive and all-embracing. Unlike Padmore, a man who had been born into a comfortable middle-class family, McKay was born into a family of hard-working peasants. Although he was more of a prisoner of poverty and insecurity for much of his life, McKay was less deferential towards the prevailing orthodoxy about proletarian purity and solidarity than Padmore or some of the other black socialists in the inter-war period.

In an important article published in 1921 on 'How Black Sees Green and Red', Claude McKay wrote: 'I think I understand the Irish. By belonging to a subject race entitles me to some understanding of them. And then I was born and reared a peasant, the peasant's passion for the soil possesses me, and it is one of the strongest passions of the Irish revolution.' Thirteen years later in 1934, Lewis Grassic Gibbon, the Scottish socialist novelist, was another heretic on the peasant question. He said: 'I like to remember I am of peasant stock and peasant rearing'.[11] Then he was expelled by the British Communist Party for 'exaggerating the values of rural life'.[12] But because McKay had the artist's gift for seeing to the heart of problems, he made an even more heretical comment in his essay on 'How Black Sees Green and Red' when he said: 'And the Irish workers hate the English. It may not sound nice in the ears of the "infantile left" communist to hear that the workers of one country hate the workers of another. It is not beautiful propaganda. Nevertheless, such a hatred exists'.[13]

The year 1919 was a pivotal one in the development and popularisation of Leninist attitudes towards the anti-colonial struggles in the world. In an article that he published in 1919 on 'International Political Affairs', Antonio Gramsci said:

But today flames of revolt are being fanned throughout the colonial world. This is the class struggle of the *coloured peoples* against their *white exploiters* and murderers.[14]

In suggesting that there was now a class struggle between coloured peoples and the whites, Gramsci was overlooking the workers' class struggle within the ensuing conflict. From a similar Leninist perspective, John MacLean, in late 1920, argued that: 'The best interests of humanity can therefore be served by the break-up of the British Empire. The Irish, the Indians and others are playing their part'.[15]

When Claude McKay contributed an article on 'Socialism and the Negro' to the *Workers' Dreadnought* in Janaury 1920, he said: 'Some English communists have remarked to me that they have no real sympathy for the Irish and Indian movement because it is nationalistic. But, today, the British Empire is the biggest obstacle to international socialism, and any of its subjugated parts succeeding in breaking away from it would be helping the cause of world communism. In these pregnant times no people who are strong enough to throw off an imperial yoke will tamely submit to a system of local capitalism'.[16] What McKay did not realise was that

Leninist ideas on colonialism had to confront an existing – and very hostile – Marxist traditionalism with its own views on colonialism.

The British Communist Party itself was initially hostile to Leninist conceptions of the role of the colonial peoples in the struggle for socialism. Writing in *The Call*, the organ of the British Communist Party, H.S. Ryde argued that the African peoples needed to be 'educated' for self-government.[17] For the dominant sections of the Left in Britain and Western Europe as a whole, it was inconceivable that the black Africans could free themselves from imperialism. The notion that the black Africans might, moreover, play a role in the struggle for socialism was even more alien to the world-outlook of the European Left. Tom Ashcroft, who was one of the authorities on colonialism in the Movement for Independent Working-Class Education, expounded the dominant Marxist and left-wing socialist view in the pages of *Plebs*:

The African is helpless and hopeless against the existing treaties in unity arrayed against his freedom and happiness. . . . These forces, with their attendant manifold evils, must continue to animate and dominate the relations between the two continents unless some new and still greater force comes in to transform these relations, to discover some more excellent way based upon their mutual and equal benefit. The only possible power to do that lies in the labour movement, which, in the proportion as it attains self-consciousness, will become increasingly capable of appreciating the African problem.[18]

Although he probably did not know that he was pitting himself against the pre-Leninist Marxist tradition in Britain, Claude McKay made an important contribution to the development of Leninist ideas about the role of the black Africans in the ongoing political struggles. The most significant thing that he wrote about race-consciousness was a letter that he sent to Leon Trotsky when they were both in Moscow in February 1922. In this letter, McKay wrote:

The stationing of black troops for the last three years has insistently demanded the international intervention of communists.

London and New York are the chief cultural centers of the West where Negroes hold mass meetings and discuss questions which interest them. At such meetings one can meet Negroes of all types – from the mulatto totally imbubed with Western culture to the young son of an African chief whom some philanthropist is educating with the aim of converting his tribe to Christianity in the future.

In the winter of 1919–20 the soldiers of various Negro groups from all parts of Africa and America met with one another in a London club especially set aside for them by the British government and separated from white soldiers. They spoke various European languages. They had all been disillusioned with the European war, because they kept on having frightful clashes with English and American soldiers, besides the fact that the authorities treated them completely differently from the white soldiers. They were deeply aroused by the propaganda of the policy of "Back to Africa" which came from New York. In place of the former pride because they were wearing Khaki uniforms put on for "the defence of civilisation", they had become disillusioned, had begun to look at things critically, and were imbubed with race-consciousness.

I was working at that time in London in a communist group. Our group provided the club of Negro soldiers with revolutionary newspapers and literature, which had nothing in common with the daily papers that are steeped in race prejudice. Moreover, we invited some of the more sophisticated soldiers to lectures at the socialist club.[19]

McKay and Trotsky also had discussions on 'the Negro question'.

Under the influence of Claude McKay, Leon Trotsky seemed to be more sensitive to the 'ecumenical' sources of socialist consciousness. With a new sense of the significance of the First World War for the long-term prospects of international socialism, he recognised the new material factors which were creating a socialist potential in African countries where extensive industrialisation did not yet exist. In a letter that he sent, to McKay, he wrote:

Dark-skinned peoples, like natives of colonies in general, preserve their conservatism and intellectual immobility only to the extent that they remain in their customary economic conditions and daily routine. When the hand of capital and, all the more so, the hand of militarism mechanically uproots them from their customary conditions of existence and compels them to risk their lives for complex and new problems and conflicts (conflicts between the bourgeoisie of different nations, conflicts between classes of one and the same nation), then their stubborn conservative states of mind break down at once, and revolutionary ideas find quick access to a consciousness thrown off its equilibrium.[20]

By the time he encountered C.L.R. James in 1938, Trotsky had reverted to a more orthodox Leninist attitude towards the Africans and Afro-American workers and peasants.

By 1922 Claude McKay had made the 'magic pilgrimage' to Soviet Russia. In the intellectual confusion in socialist and communist circles in the early 1920s, he appeared to be an orthodox communist. This certainly appeared to be the case in 1923 when he addressed the delegates to the Fourth Congress of the Third International in Moscow. But the most interesting evidence of the transmutation of McKay's 'Leninism' was seen in the article he contributed to *International Press Correspondence* in November 1922 on 'The Racial Question: The Racial Issue in the United States'. Although he attempted to reconcile race-consciousness with 'Leninism', he nonetheless focused on the race-consciousness of the Afro-Americans. As he put it: 'The blacks are hostile to communism because they regard it as a "white" working-class movement and they consider the white workers their greatest enemy, who draws the color line against them in factory and office and lynch and burn them at the stake for being colored'.[21]

When he left Russia in May 1923, Claude McKay was determined to retain his freedom as an artist and writer without being imprisoned by the constraints of communist activism. As Wayne F. Cooper puts it: 'His Russian journey proved to be only a grand finale to his radical activism. From the beginning of his association with the *Liberator*, McKay stressed his ultimate independence as a writer and a poet'. He was also by then deeply disillusioned with the racism among the European and American communists he encountered in Moscow.

Although Claude McKay spent spells in Europe and Africa between 1923 and 1934 before he took up permanent residence in America, he was already a leading light in the Harlem Renaissance. With the publication of his fourth volume of verse, *Harlem Shadows*, 1932, he gave an enormous impetus to the black Renaissance of race-conscious poetry, prose and song of a new generation of black writers and artists. In 1928 McKay published the remarkable novel, *Home to Harlem*.

This astonishing novel demonstrated indirectly that Claude McKay was, at a deep emotional and artistic level, a champion of socialist ideas and values. What he believed in an authoritarian age of socialism-from-above was socialism-from-below – a humane, humanistic and democratic socialism. In evaluating and sketching in what *Home to Harlem* was about, Wayne F. Cooper says:

Home to Harlem appeared at the height of this new interest in black culture and quickly reached bestseller status. As McKay had foreseen, its unblushing depiction of the seamier side of Harlem life generated a storm of protest in the Negro press. In telling the story of Jake Brown, the novel's working-class hero, McKay sketched in a rogue's gallery of Harlem "low life" characters. Love-starved "grass widows" and the "sweetman" who preyed upon them, pimps and prostitutes, homosexuals and drug addits, loan sharks and labor scabs, alcoholics, gamblers, sado-masochists, and corrupt cops – all were found in *Home to Harlem*. In 1928 the existence of such types in black communities, though privately acknowledged, was not publicly advertised in respectable black publications.[22]

But whether they were black or white advocates of socialism-from-above or intellectual elitism, McKay never displayed solidarity with them. In an age when socialism was increasingly authoritarian and dictatorial in the dominant sections of the labour movement in America and Europe, McKay's emotional and intellectually articulate sympathy for socialism-from-below was, in circumstances where being an advocate of race-conscious created consternation, an additional heresy.

Nevertheless, the sharpest criticism of *Home to Harlem* came from W.E.B. Du Bois. An advocate of the special role of the black middle class – the Talented Tenth – in the struggle for black rights, Du Bois was not sympathetic to socialism-from-below. In making a major criticism of McKay's novel, Du Bois said that, if the black workers were happy with the way-of-life described in *Home to Harlem*, it was difficult to see how any progress could be made by the Afro-American working class. Although McKay defended the 'primitivism' in the novels and poems he produced in the 1920s, James R. Giles explains how McKay responded to the criticisms from the black bourgeois intelligentsia:

Progress must come from within the black community, instead of being imposed from without. By maintaining his pride in his blackness and the heritage it implies, the black common man will determine his own progress. Always a believer in community solidarity, McKay advocated a "spontaneous", controlled spiritual and economic rebirth for his people. Any control, even from the black intelligentsia, might dilute the African heritage in the name of a strictly Western concept of advancement.[23]

In the 1920s Claude McKay worked with 'a small but talented group of black socialists' in Harlem.[24] With A. Philip Randolph, Chandler Owen and W.A. Domingo, McKay attempted to win Marcus Garvey over to socialism. Though they failed, they were not unsympathetic to Garvey's 'Back to Africa' propaganda. But in the light of George Padmore's expulsion from the Cominterm as a black nationalist in 1933, the Afro-American socialists' support for black nationalism in the 1920s was a harbinger of the growth of Pan-African sentiments in European and American labour movements later on. There was, for example, a fascinating piece of dialogue in *Home to Harlem*, in 1928, about black attitudes to Africa:

Had Jake ever heard of the little Republic of Liberia, founded by the American Negroes? And Abyssinia, deep-set in the shoulder of Africa, besieged by the hungry wolves of Europe.[25]

Meanwhile, George Padmore was making a considerable impression in the black community in Harlem, New York. Although he organised demonstrations at Fisk University against racialist segregation, he did not possess Claude McKay's spontaneous sympathy for socialism-from-below. Lacking McKay's democratic scepticism about the 'wisdom' of the Talented Tenth in America, Padmore was less critical of such black leaders as Alain Locke. While Padmore was critical of some teachers at Fisk University, he 'would say that as long as the students had people like Professor Alain Locke they would be safe'.[26] Moreover, by 1931, Padmore was criticising A. Philip Randolph at a time when McKay was still co-operating with the black working-class socialists in Harlem.[27]

George Padmore went to Fisk University in Nashville, Tennessee in 1924 with the intention of studying medicine. He was almost immediately involved in trouble with the Ku Klux Klan; and in 1927 he 'enrolled at the Law School of Howard University, presumably because the Communist Party, which he joined shortly after reaching the Greenwich Village campus, wanted him to do so'.[28] In 1929 he went to Moscow, where he was appointed head of the Negro Bureau of the Red International of Trade Unions (Profintern) and helped to organise the first international conference of Negro workers a year later. By 1931 he was made the editor of the *Negro Worker*. With over 5,000 contacts in various colonial countries, Padmore was already a formidable figure.

II

By 1923 Claude McKay was lost to the cause of Leninist socialism, though as a thinker, poet and novelist he tried to foster the values of libertarian socialism-from-below. As McKay abandoned practical socialist activity, the Third International devoted increasing attention to the problem of colonialism. As Cedric J. Robinson puts it: 'Starting with the efforts of Otto Huiswoud, Claude McKay and Sen Katayama, it had become increasingly clear to the leadership of the Cominterm that only a special programme could attract large numbers of black workers to the movement. After 1922, the tutelage and training of black cadres in the Soviet Union was taken quite seriously'.[29] Yet despite the systematic efforts of the Third International in the 1920s and 1930s to attract and train black socialists for work in Europe, America and Africa, they could not overcome the overt or latent 'nationalist' sympathies of the black socialists.

As Claude McKay became increasingly absorbed in a conflict with the Stalinists in America in the early 1930s, George Padmore was becoming disenchanted with the opportunist functionaries in the Third International. In August 1933 the Third International suddenly dissolved the International Trade Union Committee of Negro Workers. Padmore immediately resigned in disgust from all his positions and was expelled from the Third International as 'a petty-bourgeois nationalist' a few months later. A major reason for the decision to dissolve the International Trade Union Committee of Negro Workers was Stalin's desire to improve relations between the Soviet Union and France.

If the communists in America were responsible for depriving Claude McKay of making a livelihood in the 1930s, he did not suffer from the intense universal denunication directed at George Padmore. This was partly because Padmore had more influence in black communities in the colonial countries. As a highly placed functionary in the Third International, he was more dangerous than such black literary heretics as Richard Wright or Claude McKay. But the unlimited abuse heaped upon Padmore was not unconnected with his already growing sympathy for the ideas of Pan Africanism.

In the early 1920s the Third International allowed the communist parties outside of the Soviet Union a certain degree of autonomy. But whether we examine the early period of world communism, the ultra-left 'third period' (1928–33) or the period of the 'popular front' (1934–39), the Communist International did not tolerate what was characterised as race-consciousness. In Africa, for example, communist propaganda was focused on the indigenous Africans who had been proletarianised. This was summed up, in 1921, by David Ivon Jones, when he wrote: 'Africa's hundred

and fifty million natives are more easily assessible through eight million or
so which comprise the native population of South Africa and Rhodesia.
Johannesburg is the *industrial university* of the African native'.[30]

The Third International was always critical of W.E.B. Du Bois and the
Pan-African movement. A constant source of annoyance in the international communist movement, middle-class black – and Scottish and
Welsh – nationalism was seen as inimical to the cause of proletarian
internationalism. So when George Padmore was expelled from the Communist International in 1934 for expressing 'an incorrect attitude' towards
'the national question', the Stalinists began to unleash undreamt of
revolutionary forces in Africa. What his specific heresy consisted of was
'striving towards race unity instead of class unity'. Moreover, the black
heretic was accused of having developed contacts with black nationalists in
Ethiopia and Liberia shortly after Claude McKay had published his novel,
Home to Harlem.[31]

By 1933 George Padmore was shocked by the Communist International's 'discovery' of the virtues of 'the grand democracies' and the
League of Nations. As Peter Fryer puts it: 'He told his nephew afterwards
how he had been sent a series of directives from Moscow instructing him to
stop attacking French imperialism, then British imperialism, then American imperialism, till he was left with the Japanese – and, as he observed
with some asperity, they were not the ones that had their boots across the
black man's neck'.[32]

Although C.L.R. James was always more of an 'orthodox' Marxist than
George Padmore, he was also sympathetic to black nationalism. Even in
1938, when he produced his pioneering work on *A Short History of Negro
Revolt*, he did not attempt to conceal his sympathy for Pan-Africanism. In
the final two sentences of that book, he said:

Yet the Garvey movement like the International Commercial Union in South
Africa in its best days, though it actually achieved little in proportion to its size, is of
immense importance in the history of Negro revolts. It shows the fires that
smoulder in the Negro world, in America as in Africa.[33]

Socialism and nationalism were still inseparable in the lives of many black
socialist intellectuals.

When they met in London in 1935, Padmore told C.L.R. James why he
had stayed in Moscow and Hamburg despite his growing doubts about the
communists' opportunism in relation to the struggle for African freedom.
As James puts it:

He lived in the Kremlin. But nevertheless he called them "those people" and it
became clear to me afterwards – and I have been told even that much – that he had
never been completely swept away by the Stalinist conception of Marxism. He said:
"I lived there; I saw what was going on". He gave me some examples which I have
no time to tell you now. But he said: "I stayed there because there was a means of
doing work for the black emacipation and there was no other place that I could
think of".[34]

With the passage of time, it became obvious that 'those people' – Stalin and the Stalinists – were abandoning the black people in the colonial countries to the needs of Russian foreign policy. It was the needs of Russian foreign policy which led Joseph Stalin to give material aid to Mussolini during the war in Ethiopia.

The major turning-point in the growth and, more importantly, the *black socialist* orientation, of the Pan-African movement throughout Europe and America was the Italian fascists' attack on Ethiopia (or Abyssinia) in 1935. In the very opening sentence of his essay on C.L.R. James, Ferruccio Gambion, the Italian socialist historian, wrote: 'In our neighbourhood, we were feeling that we were with the others, with the Ethiopians, with the Spanish', said Margitt, a rank-and-file militant woman in the Po Valley, Italy, as she recalled the mid-1930s. Moreover, in criticising Eugene D. Genovese, the American historian, Gambion argues that:

Whoever believes that "during the twentieth century the prestige of the Russian revolution and its subsequent consolidation of state power long guaranteed the hegemony of the Stalinist Third International over revolutionaries throughout the world" would be well advised to re-examine the history of Pan-Africanism as well as other anti-colonial movements after the Stalinist alliance with "the grand democracies".[35]

The American and European Left's response to the black Africans' resistance to imperialism, whether through strikes, uprisings or revolts, had seldom been very enthusiastic. When Norman Leys, who had been a member of the communist League against Imperialism and a doctor of medicine in Kenya, published a book, *Kenya*, in 1926, he expressed the typical attitude of the European Left when he said:

If, some morning, the readers of this book open the morning paper over their breakfast coffee and read of some other Chilembwe or Thuku, they must not expect that some particular act of policy or the unwisdom of some Governor is the cause. They should look on the rising as a by-product of the system under which the very coffee they are drinking is produced. Nor must they blame the Governor or the Colonial Secretary for repressing the rising with slaughter. That is the kindest way of dealing with native risings. The fact that most of the people who engage in them are in no real sense criminally inclined make it no less necessary to shoot them. Those who object to the shooting must go deeper.[36]

Although Leys was hated by the white settlers in Kenya in the 1920s and 1930s because of his exposures of their exploitation and ill-treatment of the black Africans, he was always incapable of recognising the growth of black-consciousness after the First World War.

Not surprisingly, the European Left's support for the struggles of the black Africans in Ethiopia was, from the standpoint of black socialists, disappointing. In Europe and America the black socialists who called for workers' (as distinct from League of Nations) sanctions were often dismissed as nationalists; and the white Left's lack of adequate support for the

Africans in Ethiopia played a major role in creating a socialistic Pan-Africanist movement in the heartland of classical industrial capitalism. For although Pan-African movements existed in other European countries, Pan-Africanism was most solid and influential in Britain between the outbreak of the war in Ethiopia and the international Pan-African Congress in Manchester in 1945.

In 1931 George Padmore published his pioneering study, *The Life and Struggles of the Negro Toilers*. While the strikes, uprisings and revolts of the black Africans were sometimes alluded to in the emphemeral pamphlet literature of the European Left, the major chronicle of militancy and disaffection in black Africa was initially provided by Padmore. Indeed, the major theme of his book was what he called 'the revolts, uprisings and strikes in the different sections of the black world'. What was particularly interesting about *The Life and Struggles of Negro Toilers* was the sharp attack on racism in the Red International of Trade Unions. With characteristic bluntness, he concluded his critique by saying: 'The problem of national equality has not been sufficiently appraised even by many Profintern supporters, while in the ranks of those sections of the working class which still follows the reformist and the reactionary leadership the "race struggle" in most cases, we regret to say, overshadows the class struggle.' But the attraction of the Red International of Trade Unions for George Padmore before the advent of the 'popular front' period in communist history was its constant struggle against 'all colour bars' as well as its unrelenting fight against imperialism.[37]

In the summer of 1935 the Italian fascists' invasion of Ethiopia created bitter conflict between the Independent Labour Party on the one hand and the Stalinist Socialist League and the Communist Party on the other hand. The conflict within the Left in relation to what was happening in Africa was seen throughout the European labour movement as a critical development. With its new faith in the efficacy of the League of Nations as an agency of anti-fascism, the communists were no longer willing to foster or support the spontaneous struggles of the black Africans anywhere.

In October 1935 the British *Daily Worker* published the Communist International's manifesto on the Italo-Abyssinia crisis which concluded with the ostensably ringing words:

Workers of all lands, unite.
Not a single train, not a single ship in support of the
Italian war in Abyssinia.
Hands off the Abyssinian people.
Long live the Soviet policy of peace.[38]

Then the International Secretariat of the communist League against Imperialism published a pamphlet urging anti-imperialists throughout the world to demand 'the complete independence of Abyssinia, the stoppage of all munitions and financial aid to Italy and the closing of the Suez canal to all Italian military transport'.[39] But although such demands did not appear to be too different from the early anti-imperialist stance of the Communist International in Lenin's time, the Popular Front policy of protecting the black Africans in Abyssinia against the fascist (as distinct from the democrat) imperialists was to depend on sanctions applied by the League of Nations.

In contrast to George Padmore and C.L.R. James, Jomo Kenyatta defended and campaigned for the communists' Popular Front policy. While Padmore, James and others agitated for strikes and workers' boycotts against the Italian fascists, Kenyatta appealed to the Left in Europe and America to depend on League of Nations sanctions and 'democratic pressures'.[40] As Reginald Reynolds recalled:

Some Labour Party rebels, now well to the left of the communists, were also willing to join in forays against imperialism. But most important was the effect of the new Soviet policy on the colonial people. ... The League against Imperialism abandoned all propaganda relating to the French colonies ... (and) French colonials in revolt were denounced as "fascists".[41]

As the crisis in Abyssinia developed, it was difficult for the communists to persuade independent socialists that the revolts of the black Africans were inspired by fascism.

Moreover, the Italian fascists' war on Ethiopia created splits in the British Independent Labour Party and eventually vitiated its effectiveness as a significant socialist group in the European socialist movement. The split was created by the irreconcilable attitudes in relation to workers' sanctions versus League of Nations sanctions. Writing in 1935, Fenner Brockway said: 'Mussolini depends . . . on the co-operation of the workers in other countries. Unless the workers of other countries provide him with the war materials which he needs he cannot maintain his attack upon Abyssinia'.[42] In opposition to the black socialists, James Maxton and the Parliamentary group of the Independent Labour Party told the Party conference in 1936 that 'working-class sanctions could not be distinguished publicly from League of Nations sanctions and would help to create a war psychology against Italy'.

One of the interesting aspects of the annual conference of the Independent Labour Party in 1936 was the bitter attack directed at the so-called heretical 'black nationalism' of C.L.R. James. In describing what happened, Fenner Brockway said:

He (James) appealed as a black worker for help for the black population of Abyssinia; this had an emotional effect, but was used to support the argument that the case was nationalist rather than socialist. My main argument was directed against the view that international working-class action involved support of the capitalist Governments in their imperialist aims. I urged that direct action by the workers would be as distasteful to their Governments as it would be to Italy.

Before a majority of the delegates voted to support the policy of the League of Nations, John McGovern spoke for the Parliamentary group when he said that 'Haile Selassie was as much a dictator as Mussolini'.[43]

But none of the black socialists – or black nationalists – in Europe or America regarded Haile Selassie as an enemy, though Padmore had more reservations about him than James or Kenyatta. Furthermore, in 1935 such leading black socialists as George Padmore, C.L.R. James, Dr Harold Moody, Jomo Kenyatta, Ras Makkonnen, Arnold Ward, Chris Jones and others came together to form the International Friends of Abyssinia. Despite their sometimes conflicting political affiliations within Britain, they became increasingly aware of their blackness. Indeed, their common sense or awareness of being black transcended their latent antagonisms between Stalinism, Trotskyism, independent socialism and bourgeois nationalism. Jeremy Murray-Brown described what happened when the Emperor of Ethiopia arrived in London on 2 May 1936:

Kenyatta and the Friends of Ethiopia were waiting to demonstrate their solidarity with the Emperor. According to one eyewitness account, an African in the crowd broke through the polite cordon of officials. It was Kenyatta. Contemptuous of protocol, he went up to the Emperor and embraced him man to man. It was a moving scene between two exiles.[44]

The crisis in Ethiopia was responsible for the making of George Padmore as the leading figure in the Pan-African movement in Europe. With new contacts in Europe such as Daniel Guerin, he became much more sympathetic to socialism-from-below. Like Claude McKay and C.L.R. James, Padmore's disgust with Stalinism led him into the camp of democratic socialism. But although the Italian fascists' attack on Ethiopia was a decisive factor in the intellectual development of both C.L.R. James and George Padmore, the dimension of class conflict could not be ignored.

When he published an article in the *New Leader* in April 1936, C.L.R. James wrote: 'It is necessary to support the anti-imperialist movements arising among the "coloured" peoples in all countries in connection with the Abyssinian crisis, and to create a firm alliance between the international working-class movement and the suppressed peoples.' In a letter that he published in the same newspaper in June 1936, he sought to explain why he had tried to enroll in the Abyssinian army under Emperor Haile Selassie:

My hope was to get into the army. It would have given me an opportunity to make contact not only with the masses of Abyssinians and other Africans, but in the ranks with them I would have had the best possible opportunity of putting across the international socialist case. I believe also that I could have been useful in helping to organise anti-fascist propaganda among the Italian troops. And finally, I would have had an invaluable opportunity of gaining actual military experience on the African field where one of the most savage battles between capitalism and its opponents is going to be fought before very many years. As long as the Emperior was fighting imperialism I would have done the best I could.

Under Padmore's inspiration many whites as well as some black communists joined the International African Friends of Ethiopia; and James said that he 'broke at once' with them when they decided to support League of Nations rather than workers' sanctions.[45]

But although Claude McKay had too many personal problems in 1935 to allow him to campaign for Ethiopia, he remained sensitive to what was happening there. In any case, the Ethiopian crisis drew the black socialists throughout the world closer together than ever before. While Claude McKay struggled against crushing and soul-destroying poverty, Padmore earned a living by private teaching and journalism. Though he never joined the British Independent Labour Party, Padmore became its colonial expert after James's departure to found a Trotskyist group, collaborating closely with Fenner Brockway, Reginald Reynolds and others. Before he went to America in 1938, James had had an enormous influence on Padmore's attitudes to Africa and the black Africans. With the collapse of the International African Friends of Ethiopia, the International African Service Bureau was founded in London and helped to make Padmore a major figure.

In the meantime George Padmore and C.L.R. James developed an independent analysis of international politics from the standpoint of the colonial peoples. Although Padmore and Claude McKay were increasingly accused of 'Trotskyism', they were really black socialist heretics. But they did not just develop heretical views on the question of black socialism. They also questioned, challenged and developed an independent theoretical analysis of 'the actually existing "socialism"'. Though Padmore and McKay never met or collaborated, they shared many common political attitudes. Writing in the New York *Socialist Call* in 1937, Claude McKay said: 'I am against all dictatorships, whether they are social or intellectual. I believe in the social revolution and the triumph of workers' democracy, not workers' dictatorship'.[46] Then in 1938 he wrote an article in which he criticised the communists for suppressing movements for independence in colonial Africa.[47] He remained sympathetic to the concept of race-consciousness.

Whether race-consciousness was a valid or an appropriate weapon for African or West Indian socialists to use or not, George Padmore and Claude McKay were certainly not racists. They actually fought fascism and racism every inch of the way. Yet the communists in Europe and America either implicitly or sometimes explicitly accused them of racism. In a review of George Padmore's book, *Africa and World Peace* Reginald Bridgeman wrote:

What did the slogan "Africa for the Africans" mean? William I. Paterson, political leader of the American Negroes, pointed out when reviewing Padmore's *How Britain Rules Africa*, that there are white Africans as well as black: there is an African bourgeoisie, African landlords, as well as an African proletariat, toilers and farmers. What Africans is Africa for? ... Ignoring the economic causes of imperialism, he (Padmore) implied that the white peoples oppress coloured peoples and so can be represented as inferior, and echoing Nazi racialism, he declared a race war from the platform of the Pan-African Federation.

Padmore had, indeed, argued that 'The future of Africa belongs to the blacks, for they are the most oppressed on earth'. But he had also praised the white European socialists who were struggling for African freedom.[48]

This was the backdrop against which the independent Left in Britain decided, in 1939, to establish the British Centre against Imperialism. Its inaugural conference was actually dominated by the colonial delegates from Africa, India and the West Indies rather than those from Europe. When the committee met in April 1939, it was decided to give top priority to developing 'contacts' among the trade union and colonial workers' organisations.[49] However, the outbreak of the Second World War destroyed the British – and particularly the French – Centre against Imperialism, though they were reconstituted in 1946.

III

In a centenary pamphlet published in 1938, the Anti-Slavery and Aborigines' Protection Society declared that one of its aims was 'to secure the general acceptance of the doctrine that the child races of the world constitute for the stronger races a Sacred Trust'. This was exactly the conception of Africa and the black Africans that George Padmore and the Pan-Africans protested against before the outbreak of the Second World War. In an article published in *International African Opinion* in September 1938 articulating the views of black socialists like Padmore, C.L.R. James wrote:

It is clear that Sir Stafford Cripps has the typical vice of many European socialists, even revolutionaries. He conceives Africans as essentially passive recipients of freedom given to them by Europeans.

How comes it that such a man wants to transfer "trusteeship" to a new order? When and where has any people governed any other peoples as trustees?[50]

With the outbreak of the war in 1939, George Padmore made it plain that the struggle for the emancipation of the black Africans had now begun in earnest. Even before the war broke out, Padmore's friend, Chris Jones, 'the leader of the negro dockers in Britain', contributed an article to the *New Leader* in which he said: 'The imperialists' difficulties must be our opportunity to strike a blow for freedom'. In July a 'Conference of the Negro Races' in London was addressed by George Padmore, Dr Harold Moody, P. Blackman, Dr Otto Wallen, Jomo Kenyatta, Chris Jones and Ras Makonnen. A report of the conference in the *New Leader* revealed the bitter divisions opening up between the advocates of Pan-Africanism and the British communists:

In his usual forceful way, he (George Padmore) demanded that, as the conference had been convened by Negro organisations to put the case for the Africans and peoples of African descent, they should be given the majority position on the Standing Orders Committee, so that it could be truly declared that the Africans were the principal elements in shaping the conference policy. The motion was put to the conference, and although it had the full support of the Negro delegation, it was voted down by the supporters of the Communist Party.[51]

The Pan-Africans in Britain never again trusted or co-operated with the communists.

Throughout the war years George Padmore kept up an unrelenting opposition to British imperialism in Africa. In a critique of British policy in the Empire published in the *New Leader*, in 1941, Padmore asserted that the imperialists were treating 'the blacks like the Nazis treat the Jews'. In attempting to radicalise the Pan-African movement, he said: 'A socialist must be anti-imperialist and an anti-imperialist, to be consistent, must be a socialist.' In the same year, Chris Jones told the Independent Labour Party summer school that 'for forty years he had been a rolling stone in every part of the world and that he had yet to find a spot where under white domination elementary freedom is granted to the subject races'.[52]

Towards the end of 1941, Padmore informed the readers of the *New Leader* that 'Mr P. de Vere Allen, Principal Adviser in Kenya, reporting on the causes of the strikes in Mombassa in 1940, stated that he did not favour trade unions for Africans, believing that they were not ripe for trade unions.' He used this piece of evidence effectively to expose the British government's claim that it was helping trade unionism in the colonies. Then in an article in the Scottish socialist newspaper, *Forward*, in 1942, Padmore criticised 'the British Labour movement for defending British colonial interests whenever they were threatened'.[53]

Moreover, George Padmore played a crucial role behind the scenes in organising the West African students in London. In April 1941 the West African Students' Union established links with such British socialist newspapers and organisations as the *New Leader* and the Independent Labour Party. In putting the views of the increasingly militant West African students, F.O.B. Blaize, the secretary of the West African students, 'strongly urged the British government to grant the British West African colonies and protectorates internal self-government now'. Meanwhile, Padmore focused on the fact that the Atlantic Charter did not envisage freedom for the 'coloured peoples'.[54]

As the Second World War unfolded, the Africans and West Africans in Britain became more militant than ever before. With considerable encouragement from George Padmore, Learie Constantine not only fought the 'colour bar' in British hotels, but he also identified with the activities of the International African Service Bureau. As Peter O. Esedebe has summed up:

The war itself brought to a focus objects of long standing agitation as well as new issues some of which served to intensify the militancy of the exiles. It raised in sharp outline such questions as the nature of freedom and liberty, the powers of the state, the rights of the individual and the colour problem.

In the early 1930s Constantine had introduced C.L.R. James to working-class socialists in the Independent Labour Party. But although Constantine contributed a few articles to *The Keys*, the organ of the League of Coloured Peoples, in the 1930s, he did not play a prominent role in the agitations initiated by the Pan-Africanists until towards the end of the Second World War.[55]

George Padmore's close friend Chris Jones died in September 1944, but other recently arrived Pan-Africans took up where he left off.[56] One such newcomer to the Pan-African movement in London was Peter Abrahams, the black South African journalist and novelist. With assistance from Padmore, Abrahams became a leading figure in the fifth Pan-African conference in Manchester.

In describing the impact of the Second World War on the radicalisation of the Pan-Africans in Britain, Peter O. Esedebe says:

The moderates' criticisms of the colonial regimes, hitherto tempered with polite phrases, henceforth assumed a tone of marked harshness and hostility. . . . The new militancy culminated in the 1945 Manchester Pan-African meeting – the adoption of the strategy of "positive action" and the enlisting of mass support in Africa and the West Indies.

At a specially organised conference of the League of Coloured Peoples held in London in July 1944, Arthur Creech Jones, who still belonged to the independent Left, helped in the drafting of the 'Charter for Coloured Peoples' in which the demand was made for 'full self-government' for colonial peoples 'at the earliest possible opportunity'.[57] But when he became the Colonial Secretary in the first 'majority' Labour Government, he was much less enthusiastic about colonial freedom.

Under the inspiration of George Padmore the Pan-African Federation took the lead in April 1945 in preparing 'A Manifesto for Presentation to the United Nations Conference in San Francisco'. Promulgated and supported by the League of Coloured Peoples in co-operation with the West African Students' Union (London), the Negro Welfare Association (London), the Negro Welfare Centre (Liverpool and Manchester), the Coloured Men's Institute (East London) and endorsed by the African trade unions in the Gold Coast, Nigeria, Gambia and British Guiana, the extensive manifesto expressed a new and determined mood:

The present inferior political, economic and social status of the African peoples militates against the achievement of harmonious co-operation among the peoples of the world. International co-operation demands the abolition of every kind of discrimination on account of colour, race and creed, wherever such discrimination exists. The present system of exploitation by which the bulk of the wealth produced in Africa goes to enrich foreign monopoly firms and individuals must be replaced by systematic planning and development whereby in the first place the Africans themselves shall be the principal beneficiaries of the wealth produced, then an equal opportunity shall be afforded to all nations in the exchange of products.[58]

Although this very important document of Pan-Africanism was not discussed in the British socialist or Labour press, the implication of this new militancy soon became clear.

In 1945 the British Left with the exception of the small Independent Labour Party and the National Council of Labour Colleges did not really understand the impact that the Second World War had had on black Africans. In an article in *Left News* in June 1945, for example, Anopheles (Great Britain) noted that 'there have been, in the past, many fields of action in which the British socialist movement did not appear to be actively interested, and Nigeria and the other colonies of West African had been one of them'. But in a second article in the same issue of *Left News*, Anopheles wrote: 'In fact, there is a general feeling among many of the Africans that it would be as well to leave it all to the great and wise British government.' Within a few weeks, P.S. Hellicar sent a letter to the editor of *Left News* in which he called for 'Home Rule for Black Africa'. In doing so, he asked: 'What about an African saying what he thinks about regaining African freedom? Perhaps we may get something new'.[59]

In a review of Joyce Cary's book, *The Case for African Freedom*, Dr Kojo-ow Dzifa wrote: 'So long as the authorities regard themselves and the Africans in a master-servant relationship, so long as they think of human rights purely in terms of charity, they can never provide for the equal citizenship which the Africans desire.' When he published a long article on 'The Political Psychology of Africans and Europeans' in *Left News* in January 1946, Dzifa included a section on the road to Black Home Rule in Africa. In discussing the transitional steps to be taken towards Home Rule in Africa, he said:

Accordingly the first step in initiating African progress lies in the emergence of a small but vigorous and democratic group of African educationalists, aesthetes, scientists, economists and statesmen. Their task shall be to devise such curricula for their own people as would cover every aspect of life in simplified illustrations, to crystallise the new feeling for growth and give it orderliness and direction. Without such a vanguard modern Russia, China and Turkey could not have come into existence.[60]

With the exception of George Padmore and the small independent Left in Britain and America, most socialists remained ignorant of what was happening in Africa. When he reported on – and reflected Padmore's views – on the Pan-African Congress in Manchester in 1945, Peter Abrahams asserted that 'the European Left, with rare exception', had 'forfeited its right to the leadership of the struggle against imperialism'.[61] With prophetic insight, Padmore and Abrahams insisted that the 'colonial struggle' had entered a new phase.

Although the small minority of left-wing socialists could not exert any real influence on political events in Britain or Africa, the independent Left did at least appreciate the significance of the growing Pan-African movement. Writing in the *New Leader*, Frank A. Ridley said:

The Pan-African Federation, an institution of much greater historical significance than the United Nations Organisation, has an invaluable role to play in Africa itself and in Britain. (The standpoint of "Pan-Africa" is well-known to readers of the *New Leader* from the many admirable articles on colonial problems by George Padmore, one of the ablest leaders of the Federation).

But although the 'colour bar' had been 'one of the most important single factors in the growth of colonial bitterness', the Pan-African Federation had, in 1945, published an open letter to the Labour government welcoming its success at the polls and making 'a series of constructive suggestions on colonial problems'. By 1946 the Pan-Africanists had decided to go it alone. In declaring this new policy – a policy no doubt influenced by Padmore – Peter Abrahams said:

There are dangers implicit in it. . . . Dangers of a black-white struggle without a socialist basis. . . . But then "white chauvinism" has had a long day. However, two evils do not add up to anything but evil. Labour's first post-war statement had added materially to those dangers.[62]

In a book of 450 pages, *The Colonial Empire: A Comparative Survey from the Eighteenth Century* published in 1965, D.K. Fieldhouse managed to avoid making a single reference to George Padmore or Pan-Africanism. And yet the events which began to unfold with the organisation of the Pan-African Congress in 1945 provided the first solid evidence that the process of de-colonisation was now underway.

In assessing the significance of the Pan-African Congress in Manchester, Imanuel Geiss said:

Likewise absent from Manchester were representatives of the white abolitionist and philanthropic elements, in former days so closely associated with the missions. Pan-Africanism had indeed to a large extent become emancipated, both politically and socially: "The days of dependence upon the thinking and direction of their so-called left-wing European friends who had so often betrayed them were over. From henceforth Africans and peoples of African descent would take their destiny into their own hands and march forward under their own banner of Pan-Africanism in co-operation with their own selected allies". It no longer sought moral and political support from the outsiders, as had still been the case under Du Bois. . . . The Pan-Africanism in 1945 no longer asked modestly for some form or recognition or for favours from on high: it demanded political and social rights.

Moreover, what was also important about this conference was what George Padmore called its 'plebeian character'. This very important, though little-noticed, gathering was, as he put it, 'a mass movement intimately identified with the under-privileged section of the coloured colonial population'.[63]

Even without the alienation that the first 'majority' Labour government created between the Pan-Africanists and the wider labour movement, the Pan-African Congress would have been a milestone marking the Pan-Africans' determination to achieve self-government in Britain's African colonies.[64] As the Pan-Africans' disenchantment with the Labour government deepened during the next two years, black nationalism was accelerated everywhere. In 1946 Peter Abrahams wrote:

Today it is agreed by everybody, Left, Right and Centre, that there is a deep-rooted and abiding distrust of Britain's policy and intentions towards the black colonial Empire. The colonial peoples have not the slightest iota of faith in the good intentions of the Labour government towards them.

In that same year Jomo Kenyatta attended a socialist conference at Clacton where 'he joined in attacking Creech Jones over the Labour government's colonial policy'. Then he returned to Kenya, where the Mau Mau uprisings would soon cause consternation.

George Padmore was responsible for forming the Pan-African Federation – a 'loose association' of existing groups of Pan-Africanists – in 1944. This organisation had helped to organise and radicalise black Africans in various countries in the West as well as in Africa. But it was the International African Service Bureau which initiated the most important practical steps in the decades-old anti-colonial movement in British Africa. As Margaret Busby has explained in an introduction to a selection of the writings of C.L.R. James:

James was to write in a letter to Padmore in 1945: "George this young man (Nkrumah) is coming to you . . . do what you can for him because he's determined to throw the Europeans out of Africa". It was under the auspices of the Bureau that Nkrumah was to go from London to the Gold Coast in 1947 to begin his preparations for the revolution that was to initiate a new Africa.

A major aspect of the tragedy of the late twentieth century is that the struggle for de-colonialisation in Africa began 'without a socialist basis'. Despite the presence of George Padmore and other independent socialists in the Pan-African movement, the nationalist – and later on the Stalinist – elements soon gained control in many parts of Africa. In criticising Imanuel Geiss's argument that industrialisation in Africa was the cause of the 'the strikes, mass-demonstrations and boycotts', Peter Esedebe insists that he 'missed the point'. As Esedebe sums up: 'The explanation for both the militancy and the deep involvement of the trade unions in post-war nationalist movements lies more in the newly acquired nationalist ideas of the returned soldiers and the Manchester deliberations than in any other factors.'[65]

Despite the efforts of George Padmore and the small independent Left to foster the break-up of the Empire, the broad labour movement was quite content to tolerate the exploitation of the black Africans after the election of the Labour government. Almost completely unaware of the significance of Pan-Africanism, the labour movement's indifferent to what was happening amongst black Africans ensured that the Pan-Africans would, as Peter Abrahams predicted, 'go it alone'.

IV

By 1944 the Pan-African movement was gaining irresistable strength and political influence under the leadership of George Padmore. At the same time, Claude McKay was baptised in the Catholic Church in Chicago. As a result of a constant racial insults and the abuse heaped upon him by the Stalinists as well as bitter poverty and disappointments, he died in 1948 a very sad and disillusioned man.

The real tragedy of the last phase of Claude McKay's life was the failure of the democratic Left to make enough space for him to live and function in. In analysing why McKay became a Roman Catholic, James R. Giles said: 'Ellen Tarry's generosity began to represent Catholic benevolence to McKay; and he contrasted that generosity with the indifference and neglect of his former leftist associates. Thus, one feels that a unique combination of personal gratitude and resentment had much to do with his choice of a last philosophical home'.[66] In summing up McKay's predicament in those last years, Wayne F. Cooper says: 'Having found no place for himself within the black community and having rejected a servile role as a spokesman for either capitalism or communism, McKay turned to the Church simply for personal salvation'.[67]

Although George Padmore was much less detached about 'communism' than Claude McKay, he became increasingly critical of Stalin and Stalinists. As early as 1945 Padmore persuaded the Pan-African Congress in Manchester to support a policy of non-alignment, though the 'trend in the British Labour Party was still for close co-operation with the Soviet Union'.[68] With the passage of time, he became even more disillusioned with the white European Left. When he published, *Pan-Africanism or Communism* in 1956, he wrote: 'Lenin saw clearly what Marx, having died before imperialism attained its zenith, was unable to see, the gradual corruption of the European socialist movements though their "bourgeoisification".'[69] This was real heresy.

Although Ghana did not achieve her formal independence until 1957, Kwame Nkrumah had already wrested power from the British in the Gold Coast by 1951. On the declaration of independence, Padmore was appointed the Head of the Department of African Affairs. In assessing the significance of Padmore's role in Ghana's struggle for independence, C.L.R. James has written:

About Padmore I have written that he was one of the finest political organisers of the twentieth century. I not only wrote this. It was asked of Macmillan: "What was the thing in your ministry that you remember and are most proud of?" and he had the nerve to say: "The granting of freedom to African territories". I remember the difficulties Padmore had in mobilising the freedom movements. Unfortunately, Padmore lived only one year after, then he took ill and died. I think it was the *New York Times* with which Padmore kept up an unceasing conflict and it was the broadcasters in the United States that gave him the title "Father of African Independence".[70]

Suspected of harbouring Trotskyist sympathies and critical of the associates with whom Nkrumah had surrounded himself, Padmore was, according to Frank Maitland, very disillusioned with the new Ghana.[71]

As independent socialism was increasingly crushed throughout the world between the end of the Second World War and George Padmore's death in 1959, a resurgent Western capitalism and an aggressive Stalinism combined forces to thwart the emergence of democratic socialist forces from below. In such circumstances, there was no longer a spiritual or philosophical home for black heretics who believed in socialism-from-below.

But if disillusionment with the European socialist movements played a major role in the development of Pan-Africanism, George Padmore had probably lost any real hope of socialism in Africa when he went to Ghana in 1958. In a moving account of Padmore's last appearance before a socialist audience in London, Frank Maitland, a veteran socialist and activist in the Independent Labour Party, said:

I went to the farewell meeting that the Ghanaians put on for George and I especially remember that a young trade union leader told the meeting that he had come to London to ask the Trades Union Congress to help the Ghanaian unions to organise themselves to take over the industries there and the Trades Union Congress turned them down flat. When I took part in discussion, I reminded them that if they were going to replace the white colonialists with black capitalists, black generals, black landlords, black bankers, etc., they would not be making a socialist revolution but only changing colours. So that when I came to shake hands with George, he was not willing to say anything – not that I minded because I understood what was going on and why he went.[72]

Chapter 8

Clara Zetkin and Countess Markievicz: Socialist women

What I mean is that they (socialist mothers) must, above all, teach that equality is not something that is given, it must be deserved and won; and that women will conquer equality with men just as soon as they are inwardly freed from the feeling of inequality of sex dependence, and not one hour earlier.

Dora Montefiore

Though they were important figures in the German and Irish socialist movements before the First World War, Clara Zetkin (1857–1933) and Countess Markievicz (1868–1927) did not bequeath so rich an intellectual legacy to posterity as Rosa Luxemburg and other socialist women. Although they both experienced the security of material comfort and the privilege of higher education during their formative years in Germany and Ireland, they eventually reflected rather than confronted the crises of international socialism unleashed by the First World War. In contrast to Rosa Luxemburg and Sylvia Pankhurst, Zetkin and Markievicz increasingly compromised their socialist principles in the interests of *realpolitik*.

Clara Zetkin died when she was seventy-five years of age; Countess Markievicz when she was sixty-nine. Both died in tragic circumstances as socialist martyrs whose 'martyrdom' was somewhat inauthentic. And yet they were formidable socialist women before the First World War, and the tragic circumstances surrounding the last years of their lives could not have been foreseen before the advent of the Third International.

Although Clara Zetkin and Countess Markievicz attracted considerable attention from left-wing writers and historians in the early 1920s, the contemporary Left is not sure about their collective attitude to the socialist women who were active before the decline of the world-wide women's movement in 1920. Those historians who are sympathetic to Leninist interpretations of the socialists' experience before and after the First World War do not know where to place Markievicz in the Pantheon of 'Labour's mighty dead'. So they tend to ignore her altogether. In evaluating the role of Zetkin in socialist history, Leninist historians have ignored the pernicious role she played in socialist politics after 1919.[1]

Clara Zetkin and Countess Markievicz were not practitioners of *realpolitik* before the post-First World War period. During the previous age of socialist idealism and innocence, they expressed the latent *emancipatory* impulses of working-class people in their own countries. But although Zetkin was a socialist feminist, Markievicz was not a *consistent* feminist of any sort. Nevertheless they were both representative of the new age of socialist idealism – an age in which socialist women's liberatory immersion with working people contributed to socialists' confidence and led them to anticipate workers' revolutions.

I

Clara Eisser was born in a peasant village in Saxony in 1857. But although she was the eldest child of the local schoolmaster, she belonged to a well off, ambitious family. Her mother, Josephine Vitale, was a highly educated woman from the upper bourgeoisie in Leipiz. With progressive, enlightened and socially-conscious parents, Clara was encouraged to identify with the poor and unfortunate. This was the milieu in which she spent the first fourteen years of her life.[2]

As Eissner was growing up, the German universities did not admit women students. However, she was surrounded by middle-class men and women who believed in women's rights; and she was admitted to the teacher training college of the Von Steyher Institute in 1872 when she was fifteen. From the 1860s onwards Saxony had been the birthplace – and a stronghold – of the organised working class and the women's rights movement and Zetkins' parents and their friends had enlightened and progressive views about women.

Already a veteran socialist woman by 1889, when the Second International was founded in Paris, Clara Eissner was predestined to become a socialist feminist. Clearly, however, Eissner's socialist feminism was environmentally conditioned within a specific middle-class milieu. Nevertheless some of Eissner's extended family disapproved of her socialist activities, and she did not hesitate to break off personal relations with them.[3]

During the years of the illegality of the German Socialist party, Clara Eissner was an active socialist. In the 1870s and 1880s she lived abroad and took part in the activities of the socialist movements in France, Austria and Italy. The turning-point in Clara's life came in 1881 when she met and married a Russian revolutionary socialist, Ossip Zetkin. When Ossip died from tuberculosis in 1889, Clara Zetkin returned to Germany with her two young sons, Maxim and Konstantin. As soon as she returned to Germany, she became very friendly with Bebel. Thus she began to work on the illegal German socialist newspaper, *Sozial demokat*.[4]

As the women's movements developed into mass movements in countries throughout the world between 1889 and 1914, women like Rosa Luxemburg, Clara Zetkin and Countess Markievicz increasingly articulated the frustrations of working-class and middle-class women. But although women like Countess Markievicz in such countries as Ireland could begin to play a prominent role in politics, they did not always represent or express the aspirations or frustrations of middle class – and still less, of working-class-women. Indeed, the Irish women's movement was even smaller than the tiny socialist or labour movement.

Constance Georgina Gore-Booth was born at Lissadell, County Sligo in 1868. The eldest of three children, Constance was the daughter of Sir Henry Gore-Booth. One of the largest landowners in Ireland, Sir Henry was really a backward-looking traditionalist who did not believe in women's rights. Not surprisingly, Constance was not a consistent feminist, still less an uncompromising socialist feminist. From 1919 onwards the communists portrayed Countess Markievicz as a veteran socialist woman of international stature, though she had not always supported the agitation to give women the right to vote.

Although Countess Markievicz was brought up in a very conservative milieu, she eventually became an Irish nationalist who identified with the 'socialism' of James Connolly. Lacking the specific higher education and training in the methods of pedagogy acquired by such women as Clara Zetkin and Rosa Luxemburg, Constance Georgina Gore-Booth did not possess the latent traits of an intellectual or a thinker. Though she displayed an early talent for painting and wood-carving, Constance was subsequently very critical of the 'education' she had received as a young woman. In 1900 she went to Paris to study painting; and she met and married Count Casimir Markievicz.[5]

The marriage was not a very happy one; and the Countess increasingly went her own way. It was significant that Constance Georgina Gore-Booth should have become an actress. As a forty-year old actress, she discovered and then identified with Irish nationalism. In glancing back to the political 'education' she had received as a young woman, she explained that Irish history had been 'taboo'. Despite what Sir Henry Gore-Booth had said during Constance's youth about the irrelevance of Irish history, the Countess did become embroiled in Ireland's wrong-resenting sense of suffering from historic-grievances. In 1908 she discovered a portrait of Robert Emmet, the Irish patriot, and she joined the struggle for Irish freedom.[6]

In a major study of *Women and American Socialism, 1870–1920*, Mari Jo Buhle has insisted that:

The distance between formidable figures like Clara Zetkin and the average comrade kept the woman question at a relatively abstract theoretical plane in Germany, while women in the United States engaged in an almost continuous, rough-and-tumble debates with experimentation and argument at nearly every level of the movement.

In eschewing the temptation to fashion 'a saga from the biographies of leftist heroes like Lucy Parsons, Emma Goldman, "Mother" Jones, or Elizabeth Gurley Flynn', Mari Jo Buhle focuses on rank-and-file women in the American socialist movement.[7] However, if the *exceptionalism* of American socialism was seen in the greater prominence of rank-and-file women in class-cum-feminist struggles, Countess Markievicz owed her post-1916 prominence in socialist history to the *relative* absence of socialist women in modern Ireland.

Before Countess Markievicz campaigned for militant workers in Dublin in 1913, Clara Zetkin had been immersed in class struggles for several decades. Just as the thought-worlds of Antonio Gramsci and Rosa Luxemburg did not impinge on each other until the Bolshevik revolution, so were Clara Zetkin and Countess Markievicz excluded from a common communist calendar of socialist 'saints' and 'martyrs' until the Third International's 'historians' began to re-write working-class history in 1919.

Yet despite the important differences in the experience and history of socialist women in Germany and America before the First World War, Clara Zetkin was successful in raising important questions about socialist theory in relation to the struggle for women's emancipation from patriarchy. Moreover, although male chauvinism existed in most socialist movements before the disappearance of the international women's movements in 1920, it was particularly pernicious in the English labour movement. As the women's movement was in the process of disintegration in 1920, Shaw Desmond could depict a major socialist woman in the language of right-wing traditionalists: 'And Clara Zetkin of the *motherly bosoms* and the great expansive mouth is driving with me once more in a London hansom, telling me of her hopes and fears for the international socialism that was to her life itself'.[8] The real importance of Zetkin's ideas on socialist feminism before the outbreak of the First World War was their prefigurative attempt to reach out to a new conception of the better socialist world to come.

Certainly, the Second International as an organisation was much more sympathetic to the agitations of socialist (as distinct from bourgeois) women for *emancipation* than the Third International under Lenin. Although the progressive ideas and agitations of socialist women in the Second International were important in *ameliorating* the existing oppression of working-class women, many socialists failed to live up to high ideals they sometimes subscribed to. As Richard Evans puts it: 'The writings of Bebel and Zetkin were the basis for socialist theory on women's emancipation in every country, but socialist practice was another matter'.[9]

Unlike Clara Zetkin, Rosa Luxemburg was not a feminist. Yet Luxemburg was much more progressive in relation to sexual questions than either Zetkin or Markievicz. At a time when Wilhelm Liebknecht and August Bebel were arguably expressing 'generally repressive sexual attitudes', Zetkin refused to 'accept birth control or abortion'.[10] Moreover, it was Luxemburg who questioned socialist orthodoxy in sexual questions. As David Kennedy put it: 'In 1913 Rosa Luxemburg in Germany and Anatole France in France proposed that workers undertake a "birth strike", a cessation of childbearing in order to stop the flow of exploited manpower into the industrial and military machines'.[11]

So although Clara Zetkin was a socialist feminist – a feminism environmentally – conditioned by her untypical formative milieu in Saxony – and Countess Markievicz was not, they did not develop a really progressive prefigurative socialist sexual morality. While Zetkin and Luxemburg were on the extreme Left in the German socialist movement, they did not always agree about either the sexual or the political dimension of socialist politics.

Zetkin's major achievement before the First World War was the creation of the Socialist Women's International. As founder and secretary of this international women's organisation, she also published her magazine, *Die Gleicheit*, as an organ of international socialist women. In encouraging working-class women to read and think for themselves, Zetkin sought to instill deep socialist convictions in the minds and hearts of working people.[12]

Clara Zetkin was too radical for the German socialists, and by 1908 she had ceased to be a powerful figure in the German Social Democratic Women's Movement. Engaged in a succession of political disputes with other socialist women in pre-war Germany, Zetkin was defeated by moderate and right-wing socialist elements including Karl Kautsky and Louise Zeitz. As J. Strain explained: 'Zetkin led the SPD women in Wurttemburg but her influence on the national level was gradually surrendered to Zietz who had frequent face-to-face contact with socialist women all over Germany.' By 1914 Zetkin was one of a small minority of radical, left-wing socialist women within the German socialist movement.[13]

Yet Zetkin and Markievicz had one thing in common during the decade before the outbreak of the First World War. They had both belonged to an almost existentialist world of the *avant-garde*. In contrast to the very intellectual thought-world occupied by Zetkin and Rosa Luxemburg, Markievicz was immersed in the world of Irish nationalism and the Abbey Theatre. As Amanda Sebestyen put it: 'Constance was moving towards politics, he (the Count) wanted to stay in the theatre – in their original Bohemian life, one foot in *avant-garde* nationalism but the other in Dublin Castle.' Although the Gore-Booth sisters had founded a woman's suffrage society in Sligo in 1896, and although Constance was an *'advanced' woman* in a society where the women's movement was small and lacking in real influence, she did not attach a high priority to the woman question.[14]

The turning-point in Countess Markievicz's life came in 1913 when she helped James Connolly to fuse the *avant-garde* literary Nationalist movement with the small socialist movement in Dublin. In contrast to Zetkin, Markievicz did not have much of a record of socialist activity before the First World War. However, the dramatic conflict in Dublin in 1913 between capital and labour pushed Countess Markievicz into the forefront of the international labour scene at a moment when Zetkin was fading into the background.

The Dublin strike in 1913 attracted sympathetic attention throughout Ireland, Scotland, Wales, France, Germany and America. The world of Labour was, as Desmond Ryan put it, 'stirred to the very depths' and money to support the strikers and their families poured in from countries throughout the world. In depicting the role of Markievicz in the struggle, Ryan summed up:

Madame de Markievicz was the most prominent Republican personality who, whole-heartedly, associated herself with the workers' side in the struggle upon many platforms, and in the communal kitchen she organised in Liberty Hall to feed the strikers' wives and children, winning the gratitude and admiration of James Connolly by her vigorous advocacy and untiring efforts.

One of the most significant aspects of this bitter struggle between labour and capital was the appearance of the Citizen Army under Captain Jack White.[15]

Although Irish socialism was increasingly submerged in bourgeois nationalism after 1913, the Labour scene in Dublin had already been transformed beyond recognition. As W.R. Ryan argued: 'Withal it was plain and palpable that Labour in Dublin had suffered a spiritual revolution.' In depicting the crucial role of Francis Sheehy-Skeffington and Countess Markievicz, Ryan emphasised that: 'The incoming of men and women, more socially favoured, to help in any and every fashion, from street-corner speaking to cooking and serving in Liberty Hall and elsewhere, was a new feature in labour struggles in the capital'.[16]

II

In 1915 Clara Zetkin organised in Bern an international women's conference against the war. When she returned to Germany, Zetkin was imprisoned for a brief period. Throughout the rest of the First World War, she was active in anti-war activities. A prominent figure in the Spartacus League and the Independent Social Democratic party, she worked alongside Karl Liebknecht, Frantz Mehring and Rosa Luxemburg.

In 1915 Zetkin issued an anti-war manifesto to 'Women of the Working People' in the world at large. Adopted by the illegal conference in Bern attended by delegates from Britain, France, Germany, Italy, Poland, Russia, Holland and Switzerland, she was responsible for the first organised expression of socialist opposition to the war. The manifesto ended with the challenging words: 'Down with war! Break through to socialism'.[17]

On New Year's Day, 1916, Karl Liebknecht, Clara Zetkin and others met in secret in Berlin to establish *Gruppe Internationale*, which became the Spartacus League in November 1918. This was, in late 1918, the nucleus of the German Communist party (KPD). In 1916 and in 1917 Zetkin worked closely with Liebknecht in spreading socialist as well as anti-militarist propaganda. In May, 1917, the executive committee of the Social Democratic Party of Germany (SPD) removed Zetkin from the editorship of *Gleicheit*. Although the SPD leaders argued that her articles were out of touch with the feelings of working-class women, they were really angered by *Gleicheit*'s attacks on the 'majority socialists' enthusiasm for the war.[18]

What was not in doubt in 1914 was Clara Zetkin's profound emotional commitment to left-wing socialism. At the very outbreak of the war the small group around Zetkin, Luxemburg, Leibknecht and Mehring issued a statement announcing their intention of opposing the imperialist war and the war policies of the official SPD leadership. They also welcomed the Russian revolution in 1917 with great enthusiasm, though Luxemburg was much more critical of certain aspects of Leninism than the other three leaders of the future Spartacus League.[19]

While Clara Zetkin, Rosa Luxemburg and Karl Liebknecht were preparing to oppose the war at the beginning of September, 1914, Countess Markievicz and James Connolly were already making their own insurrectionary plans in Ireland. As early as 25 September, 1914, Markievicz and Connolly were planning to seize the Mansion House in Dublin where John Redmond and H.H. Asquith were addressing an army recruiting meeting. However, the plan was abandoned when it was 'discovered that soldiers were in occupation of the Mansion House'. But on the same evening Markievicz and Connolly addressed a mass meeting at Stephen's Green. In a vivid description of this meeting, R.M. Fox wrote: 'Citizen Army men armed with rifles and bayonets guarded this meeting, standing side by side with Royal Irish Constabulary men gripping their carbines. The rifles and bayonets of both sides glinted under the street lamps and the situation was tense – especially as the Citizen Army had no ammunition'.[20]

From the outbreak of the First World War, Countess Markievicz and James Connolly were waiting their opportunity to initiate a nationalist-cum-socialist revolt. When the opportunity came in April, 1916, they did not hesitate to confront the military might of British imperialism. But in restricting himself to the comment that Irish Labour was 'divided on the issue of the (Easter) Rising' in 1916, R.M. Fox was concealing the historical fact that most socialists had been hostile to Connolly's nationalist role in the events of 1916. In a statement characterising the hard-Left's response to the Easter Rising, the editor of *The Plebs*, the organ of the movement for independent working-class education in Britain, wrote: 'The tragedy of the revolt, from the socialist point of view, is that "romantic nationalism" was so largely the inspiration of it; and that Connolly – the Industrial Unionist, the sane writer and thinker – should have been goaded by circumstances into sharing in it'.[21] He was not, of course, goaded into it. Countess Markievicz and James Connolly had decided upon the *efficacy* of a nationalist uprising in August, 1914.[22]

Although the communists did not really transform socialist women like Countess Markievicz into important mythical figures until the beginning of 1919, the historical processes unleashed by the First World War contributed immensely to the decline of the women's movement and the significance of socialist women in labour movements. Vladimir I. Lenin was much less sympathetic to the preoccupations of socialist women than many of the leading figures in the Second International. Unlike Leon Trotsky, he did not display any sympathy towards sexual experimentation or modern psychology. Women's role in Bolshevism was not very prominent after 1917, and 'the Bolsheviks sometimes tended to regard the emancipation of women as something that would have to wait until after the revolution'.[23]

As the communists discovered the importance of the Irish socialist tradition epitomised by Countess Markievicz and James Connolly, Irish socialism was being increasingly submerged in bourgeois nationalism. By 1920 Ireland was in a state of revolution. In 1920 the British government tried to settle the Irish question by an Act establishing two strictly subordinate Parliaments, one for the six north-eastern counties and one for the rest of Ireland.

The character of the political struggle in Ireland, and particularly the methods of the Black and Tans, a special force of ex-servicemen imported into Ireland to wreak 'reprisals', had shocked the civilised world. In July, 1921, a truce was signed with the Irish leaders, and negotiations began, during which the British government succeeded in dividing their Irish opponents. Arthur Griffith, the founder and intellectual leader of Sinn Fein, and P.W. Collins, the brain of the Republican army were prepared to compromise, and on 6 December signed a treaty by which Ireland, outside the six north-eastern counties, was constituted a Free State within the British Empire. The treaty was promptly repudiated by the Sinn Fein President, Eamon de Valera, and the more militant Republicans, but was accepted by a small majority of the Dail in January, 1922, and confirmed by the Irish electorate in June.[24]

Although Constance Markievicz was sentenced to death for the role she had played in the Easter revolt, she was granted an amnesty in June 1917 on account of her 'sex alone'. In prison she had wanted to die alongside such executed comrades as James Connolly; and she began to receive instruction in the Catholic faith before she was released from prison. A Sinn Fein candidate during the general election of 1918, Constance was elected as the member of Parliament for the St. Patrick's Division of Dublin. The first woman to be elected to the House of Commons, she was doubly assured of her place in Irish as well as in British history.[25]

But Markievicz lost all sense of political direction after the 'legal' murder of James Connolly. Yet despite the communists' attempts in 1919–21 to portray her as an almost mythical figure of heroic stature, Markievicz moved increasingly to the Right and allowed herself to be used by an evolving bourgeois-nationalist Establishment in Dublin. Although she became known as the Red Countess on the Clyde – then a 'red centre' in the west of Scotland – she was unhappy with this description and perception of her political position. As R.M. Fox explained: 'Incidentally it might be mentioned that, although she was a firm believer in and a keen advocate of Connolly's revolutionary ideas, she did not care for the label of Red Countess – it was not distinctly Irish enough for her. She preferred the appellation given her on the Continent, where she was the Green Countess'.[26]

When Eamon de Valera played a major part in forming the first Irish

Cabinet in the Free State, Markievicz was chosen as the Minister for Labour. Far from behaving in a distinctly socialist way, she became a *conventional*, though progressive, politician. Although she worked with a group of Irish women, the Countess did not attach more importance to the woman question after the First World War. And yet she was a complex nationalist personality, not an authentic *socialist woman* in the years after 1916.

Constance Markievicz was opposed to the Treaty with Britain. When she opposed the Treaty in the Dail in January 1922, she said:

Looking as I do for the prosperity of the many, for the happiness and content of the workers, what I stand for is James Connolly's ideal of a Workers' Republic, a Co-operative Commonwealth. . . . Can any Irishman take that oath honourably and then go back and prepare to fight for an Irish Republic, or even to work for the Republic?[27]

However, in contrast to Clara Zetkin, Markievicz became very critical of 'State socialism' and Bolshevism in communist Russia. By 1922 she had ceased to be a socialist woman. Identifying with James Connolly's ideas in speeches in the Irish Parliament, she became muddled, confused, extremely nationalistic, and disoriented in practice. In attempting to explain what she meant by a Workers' Republic when she spoke in the Dail in 1922, she was incoherent. As Sean O'Faolain observed: 'When she comes to answer the charge that she does not know what she means by the term Republic, her reply is of the feeblest'.[28] If she had not become more and more caught up in the opportunism and *realpolitik* of the early 1920s, she might have escaped the tragic fate that engulfed Clara Zetkin after the execution of Rosa Luxemburg.

Although there were powerful objective factors motivating the decline of the international women's movement (including the autonomous socialist women's movement) from 1920 onwards, Clara Zetkin and Countess Markievicz were incredibly *dependent* on their respective mentors – Rosa Luxemburg and James Connolly. With the murder of Luxemburg in 1919 and the legal murder of Connolly in 1916, Zetkin and Markievicz at first reflected and then fashioned the growing tragedies and crises of international socialism. Moreover, the disappearance of their socialist mentors was responsible for their confusion and theoretical disorientation, not innate moral corruption. What the First World War demonstrated in practice was the importance of the factors socialist had debated for decades beforehand – the role of the individual and the place of accidents within the historical process.

Elected to the Reichstag as a communist deputy in 1920, Zetkin spent most of the last decade of her life living in Moscow. During the years between 1920 and her death in 1933, she became an uncritical 'communist' functionary and bureaucrat. The first signs of her lack of socialist resolve and determination were seen in 1922 when she betrayed Dr Paul Levi who had also been elected as the other communist deputy to the Reichstag in 1920. Then she began to *reflect* the end of the era of socialist innocence in international labour history.[29] In the very early 1920s Zetkin was close to those in the German Communist party who were critical of Moscow's leadership of the Third International. Yet she was soon absorbed by the powerful and developing bureaucracy in the Third International.

III

Although Clara Zetkin initially accepted, approved of, and encouraged Paul Levi's criticisms of the Russian leaders in the Third International, she always refused to break with them officially. After the murder of Rosa Luxemburg, she became very critical of the Left as well as the ultra-left in the German communist movement. In tracing Zetkin's zig-zags inside German communism, Rosa Levine-Meyer's portrayal of the once major socialist woman in Germany was not very flattering.[30] By 1925 when Zetkin was proposed as a Presidential candidate by such right-wing communists as Wilhelm Pieck, this was rejected because most delegates regarded her as 'an outspoken Right-Winger'.[31] When Zetkin was elected as the president of the new organisation, the German Red Women's and Girls' League in the same year, socialist feminism had ceased to be important in the international communist movement.[32]

With the rise of fascism, Stalinism and milder forms of bourgeois nationalism, socialist feminism was eradicated. Despite countless eulogistic biographies of Zetkin and Markievicz, they really became tools of different sorts of Establishments during the last phases of their lives. Although Philip S. Foner made assertions about Zetkin's democratic socialist aspirations during the last phase of her life, she was actually a willing tool of Joseph Stalin and the Russian bureaucracy.[33] Even before Stalin's rise to power, she came back to Germany from Russia with instructions from Lenin to 'burn Luxemburg's manuscript on the Russian revolution'. After initially supporting Paul Levi's plans to publish Luxemburg's important critique of Lenin and Bolshevism, Eliżbieta Ettinger says that: 'Zetkin wrote to Paul Levi to ask him to refrain from publishing the disputed manuscript'.[34]

The tragedy of Zetkin's last years was that she used superb socialist rhetoric to defend a profoundly anti-socialist *praxis*. Despite desperate illness, she returned to Germany in 1932 to open the new Reichstag. As the oldest deputy, she was allowed to give the opening speech before she went back to Stalin's Moscow to die. Furthermore, she was probably being very sincere when she said: 'I open the Reichstag in accordance with my duty as the oldest member, in the hope that despite my present ill-health I will live to open the first council-congress of Soviet Germany'.[35] The best assessment of Clara Zetkin has been provided by Eliżbieta Ettinger:

Capable of assimilating but not of creating ideas, "she never had her own opinion", Luxemburg wrote to Leon Jogiches; and she reported, "her entire speech was a *literal* repetition of my last five articles". Luxemburg's assessment proved right when, towards the end of her life, Clara Zetkin became Stalin's mouthpiece.[36]

Furthermore, Countess Markievicz increasingly moved against the Irish working class. Despite was R.M. Fox said about her attempts as the Minister of Labour to 'further the democratic ideals for which she stood', the objective reality was otherwise.[37] Far from identifying with the Irish strikes and strikers who raised the 'red flag' and attempted to form Soviets in various parts of Ireland in 1921, she became a practitioner of *realpolitik*. In summing up, Mike Milotte says:

Fearing that such activity would "disrupt the Republican cause", Markievicz recommended ameliorative action "to show the workers that we have their interest at heart", but her Cabinet colleagues preferred to retaliate.[38]

If Clara Zetkin and Countess Markievicz were absorbed by fundamentally anti-socialist bureaucracies during the last phase of their lives, this was not predestined or preordained. Because they had been rather *uncritical* socialist women before the cumulative crisis of international socialism deepened towards the end of the First World War, they did not have the intellectual or inner psychological resources to stand against the powerful anti-socialist currents of the early 1920s. However, they did not fail as advocates of militant, democratic socialism because they were socialist *women*, but because the 'balance of class forces' had created seemingly insoluble problems for socialists and the *socialist idea*.

Chapter 9

Leon Trotsky and C.L.R. James: Socialist fugitives

Socialism is about abolishing the domination of people by other people, about collectivism which is nobody's prison, about social equality and justice, about making people conscious of their power and able to control their destiny here and now.

Teodor Shanin

Leon Trotsky was murdered in 1940 by a GPU assassin, but his political legacy of hostility to all ruling classes continues to haunt the existing social order in Russia and Eastern Europe as much as in the West.[1] No longer a fugitive in the mid-1980s, the confident, optimistic and hard-working octogenarian, C.L.R. James is unique among the major figures of late twentieth-century socialism. In contrast to such influential left-wing politicians as Francois Mitterrand and Mario Soares, James does not hold office and he is not a member of any political party. A writer, speaker and lecturer, he is more of a prophet than a politician.

With the publication of three major collections of the writings of C.L.R. James – *The Future in the Present* (1977), *Spheres of Existence* (1980) and *At The Rendezvous of Victory* (1984) – and hour-long interviews on British television, the titanic revolutionary socialist scholar has become a *living* historical figure in the way that Eugene V. Debs was a legend before his death in 1926. Of the major figures of contemporary militant socialism – for example, Ernest Mandel, Paul Sweezy and Hal Draper – only James seems to express – and speak to – the latent forces of progressive, libertarian change with the combined and cumulative wisdom of the nineteenth and twentieth centuries.

Lev Davidovich Bronstein (1879–1940) was born into a family of well-to-do Jewish farmers in the Russian village of Yanovka near the Black Sea. Although he only adopted the pseudonym Leon Trotsky when he escaped from a Tsarist jail in 1902, he was alienated from the society around him at an early age. Despite his unwillingness to acknowledge it, Trotsky's Jewishness almost certainly played an important part in alienating him from Tsarist society. Culturally, spiritually and temperamentally, he was always an outsider.

C.L.R. James, who was born in 1901, did not feel himself to be an outsider. He was born into a comfortably-off middle-class family in Tunapuna, near Port of Spain, in Trinidad. His father was a sportsman and the head of a teachers' training college. His mother had an enormous influence on his formative development, because 'she read perpetually and as she put the books down I picked them up'. With a rebellious, questioning temperament, he eventually rejected the colonial world he was brought up in. A voracious reader when he was still a schoolboy, English novelists such as William Thackeray led him to anti-colonialism and ultimately towards socialism. As he explained in the autobiographical volume, *Beyond a Boundary*: 'I laughed with satiety at Thackeray's constant jokes and sneers and jibes at the aristocracy and at people in high places. Thackeray, not Marx, bears the heaviest responsibility for me.'[2]

In challenging established opinion with all its institutions and institutionalised values, Leon Trotsky and C.L.R. James required the immense confidence, pride and dignity they had forged for themselves during their formative years in Tsarist Russia and colonial Trinidad. Although nineteenth-century Marxism engendered an internationalist socialist world-outlook amongst a minority of working-class men and women and peasants, it could scarcely cope with the cumulative crises of the 1920s and 1930s without questioning some of its own orthodox assumptions. But while Trotsky restricted his own role to questioning the traditions of the Second International, James would eventually question the attitudes and assumptions of the Fourth International.

Most of Trotsky's major achievements were behind him by the time C.L.R. James was *converted* to revolutionary socialism in the early 1930s. By 1929 Trotsky was, as he acknowledged later, living on 'a planet without a visa'. A new world of 'totalitarian collectivism' was already creating a unique type of *socialist fugitive*. While Trotsky had been a fugitive in Tsarist times, he had not been deprived of the right of political asylum until the advent of the totalitarism created by Stalinism and capitalist economic crises. Certainly, when Trotsky and James met in Coyoacan in 1939, they were both undoubtedly socialist fugitives.

During his fifteen-year sojourn in America between 1938 and 1953, C.L.R. James was objectively a socialist fugitive. As Paul Buhle puts it in his stimulating introduction to the book he edited, *C.L.R. James: His Life and Work*: 'Unlike other intellectual giants whom immigration brought to American radicalism – Morris Winchevsky, Daniel De Leon and Moissye Olgin, to name three – James was Black and an illegal. He had to keep a low profile.' Then he was deported from America in 1953. When James returned to Trinidad in 1965 as a cricket correspondent to report the Test series, Dr Eric Williams, the 'Marxist' Prime Minister, put him under house arrest.[3] Before the break-up of Stalinism and McCarthyism in the mid-1950s those men and women like Trotsky, James, Raya Dunayevskaya and Abraham Leon who fought for democratic socialism were forced to accept the status of fugitives.[4]

Although their lives only impinged on each other for a few brief years in the late 1930s, Leon Trotsky and C.L.R. James had a great deal in common. More than most other Marxist scholars with the exception of Franz Mehring and Georgy Plekhanov, they produced *sustained works* of *literary criticism* in which they probed the peculiarities of modern totalitarian and elitist capitalist societies. They were both deeply hostile to the totalitarian practice of putting, in Max Eastman's phrase, 'artists in uniform'. They shared many other common attitudes and theoretical preoccupations.

In the 'dark times' of the late 1930s Trotsky and James were very aware of the major crisis of 'Marxian' socialism. Meanwhile, the distinctive cultural and political backgrounds they had emerged from – Trotsky's cosmopolitan background in the milieu of Second International socialism and James's background in a self-conscious literary conclave of West Indian nationalists in the 1920s – shaped the responses with which they met the crossroads-crisis of 1939–40.

The distinctive backgrounds of the two titans of twentieth-century socialism played a major role in their fundamental attitudes to life as well as politics. While Trotsky remained austere, puritanical and intransigent in his attachment to the authoritarian traditions of Bolshevism, James displayed great enthusiasm for good booze, women, sport and nightlife in multi-racial New York. Unlike Trotsky who thought that working men's participation in sport, whether football or cricket, was a diversion from the class struggle, James wrote: 'In my private mind, however, I was increasingly aware of large areas of human existence that my history and my politics did not seem to cover.' Later on, he observed that:

In 1940 came a crisis in my political life. I rejected the Trotskyist version of Marxism and set about to re-examine the reorganise my view of the world, which was (and remains) essentially a political one. It took more than ten years, but by 1952 I once more felt on solid ground, and in consequence I planned a series of books.[5]

I

Leon Trotsky spent a large part of his early adult life in Tsarist prisons. With the exception of the brief sojourn he spent in Vienna before the First World War, he often displayed the embattled attitudes and mentality of an outsider and the permanent intransigence of a socialist fugitive. Even when he was at the pinnacle of his power in the Kremlin in 1923, he saw political consciousness and the ongoing de-radicalising processes through the sort of personal and subjective lens that he depicted as un-Marxist in the life of Joseph Stalin. Although he insisted that 'the changes in *the anatomy* of revolutionary society' was primary, he focused on the *psychological* aspect in explaining the rise of Stalinism:

Gossiping over a bottle of wine or returning from the ballet, one smug official would say to another: "He can think of nothing but permanent revolution". The accusations of unsociability, of individualism, or aristocratism, were closely connected with this particular mood. . . . It was because of this that I lost power, and it was this that determined the form which this loss took.[6]

For an orthodox Marxist, Trotsky attached an inordinate and surprising importance to the *psychological* factor in socialist politics. As a school boy, he hated and fought against injustice. When he was only ten years old, he was expelled from school for a year because he joined in a demonstration against a teacher who had bullied another boy simply because he was of German origin. In his autobiography, *My Life*, he described this incident with intense passion:

Such was my first political test, as it were. The class was henceforth divided into three distinct groups: the tale-bearers and envious on one side, the frank and courageous boys on the other, and the neutral and vacillating mass in the middle. These three groups never quite disappeared even in later years.[7]

A socialist fugitive for a large part of his life, C.L.R. James never developed the embattled mentality of a fugitive. Far from behaving like a fugitive, he was always a warm-hearted human being who never lost the 'common touch' or the ability to move with ease and communicate with 'the mariners, renegades and castaways' in the language of the market place. Because the formative experiences, responses and political attitudes of the two men provide the key to understanding their 'Marxism', it is necessary to at least glance at their *interpretation* of the different worlds they lived in, in their early years.

In a revealing account of his early life in Odessa in the 1880s, Trotsky wrote: 'My life was not of the street, of the market-place, of sports and outdoor exercises. I made up for these deficiences when on vacation in the village. The city seemed to me created for study and reading. The boys' street brawls seemed to me disgraceful.' Moreover, although he was sensitive to the cruelty of anti-Semitism, the young Trotsky, in Irving Howe's phrase, 'entered eagerly upon the total abandonment of "Jewishness" which was becoming a tradition among Jewish revolutionaries in Russia'.[8]

By contrast, James did not express any interest in politics until after he left school. His life was spent in the streets, the back-yards and in the market-place. As he explained later about his early education: 'But this school was in a colony ruled autocratically by Englishmen. What then about the National Question? It did not exist for me'. He was, in fact, an insider. As he put it: 'The race question did not have to be agitated. It was there. But in our little Eden it never troubled us'.[9] By the late 1920s he was a leading figure in West Indian nationalist and literary circles.

Like Daniel De Leon and H.M. Hyndman before him, Leon Trotsky was always somewhat autocratic in temperament. But in contrast to De Leon and Hyndman, whose autocratic behaviour was mitigated by the milieu of the socialism of the Second International – that is, during the apostolic period of international socialism – Trotsky's autocratic behaviour was frequently magnified by the authoritarian socialism engendered by Tsarism.

Being very conscious of the authoritarian cast of Leon Trotsky's thought, Victor Serge attempted to justify it in 1940 by asserting that:

His absolute conviction that he knew the truth made him impervious to argument towards the end and detracted from his scientific spirit. He was authoritarian, because in our time of barbaric struggles thought turned into action must of necessity become authoritarian.[10]

However, the roots of Trotsky's dictatorial socialism were planted long before the advent of 'totalitarian collectivism' in the 1920s. This was seen in the most liberal of the Russian socialists' attitude to such a simple fundamental reality as workers' *consciousness*.

In a significant essay published in 1943, Victor Serge placed Leon Trotsky's socialism in the crucial context of the nineteenth-century Russian intelligentsia. Since the Russia intelligentsia played a more important role in shaping the authoritarian character of twentieth-century 'Soviet' socialism than the proletariat, Serge deserves to be quoted at length:

The greatness of Trotsky's personality was a collective rather than an individual triumph. He was the highest expression of a human type produced in Russia between 1870 and 1920, the flower of half a century of the Russian intelligentsia. Tens of thousands of his revolutionary comrades shared his traits – and I by no means exclude many of his political opponents from this company. Like Lenin, Trotsky simply carried to a high pitch of individual perfection the common characteristics of several generations of Russian revolutionary intellectuals. Glimpses of the type appear in Turgenev's novels, notably Bazarov, but it comes out much more clearly in the great revolutionary struggles. The militants of the Narodnaya Volya were men and women of this stamp; even purer examples were the Social-Revolutionary terrorists of the 1905 period, and the Bolsheviks of 1917. For a man like Trotsky to arise, it was necessary that thousands and thousands of individuals should establish the type over a long historical period. It was a broad social phenomenon, not a sudden flashing of a comet, and those who speak of Trotsky as a "unique" personality, conforming to the classical bourgeois idea of the "Great Man", are much mistaken.

But in contrasting the integration of Trotsky's thought and action with 'the after-dinner heroism of Western socialists', Serge was unwittingly raising grave questions about the prospects of world socialism. For if socialism had been impossible in Western Europe, the dim prospect for world revolution after 1917 surely made Stalinism inevitable.[11]

While Trotsky's environmentally-conditioned authoritarian socialism was forged in the milieu of the disaffected Russian intelligentsia, the socialism of C.L.R. James crystallised in the West Indies and in working-class communities in England. Although James became a liberal type of socialist in the West Indies in the late 1920s under the impact of the world-shattering Russian revolution, his socialism was bookish, literary and abstract until he came to live in England in 1932.[12]

The year before Hitler came to power in Germany was a decisive one in the political development of C.L.R. James. As Margaret Busby explained:

In 1932 he came to England with the encouragement of an old acquaintance and cricketing opponent, Learie Constantine, whom he was to help write his autobiography, and for a while James lived in Constantine's adopted town of Nelson, Lancashire. He had brought with him his first political book, *The Life of Captain Cipriani*, a pioneer work arguing the case for West Indian self-government which was published that year in Nelson with Constantine's assistance, and later in a shortened version by Leonard Wolfe's Hogarth Press in London.

In his own autobiography, *Beyond a Boundary*, James explained that between 1932 and 1938 'fiction-writing drained out of me and was replaced by politics'. Moreover, he depicted the process which led him to revolutionary socialism: 'I soon made friends in the local Labour Party, attended their meetings, spoke to them. Some of Constantine's intimate friends who came to the house often found congenial company in me, apart from cricket. My Labour and socialist ideas had been got from books and were rather abstract. These humorously *cynical* working men were a revelation and brought me down to earth'.[13]

In contrast to Trotsky, C.L.R. James was sympathetic to existentialism and nationalism. Without abandoning the radical spirit of Marxism, he increasingly rejected much of Trotskyist orthodoxy. But the key to James's socialist heterodoxy resides in the West Indian milieu in which he formed his early intellectual attitudes, just as Trotsky's orthodox socialism was formed within the Russian intelligentsia depicted by Bertram D. Wolfe as being 'precariously suspended as in a void between an uncomprehending autocratic monarchy above and an uncomprehending, unenlightened mass below'.[14] James's deep involvement with the common ruck of humankind was the decisive factor which allowed him to analyse and rescue the essence of Marxism from the cumulative crises which crystallised with the birth of 'totalitarian collectivism' in Russia and Germany in the 1930s.

For Trotsky the genesis of socialism as a potential reality really existed in the bold and innovative ideas of artists and radical intellectuals. Towards the end of his life, he put the argument thus:

Not a single progressive idea has begun with a "mass base", otherwise it would not have been a progressive idea. It is only in the last stage that the idea finds its masses – if, of course, it answers the needs of progress. The more daring the pioneers show in their ideas and actions – the more bitterly they oppose themselves to established authority which rests on a conservative "mass base" . . .

In contrast to this approach to the socialist struggle, James saw 'socialism' within workers' day-to-day lives. No matter how *potential* this socialism was, it could be seen vibrating, pulsating and struggling to articulate itself in the midst of ruling-class repression. As Gregory Rigsby observes: 'In his short stories and in his novel *Minty Alley*, James creates this human fellowship. As early as 1929, in his short story "Triumph", James deliberately sets the action among characters who did not enjoy a high standard of living – the porters, the prostitutes, cartermen, washer-women, and domestic servants of the city. Yet despite their material deprivations, these people enjoy a liveliness and vitality which is the essence of the good life.'[15]

In a perceptive and brilliant essay on 'Trotsky's Place in History', C.L.R. James made an interesting point when he said: 'Being determines consciousness. In the struggle for socialism he strides through the world, a titan among men, excelling in every field he touched. An exile half his life, persecuted as no man has been persecuted, he lived the fullest life of any human being hitherto. The field of being which he chose developed his consciousness to a pitch reached by few men. That consciousness he did his best to pass on to us.' This was, in 1940, an orthodox Trotskyist attitude to class-consciousness, though James would soon make a new distinction between Marxists and 'economic materialists'.[16]

Nevertheless, the comment about Trotsky's choice of a 'field of being' was full of insight and significance. For what Marx meant by social being was something like collective being (social experience) and by social consciousness he indicated something like common cultural life. Leon Trotsky's social being was a part of the collective existence of the nineteenth-century Russian intelligentsia and the common cultural life of that intelligentsia was cast in an authoritarian mould of fugitivism. In sketching in the common cultural life of the nineteenth-century Russian intelligentsia with its excessive emphasis on literature and ideas, Bertram D. Wolfe said:

Not having much else to live by, they acquired the power of living by ideas alone. "The thoroughly true-to-type intolerance of the Russian intelligentsia", observes Berdyaev, "was self-protective; only so it could preserve itself in a hostile world; only thanks to fanaticism could it weather persecution".[17]

From his conversion to Marxism in 1896 the fanaticism was always present in Trotsky's life. Even such a sympathetic biographer as Joel Carmichael identified Trotsky's typical obsession with the Revolution as an Idea:

Young Bronstein found it quite incomprehensible, for instance, how anyone with even the slightest profession of revolutionary interest could show any concern at all for parents, relatives, or friends. The slightest weakness in this respect was already, in his eyes, a sort of treachery to The Revolution.[18]

Although socialist intellectuals in the West had always merged their literary with their political interests, literature and literary criticism assumed a different function in Tsarist Russia. In the absence of direct political discussion or the dialogue so essential to 'civil society' in the West, Russian literature was, in Bertram D. Wolfe's phrase, 'but another form of social criticism in the second degree'. The inseparability of literature and politics, together with the Bolshevik conception of the role of the 'vanguard Party' in working-class struggles, was a product of actual Russian life in the late nineteenth century. Trotsky's programmatic recipes for working-class politics in the West in the later twentieth century never escaped from the world-view he developed in his youth in Tsarist Russia. This was why he sent a letter to the founding conference of the Fourth International in 1938 emphasising the inseparability of imaginative literature and socialist politics:

To prevent the shipwreck and rotting-away of humanity the proletariat needs a perspicacious, honest and fearless leadership. No one can give this leadership except the Fourth International basing itself on the entire experience of past defeats and victories. Permit me, nevertheless, to cast a glance at the historic mission of the Fourth International not only with the eyes of a proletarian revolutionist but with the eyes of the artist which I am by profession. I have never separated these two spheres of my activity. My pen has never served me as a toy for my personal diversion or for that of the ruling classes. I have always forced myself to depict the sufferings, the hopes and struggles of the working classes because that is how I approach life, and therefore art, which is an inseparable part of it.[19]

Seen in this context, Trotsky's attitude to imaginative literature was utilitarian rather than enlightened.

In contrast to Trotsky, C.L.R. James did not live by ideas alone. Being much closer to the spirit of classical Marxism than Trotsky, he saw the potential of the socialist reality in the lives of ordinary people, not in the ideas of artists or radical intellectuals. Yet Trotsky had a major influence on his initial development as a socialist thinker and activist. As he told the editors of the American *Radical History Review*: 'When my autobiography is published you will understand how I became a Marxist. I became a Marxist through the influence of two books I read. One was Trotsky's *History of the Russian Revolution* and the other was *The Decline of the West* by Oswald Spengler. What Spengler did for me was to discover pattern and development in different types of society. It took me away from the individual and the battles and the concern with the kind of things that I had learned in conventional history. Trotsky did that also by his reference to historical development in the *History of the Russian Revolution*'.[20] But the seeds of James's socialist heresy were already germinating before he came to England in 1932.

In a recent self-evaluation of two of the things he wrote in the late 1920s, James says.

In *The Life of Captain Cipriani* I dealt with the political issues and what the political parties were doing, and with what the middle-class people in general thought about domination by the British system. In "Triumph" I do something entirely different: I speak about the actual life of the ordinary people, living in the towns. . . . People still live that way, but now they are conscious of it and very hostile; in those days, the people in "Triumph" took it for granted. I was concerned with their immense vitality and the way they met their problems.[21]

The same ability to listen to and learn from working people was to characterise the socialist activities of C.L.R. James into the late twentieth century. But his growing antagonism to the Bolshevik concept of the 'vanguard Party's' monopoly of historical truth and 'scientific' certitude was already latent in the fiction-writer of the 1920s.

II

Of all the socialist critics of V.I. Lenin's Bolshevism between 1902 and 1917, Leon Trotsky was the most eloquent, persuasive and persistent. Although he maintained a position quite distinct from either the Bolsheviks or the Mensheviks until the October revolution in 1917, he was not without considerable sympathy for the Mensheviks. In summarising Trotsky's critique of Lenin as early as 1904, Isaac Deutscher said:

Lenin had bullied the revolutionary intelligentsia into a Marxist orthodoxy, into an unconditional surrender to Marx's authority, hoping that in this way he would train men of the intelligentsia into reliable leaders of an immature and timid labour movement. But Lenin was merely trying to force the pace of history: for to be in possession of a proletarian doctrine, such as Marxism, "was no substitute for a proletariat". Lenin distrusted the masses and adopted a haughty attitude towards their untutored activities, arguing that the workers by themselves could not rise from trade unionism to revolutionary socialism, and that socialist ideology was brought into the labour movement from "the outside", by the revolutionary intelligentsia. This Trotsky wrote, was the theory of an "orthodox theocracy"; and Lenin's scheme of organisation was fit for a party which would "substitute" itself for the working classes, act as proxy in their name and on their behalf, regardless of what the workers felt and thought.[22]

A leading figure in the Russian revolution of 1905, Trotsky would soon produce his epoch-making book, *Permanent Revolution* – a book in which were locked up the 'contradictory' attitudes which led him to Bolshevism in 1917.

The most startling proposition in *Permanent Revolution* was the assertion that: 'It is possible for the workers to come to power in an economically backward country sooner than in an advanced country'.[23] But the bold, daring and innovative cast of Trotsky's revolutionary thought was allowed to conceal his closeness to the authoritarian socialism of Lenin. Moreover, despite the importance of socialist consciousness within the small early twentieth-century Russian working class – the central pivot of the concept of the socialist revolution in permanence – Trotsky did not face the question squarely. As Baruch Knei-Paz has argued:

It is clear that here, in Trotsky's discussion of the proletariat and socialist consciousness, the most conspicuous elements of "voluntarism" are revealed. He made more concessions to "elitism" as well here than anywhere else in his early writings. . . . And although he acknowledged the limits of the workers' socialist consciousness, he made less of this than he perhaps should have. Many years later, after 1917, he would, in contrast, continually stress the limits. All the "minuses" of the proletariat, he would then write, their "illiteracy, backwardness, the absense (among them) of organisational habits, of system in labour, of cultural and technical education . . . we are feeling at every step". This would mean that the Russian workers' past had badly prepared them for socialism; and that the absence among them of a "socialist consciousness" would complicate and transmute the tasks of the post-revolutionary regime.[24]

The life that Leon Trotsky lived before the outbreak of the First World War was faraway – that is, spiritually, intellectually and socially – from the Marxists' theoretical world of 'permanent revolution'. From 1907 to 1914, he lived in Vienna with his second wife, Natalya Sedova, and two sons. No matter how much he might deny it later on, a new world was opened up for him. Here he met Alfred Adler, the *socialist* psychologist. As Robert Wistrich put it: 'It was this early contact with the new science that was being pioneered in Vienna that was at the origin of Trotsky's later fascination with Freud and his attempts to reconcile psycho-analysis with Marxism'.[25]

Before 1917 Trotsky was very conscious of the faults and political weaknesses of the Russian intelligentsia. In summing up his pre-war critique of the Leninists' vanguard elitism, Robert Wistrich says: 'The estrangement of the Russian intellectuals from the masses led them to exaggerate their sense of "closeness" and to indulge in delusions of grandeur. Since the early nineteenth century they had acted by proxy for weakly-developed or non-existent social classes. It was also significant that Trotsky thought the socialist intellectuals in the West were, in Wistrich's phrase, 'more organically tied to the programmes and class interests of the labour movement'.[26]

By the time that he wrote his autobiography, *My Life*, while he was an exile in the late 1920s, Leon Trotsky tried to bury the illusions he had developed about European socialism before 1917. In discussing this aspect of his life in pre-war Vienna, Wistrich says:

The scarcely veiled hostility behind Trotsky's description of the Viennese Marxists clearly suggests a backward projection of later Bolshevik attitudes. At the same time, the soft, cosy *Gemutlichkeit* of the Viennese atmosphere did not grate on Trotsky nearly as much as he implied. . . . Perhaps the Bolshevik Commissar of later years did not like to think of himself as having hobnobbed with these socialist intellectuals who had singularly failed to live up to his expectations.[27]

To speak about a backward projection of later attitudes is a very polite way of saying that Trotsky had competed with Stalin in the process of re-writing history. Though his motivation was more generous and progressive than Stalin's, he carried this practice to quite preposterous lengths. Thus when he compared the contributions of Jean Jaurés and August Bebel to Western socialism before the outbreak of the First World War, he said: 'Their deaths marked the line where the progressive historical mission of the Second International ended'.[28]

Although Trotsky was relatively more open-minded about scientific research than the Marxists and conservative academicians in the Russian universities in the early 1920s, he was blinkered in his attitude to open-ended, impartial scientific research. In his brilliant, though often uncritical and eulogistic biography, Isaac Deutscher sketched in Trotsky's defence of the Freudian school of thought against 'Pavlov's followers who were bent on establishing a virtual monopoly for their own teachings'.[29] Indeed, Trotsky's dogmatic Bolshevik attitudes alienated many socialists who were otherwise sympathetic to his struggle against Stalinism. By the 1930s his attitudes had really hardened. When Alice Ruhle-Gerstel described discussions with Trotsky at that time, she said:

At one of these lunches – it may even have been the first time, I don't quite remember – the conversation came round, via the Furtmullers and the Adlers, to individual psychology. Lina Furtmuller had visited the Trotskys in France two years before, and had once again tried to bring them round to the psychological view of Alfred Adler . . . I unfolded my own Adlerian standpoint, but Trotsky showed more interest in Freud. I tried to show that while Freud was cleverer, more scientific, more profound, and Adler shallower and woolier, the latter's work did have a solid socialist foundation, whereas Freud's attitude was reactionary in comparison. Trotsky would have none of it: how can science have an "attitude"? The job of science is to research, and politicians then have to make use of its results in one way or another. . . . If someone studies astronomy or mathematics he does not have an "attitude"; he researches.[30]

The hardened, intransigent and authoritarian attitudes that Leon Trotsky developed towards politics and scientific research in the 1930s were, though not inevitable, rooted in the whole history of the nineteenth-century Russian intelligentsia. In re-writing the history of the years he spent in Vienna before the First World War, he was interested in emphasising the *discontinuity* in the history of international socialism. For although the crisis of socialism was, as Julius Braunthal put it, 'engendered by the collapse of an illusion – the illusion that the Second International could prevent the outbreak of a European War', the war nevertheless allowed the Bolshevik Party to create the October revolution.[31]

A major strike of women textile workers in St Petersburg on 8 March 1917 marked the beginning of the first – or February – revolution. When the entire garrison went over to the side of the workers, the Russian revolution had won its first major battle. In describing the way in which V.I. Lenin's political perspectives changed during the fateful year of 1917, Joel Carmichael said: 'On his return to Russia in April, Lenin had dropped his traditional perspective and veered over to the idea that it was possible for the working class to conduct The Revolution through its "bourgeois" phrase; by September he thought the situation ripe for the Bolshevik Party itself, "representing the vanguard of the Russian proletariat" to seize power "on its behalf" and "in the interests" of The Revolution. With that as a starting-point a specific action was needed – a conspiracy. A putsch naturally required secrecy and precision'.[32]

Nevertheless, the October revolution was a dramatical turning-point in the history of the revolts, uprisings and struggles of working people and peasants throughout the world. In evaluating Trotsky's epic *History of the Russian Revolution*, C.L.R. James said:

Milton says that a great book is the precious life-blood of a master spirit. True. But in the *History* is the precious life-blood of many master spirits; and also of the Russian people, of the French proletariat, in 1848 and 1870, of Ironsides and Jacobins and sansculottes, of the abortive German revolution of 1918, of the Chinese and other nationalist revolutions. All, all are there. All had contributed their sufferings, their hopes, the wisdom that was drawn from their experiences. A hundred years of socialist thought and proletarian struggles have gone into the making of that book, the first of its kind. No one will every again be able to write like it again for generations. It is the first classic of socialist society and it will never be superseded.

In setting out what differentiated Trotsky from the arm-chair socialist intellectuals of the academy, James focused on his attitudes to the 'masses':

He had a passionate faith in them and no great work for socialism, theoretical or practical, can be done without it. . . . More than once the *History* refers to the freedom from drudgery of the domestic servants. Of the many passionate outbursts in the *History* one of the most remarkable is the description of the horny hands and harsh voices of the Paris workers intruding themselves on the political stage where the silken gentlemen are setting the fate of the nation. His chapters on the revolution in the autobiography are instinct with a *hot sympathy* for humanity in *the mass*.[33]

But Leon Trotsky was actually aloof from working-class men and women for most of his political life. Like Trotsky, C.L.R. James, the 'Trotskyist', was also more interested in the 'masses' than in individuals until a political crisis developed in his life in 1940. Moreover, although Trotsky was devoted to the socialist project as he understood it, James did not notice the fact that Trotsky was compelled to invent a fictitious character, 'a collective Markin', who embodied all the virtues of the 'proletarian' makers of the Bolshevik revolution.[34] In any case, Trotsky was often confused in later years about who – or what – actually made the revolution. As Walter Laqueur puts it: 'Trotsky was in two minds about the revolution: "It was led by conscious workers educated for the most part by the party of Lenin", he wrote on one occasion. On another he said that it was a spontaneous uprising spurred by universal indignation; the Bolsheviks were a headless organisation with a scattered staff and weak illegal groups'.[35]

Although C.L.R. James was to play a major role in the small Trotskyist movement in the 1930s, the half-repressed and sub-conscious theoretical differences that he discussed with Trotsky in those years had a tone of *premonitory* 'inevitability' about them. If Trotsky's socialism was often abstract, James could not divorce socialism from the day-to-day lives and experiences of ordinary people. This was seen in his alienation from the black middle class in the West Indies even before the October revolution. As he explained much later:

I was fascinated by the calypso singers and the sometimes ribald ditties they sang in their tents during carnival time. But, like many of the black middle class, to my mother a calypso was a matter for ne'er-do-wells and at best the common people. I was made to understand that the road to the calypso tent was the road to hell, and there were plenty of examples of hell's inhabitants to whom she could point.[36]

Moreover, C.L.R. James came to political, though nationalist, consciousness in the shadow of the Russian revolution. In his interesting essay on 'The making of an intellectual, the making of a Marxist', Richard Small says that 'ribald ditties were not all that were being sung in those tents'. Also he speculates about whether the young James ever heard the left-wing, anti-imperialist songs of the Calypsonian, Patrick Jones, in 1920. Certainly, in the short stories, 'La Divina Pastora' and 'Turner's Prosperity' that he published in 1927 and in 1929, James was interested in portraying the 'yard life' of the commonalty rather than 'high politics'.[37] Notwithstanding the influence of Trotsky's *History of the Russian Revolution* at this time, the lives of Trotsky and James had not yet converged or interacted.

By 1923–24 Leon Trotsky no longer had any real power in 'Soviet' Russia. In alluding to Trotsky's growing conflict with the developing Stalinist bureaucracy, some of his biographers have used Biblical language to describe his isolation within Russia. In *The Tragedy of Leon Trotsky*, Ronald Segal devoted a whole chapter to what he called 'The Fall' of the founder of the Red Army and co-architect of the October revolution. But Trotsky's real tragedy was that he identified himself with the repressive, authoritarian tradition of Bolshevik Leninism from 1923 onwards. As Joel Carmichael argued:

The impulse to treat Marx's writing as Holy Writ, typical of Russian Marxism and especially among Russian Jewish Marxists, was plainly a translation of old traditions into a new idiom that despite apparent secularisation retained the aroma of a millennial piety.

Trotsky's cluster of shortcomings, all rooted in the unconscious sources of his character, obliged him to concur in the ikonisation of Lenin. Lenin whilst alive had become his only bulwark, as it seemed against his obliteration by the evolving apparatus; after Lenin's death Trotsky hoped that Lenin, incarnate in the "legacy of Lenin', would go on playing the same role.[38]

The cumulative crises of socialism were growing with frightening rapidity. Then in 1928 Joseph Stalin was responsible for forcing Trotsky into permanent exile. Yet despite being compelled to live in several countries before he found political asylum in Mexico in 1937, he continued to defend the counter-productive Leninist heritage. It was as if the pre-1917 Trotsky had not existed.

By producing articles, books and theses, Trotsky sought to defend the Bolshevik revolution in a completely uncritical way. Although the 'Trotskyists' in the West were in a very small minority in the late 1920s and 1930s, they did exist. Not only did they exist in very unfavourable – and often daunting – conditions – but they fought for libertarian socialism. C.L.R. James was, for example, attracted to 'Trotskyism' because of the 'Trotskyists' defence of libertarian socialist ideals rather than Trotsky's orthodoxy. Besides, the most remarkable thing about the Trotskyist newspapers and journals of that period was the open, critical and creative debates which raged in their pages – not Trotsky's attempt to impose Leninist orthodoxy on a recalcitrant rank-and-file.

III

With the Wall Street crash and the deepening economic crisis of Western captialism between 1929 and 1939, the Trotskyist movement in Britain, Germany, France, Italy and, above all, America attracted outstanding socialist intellectuals. But they were from Trotsky's point of view difficult and troublesome, and they insisted on debating luxurious questions about the early phase of the Russian revolution. They raised awkward questions about why Trotsky had advocated 'the militarisation of labour' in 1919, why he had suppressed the Kronstadt rebellion in 1921 and why he had not repudiated dictatorial practices. Though he was obviously irritated and annoyed, Trotsky did respond to their criticisms.

Surrounded by very real enemies in Coyoacan, Trotsky developed the outlook of a socialist fugitive. Although his role in 'the trade union debate' in Soviet Russia in 1921 was frequently cited against him, he did not require to respond with the defensive arguments of a fugitive. Trotsky could have identified himself with democratic motives. For as early as 1934 Arthur Rosenberg insisted that Trotsky's objective in that debate was 'the restoration in Russia of working-class democracy by means of the trade unions'.[39] However, Trotsky chose to identify with the last years of Lenin's authoritarian rule by decree.

This was particularly clear in the discussion in France, Italy and America on the Kronstadt rebellion. In criticising the article that Leon Trotsky published in the *New International* in April 1938, Dwight MacDonald demonstrated that 'his lengthy argument boils down to an identification of all the elements which opposed the Bolsheviks as "petty bourgeois"'. Furthermore, MacDonald emphasised that he had ignored the question of the 'mass executions which took place for months after the rebels had been crushed'. In an exceptionally perceptive paragraph, McDonald linked Trotsky's attitude to Kronstadt to the unresolved questions that Trotsky evaded in 1935 when he published his book, *The Revolution Betrayed*:

In *The Revolution Betrayed*, Trotsky demonstrates that Stalinism is primarily a reflection of the low level of productivity and economic development of Russia. But even if one accepts this analysis, as I do, an important contributory cause may still be found in certain weaknesses of Bolshevik political theory. Is it not the duty of Marxists today relentlessly to search out these weaknesses, to reconsider the entire Bolshevik line with scientific detachment? My impression is that Trotsky has shown little interest in any such basic reconsideration. He seems to be more interested in defending Leninism than in learning from its mistakes.[40]

When he replied to such socialist critics as Dwight MacDonald, Victor Serge and Boris Souvarine, Trotsky denounced them as idealists and pacifists. In admitting to and glorying in his personal responsibility in suppressing the Kronstadt rising, he attributed the so-called 'excesses' to the 'Iron Laws' of history. As he put it: 'The main point is that "excesses" flow from the very nature of the revolution which in itself is but an "excess" of history'. But in doing so, he described a meeting of communist-seamen he had addressed in Petrograd before the decision was taken to crush the Kronstadt rebels: 'Dandified and well-fed sailors, communists in name only, produced the impression of parasites in comparison with the workers and Red Army men of that time'.[41] It was axiomatic that the dandified and well-fed could not possess any socialist idealism. Impoverished fugitivism was an essential pre-condition for authentic socialist convictions.

By the early 1930s the American intelligentsia had been radicalised. But Leon Trotsky and the Trotskyist activists were schizophrenic in their attitudes to intellectuals. Trotsky's relationship with the literary Trotskyists did not, as Joel Carmichael put it, 'sit well with the leaders of the Socialist Workers' Party, who were irritated by the glamour he made available to the rootless intellectuals'. In an article published in 1935, John G. Wright reflected Trotsky's own attitudes towards the intelligentsia in the West.

The average intellectual is no better off economically than the average white-collar worker; the freelance intellectuals who haunt the Bohemias of the metropolitan centers are even less fortunate. Except in rare cases, intellectuals function, not as factors in capitalist economy, but as part of the social institutions stemming from it. So long as these institutions maintain them in comparative comfort, they will remain loyal to the class that supports them. The impact of the crisis, however, has hurled crowds of helpless intellectuals and professionals into space, like so many dissociated atoms. . . . These discontented and dislocated people are among the most inflammable elements in contemporary society.

The intelligentsia was a microcosm of capitalist society. Unfortunately, intellectuals were 'prone to idealise revolution in the first flush of their enthusiasm, only to remain on the sidelines or run for cover into the opposing camp when they come face to face with the revolution itself'.[42]

While the French and the American Trotskyist intellectuals were raising critical questions about the relevance of Bolshevism to the major economic and political crises of Western capitalism, C.L.R. James was at work in England. In addition to his agitational work in the Independent Labour Party, the International Friends of Ethiopia and the International African Service Bureau, he produced a spate of books on historical and political subjects. In 1937 he published *World Revolution, 1917–1936: The Rise and Fall of the Communist International* and in 1938 he published *The Black Jacobins: Toussaint L'Ouverture and the Haitian Revolution*. On the surface an orthodox 'Trotskyist' intellectual, James was already a dissident with a touch of anarchist disaffection.

Despite his constant protestations of orthodoxy, C.L.R. James – the James who published the novel, *Minty Alley*, in 1936 and *A History of Negro Revolt* in 1938 – was much closer to the traditions of the independent left-wing intelligentsia than he acknowledged. Certainly, the *Black Jacobins* was a masterpiece – a classic of Marxist historiography. Eugene D. Genovese, the authority on the Afro-American slave revolts says: 'Any consideration of the revolts should begin with C.L.R. James's great historical work and Marxist interpretation, *Black Jacobins and the San Domingo Revolution*'.[43] In awe of his work as a Marxist historian, the American Trotskyists were less happy with some of his political attitudes. When Joseph Carter reviewed *World Revolution, 1919–1936*, he said:

The real weakness of the book is its treatment of the role of the party and the leadership . . . He accepts Lenin's 1903 position as applicable today. Yet in the explanation of it he writes that it was conditioned by the existence of Tsarism.[44]

In the early 1930s the American and other Trotskyists refuted the notion that the Left was living through a process of de-radicalisation. For them, the world revolution had begun in 1917. In rejecting the forebodings of 'the doom-haunted middle-class intellectuals', a reviewer of Celine's novel, *Journey to the End of the Night*, ridiculed them for wondering 'whether the book is "a prelude to revolution or better a mournful overture to that suicidally irrational era . . . upon which the human race appears to be entering"'. To the Trotskyists who were 'more aware of the inexorable forces assembling for revolution', Celine's novel 'seems less an overture and more a cacaphonous finale to the mad symphony of individualism'.[45]

By 1934 Leon Trotsky and the Trotskyists were isolated from the independent working-class movements in America and Western Europe. The petty-bourgeois individualism so long despised by all socialists had played a major role in the rise of Nazism in 'civilised' Germany. In commenting on Trotsky's forlorn attempts to arouse the international, and especially the German, labour movement to the dangers of fascism, Irving Howe says:

Had Trotsky's advice been followed the world might have been spared some of the horrors of our century; at the very least, the German working class would have gone down in battle rather than allowing the Nazi thugs to take power without resistance. But Trotsky was not heeded. His flow of articles and pamphlets barely reached the larger left-wing public.

By now the escalating workers' revolts in France and Spain had persuaded Trotsky to attempt to create a Fourth International. No longer an oppositional critic within the world communist movement, he tried to create an entirely new revolutionary leadership.[46]

During the crucial conflict throughout the world in the late 1930s between the forces of capitalism and socialism, Leon Trotsky unwittingly vitiated his own efforts to build a militant international socialist movement by defending totalitarian Russia as a socialist society. With analytical sharpness and passion, Joseph Carter demonstrated that Trotsky's fugitive attitudes had crystallised between 1917 and 1921. In 1920 Trotsky had argued that the socialist character of Soviet Russia rendered the traditional role of the trade unions as instruments of class struggle both irrelevant and outmoded. In this he was, as Carter put it, 'repeating the argument which up to that time was common to all Bolsheviks in their struggle against the Menshevik conception of the "independence" of trade unions'. In sketching in the real situation in 'Soviet' Russia, Carter said:

Among the workers, dissatisfaction developed in the face of the inability of the Soviet regime to satisfy their material needs. At the same time a tremendous bureaucracy had developed – an officialdom, separated from the masses, and composed in large measure of bureaucrats and specialists of the old regime.[47]

Despite the Hitler-Stalin pact in 1939, Leon Trotsky persisted in urging 'the unconditional defence of the Soviet Union'. When Max Shachtman, Joseph Carter, C.L.R. James and others argued that Russia was 'essentially no different now from any other Imperialist power', Trotsky 'insisted that his followers should continue to defend unconditionally the "gains of October" against all foreign capitalist governments'.[48] Although the controversial question of whether Russia is socialist or not remains unresolved in working-class movements throughout the contemporary world, the totalitarian – or 'bureaucratic collectivist' – societies in Russia and Eastern Europe continue to do violence to the socialist idea.

In an article in which he developed the theory of 'bureaucratic collectivism', Joseph Carter argued that: 'The administration of the state and the economy in culturally isolated Russia, while controlled by the Bolsheviks, was in the hands of a bureaucracy. The Bolsheviks expected, and worked for, the extension of the Russian revolution into the more advanced industrial countries which would break the imperialist encirclement, raise the Russian industrial and cultural level, and thus create the pre-conditions for complete workers' democracy'. Confronted with the unexpected advent of Stalinism and the destruction of the 'political power of the working class and the strengthening of state property and planning', Trotsky could neither acknowledge that Russia was no longer a workers' state or defend the theses developed in *The Revolution Betrayed*. The intellectuals in the small, isolated and embattled Fourth International were in revolt and Trotsky was really unreceptive to new ideas. Carter explained his response thus:

He now affirmed that it was the state-owned character of property which determined the socialist character of the economy and the proletarian nature of the state. The bureaucracy's expropriation of the political power of the working class, he added, only signified that Russia was a "degenerated" workers' state, politically dominated by a Bonapartist bureaucracy.[49]

Trotsky faced the intellectuals' criticisms within the Trotskyist movement by questioning the motivations of the critics – not by answering the actual criticisms. But if bureaucratic collectivism was everybody's prison, Leon Trotsky exhorted the Western labour movements to defend it at all costs in the name of international working-class solidarity.

Meanwhile, Leon Trotsky urged socialists to defend the betrayed revolution, though critics like Max Shachtman, Joseph Carter and C.L.R. James suggested that the real political function of 'Soviet' Russia was to destroy the intellectual content of Marxism. In defending 'communism and terrorism' during the early years of the Russian revolution, Trotsky gave his critics within left-wing socialist circles the chance to raise questions about 'Bolshevik amoralism'. When he responded by arguing in a pamphlet, *Their Morals and Ours* that moral standards were historically relative and conditioned by the needs of the class struggle, he alienated many devoted socialists. The most devastating critique of *Their Morals and Ours* was subsequently formulated by a scholar who had once been an orthodox Trotskyist, Irving Howe. In a paragraph of great eloquence, he said:

In responding to the vicious conduct of the Stalinist regime, he found himself resorting spontaneously and passionately to the kind of humanitarian or supra-class moralism that he dismissed on other occasions. He wrote, not just about the reactionary drift of Stalinism, but also about its "baseness" and "perfidy" – terms taken from the traditional moral lexicon and implying a preference for their opposites, "nobility" and "integrity". The "elementary moral precepts" now played a strikingly large role in his battle against the Stalinist dictatorship. Repeatedly he charged it, in effect, with violating that "moral sense" which his essay tended to minimise.[50]

In contrast to C.L.R. James, Trotsky saw the survival of capitalism in somewhat conspiratorial terms. From Trotsky's perspective, the existence of revolutionary consciousness amongst the 'masses' was quite evident, though in a very ethereal sense. Therefore the impoverished 'masses' had to be separated from the 'labour aristocracy' and the capricious petty-bourgeois intellectuals. With the authentic leadership of the Fourth International, the revolutionary passions of millions of working people in America, Western Europe and the colonial world would be unleashed.

Trotsky saw a correlation between working-class impoverishment and revolutionary socialist consciousness. When he belatedly discovered Jack London's novel, *The Iron Heel*, he argued that the growth of wealth at one pole and of misery and destitution at the other was responsible for 'the accumulation of social bitterness and hatred' perceived by London even before the First World War.[51] Socialist consciousness was reduced to a function of working-class misery and destitution rather than idealistic visionary aspirations. Human courage, fidelity, creativity and unselfishness seemed to be restricted to an 'impoverished' working class and a few unrepresentative socialist intellectuals of petty-bourgeois origins.

Furthermore, Trotsky did not understand the force of nationalist passions amongst the Afro-Americans as a motivating-engine of the class struggle. As he told C.L.R. James in 1939: 'The Negro can be developed to a class standpoint only when the white worker is educated. On the whole the question of the colonial people is in the first instance a question of the development of the metropolitan worker'.[52] In contrast to James, he did not see the growing creativity and disaffection within the Afro-Americans, the dawning of a consciousness hungering for civil rights or the eradication of lynching and racialist discrimination.

Trotsky was distrustful of C.L.R. James's version of socialism and the publication of *World Revolution, 1917–1936* gave him the opportunity to assert that the Black Marxist did not understand 'the dialectic'. What Trotsky did *not* understand was 'the dialectic' of the struggles of the colonial peoples and the Afro-Americans. With Claude McKay, George Padmore, Richard Wright and many other Black Marxists, James was already aware of the power of nationalist passions in the struggles of the colonial peoples. Although he argued at the annual conference of the Independent Labour Party in 1936 for workers' sanctions versus League of Nations' sanctions, James was actually accused of advocating black nationalism.[53] Furthermore, John McGovern attacked Haile Selassie as a dictator.[54]

But although C.L.R. James fought for some of the ideas of Bolshevism in the 1930s, he was far in advance of Leon Trotsky in anticipating the later revolts in the colonial world as well as in Afro-American communities. In contrast to Trotsky, he always focused on the autonomy of the colonial peoples in Africa and Asia and the Black people in America without stressing any necessity for superior 'vanguard' Bolshevik leadership. In criticising the English Bolshevik he was so familiar with in the late 1930s, he wrote:

He speaks always of the English revolutionaries winning power in England and then "granting" freedom to Africans. . . . He sees Africans as incapable of independent action on a large scale, unable to organise a revolutionary struggle, to seize power and hold it.[55]

And yet both Trotsky and James were, from quite different theoretical perspectives, optimistic about the coming upheavals within the industrial capitalist world and colonial hinterlands.

Towards the end of his life Trotsky was convinced that capitalism was writhing in its 'death agony'. With socialist revolutions being imminent, he was afraid that the inexorable forces of the revolution would be diverted by the vaciliating, petty-bourgeois intelligentsia. When Trotsky and James discussed black nationalism in Mexico in 1939, they clashed on the question of the role that Black intellectuals could play in the struggle for the emancipation of the Afro-American people. While Trotsky asserted that the Afro-American intellectuals kept 'themselves separated from the masses, always with the desire to take on the Anglo-Saxon culture and of becoming an integral part of Anglo-Saxon life', James disagreed. In arguing at length against Trotsky's evaluation of the role of the Black intellectuals, he said:

Also they are very much isolated from the white bourgeoisie and the social discrimination makes them less easily corrupted, as, for example, the Negro intellectuals in the West Indies. ... Also what has happened to the Jews in Germany has made the Negro intellectuals think twice . . .[56]

But although Trotsky insisted that it was necessary to 'make *use* of every intellectual who can contribute to our party', he provided a list of capricious intellectuals whose individualism impeded the socialist struggle. In summing up, he said: 'The First International had trouble with the poet, Freilgrath, who was also very capricious. The Second and Third Internationals had trouble with Maxim Gorky. The Fourth International with Diego Rivera. In every case they separated from us'. But when he depicted C.L.R. James, in 1940, as 'a Bohemian free-lancer', he made an extremely interesting comment.[57] As a freelance socialist, James was able to survive the debacle of the Second World War.

IV

In 1939 a faction within the American Socialist Workers' Party broke away to form the Workers' Party. Led by the dynamic Max Shachtman, the Workers' Party attracted many brilliant and outstanding writers, novelists and intellectuals. C.L.R. James joined and remained in the Workers' Party until 1947. The Workers' Party argued that Russia was a bureaucratic collectivist society, while a minority within it led by Freddie Forest (Raya Dunayevskaya) and J.R. Johnson (C.L.R. James) portrayed it as a totalitarian state-capitalist society. In 1947 the Dunayevskaya–James group re-joined the Socialist Workers' Party, but left it again in 1951 to form their own News and Letters group.

Like Leon Trotsky, C.L.R. James attached an enormous importance to the role of intellectuals in capitalist society. But although James spent a lot of time participating in the day-to-day social activities of Black and white workers in America, he nevertheless produced innumerable articles on a wide variety of subjects. With great sensitivity and astuteness as a *socialist* literary critic and historian, he produced articles on imaginative literature and the latent disaffection of the Afro-Americans. In a series of outstanding articles on the 'Tercentenary of the English Revolution, 1649–1949" he focused on what was new and innovative in the struggles of the 'ancestors of the proletariat' when he said:

The new in literature was the straightforward, plain, simple prose style. And the men who created it were the Puritan preachers, not Dryden, Addison and Steele, as all the bourgeois school books say. The Puritan propagandists were the founders of the style which is the basis of modern English to this day.

They did more. In their efforts to dramatise their theological doctrine, they introduced the autobiographical narrative, dialogue, and the dramatic scene, all of which were the direct ancestors of the modern novel. Haller recognises that not only *Paradise Lost* but *Pilgrim's Progress* and *Robinson Crusoe* came directly from the left-wing Puritans.

The three books which represent bourgeois society before the rise of the working-class movement are *Pilgrim's Progress*, the struggle of the poor; Defoe's *Robinson Crusoe*, the odyssey of the individual capitalist, and Swift's *Gulliver's Travels*, the revolt (without hope) against the immorality and corruption of bourgeois society.[58]

A major aspect of the English revolution of 1649 was, in James's view, the outstanding literary achievements of the dissenters. Furthermore, the 'very finest exponents of the new plain straightforward style were not the preachers but the Leveller pamphleteers'. Literary trends were just as important as economic trends in assisting socialists to understand what was happening. In functioning as a socialist writer and agitator during and after the Second World War, he always tried to grasp what was new in the experiences and activities of working men and women. Just as they had been important in the past, so they were the innovators of the present. But although past and present merged and fused in James's writings, he was and remained much more optimistic – often unrealistically optimistic – than most of the anti-Stalinist socialists on the Left.

The Second World War and its aftermath actually created a major crisis in the ranks of the Trotskyist movement and the independent Left. With unmoveable confidence Trotsky had, in 1939, written that: 'If this war provokes, as we firmly believe, a proletarian revolution, it must inevitably lead to the overthrow of the bureaucracy in the USSR and regeneration of Soviet democracy on a far higher economic and cultural basis than in 1918'.[59] Yet despite his revulsion over totalitarian thought-control and the 'show trials' in Moscow in the late 1930s, Trotsky remained ambiguous about the 'Soviet' bureaucracy's commitment to fostering socialist revolution in other parts of the world.

During the discussions between Leon Trotsky, C.L.R. James and other leaders of the world Trotskyist movement in 1939, Trotsky criticised the 'lack of dialectical approach' and 'Anglo-Saxon empiricism' in James's book, *World Revolution*. A number of the disagreements beween the two socialist thinkers impinged on the debates in the wider socialist movement for a long time afterwards. In contrast to James, Trotsky denied that the Soviet bureaucracy had 'sabotaged the Chinese revolution'. Even in 1927 Russia was, in Trotsky's opinion, still interested in fostering socialist revolution in other parts of the world. Having researched the history of the Third International, James knew better. Being more optimistic about the prospects of proletarian revolts and uprisings than Trotsky, they also disagreed about the socialist potential of the Afro-American workers.[60]

In 1940 James produced a remarkable assessment of Richard Wright's novel, *Native Son*, long before anyone else anticipated the 'explosions' of the Afro-American people in the 1960s. A participant in the social activities of the black Americans in city and rural communities, he was particularly sensitive to the significance of the central character in Wright's novel:

Black Bigger Thomas, native, stifled by and inwardly rebellious against white America's treatment of him, by accident murders a white girl. For him this murder is the beginning of a new life. In striking such a blow against his hated enemies, in the struggle to outwit them and evade capture, his stunted personality finds scope to expand. Before he is sentenced to death, the sincere efforts of two white communists to save him teach him that all whites are not his enemies, that he is not alone, that there is a solidarity of all the oppressed.

By insisting that Bigger Thomas was 'a symbol or prototype of the Negro masses in the proletarian revolution', James explained that much more than Thomas's 'desire to live was at stake':

It was the bursting pride of a spirit long cramped and oppressed that found itself free at last. All students of revolutionary history know it: the legions of Spartacus, Cromwell's Ironsides, the Paris enrages, the Russian workers defending Petrograd against Udenitch, the Spanish workers defending Madrid, the march of the Chinese communists across China in 1936.

The accumulated experience of generations of Afro-Americans was creating the potential for socialist revolt. In looking below the surface of American society, James argued that the Afro-Americans' hatred of their treatment in a racist community would be 'one of the most powerful forces in the Negro revolution'. But although imaginative literature could not be divorced from politics, he was opposed to 'socialist realism'. In identifying Wright's major achievement, he said:

The artist, by methods compounded of conscious logic and his own intuition, observes society and experiences life. He comes to his conclusions and embodies them in character, scene and dramatic situation. According to the depth of his penetration and the sweep of his net, his capacity to integrate and reproduce, he writes his novel, paints his picture, or composes his symphony. Psychologist, historian, politician, or revolutionary, drawing on his own experience, sees symbols, parallelism, depth and perspective unsuspected by the creator.[61]

Like Trotsky, James was more critical of socialist intellectuals than independent artists and novelists.

By 1940 C.L.R. James was beginning to reject the Leninist conception of the role of the 'vanguard Party' in workers' struggles. A prominent, though fugitive, member of the Workers' Party, he took part in a sharecroppers' strike in South-East Mussouri in 1942. In preparing a report for the Workers' Party newspaper, *Labor Action*, he was already hostile to Trotskyist elitism. In a recent account of his role in that strike, he said:

So I sat down with my pen and notebook and said, "Well, what shall we say?". So (I used to call myself Williams) they said, "Well, Brother Williams, you know". I said, "I know nothing. This is your strike. You are all doing it. I have helped you, but this pamphlet has to state what you have to say".[62]

In contrast to the Trotskyists, James refused to impose 'vanguard' wisdom and certitude on struggling workers and sharecroppers.

Before his death Trotsky had predicted that the Second World War would result in the disintegration of Stalinism and the outbreak of socialist revolution in Europe. In his massive study of the politics of the Second World War, Gabriel Kolko documents the revolts and uprisings of working people throughout Europe. In stressing that the ruling classes in America and Britain could not afford to assess the threat of socialist revolution 'too conservatively', he concluded that: 'No one knew that the Left's leaders and premises condemned them to passivity, or what the critical ingredients were that made men revolt'.[63] Despite the massive and widespread revolts and growth of communist movements, the socialist revolutions anticipated by Trotsky were actually strangled by Stalin and the Russian bureaucracy. As Stanley Weir puts it: 'New conditions were an aid to organisation from the top down only. Each expansion of Russian control in Europe, moreover, brought the round up and disappearance of Trotskyists. There would be no quick recouping of the Russian revolution or any revolution in Western Europe'.[64]

As early as 1943 the *Daily Worker*, the organ of the British Communist Party, said that 'anyone who seriously believes that the Party is today simply fighting for a socialist revolution ought to be put in a cage'. Furthermore, when the Italian revolution erupted in 1943, the Communist Party published a statement in the *Daily Worker*:

A large part of the port workers (in Genoa) have left their work. "Communist demonstrations have taken place, the demonstrators carrying red flags and singing the Internationale". The *Daily Worker* asserts that this is German propaganda . . .[65]

Contrary to Trotsky's expectations, the communists proceeded to de-radicalise the spontaneous revolts and socialist movements in Europe and America.

While the Fourth International acknowledged that socialist revolution was not on the agenda at the end of the Second World War, the Trotskyist movement did untold damage to the socialist goal of abolishing the domination of people by other people by equating socialism with totalitarian State ownership of the means of production. In celebrating the 28th anniversary of the Russian revolution in 1945 against a background where a 'reactionary bureaucracy' imposed 'a totalitarian regime on the Russian masses', the Fourth International insisted that:

But thus far, as in the case of the great revolutions of the past, the reaction has not swept away the fundamental conquests of the revolution; in this case, the new, more advanced property forms – nationalised property.[66]

By 1946 a new 'optimism' developed in the ranks of the Trotskyist Fourth International. In arguing that 'the first phase of the European revolution' was already evident, Ernest Mandel portrayed the develop-ment of 'dual power' and the 'independent initiative by the working class and the petty-bourgeois masses, or, at all events, of their vanguard'. At the same time, Michel Raptis defended the role of the Red Army in Eastern Europe in stimulating 'a revolutionary movement with workers taking over the factories and peasants seizing the land'.[67]

Far from being too critical of Stalinism in Russia or Eastern Europe, in 1948 the Fourth International embraced 'progressive Titoism' utterly uncritically. In an article on 'The True Testimony of Trotsky' in which he criticised the libertarian socialist analyses of C.L.R. James and Max Shachtman, Ernest Mandel argued that the Stalinist bureaucracy itself was progressive. As he put it: 'The ponderous totalitarian lid still hides from the world the powerful process of discontent with Stalinism among the *Russian communist vanguard*'. By 1951 Michel Pablo was arguing that in China, Vietnam, Korea, Burma and the Philippines the international communist movement should be supported because it was in the 'van-guard' of the anti-capitalist and anti-imperialist struggle'.[68] It was now the duty of all genuine socialists to support totalitarianism as a step towards the eventual emancipation of humankind. This was a far cry from Trotsky's admonition to the ultra-pessimistic prophets of *permanent totalitarianism* to 'develop a new minimum programme to defend the interests of the slaves of the totalitarian bureaucratic system'.

In the midst of such confusion about the nature of socialism, C.L.R. James wrote a perceptive review of the novels by Norman Mailer and

William Gardner Smith, *The Naked and the Dead* and *The Last of the Conquerors*. He again contrasted the superiority of the creative imagination of the artist and the writer with the 'administrative efficiency' favoured by intellectuals in response to the 'social chaos and crisis' of the contemporary world. While thinkers like Ernest Mandel succumbed to Stalinist totalitarianism in the years immediately after the Second World War, James explained the secret of maintaining an independent socialist position:

The primary condition of strength is to see the enemy in all its amplitude. A babel of self-contradictory tongues, professional journalistic and unashamedly amateur, serve by their combined obfuscation no purpose except to protect the tottering foundations of a decayed bourgeois culture from serious examination.[69]

Although C.L.R. James did not produce an extended essay on the Hungarian revolution of 1956, the innovative Hungarians had a big impact on his thinking about modern socialism. In many essays written on a variety of topics after 1956, he described the Hungarian revolution as one of the major events of modern times. Despite the fact that James and Raya Dunayevskaya developed serious political disagreements before he was deported from America, the subsequent work she published on *Marxism and Freedom* and *Philosophy and Revolution* was influenced by 'the Black Marxist scholar'. And it was in *Marxism and Freedom* (New York, 1958) that Dunayevskaya provided one of the earliest and most penetrating analyses of the East German workers' revolt of 1953 – the major prelude and harbinger of the Hungarian revolution.

By 1958 C.L.R. James had completed his major books on history, politics and literature. When he published *Mariners, Renegades and Castaways* in 1953 as a protest against his *deportation* from McCarthyite America as *an alien*, he again criticised intellectuals for being divorced from work and working men and women. In summing up his critique of the intellectuals' role in modern societies, he said: 'In the two or three words which is all the narrow back of a book will take, the intellectuals of our time have placed their diseased stamp upon the literature of our age, as they have placed their diseased stamp upon its psychology. . . . Yet how light in the scales is the contemporary mountain of self-examination and self-pity against the warmth, the humour, the sanity, the anonymous but unfailing humanity of the renegades and castaways and savages of Pequod, rooted in the whole historical past of man, doing what they have to do, facing what they have to face'.[70]

In 1958 C.L.R. James published *Facing Reality*, a major analytical critique of modern society from a socialist perspective. By insisting on 'the realism of socialism' as the 'invading society' within the contemporary world, he distanced himself from Trotskyism, Stalinism and State capitalism. In focusing on such obsolete concepts as the 'vanguard Party' and the absurdity of equating socialism with state planning, he went on to sketch in the requirements of a socialist strategy for the modern world:

What the people need is information of where they are, what they are doing, what they have done in the past. . . . Even in the fully established socialist society, those with intellectual gifts and inclinations will have an indispensable function to perform, to master the material in any given social sphere and so present it to the people that it is easy for them to decide what to do.[71]

In the same year, James wrote *Nkrumah and the Ghana Revolution*, though it was not published in Britain until much later. This book revealed some of his serious weaknesses as a socialist thinker. Rather than acknowledge that the socialist idea was undergoing a very real cumulative crisis, he developed a quite different analysis for Africa:

The man at the helm is the African intellectual. He succeeds – or independent Africa sinks. . . . Yet Western racial prejudice is so much a part of the Western outlook on life that the African intellectual continues to be looked upon as some kind of primitive barbarian climbing the sharp and slippery slope to civilisation.

This argument was, however, at odds with what he said in *Facing Reality* about the working class and peasantry no longer needing 'proletarian Jesuits'.[72]

In recent years C.L.R. James and E.P. Thompson have frequently been compared and contrasted. As committed socialist scholars and activists, they have had much in common – a passionate interest in the history of the commonalty, hostility to totalitarianism and involvement in the lives of ordinary men and women. Unlike Thompson, however, James has taken refuge in an increasingly facile optimism. He has really refused to face 'the crisis of socialism' in theory and practice. Their quite distinctive responses to the 'underdeveloped' world are also interesting. For in contrast to his earlier optimism about 'winning causes' in Asia or Africa which 'were lost in England', Thompson has now opted for a far less optimistic perspective. Thus he sounds a note of fatalism: 'Without time-discipline we could not have the insistent energies of industrial man . . . whether this discipline comes in the form of Methodism, or of Stalinism, or of nationalism, it will come in the developing world'. Instead of endorsing Engels' comment that 'History is the most cruel of Goddesses', James actually defends *forced* industrialisation when he says: 'The only advantage he (the African intellectual) has is that Africa is so backward that he will be guilty of violences far closer to Mussolini's cruelties than to the unbridled savagery of Hitlerism or Stalinism seeking "to catch up with and surpass"'.[73]

But whatever his faults as a socialist practitioner, C.L.R. James has made major contributions to Marxist historiography. In referring to *Black Jacobins*, Eugene D. Genovese says that 'one great book should be enough for a lifetime'. He (James) has also produced many brilliant and perceptive essays on literature and art, and he still refuses to be silent in the face of oppression and injustice. In a warm tribute to him a few years ago, E.P. Thompson said:

Tom Mann and C.L.R. James have one thing in common. On his eightieth birthday, Tom said: 'I hope to grow more dangerous as I grow older'. C.L.R. James has already shown that he intends to do the same.

Chapter 10

Leszek Kolakowski and Frantz Fanon: Totalitarian and colonial labyrinths

The weapon of criticism is undoubtedly inadequate. Who on that account would choose to surrender it?

Harold Rosenberg

In the totalitarian and colonial labyrinths in which militant socialists lived during and after the Second World War, day-to-day existence was hazardous. For oppositional socialists in totalitarian Poland or in the French colonies, human existence had become an almost permanent nightmare. Leszek Kolakowski (1927–   ) was born in Radom, near Warsaw, on 23 October 1927. Because he lived at the geographical crossroads where totalitarian Nazism came face-to-face with Russian 'communism', he experienced 'the terrible hell of the twentieth century'. Although he has written very little about the impact of existentialism on his intellectual formation in Poland after the Second World War, Kolakowski was no stranger to the existentialist experiences of critical and creative left-wing oppositionalist thinkers elsewhere in the world.

Although Leszek Kolakowski identified with left-wing 'Marxist' critiques of 'the actually existing socialism' in Poland during the decade between 1956 and 1966, there was a strong element of opportunism in his writings. But it was the opportunism of an oppositionalist who valued the traditions of the Polish past, and not the opportunism of a careerist. He was always more interested in emphasising what socialism was not than in what it might become. Furthermore, in reflecting and in fashioning the tragedies and crises of international socialism since the Second World War, he shared the characteristics of passionate *nationalism* and elitism with Frantz Fanon. For in spite of the existentialist labyrinths in which they lived Kolakowski and Fanon belonged to the tradition of socialism-from-above. Unlike C.L.R. James, they always displayed the world-view of fugitives.

Yet despite Kolakowski's quite recent rejection of existentialist philosophy in a major three-volume work on Marxism, he obviously shared some of the same subjectivist – or existentialist – feelings as such other oppositionalist socialists as Frantz Fanon. While the *mature* Kolakowski now insists that 'the most we can do is negatively to transcend the existing world' rather than anticipate 'Utopia in positive terms', the passionate rejection of totalitarianism. 'I have lived there, I have suffered it, I know' – has come out of the cumulative consciousness of a man who has gone to the very existentialist edge of human existence.

In contrast to Leszek Kolakowski, Frantz Fanon (1925–61) was always very disaffected from the society he was born and reared in. He was born in Martinique in 1925; and he, died in the National Institute of Health in Bethesda, in 1961. Although he was one of six children, Fanon belonged to the black Martinican upper class. However, he belonged to a strange elite – an elite with a dual-identity. During his formative years, he was steeped in French traditions and culture. Yet Fanon's early life was, in the phrase of C.L.R. James, 'circumscribed by the books available'. In the labyrinth of a privileged way-of-life, he was already ultra-sensitive to the racist behaviour of the French army of occupation of Martinique. At an early age, the racism of the French troops contributed to his profound sense of alienation from the society in which he lived.[2]

An opponent of fascism and the Vichy administration, the eighteen year old Frantz Fanon fought with the de Gaulle forces in North Africa during the closing stages of the Second World War. In depicting Fanon's initial development as a black nationalist, C.L.R. James said: 'He was sent to North Africa and there he received his first lesson in overt racism by the French troops against the Africans. The experience was traumatic and unforgettable by Fanon even after his unit had been posted to France, where he also witnessed and was subjected to racial discrimination.' When he returned home at the end of the war, he became a disciple of Aimé Césaire.[3]

If Marxism was, as Harold Rosenburg argued, 'unthinkable apart from its premise of proletarian victory and its all-liberating effects', militant democratic socialism-from-below was not on the agenda after the Second World War. And although both Kolakowski and Fanon were major radical figures, they were – at least before Kolakowski's disillusionment with all forms of socialism – committed to socialism-from-above. Within the context of Max Eastman's three distinctive motivations in transforming individuals into socialists, Kolakowski and Fanon belonged to the third group of those 'yearning with a mixture of religious mysticism and animal gregariousness for human solidarity'.[4]

I

In volume three of the *Main Currents of Marxism: The Breakdown*, Leszek Kolakowski displays a sensitive awareness of Polish national history and cultural traditions before, during and after the Second World War. When he joined the Polish Communist Party in 1946 at nineteen years of age, he was obviously not an innocent abroad. In circumstances where most university teachers were drawn from the pre-war ruling class, he taught at the University of Lodz from 1947 to 1949 and at the University of Warsaw from 1950 and 1968. He played a prominent role in the 'Polish October' in 1956, and he soon attracted the attention and the adulation of the independent Left in Europe and America.[5]

In the brilliant, generous, polemical and haughty 'Open Letter to Leszek Kolakowski', E.P. Thompson would ultimately accuse him, in 1973, of betrayal. Yet despite Thompson's protestations to the contrary, Alasdair MacIntyre understood Kolakowski's unique 'socialist' stance against totalitarian collectivism in 1958 when he said: 'Kolakowski and others like him stress the amorality of the historical process on the one hand, and the moral responsibility of the individual in history on the other'. As well as perceiving that Kolakowski was already reducing himself to the role of 'a spectator' of the ongoing class struggles in Poland, MacIntyre criticised him for 'taking a Stalinist view of historical development and adding liberal morality to it'. By insisting that the moral content inherent in Marxism could not be revived without participation in existing class struggles, MacIntyre was being remarkably prophetic.[6]

Despite the false hopes placed on Kolakowski by authentically critical democratic socialists in the West in the 1950s and 1960s, he was essentially a liberal spectator rather than a democratic socialist fighter. Far from really distancing himself from totalitarian collectivism in Poland after the Second World War, Kolakowski co-operated with it as the price of preserving some of the nation's cultural traditions and history. Yet despite the most devastating and far-reaching criticisms he developed in the article on 'The Fate of Marxism in Eastern Europe', the mature Kolakowski does not really criticise State 'Marxism' in contemporary Poland very sharply or fundamentally.[7]

Far from criticising intellectual life in totalitarian Poland after the Second World War, Leszek Kolakowski actually praises State 'Marxism' to the high heavens. Despite the labyrinths created by totalitarianism in the late 1940s and early 1950s, socialism-from-above was more positive than negative. As he puts it: 'Some members of philosophical faculties were left in their jobs but ordered to confine themselves to teaching logic; others again were given posts under the Academy of Sciences, where they did not come into contact with students'. Moreover, in the Stalinist years 'the State was quite generous in subsidising culture, so that a good deal of rubbish was produced, but also much work of permanent value'. Although the content of intellectual life was totalitarian, a 'primitive and stereotyped Marxism' implanted 'fruitful and rational ideas that were part of its tradition'.[8]

In contrast to Raya Dunayevskaya, who emphasised the crucial role of Polish and Eastern European working-class revolt against totalitarian collectivism in 1956, Kolakowski insists that 'revisionism in Poland, where the critical movement in the 1950s went much further than in the rest of Europe, was the work of a numerous group of Party intellectuals'.[9] Just as Frantz Fanon was a passionate advocate of black consciousness, so was Kolakowski a defender of the Polish ruling class elements who went into university teaching in post-war 'communist' Poland. Quite independently of the Russians, Polish Marxism had its own national traditions.[10] In depicting such traditions in Polish intellectual life before the Second World War, Kolakowski was implicitly justifying his own involvement with the

Polish Communist Party after the Yalta arrangements which consigned Poland to the sphere of Soviet influence. By working within the new social order, the critical Polish intellectuals like Kolakowski were celebrating the fact that Poland had not been absorbed into the USSR. But the most striking aspect of the mature Kolakowski's *Polish nationalism* resides in the refusal to unmask totalitarian collectivism for what it actually became after the war.

Nevertheless E.P. Thompson denounced Leszek Kolalowski for emphasising the totalitarian aspects of 'communist' Poland. But a more careful interrogation of Kolakowski's recent writings would have revealed a visible softening in his criticism of totalitarian 'communist' societies – at least in Poland. As happened to Frantz Fanon earlier on, Kolakowski's traditionalist nationalism has grown much stronger with the passage of time. In defending Polish exceptionalism within Eastern Europe, he emphasises that the Catholic University of Lublin – 'a fact unparalleled in the history of socialist States' – was never suppressed and functions to this day'. Further, despite its 'destructive and obscurantist elements', the Polish 'Marxist' habit of envisaging cultural phenomena as aspects of social conflict, of emphasising the economic and technical background of historical processes and generally studying phenomena in terms of broad historical trends', was a very positive feature of 'the actually existing' socialism.[11]

In lambasting the cultural bureaucrats and hacks in the East and the West, C. Wright Mills put Leszek Kolakowski into the forefront of the international radical scene in 1958 when he published the influential study, *The Causes of World War III*. In criticising the warmongers in the East and the West, he wrote: 'I can no longer write with moral surety unless I know that Leszek Kolakowski will understand where I stand – and I think this means unless he knows I have feelings of equal contempt for both leading types of underdeveloped cultural workmen of the overdeveloped countries of the world'.[12] Unlike Kolakowski, Mills was a rebel, a romantic, an iconoclast and a visionary. In contrast to the critical Polish thinker, Mills unique brand of socialism made him 'impervious to the outraged cries of the genteel academic world of *noblesse oblige* and immune to the hardships of underground life'.[13]

The small independent Left in the West in the 1950s was so desperate to acknowledge any challenge to 'the actually existing socialism' in Eastern Europe that it could not understand what Leszek Kolakowski really stood for. In citing the article produced by the young Polish philosopher at the height of the revisionist ferment in 1957 on 'What Is Socialism?', Irving Howe subsequently insisted that the series of epigrammatic sentences describing what socialism was not could be interpreted as an indication of what it should be. In quoting some of Kolakowski's epigrammatic sentences, Howe thought he could perceive what the Polish revisionists really wanted. Some of those sentences read as follows:

A State which considers itself solidly socialist because it has liquidated private ownership of the means of production.

A State which knows the will of the people before it asks them.

A State in which the philosophers and writers always say the same as the generals and ministers, but always after them.

When he cited Leszek Kolakowski as a model socialist thinker in an article published in 1965 on 'New Styles in "Leftism"', Irving Howe simultaneously criticised Frantz Fanon as a nationalist–revolutionary with strong authoritarian traits in his writings.[14] In criticising Fanon at that time, Howe was in a small minority of a minoritorial Left. It was not until 1972, however, that Fanon's new style in 'leftism' would be defended by such an eloquent spokesperson for the revolutionary role of the 'lumpen-proletariat' in the Third World as Peter Worsley, the English sociologist.[15]

Although post-war totalitarian ' 'communism' compelled Leszek Kolakowski to survive in the existentialist labyrinths of pre-war culture and intellectual traditions, he did not develop a penetrating critique of twentieth-century totalitarianism. By emotionally locating himself within the recent traditions of Polish nationalism, he survived in a sub-existentialist world committed to the preservation of a 'loose, uncodified (Polish) Marxism'. Marxism in Poland did not, in the opinion of the mature philosopher, 'descend to the Soviet level', and it preserved some elements of 'rational thought'.[16]

Because Leszek Kolakowski's critique of 'the actually existing socialism' was circumscribed by a deep emotional attachment to the Polish past and its preservation is a complex post-war world, it was inevitable that he would end up rejecting the socialist project altogether. Lacking an Orwellian grasp of the real nature of totalitarianism in Poland, he could not contribute to a resurgence of socialist internationalism. When he ultimately described Marxism as 'the greatest fantasy of our century', he was simultaneously reflecting and contributing to the tragedies and crises of late-twentieth-century socialism.[17]

At the other end of post-Second World War Two Europe, Frantz Fanon, a brilliant black socialist thinker, was struggling for survival in the sub-existentialist world of left-wing writers and thinkers. Seen through the lens of the 1980s, he had always been 'plagued and embittered by his encounters with racism'.[18] As a student in Paris in the late 1940s, Fanon was discovering the writings of Aimé Césaire and the traditions of European socialism. Under the fleeting influence of the French Communist Party, he was identifying with the dreams and hopes of *the Internationale*. But in conditions where the French communists were supporting the status quo created by the Yalta and Potsdam agreements, Fanon's latent disillusionment with European socialism was already predestined to contribute to the tragedies and crises of modern socialism. Unlike Kolakowski, however, Fanon at least attempted to work with 'the wretched of the earth' in capitalist Europe and the Third World.

During the working-class revolts and 'explosions' in Poland and Hungary in 1956, Kolakowski was a major figure in the 'revisionist' movement of dissident intellectuals. Far from lauding the courageous role of the Polish and Hungarian workers in mounting the first earth-shattering challenge to Stalinism, he made a restricted and restrictive appeal to the intellectuals. He did not focus on the workers' revolts in any of his writings, then or later. He belonged to the elitest tradition of the authoritarians of the Left.

In 1956 the critical intellectuals were the agency of change and hope, not the unlettered and brutish working class. Although the rationalism and 'the magic of the intellect' he attached so much importance to had to reside in subterranean labyrinths, he wanted to modify Polish 'communist' dictatorship by appealing to reason and common sense. While Kolakowski had the temperament of a survivor, Fanon had the temperament of a fighter. Furthermore, although Fanon was a trained scientist, he was too much the uncompromising revolutionary to place excessive hope on reason and rationalism. As he put it in one of his essays: 'I do not carry innocence to the point of believing that appeals to reason or to respect for human dignity can *alter reality*'.

II

When Frantz Fanon was completing his medical training in Paris in 1949, he discovered the little-known book, *General Psychopathology*, by Karl Jaspers on existentialism. In summing up the importance of this discovery, C.L.R. James said: 'The book relieved Fanon of depression and his work became of greater importance to him than his race'.[19] He was not yet a revolutionary practitioner.

A turning-point in Fanon's life came in 1952 when he married a white woman, Josie Dublé. At the same time, he was admitted to the residency programme at the hospital of Saint Alban Mende. In 1954 he became a qualified psychiatrist; and before very long he obtained a post as a psychiatrist in the hospital in Blida in Algeria. When he published his first book in 1952, he was not yet completely disillusioned with the white European Left. It was not until 1956 that the process of disillusionment with the European Left had culminated in another crisis in socialist history. Yet it was not until 1970 that a major European historian would acknowledge in print the role of the European Left's 'paternalism' in creating the illusion of African 'backwardness'.[20]

Out of the experience at the hospital in Blida in Algeria, where a black revolution was in full spate, he produced the influential book, *Black Skin, White Masks*. In 1952 he had still been dedicated to the integration of black and white on the basis of equality. By 1956 he had repudiated the European Left altogether. The tragedy anticipated by Peter Abrahams in 1945 of a conflict between blacks and whites without a socialist basis had come to pass. In a comment summarising his new stance in 1956, Fanon said that 'for a long time now history has been written without the Left in Europe'.[21] By then, 'having witnessed the outbreak of the Algerian revolution, and increasingly aware of the rising independence movements in the black colonies, his project had become that of a political militant'.[22] It was also destined to deepen the cumulative crisis of international socialism.

Yet in 1952, when he published *Black Skins, White Masks*, he was still committed to the goals and objective of socialism as expounded by the most progressive thinkers and militants who belonged to the traditions of the Second International. A self-conscious member of the black elite, Fanon was already under the influence of such black francophone writers as Césaire. But although black resistance to the 'colonisation of the personality' was part of an established literary tradition, the black nationalist literary tradition was itself 'part of a wider social movement of resistance to colonialism which was not just intellectual or literary'.[23] In contrast to Leszek Kolakowski, Fanon emerged as a political militant at a historic moment when he could merge with a social movement hostile to the established social order in the Third World.

Linked by the events of 1956, Kolakowski and Fanon symbolised the cumulative tragedies and crises of twentieth-century socialism. In protesting against the opportunism and world-outlook of orthodox communism, they both inspired the first stirrings of an indepedent Left in the West. When the French Communist parliamentary deputies voted in favour of special powers that enabled the Government to do virtually as it liked in Algeria, Frantz Fanon suffered an agony of genuine outrage. He was not alone. In resigning from the French Communist Party in March 1956, Aimé Césaire said: 'What I desire is that Marxism and communism should serve the black people, not that the black people should serve Marxism and communism'.[24] Fanon was just beginning to move in the same direction, a mere year after he published *Black Skin, White Masks*. He was not, however, a harbinger of an independent, democratic socialism-from-below.

It was unfortunate for the history of international socialism that Frantz Fanon was picking up his 'Marxist' ideas and world-view from Jean Paul Sartre, Césaire and other existentialist thinkers who had no roots in workers' organisations or experiences. In merging Sartre's evolving existentialism with Parisian 'Marxism', Fanon became increasingly preoccupied with the black 'wretched of the earth' at the expense of the Western working class. In looking for the crucial moments in Fanon's development as a revolutionary advocate of a restrictive black Marxism, Peter Worsley said:

His connection with Sartre also reinforced his detachment from orthodox French communism because Sartre and his followers were actively engaged in initiatives against the Algerian war, notably the anti-conscription activities of the Jeanson movement. It was the experience of Algeria, the revolutionary storm-centre to which he naturally gravitated, that finally transformed him into a revolutionary.[25]

Yet Fanon seems to have been more interested in world political developments in 1956 than Kolakowski. Thus Frantz Fanon described the upheavals and suppression in Budapest and Suez as being the really decisive moments in the growth of *mass murder*. Unlike Kolakowski, he did not, however, develop illusions about the existence of freedom anywhere else in the world. Nevertheless in common with Kolakowski, Fanon did not analyse the murderous irrationality of fascism or Russian totalitarian collectivism.[26]

The real turning-point in Frantz Fanon's life came in 1957 when he got caught up in a pro-FLN doctors' strike. By then, he had encountered appalling cases of mental breakdown, neurosis and psychosis. However, he did not see these problems as being latent in the 'human condition'. As Peter Worsley explained: 'Rather he diagnosed them as a result of social strains specific to a particular kind of society – colonialism, and a colonialism at the end of its tether, ready to do anything to human beings in the effort to preserve colonial domination'.[27] He was now destined – however unwittingly – to contribute to deepening the cumulative crises confronting modern man.

It was actually a major tragedy of twentieth-century socialism that Frantz Fanon rejected the socialist assumption of the *common* class interests of all underprivileged and oppressed men and women, irrespective of their creed or colour. Although the words of Fanon's last and most influential book came from the Internationale – *Les Damnés de la Terre* – he had now succumbed to an anti-white black nationalism in which the historical process would henceforth be shaped by the 'lupenproletariat' in the Third World.

While the first signs of profound discontent and disillusionment with the European Left had been seen at the Pan–African Congress in Manchester in 1945, this was simply one among many harbingers of a growing hatred amongst black intellectuals and thinkers for *white Europe* and the West. This black nationalism had already been foreshadowed in Aimé Césaire's lines:

I give my support
to all that is loyal and fraternal to all that
has the courage to be eternally
new to all than can give its heart and fire . . .
Europe
pompous name for excrement.[28]

This hatred, not just for imperialism or the white ruling class, but of 'Europe', *tout court*, quite obviously dominated the existentialist thought-world in which Frantz Fanon survived and studied in Paris after the Second World War.

The independent Left in the West – or rather some members of it – criticised Frantz Fanon before they criticised Leszek Kolakowski. In criticising Fanon for accepting and fostering totalitarian 'methods and values', Irving Howe wrote as follows as early as 1965:

Fanon tried to locate a new source of revolutionary energy: the peasants who, he says, "have nothing to lose and everything to gain". He deprecates the working class: in the Western countries it has been bought off, and in the undeveloped nations it constitutes a tiny "aristocracy". What emerges is a curious version of Trotsky's theory of permanent revolution, concerning national revolts in the backward countries which, to fulfil themselves, must become social revolutions: Fanon assigns to the peasants and the urban declassed poor the vanguard role Trotsky had assigned to the workers.[29]

When he retrospectively attacked the 'ideological fantasies' of the New Left in Europe and America of the 1960s, Kolakowski wrote: 'Apart from leaders of the Third World and Western ideologists interested in the problems, like Frantz Fanon and Regis Debray, the student New Left especially admired Negro leaders in the United States who advocated violence and black radicalism'.[30]

In *The Wretched of the Earth*, Frantz Fanon articulated profoundly un-democratic sentiments. What he really wanted was the single Party totalitarian State in the Third World, though he criticised the vanity of such dictators as Nkrumah. Despite his very acute insights into the process of oppression in the French colonies, he did little to contribute anything to libertarian socialist thought. At a moment when Kolakowski was unobstrusively moving further away from 'Marxism' in totalitarian Poland in the late 1950s, Fanon was making an independent contribution to the growth of an African totalitarianism. As he wrote in *The Wretched of the Earth*: 'Only those underdeveloped countries led by revolutionary élites who have come up from the people can today allow the entry of the masses upon the scene of history'.[31] Socialism-from-above had come to Africa and the Third World just as the European Empires and the worst phase of Stalinism were beginning to break-up and disintegrate.

If a major aspect of the tragedy of international socialism in the 1960s was the role played by Fanon's ideas in America in transforming the revolt of class into a revolt of colour, the rebels and the disaffected in the world, though not always the underprivileged, at least understood what he had said. Fanon was better understood than Kolakowski. But because Kolakowski couched 'the weapon of criticism' in the language of 'Marxism', he reinforced the crises of twentieth-century socialism by creating illusions among independent socialists in the West about the strength of genuine intellectual socialist opposition within Eastern Europe. For although he employed a 'revisionist Marxist jargon, this was – though it was not clear for a long time afterwards – because he was attempting to survive as a defender of Polish national culture and traditions in the midst of totalitarian conditions. Though Kolakowski was not a socialist fighter, he had never been a mere survivor.

Moreover, if the heady days of 1956–57 inspired independent socialists and socialist movements everywhere, E.P. Thompson had not understood Kolakowski when he attacked him for wanting to blur and merge Marxist with non-Marxist philosophies.[32] Yet in a precipitate critique of 'the actually existing' totalitarianism in Poland in the 1950s, Kolakowski was already anticipating that the Trotskyists, Stalinists and détente Liberals and conservatives would ultimately accept the legitimacy, if not the authenticity, of a modernised 'Stalinist' Marxism in the universities of Russia and Eastern Europe. With a growing realisation that the weapon of criticism was inadequate in the modern world, he became more of an uncritical critic.

After his expulsion from the Polish Communist Party in 1968, Kolakowski began to repudiate the socialist goal of a classless society as an impossible Utopia. This was done in such important essays as 'The Myth of Human Identity' and 'The Meaning of Tradition'. In suggesting that the class struggle for the distribution of the surplus product would almost certainly go on in societies in which the means of production, distribution and exchange existed under common ownership, he was being increasingly drawn towards the elementary freedoms of speech and assembly in the 'democratic West'. Despite the essay that he published in *Encounter* on 'Intellectuals, Hope and Heresy' in October 1971 – an essay in which he savaged the New Left in Europe and America for its irrational behaviour – Kolakowski retained a deceptive reputation as a radical 'socialist'.[33] This was not just the consequence of the independent Left's comparative failure to understand the nature of totalitarianism in Russia and Eastern Europe. It was also a result of the essay he published in the *Socialist Register* towards the end of 1971 on 'Althusser's Marx'.[34]

It was symptomatic of the tragedy and crisis of international socialism and the parochialism of the English Left that E.P. Thompson could savage Kolakowski in 1973 for suggesting that 'human evil' might be rooted in biological rather than in social circumstances and yet appeal to his inherent 'socialist sentiments'.[35] This peculiarly English socialist parochialism was also revealed in Thompson's insistence that the problems confronting left-wing intellectuals in the West and the East were a result of their isolation from 'large popular movements'. But in attacking Kolakowski's statement that 'religious consciousness' was 'irreplaceable' because it fulfilled a human need, Thompson was betraying his own ignorance of existentialist 'survival' in totalitarian societies.[36]

III

From the perspective of the 1980s, the absence of socialism was not simply a hiatus but a prolonged conjuncture and impasse unpredictable at the end of the Second World War. In these circumstances, the continuities and limitations of these two major socialist thinkers' ideas were environmentally-engendered. For in very different ways, Kolakowski, the Polish traditonalist, and Fanon, the *avant-garde* revolutionary, helped to preserve the international capitalist *status quo*. Socialism was not an idea whose time had come.

In their own distinctive characters and intellectual traits, Kolakowski and Fanon expressed and reinforced the crises of socialist internationalism at the end of the Second World War. As very young men, they had been radicalised by the experience of total war, mass murder and a vast impersonal system of 'irrationalism'. While Fanon summarised the profound thoughts he had formulated in a short, painful and creative life in *The Wretched of the Earth*, the culmination of what Kolakowski began to say in the 1950s found its ultimate expression in an impressive three-volume work on *The Main Currents of Marxism* in the late 1970s.

In a brilliant response to E.P. Thompson's open letter, Leszek Kolakowski used the weapons of the jester – the weapons of satire and irony – to attack the suggestion that the new societies in Russia and Eastern Europe were moving towards socialism. He also ridiculed Thompson's assertion about the existence of a late-twentieth-century 'Marxist family defined by the spiritual descendance from Marx'. But although Thompson had previously disapproved of Kolakowski's role as a jester in 'communist' Poland, the jester made a devastating point when he asked: 'Do you mean that all people who in one way or another call themselves Marxists form a family (never mind that they have been killing each other for half a century and still do) opposed as such to the rest of the world?' In depicting the tragedy of socialism in the twentieth century, Kolakowski focused on 'the great Apocalypse' likely to trigger off war 'between two Empires both claiming to be perfect embodiments of Marxism'.[37]

It was a major paradox of contemporary socialism that both E.P. Thompson and Leszek Kolakowski claimed to stand in the rationalist traditions of the Enlightenment at the same time as they refused to face up to the intellectual complexities created by totalitarian collectivism. Furthermore, because Kolakowski did not really understand totalitarianism in the way that Victor Serge and George Orwell did, he could not engage in a dialogue with Thompson on why religious sentiments had survived in so-called 'communist' societies. But in an important book, *The Crisis in Historical Materialism*, Stanley Aronowitz had explained that: 'If religion is the only place where the expression of and protest against emotional suffering (which is grounded in both exploitation and sexual repression) is possible, it will survive the creation of a new society'.[38]

In a retrospective critique of black thinkers like Frantz Fanon, Leszek Kolakowski wrote: 'The contemporary enthusiasm of intellectuals for peasant and lupenproletarian movements or for movements inspired by the ideology of national minorities is an enthusiasm for that which in these movements is reactionary and hostile to culture – for their contempt of knowledge, for the cult of violence, for the spirit of vengeance, for racism.' But although some left-wing intellectuals in the West in the 1970s did act in the spirit of intellectuals against the intellect, Kolakowski was much softer in his criticisms of their counterparts in totalitarian Poland.

Moreover, in defending the inherent rationalism of dissident Marxism, E.P. Thompson managed to overlook the *obscurantist* views of New Left thinkers like Peter Worsley, a leading New Left thinker who worked closely with Thompson in the 1950s and 1960s. In defending 'the actually existing socialism' today, Worsley argues that:

Further, whatever one's reservations about and criticisms of Soviet and other forms of State socialism, and the distortions caused by the struggle to survive and grow in a world in which capitalism is still far stronger materially and militarily, the socialism that has developed up to now – however authoritarian – is fundamentally oriented to establishing not only collectivist, but an egalitarian alternative to capitalism, and draws its ideas and ideals from the Marxist founding fathers.[39]

What united Kolakowski, Fanon, Thompson and Worsley was the assumption that 'Marxism' had displayed some 'positive' features in Eastern Europe.

However, since the end of the Second World War Marxism in Poland has been transformed into a 'science' of mumbojumbo and gobbledygook. By playing the jester – a jester deeply committed to preserving Polish national traditions in incredibly difficult circumstances – Kolakowski helped to conceal the nature of totalitarian irrationalism operating under the guise of 'socialism'. But he would not have been able to play this role in the 1950s and 1960s if allegedly 'critical' socialist thinkers in the West had not been so uncritical of Russia and Eastern Europe.[40]

In Poland – and elsewhere in Eastern Europe – the totalitarian context was decisive. The social sciences were not, and are not, therefore just very conservative. They were, and are, utterly irrational. In so far as they refuse to acknowledge such tangible problems as wife-beating, child abuse, prostitution, industrial accidents and political dissidence as *social problems*, they are not comparable to the social sciences in the West. While such problems were, and are, occasionally, discussed by Polish social scientists, they were portrayed as pathological or psychological ones. 'Socialist' society in Poland was excellent. There was, however, something profoundly wrong with the individuals who railed against it.

Because such critical thinkers as Ernest Mandel dismiss the problem of *totalitarianism*,[41] the social sciences in the Polish universities are not seen for what they really are – a medieval-like mumbojumbo. In a pertinent critique of the Polish sociologist Stanislaw Ossowska, Mandel argues: 'Here we plainly pass from a sociology based on the ideas of social class and surplus social product to a sociology based on the concept relatively vaguer and less operative, of "dominant groups". And a bridge is established between critical but revisionist sociology (and philosophy) in the socialist countries and the academic sociology of capitalist countries, which rejects Marxism in favour of a division of society into "those who command" and "those who obey"'.[42] But a sociology which refused to acknowledge the very real problems arising out of and yet impinging on the lives of workers and peasants was, and is, inherently uncritical and intellectually stagnant.[43] By insisting on the rational features of Polish Marxism, Mandel and Kolakowski were concealing the real nature of intellectual life in totalitarian societies.[44]

What Leszek Kolakowski and Frantz Fanon succeeded in doing after the Second World War was to reflect and reinforce the tragedy of twentieth-century socialism. They illuminated rather than transformed it.

Furthermore, if Leszek Kolakowski and Frantz Fanon failed to develop a critical analysis of modern totalitarian capitalism, they were quite typical of those left-wing intellectuals who had been moulded in an era of fascism and Stalinism. While Kolakowski ended up in the 'free West', Fanon ended up in Africa as, in the phrase of David Caute, 'a voice in the wilderness'.[45] In their shared isolation from working-class movements, they expressed the agonised and agonising fate of international socialism after the Second World War.

Chapter 11

Contemporary Socialism: Tragedies and crises, 1939–86

But fascism has delivered a hard blow to socialism. . . . The harm done to the socialist movement by the death of innumerable militant Marxists was grave enough, but the demonstration of the practicality of adapting working-class organisation to reactionary purposes was graver still.

Ignazio Silone

The continuity and discontinuity in the *phases* of the history of socialism since 1939 have been characterised by successive tragedies and crises. Any continuity in the historical development of socialism was destroyed by the rise of fascism. Together with Stalinist red 'communism', fascism contributed immeasurably to the tragedies and crises of world socialism after 1939.

In glancing back to the period of the Second World War – a period when the fascists' hegemony over large parts of the world marked a tragic episode in socialist history – Irving Howe challenged the *'rationalism'* of classical Marxist explanations of political developments by asking if the class interests of the German bourgeoisie 'were significantly at stake in Auschwitz and Buchenwald'.[1] Moreover, Isaac Deutscher also unwittingly contributed to the *crisis of historical materialism* by questioning the very possibility of 'historical interpretation and explanation' in relation to 'the Jewish tragedy' during the Second World War. In summing up the limitations of Marxist or any other historical explanation of the Jewish tragedy, he said: 'I doubt whether even in a thousand years people will understand Hitler, Auschwitz, Majdanek and Treblinka better than we do now'.[2]

Yet in *The School for Dictators* published in 1939, Ignazio Silone predicted with prophetic brilliance that 'every future counter-revolutionary and anti-socialist movement in the countries which are still democratic will assume a popular, even a plebeian mask'.[3] Indeed, when the GPU and the Gestapo co-operated with each other at the beginning of the Second World War in murdering socialists and communists, Boris Souvarine's comments on 'the massacre' of communist leaders from many countries in Stalin's Russia illuminated the common characteristics of the 'communists' and the fascists in using a plebeian mask to defend the established social order.[4]

In the early years of the Second World War the combined forces of Stalinism and fascism did immense damage to *the socialist idea*. The years 1940, 1941 and 1942 constituted 'dark times' for the authentic, militant democratic Left in the world at large. As Ernest Mandel puts it: 'The lights of civilisation seemed to go out one by one – in Europe, in Asia, in the USSR. Barbarism seemed to be on the move everywhere . . . Victor Serge gave one of his novels the apt title: *Midnight in the Century*'.[5]

In Europe the fascists' totalitarian hegemony was challenged throughout the Second World War, though the Left did not achieve any marked success until 1944. In America and large parts of Asia and Africa, working-class men and women and peasants challenged the status quo. However, the Socialist Party of America was pitifully weak, and the American workers' industrial militancy was circumscribed by the rise of a stronger labour bureaucracy in both the American Federation of Labour and the Congress of Industrial Organisation.[6]

I

The beginning of the end for Italian and German fascism was seen in the mass strikes of millions of Italian workers in 1943. As the *New York Times* reported in July 1943:

The first eyewitness accounts from Germany on Berlin's reaction to the fall of Italian fascism reveal that the Reich capital experienced its most troublesome day since Afolf Hitler assumed power . . . Numerous Italian metal workers in the Siemens-Schuckert plant took the lead in the Monday pause to celebrate the news, just announced by the Reich radio, singing the *Internationale*. Their German fellow-workers joined in. . . . In the afternoon illegal tracts appeared as from nowhere. . . . In the working men (sic) slums in Wedding and Moabit such inscriptions as "Hitler dead, Berlin stays red".[7]

When the Allies landed in Italy at that time, Mussolini's own Fascist Council got rid of him. Then King Victor Emanuel appointed Marshal Badoglio, the Chief of the General Staff, as his successor; and the Allies made a secret deal to keep Victor Emanuel on the throne.

Although the Italian fascists' hegemony over the working class seemed to be total and complete in 1939, it most certainly was not. In the important book by Luisa Paserini, *Fascism in Popular Memory: The Cultural Experience of the Italian Working Class*, oral history has been used as a means of documenting the workers' hostility to the fascists. Despite the contrary *impression* of Benedetto Croce, the distinguished Italian philosopher, the workers had not succumbed to fascism. While nationalist sentiments intermingled with workers' own values, Passerini sketches in the workers' resistance to Mussolini *and* 'the language of totalitarianism'.[8] But before Mussolini was caught and executed by communist partisans in April 1945, the Allies were already co-operating with the remnants of the Italian ruling class and helping them to conceal their war crimes.[9]

In a leaflet issued by the leaders of the Independent Labour Party and the Italian Socialist Party in London in 1943, the 'future of the *socialist revolution* in Europe' was eagerly anticipated. The European working class was most certainly militant; and in an appeal to 'Stand by the Italian Revolution', Fenner Brockway, Giovanni Giglio and Walter Padley reported that:

The Italian socialists are challenging Badoglio with mass strikes and demonstrations, demanding immediate peace negotiated by delegates chosen by the Italian people. The unrest in Italy has encouraged the anti-fascist forces all over Europe. Reports have come through from Hamburg that anti-Hitler posters have been displayed, and from Berlin that troops have been used to disperse an anti-war demonstration by war widows.[10]

However, if the Allies were haunted by the prospect of the spectre of communism in Europe and elsewhere, so were the 'communists'. From London to New York such leaders of the Communist Party as Harry Pollitt and Earl Browder were committed to the *status quo* as defined and re-defined by Joseph Stalin. In January 1944, Earl Browder pleaded for 'a continuation of national unity into the post-war period for a long term of years', based upon 'a compromise between the classes'. It was the task of the Left to make capitalism work effectively in the post-war period, and socialists and communists were not to 'raise the issue of socialism in such a form and manner as to endanger or weaken that national unity'. In the book, *Answers to Questions*, published in 1944, Harry Pollitt argued a similar thesis.[11]

In the talks between Winston Churchill, F.D. Roosevelt and Joseph Stalin at Potsdam and Yalta, the constant *motif* was one of *realpolitik* in the re-drawing of the map of the world. Although the communist parties throughout the world used radical rhetoric behind a plebeian mask, they were hostile to militant, democratic socialism-from-below. In a very perceptive comment illuminating the pressure the communist parties were under from 1943 onwards, Gabriel Kolko said: 'Moving from East to West, the statistics on the rise of the communist parties from the depression decade to 1944–1948 simply show that war and stability were incompatible with the Old Order'.[12]

Although a few independent socialist voices in Europe and America criticised Stalin for supporting Badogilo, the Italian fascist dictator, and 'power politics' in the world at large, they were brushed aside with contempt. When socialists throughout Europe in 1944 appealed for a regenerated Italian democracy under the promises of the Atlantic Charter and a new socialist International, they were ignored. By October 1944, however, it was clear that the Italian socialists were preparing to merge their independent identity in the Italian Communist Party.[13]

In addition to their worry about what was happening in Italy, the Allies were already worried by events in Greece and Yugoslavia in 1943. When he wrote to Churchill in August 1943, Field Marshall Jan Smuts expressed general ruling-class fears:

With politics let loose among those people, we may have a wave of disorder and wholesale communism set going all over those parts of Europe.

This may even be the danger of Italy . . .

Furthermore, as Ernest Mandel argues, there had been considerable resistance to Nazism in Germany itself. As he puts it: 'Yet between February 1933 and September 1939, 225,000 men and women were condemned by Nazi courts for political reasons'.[14]

In a vivid description of what happened in *Stalin's Satellites in Europe* towards the end of the Second World War, Ygael Gluckstein said that the Russian communists' unyielding 'opposition to any spontaneous independent and democratic action by the masses' was seen in Poland in 1944 during the Warsaw uprising. During the Second World War itself, the Polish socialists played a consistent role in leading the opposition against the fascists.

In 1940 the Polish Socialist Party formed a secret Party movement, the Movement of the Working Masses of Poland (WRN). The new movement organised a socialist militia on a territorial and a factory basis as well as an underground socialist press. As Adam Ciolkosz pointed out: 'The underground socialist press and pamphlets reached, in the course of the war, the amazing figure of 2 million copies'.[15]

With the approaching 'hour of the final and open rising against the Germans' in May 1944 the WRN reverted to the older name of the PPS. In depicting the ways in which the Russians and their Polish allies expropriated the Polish Socialist Party (PPS), Adam Ciolkosz insisted that: 'There is little doubt that the bulk of the working class of Poland, including the rank and file of the "official" PPS, remains faithful to the ideals of democratic socialism and loyal to the authentic PPS.' Even so, by 1946 he sketched in one aspect of the tragedy of socialism when he said: 'In present circumstances, no free socialist press can exist.' In 1949 the new Party was named the United Polish Workers' party; and as early as 1949 one historian noted that Gomulka 'held nationalist views similar to Tito's'.[16]

Meanwhile the French Communist Party assisted General De Gaulle to suppress the movements for national liberation in Algeria, Syria and the Lebanon. Despite Stalin's reluctance to help in the process of fomenting revolution in China, some form of socialism was now inevitable. In explaining what happened there towards the end of the war, Ernest Mandel said: 'Leadership of this resurgence was not forthcoming from the Chinese bourgeoisie, which increasingly feared it. Instead, the Communist Party of China became the leader of the national struggle for survival.' What came to China was the same thing which came to Eastern Europe – socialism-from-above, despite the genuine elements in the Chinese case of popular insurgency.[17]

In the heartland of capitalism working people were moving steadily to the Left during *Britain's War-Time Revolution*, and Hamilton Fyfe was already, in 1944, anticipating the election of the first 'majority' Labour government. In Cario the 'Forces Parliament' demonstrated their sympathy for the Left and the need for profound social change. Then in February 1946 two ships of the Royal Indian Navy mutinied before the Indians gained independence. The mutiny was motivated by such grievances as inadequate food. At the same time, however, the mutineers backed the demands of the Indian Congress for national independence. Before a number of the mutineers were shot dead, Basil Davidson described what happened: 'Carrying this anti-colonial demonstration further, Bombay trade unions declared a general strike in sympathy with the sailors. Both strike and mutiny were settled in the end by mediation through Indian Congress spokesmen.'[18]

But despite the Left's excellent prospects for coming to power democratically in Italy, the opportunity was thrown away. Although it was not obvious to many except the most critical socialists at the end of the Second World War, the communists did not want socialism-from-below. This was most obvious in Italy, though the prospects of making a democratic socialist society could not have been eradicated without the help of the fellow-travellers. In explaining what happened in Italy at the end of the War, Maurice F. Neufeld wrote: 'Under Pietro Nenni, the Socialist Party did not act like the second strongest political force in the country. Instead, it engaged in oratorical splendors and maximalist demagogery and surrendered initiative to the communists. In the fall of 1946, Nenni drew the Socialist Party even closer to the Communist Party.' In France towards the end of the war, the communists did everything in their power in inhibit the development of a popular revolution. As Peter Novick explained the communists in France followed a consistent policy of 'subordinating political goals to the war effort'.[19]

Although socialism-from-above had existed as a theory for hundreds of years, it was not really implemented on a large scale until the end of the Second World War. In the important book by Gabriel Kolko, *The Politics of War*, the role of Stalin and the communist parties in sustaining the status quo was documented in great detail. Certainly, the year 1945 was a crucial one in restoring capitalism in some parts of the world and in creating a new social order of bureaucratic collectivism elsewhere. In Greece, for example, Stalin sacrificed the Left in the interests of 'socialism in one country'. In depicting Stalin's betrayal of the communists and socialists in Greece, Kolko asserted that: 'Stalin has been utterly indifferent to the fate of the Greek people, and repeatedly assured the English (ruling class) that he regarded the nation as within their sphere of influence and vital to their security'.[20]

Despite the old ruling classes' obsessive fear of the communists, Stalin had no intention of allowing the Left to create genuine socialist societies. In Italy the communists preferred, in the idiom of Gabriel Kolko, 'to enter the intrigues of Cabinet politics, secure posts for themselves in Rome, and stress their new role as the Party of all Italians, irrespective of religion, class, or philosophy, who lived by their own labour'.[21] As early as 1945 the

French communists called upon the workers, and particularly the coal miners, to 'overcome their "deficient psychology", avoid strikes and absenteeism, and produce'. Although Europe was a crucible of workers' democracy and latent socialist revolution, the communists were just as committed to the status quo as the former ruling classes in Europe. Only the conservatism of the Russian communists stood, as Kolko put it, 'between the old Order and revolution'.

A major aspect of the cumulative tragedies and crises of the democratic Left during and at the end of the war resided in the role of the communists in restoring capitalism in many parts of the world. Although European and American imperialism and Russian bureaucratic collectivism could suppress revolution in China, the spontaneous peasants' uprisings made room for Mao's socialism-from-above. Despite the huge upsurge of workers' militancy in the heartland of capitalist Europe, the communists objectively assisted in the restoration of the status quo. But socialism-from-above in Eastern Europe did not develop without major challenges. As Ernest Mandel puts it: 'Even in Eastern Europe, independent class activity put some constraints on the Kremlin's plans – at least temporarily – in East Germany, Czechoslavakia and Hungary'.[22]

Although Joseph Stalin's authoritarian socialism-from-above was not *novel*, it was at least distinctive. In sharing the same anti-working-class attitudes as the traditional advocates of socialism-from-above and the authoritarians of the Left, Stalin did not like militant working people. As Ernest Mandel said of Stalin's attitudes during and at the end of the war: 'Stalin's whole strategy towards Europe was, of course, premised on deep distrust, especially of the German working class.' Nevertheless the socialism-from-above represented by Stalin and the Russian communists was unique in so far as Stalin was the first 'socialist' dictator who was *conscious* of his power to *impose* socialism-from-above. In April 1945 Stalin told Tito and Djilas during their trip to Moscow that: 'This war is not as in the past; whoever occupies a territory also imposes his own social system. Everyone imposes his own system as far as *his* army has the power to do so'.[23]

As early as 1943 J.F. Horrabin was so disappointed with the Left's response to the growth of Pan-Africanism that he helped to initiate a new left-wing socialist pressure group – the Socialist Vanguard Group. In one of the Group's first publications, *The Future of International Socialism*, he wrote that:

We have to draw up a socialist charter for the colonies. Brutal misrule of Africa for five centuries by Europeans has left a continent riddled with disease and poverty. Little has been done to eliminate these ghastly evils. Remember the present war can be said to have started in Africa, in Abyssinia. The riches of Africa for fifty years have caused international conflict.[24]

For J.F. Horrabin, Frank Ridley and George Padmore 'the oppressed Negro in South Africa' was 'the Jew of the colonial world'.

By 1945 the international Pan-African movement meeting in the English city of Manchester made it plain that the Africans were now prepared to go it alone without waiting for the white European socialists. Despite the efforts of the small independent Left in Europe and America at the end of the war, the labour movement did not attempt to foster the break-up of European imperialism.

The growing divisions between the black Africans and the white European socialists deepened. This was another of the cumulative crises confronting the independent Left; and in adding to the multi-dimensional crises of the independent, anti-totalitarian Left, the European labour movements' comparative indifference to the struggles of the black Africans for self-autonomy gave a new aura of tragedy to the development of international socialism. In depicting the development of a black Marxism which was innately inimical to the emergence of a militant, democratic socialism-from-below, Cedric J. Robinson said: 'At first they (the black Marxists) would believe that the answer lay in the vision of class struggle, the war between brothers, as Julius Nyerere would characterise Marxist socialist theory'.[25] But the various plebeian masks developed by such practitioners of socialism-from-above as Nyerere and Fanon had resulted in new tragedies for those independent socialists who were struggling to develop a global socialism-from-below.

Though he insisted with the benefit of hindsight that the communists 'did something to assist the struggles for colonial independence' and to assist in 'the defeat of fascism between 1942–45', E.P. Thompson ignored the communists' role in crushing independent socialists and socialism throughout the world.[26] That particular phase in the history of international socialism was suffused with tragedies and crises; and the *absence* of the communists' role in attempting to eradicate independent socialist movements in otherwise critical left-wing historiography has contributed to the impasse in which international socialism now finds itself.

II

Although the Communist parties grew enormously almost everywhere towards the end of the Second World War, the communists' role in the early post-war world as defenders of capitalism and bureaucratic collectivism contributed to the decline of independent socialist movements. In Eastern Europe the communists set out to destroy the existing socialist organisations by a mixture of deception and repression. While the socialists had been stronger in some than in other of Stalin's satellites in Europe, they were a uniform obstacle everywhere in Eastern Europe in the way of the creation of the so-called 'Peoples Democracies'.

When the Russian army entered Poland in 1944, one of its main objectives was the destruction of independent socialist movements. In Poland, Hungary, Rumania, Bulgaria and Czechoslovakia in the late

1940s, the representatives and puppets of Russian totalitarian 'communism' sought to liquidate the socialist movements. In destroying, bribing, imprisoning and incorporating independent socialists into their vast, impersonal, totalitarian machine, the communists in those countries were imposing a form of 'socialism'-from-above.[27]

In countries where the communists had mass support – for example, France, Italy and Greece – the status quo was not challenged. In Britain and America the communists' role in weakening independent socialist groups and independent left-wing journals was not inconsiderable. Nevertheless in the late 1940s and early 1950s independent socialist currents were undermined still further by the destruction of traditional working-class communities, the Cold War and McCarthyism.[28] In most of the bourgeois Parliamentary democracies with the exception of Italy, where Nenni slavishly toed the communists' ever-changing line, the traditional socialist parties increasingly moved to the Right. In Britain the radicalisation witnessed towards the end of the war was soon tamed by successive Labour Party leaders.[29] In the early post-war years, the Left in Italy was, as John L. Harper puts it, 'shell-shocked' and the 'sullen forces of the Left' were reduced to looking on from the sidelines.[30] The same pattern was evident elsewhere in non-communist Europe.

By an irony of history independent socialism remained much stronger in totalitarian Eastern Europe than it did in Western Europe. In the late 1940s it was not totalitarianism which weakened the determination of the socialists in Czechoslovakia to preserve something of their independent socialist traditions and attitudes. It was, in fact, 'the uncertainty' of the socialist leadership.[31] In East Germany, too, the independent socialists were persecuted or, in some cases, incorporated into the communists' totalitarian system with its vast apparatus of thought-control. It was only in Czechoslovakia, where the communists had some popular support in cities like Prague, that the communists could conceivably present themselves as democrats. But the communists' *coup* in Prague in 1948 was clearly an example of socialism being imposed from above.[32]

The caricatured 'socialism' in Eastern Europe after the Second World War did not just create bewilderment in the ranks of independent socialists elsewhere. It also created widespread confusion about the very possibility of democratic socialism in the modern world. However, a series of events beginning with the East German workers' rising in 1953 and culminating in Nikita Khruschev's denunciation of Stalin at the twentieth congress of the Soviet Communist Party in 1956 and the Hungarian revolution put independent, democratic socialism back onto the political map of the modern world.

The rising stream of refugees from East Germany into West Berlin in 1952 foreshadowed the mass revolt of 1953. As Stefan Brandt put it: 'To hutted camps, disused factories, air-raid shelters, exhibitions halls and private houses – month after month they came, a seemingly endless stream of miserable victims of so-called socialism.' With anger and accuracy, Brandt described the immediate background to the East German rising:

A godless and desolate Puritanism laid down the law of "socialist morals", as though Eros himself were being persecuted. Certainly he was driven out of the arts; novels, plays, films and paintings created new heroes of labour, war, revolution and ideology. Laughter died away and happiness disappeared.

However, before Russian tanks were used to drown the workers' uprising in blood, the German workers demonstrated their attachment to authentic socialism-from-below.[33]

The East German uprising was a decisive turning-point in the history of post-war international socialism. In fighting against Russian tanks as well as against their own 'communist' regime, the East German workers exposed the totalitarian nature of 'the actually existing socialism' in Eastern Europe. In summing up the significance of this important political development, Raya Dunayevskaya wrote: 'The East Germans wrote a glorious page in this struggle for they answered, in an unmistakable affirmative, Can man achieve freedom out of the totalitarianism of our age?'[34]

Out of the upheavals which began in Eastern Europe with the East German workers' mass uprising in 1953, a whole number of new socialist scholars began to make an important contribution to authentic socialist literature. In Hungary, Poland, Czechoslovakia and East Germany a new generation of dissident socialists would subsequently document the 'revolt of the mind' in the midst of totalitarian conditions and circumstances. In defending socialism-from-below against 'communist' totalitarianism, Ivan Svitak wrote: 'Marx was an internationalist, for whom national frontiers were barriers to understanding between nations and between the working classes. But the doctrine of socialism in one country, which is incompatible with Marx's appeal to the workers of the world, has created a nationalistic pattern of co-operation between unequal nations'.[35]

When he published, *Mariners, Renegades and Castaways: The Story of Herman Merville and the World We Live In*, in 1953, C.L.R. James was insisting that any hope for socialism resided in the reality of workers' lives, and not in the heads of intellectuals. In focusing on the degeneration of socialist movements, a decaying capitalism and the communists' totalitarian societies, he denounced Western intellectuals in particular in the name of classical socialist humanism by concluding that:

Some of them are men of very great gifts, but for all of them, human beings are the naked and the dead, for whom there is nothing between here and eternity, life is a journey to the end of the night, where in the darkness of midday, the neurotic personality of our time escapes into a wasteland of guilt and hopelessness.[36]

But although left-wing intellectuals in the West did contribute to socialist theory and literature in the 1940s, 1950s and 1960s, the most perceptive left-wing analysis in the post-Second World War world have come out of the experiences of those intellectuals who had to live in colonial and totalitarian labyrinths.

Moreover, although the socialist intellectuals' 'revolt of the mind' created the crucial pre-conditions for the Hungarian revolution in 1956, pre-war socialist traditions and attitudes survived in Stalin's Europe after the Second World War. Despite the Stalinists' propaganda against all independent socialist thought summed up in the dismissive phrase 'From Trotsky to Tito', leftists in the so-called 'People's Democracies' disseminated Titoist literature in the universities, factories and coal mines. Although Titoist literature was taken away and burned by the secret police in Hungary before the revolution in 1956, the resentments of the intellectuals and militant workers could not be contained within the powerful totalitarian framework constructed by the communists in the 1940s.

What was decisive in precipitating the mass revolts in Poland and Hungary in 1956 was the Khruschev denunciation of 'Stalinism' at the twentieth congress of the Russian Communist party. Yet by July 1956 several months after Khruschev's speech, an 'atmosphere of terror again prevaded' Budapest. The Hungarian revolution was certainly precipitated by writers' clubs and workers' councils. The speech made by the writer, Tibor Meray, acted as a catalyst for accumulated discontent and resentments when he said: 'The telling of truth is our most imperative inner necessity. ... It is not the State-owned automobiles, the alternating drivers, the special stores, the extra-high salaries, the protocol lists, etc., that make the journalist. It is whether or not he is a militant of truth'.[37]

In depicting the history of workers' revolts under totalitarian 'communism', Neal Ascherson emphasised the much greater independence of the rebellious working class in Hungary than in Poland. Although the dissident socialist intellectuals in Hungary articulated the grievances of the Hungarian workers, the relative autonomy of the Hungarian workers' councils did allow them to 'formulate a programme for a provisional Republic of workers' councils'. By contrast, the dissident intellectuals in Poland were able to use the workers' councils as a source of political mobilisation against 'the old Stalinist clique' in the PUWP.[38] In stressing the point made by Ascherson in more socialist language about the differences between the dissident movements in Poland and Hungary, C.L.R. James said: 'Working, thinking, fighting, bleeding Hungary, never for a moment forgot that it was incubating a new society, not only for Hungary but for all mankind.'[39]

When Joseph Stalin decreed the dissolution of the Third International in 1943, he was initiating the break-up of the hitherto all-powerful Russian hegemony over existing communist movements. Although he was unable to kill Marshall Tito of Yugoslavia by anathema in 1948, Stalin kept his satellites in Eastern Europe in a totalitarian prison. It was – and it remains – simultaneously a tragedy and crisis of socialism that totalitarian 'communism' survived the dictator's death in 1953.

Despite Stalin's death a decade after the dissolution of the Third International, and despite the weakening of the Russians' hegemony over working-class movements, totalitarian 'communism' acted as a powerful break on the development of authentic socialism-from-below. As Bertram

D. Wolfe explained : 'Somehow, Stalin held the flawed edifice together by his machine-made prestige and his wide-ranging terror, until his death.'[40]

Yet Stalinism was not entirely to blame for the decline of the independent Left everywhere. In examining the causes of the prolonged and protracted decline of the Socialist Party of America after the First World War, James C. Durham, a biographer of Norman Thomas, the American socialists' long-time leader, endorsed Thomas's own argument that the decline of socialism in America was 'the product of events largely beyond the control of socialists'.[41] An important factor in weakening the appeal of American socialism amongst Afro-Americans was the Socialist Workers' Party's hostility to 'mixed marriages' and social intercourse between black men and white women.[42]

It was a major tragedy of international socialism that the European socialists were so timid and unimaginative in the 1940s and early 1950s. As Albert S. Lindemann put it: 'For a number of years immediately following World War II an important unifying force for most democratic socialists was anti-communism. . . . In nearly all European countries democratic socialists after the war projected an image of openness, moral earnestness, and pragmatism.' But in opposition to Leon Blum's strictures against entering the Cabinets of bourgeois governments, the French and other European socialists abandoned their political independence.[43]

In Israel, too, the experiment in democratic socialism was not a success, though it began quite well. In a favourable and optimistic view, Julius Braunthal wrote: 'The State of Israel came into existence as a result of socialist initiative. Socialists have governed it since its foundation, realising socialist ideas in economic, social and cultural institutions, thereby imprinting socialism more deeply into the character of the social order than in any other country that has a democratic system of government'. However, according to Moshe Lewin, the transition to 'the post-revolutionary period' was 'very swift'. Later on he wrote with some bitterness when he confessed: 'At that time I did not realise that, at least to some extent, outcomes of romantic movements always deceive the tenets of original creeds.'[44]

If the Left lost the battle for authentic democratic socialism in Israel as early as 1955, the Hungarian workers' revolt in 1956 offered hope of the better socialist world to come. In any event, the democratic Hungarian Republic of workers' councils was soon drowned in the blood of 'at least 20,000 Hungarian dead' before the 'mass deportations of Hungarian patriots' to Russia. What Peter Fryer depicted as the *Hungarian Tragedy* was also a tragedy in the history of post-war international socialism.[45]

The two decades before the 'explosion' of the revolutions of 1968 were black, bleak and brash. In the late 1940s and 1950s international socialism moved to the Right in response to the behaviour of 'dictatorial communism' in Europe. A decisive factor in this further drift to the Right was what had happened in Prague in 1948. As Julius Braunthal explained: 'Yet the very idea that Social Democracy might approve an alliance with the capitalist United States against the Soviet Union had been unthinkable before the Prague *coup d'état'*. In surveying the history of world socialism down to the year 1968, Julius Braunthal concluded that:

The socialist idea, however, has permeated all cultural fields, has inspired the thinking of all races, has become the fundamental principle for nations containing a third of humanity.[46]

The reality was more tragic, crisis-ridden and doom-laden.

Moreover, although such independent socialist Pan-Africanists as Ras Makonnen became increasingly critical of socialists like Fenner Brockway and other European socialists, the American and European Left were very enthusiastic about the seemingly socialist revolution in the Gold Coast. What the revolution in Ghana foreshadowed and prefigured in the late 1950s, however, was a new form of authoritarian African capitalism.[47] In a study *Behind the Rape of Hungary* published in 1957, Francos Fejto, noted that 'a Red aristocracy based on a police force and foreign troops' had arisen long before 1956. And in describing the background to the rape of Hungary, Fejto argued that:

The writers and journalists made the important discovery that lies cannot contribute to progress. They discovered that the workers' socialist movement needs the truth that can be achieved by means of discussion and the free confrontation of ideas.

Tragically, very few of the left-wing African intellectuals were prepared to criticise the emerging ruling classes in Africa.[48] As Lewis Coser and Irving Howe feared when they produced their influential essay in the 1950s on the 'Authoritarians of the "Left"', socialism-from-above was coming to Africa and Asia.[49]

III

In delineating what happened in Czechoslavakia and Stalin's other satellites in Eastern Europe after the Second World War, Ivan Svitak wrote: 'Like the Soviet bureaucratic elite earlier, the Czech bureaucratic elite seized the collective ownership of the means of production . . . made the distribution of utility values its sovereign domain, installed a system of privileges and social inequality and, through terror, secured the expolitive practice of appropriation of the surplus product'. Furthermore, the new power elite in Czechoslovakia (population, 14,000,000) comprised roughly 100,000 people who 'held key positions in the State and Party apparatus'. But despite the immense political power of the 'power elite', the middle-class intelligentsia had not abandoned their sympathy for democratic socialism in the 1950s and early 1960s.

Socialist ideas were not eradicated in Eastern Europe; and there was considerable working-class support in Hungary and Czechoslovakia for the collective ownership of the means of production, distribution and exchange. There was also a strong element of popular support for the Czech 'communists' before their totalitarianism was fully developed. With the development of the Stalinist counter-revolution from above, Czech totalitarianism did not, as Ivan Svitak put it, 'need time to degenerate simply because it came into being a *degenerate* of socialist revolution'.[50] But until the year of the barricades in 1968, the *possibility* of authentic democratic socialism-from-below appeared to have been eliminated.

At the same time as he ridiculed the idea of socialism-from-below as a realistic possibility in the future, Eric J. Hobsbawm supported Stalinist socialism-from-above in the 1950s and early 1960s. However, in 1968 the political revolution in France forced Hobsbawm to revise his views about proletarian revolution. As he explained in the *Black Dwarf*: 'The events in France are totally unexpected and totally unprecedented. . . . A revolution has never yet broken out under such circumstances. Yet in Paris it did'.[51]

The years 1967–69 saw the rise of revolutionary movements throughout the Western World, though 'only black America provided a revolt by those who were exploited as well as alienated'. In 1968 there were insurrections in Poland, Italy, Spain, France, Germany, Belgium, Yugoslavia and, on a lesser scale, in Britain. In America the Democratic Convention in Chicago was, as David Caute has argued in an authoritative history of *Sixty-Eight: The Year of the Barricades*, 'accompanied by scenes of violence more suggestive of war than of a civil society bonded by shared values'. Furthermore, the French government was 'temporarily paralyzed by the most severe revolt since the Paris Commune of 1871'.[52]

In the study of the French revolution of 1968, *The Beginning of the End*, Tom Nairn focused on the spontaneity of 'the masses' and the importance of the 'student vanguard'.[53] In contrasting the hopefulness of socialist prospects in 1968 (as distinct from the 'dark times' for the Left in the inter-war period), Nairn said: 'Perhaps ours, by contrast, is a time when at last reality had begun to "tend towards the (socialist) idea" again'. But despite the widespread revolts throughout Europe and America, the biggest challenge to Western capitalism 'exploded' in France.

Without underestimating the importance of the revolts elsewhere in Western Europe, it was in France where capitalism was almost toppled. Although there were massive student and worker revolts in the Italian cities of Turin and Naples as well as student occupations at Berkeley, Madison, Washington, Milan, Turin and London, the rebellious working classes only became a decisive force in France. In America where the Afro-Americans shook a powerful capitalist society to its very foundations, the white workers' racism vitiated an all-embracing working-class solidarity. This black rebellion was already anticipated by C.L.R. James in 1940 when he reviewed the important novel, *Native Son*, by Richard Wright:

Quite often the hate is hidden, sometimes it is buried deep out of sight, sometimes it is twisted into its opposite, a passionate religiosity. But it is there, and speakers, particularly Negro speakers, can always elicit it from any Negro gathering.[54]

While the insurrections in most countries were inspired and led by 'the student vanguard', the strike wave in France put the insurrection under the control and direction of the French working class. Although the strike came quite late in Marseilles, the second city of France, it embraced 200,000 workers in 150 industrial concerns. Moreover, the workers in various parts of France displayed a developing socialist consciousness; and the workers were interested in control over their own lives, not just material improvements. Though they changed their attitude to the workers' insurrection on several occasions, the communists helped De Gaulle to restore capitalism.

As capitalism with its whole system of hierarchy and competitive individualism was being restored in France and Western Europe, the revolt of the working people in Yugoslavia and Poland was beginning to reach a crescendo. It was in Czechoslovakia, however, that democratic socialism-from-below was established. Though it was soon overthrown by half a million Russian troops with tanks and armoured cars, the Czech workers and intellectuals expressed their passionate support for the sort of classical militant socialism represented by the Second International. In summing up the significance of the Prague Spring before the Russian troops invaded the country in August 1968, Michel Salomon said: 'The European or world revolution for civil rights which began with a series of student revolts in the West and the East represents, above all, revolt against the absurd alienation of man in an industrial society. It is a revolt against dictatorship.'[55]

The Prague Spring was, in the phrase of Robert Pontillon, 'the protest of the heart and the revolt of the spirit'. But it was, above all, a democratic socialist revolt – a revolt suffused with the generosity of the spirit of democratic socialism. As Ivan Svitak put it: 'The significance of the Prague Spring for Czech history lies in the fact that antagonisms of totalitarian dictatorship appeared in their utter nakedness, that the fetishes of office temporarily lost their power over the people, and that latent antagonism between the power elite and people, the antagonism of class rule, became apparent to the entire nation.' In an important study of *The Intellectual Origins of the Prague Spring*, Vladimir V. Kusin says that in Czechoslovakia the 'genuine striving for socialism as a socially just form of democracy in conflict with communism' had had a long history.[56]

The democratic Left did not really recover from the debacle of 1968 at the hands of very different, though ruthless, ruling classes in the West and the East. It is difficult to disagree with David Caute's judgment that 'by the end of 1970 the high tide of campus rebellion had receded'. By then, the advocates of socialism-from-above were more confident than ever before; and the cumulative tragedies and crises multiplied.[57]

Nevertheless militant, democratic socialism did challenge the Iron Heel in various countries in the East and the West in the 1970s. In any case, despite the massive defeats the working classes and the intellectuals experienced in 1968, the socialists' very old traditions of resistance and de-subordination were woven into the fabric of daily life everywhere. In discussing this important aspect of workers' lives, Herbert G. Gutman said: 'Working-class cultures – even those which reject acquisitive individualism – do not necessarily directly challenge inequality and the structures and belief systems that sustain it, but the existence of these cultures themselves is a form of resistance'.[58] Unfortunately, labour historiography since the end of the Second World War has been produced largely by those who adhere to socialism-from-above, not below.

Rather than explaining the failure of the socialist insurrections of 1968 in terms of the 'balance of class forces' as Otto Bauer would have done, the authoritarian historians of the 'Left' have criticised the East German, the Polish, the Hungarian and the French workers for not evolving Leninist-type 'vanguard' parties. Even when such apparently critical, anti-totalitarian thinkers as Rudolf Bahro, the author of *The Alternative in Eastern Europe*, spoke up in defence of democratic principles after 1968, they also articulated an elitist disdain of working-class men and women's lack of creativity and insight.

Moreover, there was, and is, a constant reiteration of the argument that socialist revolts and revolutions always fail because of one factor – the absence of Leninist 'vanguard' parties. Though nationalism and religion were powerful components of the working-class insurrections in Eastern Europe, the authoritarian historians of the 'Left' have not been willing to acknowledge such factors. In this world-view from the top, too, the assumption was that nationalist movements in the Third World (as distinct from Eastern Europe), were automatically 'progressive' if they involved 'liberation' from right-wing dictatorships or 'foreign imperialism'.[59] In attributing the failure of the revolutions in France in 1968, in Chile in 1972–73, in Portugal in 1974–75 and in Iran in 1979, the 'Trotskyist' authors of *Revolutionary Rehearsals* assume that all revolutions in the late twentieth century are innately and automatically *progressive*.

In contemporary 'socialist' historiography, whether communist or Trotskyist, the dominant assumption is that the revolutions in France, Chile, Portugal and Iran would have been successful if 'vanguard' Leninist parties had existed to provide the 'correct' leadership. For Karl Marx, Frederick Engels and the classical Marxists, the possibility of failure was inherent in socialist revolts and revolutions. In contrast to the socialist historiography of the Second International, contemporary 'socialist' historiography ignores such factors as modern totalitarianism or the balance of class forces.

Although the 1970s and 1980s have not been an impressive period for the advancement of socialist ideas, socialists did at least play an important role in the overthrow of fascist regimes in Portugal, Spain and Greece. In an optimistic book *1968 and After: Inside the Revolution*, Tariq Ali argued that the events in Portugal in 1974–75 were remarkable in so far as 'Portuguese fascism (1962–74) was overthrown by an internal revolt'. However, as well as exaggerating the argument about the extent to which fascism in Italy and Germany had been overthrown by 'the intervention of outside armies', he overlooked the much greater role of the Italian and German working classes in the destruction of their own fascism. Furthermore, the decisive factors in the overthrow of the fascist regime in Portugal were a disaffected army and costly colonial wars in Africa. While the Portuguese working class did play a role in the eradication of the fascist dictators, the decisive role was played by army officers.[60]

In Portugal, Spain and Greece, however, the revolutions in the 1970s contained strong elements of socialism-from-above and socialism-from-below. Nevertheless the initiative sometimes came from above rather than below; and the socialists were a more active agency of change than the communists. As Neil McInnes put it: 'The communists made no contribution to the downfall of fascism in Portugal or to the overthrow of military rule in Greece or even to the sudden collapse of the Francoist regime's prestige (which was rather the work of anti-communist Basques).' But although 'the high tide of campus rebellion had receded' by 1970, socialist and other students in Greece destroyed the image of President Papadopoulos's 'unshakable dictatorship'.[61]

IV

What happened when the democratic socialist government of Allende was overthrown in Chile in 1973 was a major tragedy for international socialism. In helping to deepen the pessimism of the socialist intelligentsia in the West, it contributed to the cumulative crisis of socialism everywhere. But in blaming what happened in Chile in 1973 on the so-called socialist-reformism of Allende and the Chilean socialists, the dominant 'socialist' historiography of the 'Left' has reinforced the crippling, immobilising pessimism of most socialist intellectuals in the modern world.[62]

In *Revolutionary Rehearsals*, Mike Gonzalez asserts that the events in Chile in 1973 were the fault of the socialists, not the fascists. As he sums up the significance of what happened there in 1973 when the fascists' coup turned the class struggle into class war: 'Tragically, it also showed that at such a moment the enemy of revolution is reformism, the politics of those more committed to the defence of the bourgeois State (i.e. Parliamentary democracy rather than 'the dictatorship of the proletariat') than to the transformation of the world'. The Chilean socialists adhered to Parliamentary democracy as 'a stepping stone' towards socialism in the rest of the world. Yet it would seem that attempts to create democratic socialism anywhere are, from the standpoint of the dominant left-wing historiography, predestined to failure without even a latent possibility of success. But in an important essay on 'Some Problems of the Left in Chile' published as early as 1969, Miles D. Wolpin argued that the *possibility* of democratic socialism emerging in that part of Latin America could not be dismissed, except by those who preached and practised historical determinism.[63]

Despite the world-wide cumulative crisis of democratic socialism and the move to the Right in the 1970s, the history of the authentic democratic Left was not one of total doom and gloom. In Greece, Portugal and Spain the democratic Left made considerable advances. With the emergence of Parliamentary democracy in those countries, the forces of socialism-from-below began to make some *impression* on their own societies.[64]

But the massive tragedies and crises of internationalism socialism in the 1980s were already foreshadowed in the 1960s. What happened in Iran in 1979 was symptomatic of the triumph of authoritarian 'socialism' in Third World countries at large. In the historiography of the authoritarians of the 'Left', it was assumed that 'liberation' from right-wing regimes would result in socialist revolutions. In examining the role of the Iranian students in West Germany in the 1960s in persuading Western Socialists that workers, students and women would be automatically liberated if the Shah could be got rid of Walter Laqueur concluded that:

A little more thought would have shown that it was highly doubtful whether Western Marxism in any meaningful sense of the term (let alone Western Marxism) could prosper outside Europe, that whilst national liberation movements were anti-capitalist in inspiration and that while socialist phraseology was *de riguer* in these circles, they were neither socialist nor democratic and least of all internationalist in inspiration.[65]

Socialism had become imprisoned by the dogmas – or rather by authoritarian 'socialist' historians' interpretation of the canons of Leninist theory – of the least attractive or relevant parts of its own history.

In criticising the 'vanguardism' and historical determinism of the non-communist Left, Herbert G. Gutman increasingly identified with the socialist historiography of the Second International. What could not be ignored was the historical fact that for most of the time 'subordinate populations live with their exploitation'. 'Then, under certain circumstances – none of them predictable – that acceptance is transformed into opposition. Chicago in the 1880s, St Petersburg in 1905, Gdansk in the 1970s'.[66]

The most open-minded and critical democratic socialists were, and are, aware of the formidable obstacles confronting the Left in the 1980s. In confronting the reality of the late twentieth century – a period when the right-wing forces *seem* to be very powerful almost everywhere – the most critical democratic socialists have attempted to offer working-class men and women *a margin of hope* of the better (socialist) world to come. Without minimising or underestimating the power of the forces of sloth and reaction, Bill Resnick has argued that:

Not long ago, less than one human lifetime, women and children were in law and fact treated as property, racial minorities were kept in virtual slavery and segregated; bosses had near unquestioned power over the workplace, police brutality was open, explicit, unchallenged; sexual minorities and the handicapped were forced into hiding; female sexuality was extremely narrowly defined. . . . If domination still exists, often in new forms, there is no denying that the old figures and authoritarian forms have been in long-term retreat.[67]

In an important article on international socialism in the 1980s – an article in which he emphasised 'the profound crisis' of international socialism – Julius Jacobson wrote: 'For Third Camp socialists, political and social democracy and a belief in the ability and necessity of working people to govern their own lives are at the core of our socialism; we cannot recognise socialism in any other guise.' But in affirming what Third Camp socialism was for, he also insisted that it was 'against the two camps of capitalism and totalitarian communism.'

At the same time as Jacobson acknowledged the formidable problems standing in the way of the advancement of the democratic Left, he insisted on the need for socialist optimism. As he put it: 'Meanwhile, plausibility of Third Camp socialism has been advanced by Spanish events as it has been by similar events in Portugal. Twelve years ago a powerful movement from below rid that impoverished nation of a 50-year long dictatorship. And in February 1986 an absolute majority of voters elected the leader of the Socialist Party as Portugal's President. Third camp socialists find little to cheer about in Mr Soares' politics but we take heart from what that vote reflects about the consciousness of workers and peasants who supported his candidacy'.[68]

By 1986 international socialism was weaker than it had been during the heyday of the Second International between 1889 and 1914. Between 1939 and 1986 socialist struggles and achievements everywhere had suffered cruel blows and defeats at the hands of fascism, Stalinism and neo-Stalinism. Nevertheless in the midst of cumulative tragedies and crises, international socialism had survived. In assessing the possibility of a socialist future after the Austrian fascists had seized power in 1934, Joseph Buttinger did not succumb to the temptation to write a collective obituary for socialists and socialism everywhere in conditions where fascism *seemed* to be the inexorable wave of the future. While conveying the Austrian socialists' deep sense of frustration and immeasurable bitterness, he ended by acknowledging what the most perceptive socialists of 1986 were rediscovering in totally new circumstances:

In this deepest sense the Austrian socialists have not failed. Their socialism lives on like seed beneath the snow. . . . Everywhere, individually or in small groups, they search for a new way.[69]

Notes

Introduction

1. Antonio Labriola, *Socialism and Philosophy* (Chicago, 1912), p. 195.
2. Julius Braunthal, *History of the International, 1864–1914* (London, 1961), p. 355.
3. Bertram D. Wolfe, *Three Who Made A Revolution: A Biographical History* (New York, 1948).
4. Hal Draper, *The Two Souls of Socialism* (Berkeley, 1961).
5. Arthur Lipow, *Authoritarian Socialism in America: Edward Bellamy and the Nationalist Movement* (Berkeley, 1982).
6. For Leninist and Stalinist critiques of Debs, Maclean, Luxemburg and Liebknecht, see Alexander Trachtenberg, *The Heritage of Gene Debs* (New York, N.D., probably 1926); Carl Reeve, 'De Leonism and Leninism', *The Communist*, June 1928; William Gallacher, *Revolt on the Clyde* (London, 1939; Elizbieta Ettinger, *Rosa Luxemburg: A Life* (Boston, 1987); Emile Burns, *Karl Liebknecht* (London, 1934).
7. Perry Anderson, *Considerations on Western Marxism* (London, 1976), p. 6.
8. Carl Boggs, *Gramsci's Marxism* (London, 1976), p. 64.
9. Antonio Gramsci, *Selections from Political Writings, 1910–1920* (London, 1977), pp. 59–60.
10. Richard J. Evans, *The Feminists* (London, 1977), p. 228.
11. Anderson, Considerations on Western Marxism, op. cit., p. 29.

Chapter 1: The history of socialism: An overview, 1889–1939

1. Julius Braunthal, *History of the International, 1864–1914* (London, 1966), Vol. 1, p. 195.
2. Ralphael Samuel, 'Sources of Marxist History', *New Left Review*, No. 120, 1980, p. 47.
3. Edward S. Mason, *The Paris Commune: An Epsiode in the History of the Socialist Movement* (New York, 1930), p. 368.
4. Quoted in Harvey Mitchell and Peter Stearns, *The European Labor Movement and the Origins of Social Democracy* (Itasea, Illinois, 1971), p. 209.
5. G.M. Stekloff, *History of the First International* (London, 1929), pp. 366–369.
6. Thomas Kirkup, *A Short History of Socialism* (London, 1913), p. 23.
7. J.H. Harley, *The New Social Democracy: A Study for the Times* (London, 1911), pp. 76–8 and p. 207.
8. Richard T. Ely, *Socialism* (London, 1896), p. 72.
9. M. Gustave Le Bon, *The Psychology of Socialism* (London, 1899), p. 62.
10. S.P. Orth, *Socialism and Democracy in Europe* (London, 1913), p. 16.
11. S.F. Markham, *A History of Socialism* (London, 1930), p. 299.
12. Leszek Kolakowski, *Main Currents of Marxism: The Golden Age* (Oxford, 1978), p. 1.

13. Lewis L. Lorwin, *Labor and Internationalism* (New York, 1929), p. 87.
14. James Joll, *The Second International* (London, 1968), p. 17.
15. Orth, op. cit., p. 165.
16. Kirkup, op. cit., p. 351.
17. Sen Katayama, 'What It Means To Be A Socialist', *International Socialist Review*, February 1914.
18. 'Conditions in Mexico', ibid., May 1905.
19. W.A. McConagha, *Development of the Labor Movement in Great Britain, France and Germany* (Chapel Hill, 1942), p. 118.
20. Nicholas Klein, 'The Situation in Hungary', *International Socialist Review*, January 1906 and Kirkup, op. cit., p. 338.
21. Orth, op. cit., p. 110 and pp. 132–5.
22. Ibid., pp. 182–4.
23. Orth, op. cit., pp. 263–4 and 'Revolutionary Russia', *International Socialist Review*, July 1905.
24. Mitchell and Stearns, op. cit., p. 207.
25. Gerald Brenan, *The Spanish Labyrinth* (Cambridge, 1947), pp. 218–21 and p. 217.
26. C.A. Macartney, *The Socialist Revolution in Austria* (Cambridge, 1926, p. 44.
27. Orth, op. cit., p. 180 and Macartney, op. cit., p. 181.
28. Orth, op. cit., p. 339.
29. R.C.K. Ensor, *Modern Socialism* (London, 1919), p. xxvi.
30. Macartney, op. cit., p. 30.
31. Markam, op. cit., p. 84.
32. Macartney, op. cit., p. 26.
33. Dick Geary, *European Labor Protests, 1848–1939* (London, 1981), p. 115.
34. Poultney Bigelow, *Prussian Memories* (New York, 1916), p. 105.
35. J. Hunter Watts, 'In the Prison of Our Past', *Justice*, 19 July 1913.
36. A. Lazovsky, *Marx and the Trade Unions* (London, 1935), p. 169.
37. Quoted in Max Shachtman, *The Bureaucratic Revolution* (New York, 1962), p. 212.
38. Antonio Labriola, *Essays on the Materialistic Conception of History* (Chicago, 1908), pp. 68–9 and James D. Young, 'Class Consciousness, the Class Struggle and International Labour History', in *Internationale Tagung der Historiker der Arbeiterbewegung Sonderkonferenz*, edited Rudolf Neck (Wien, 1984), pp. 54–90.
39. Angela Rappoport, *Dictionary of Socialism* (London, 1924), p. 111.
40. Orth, op. cit., p. 180.
41. Kirkup, op. cit., p. 334.
42. Orth, op. cit., p. 263.
43. Kirkup, op. cit., p. 333; Orth, op. cit., p. 205; and Macartney, op. cit., p. 35.
44. Brenan, op. cit., p. 216; Walter Bateman, *The Way We Came* (Bradford, 1928), p. 45; R.H. Sherard, *The White Slaves of England* (London, 1897), p. 20; James D. Young, 'Elitism, Authoritarianism and Western Socialism', *Bulletin of the Society for the Study of Labour History*, No. 25, 1972.
45. A. Ramos Oliveira, *Politics, Economics and Men of Modern Spain, 1808–1946* (London, 1946), pp. 148–52.
46. Brenan, op. cit., p. 221.
47. Jaime De Angulo, *The "Trial" of Ferrer* (New York, 1911), pp. 6–10 and William Archer, *The Life, Trial and Death of Francisco Ferrer* (London, 1911), pp. 105–26.

48. Adelheid Popp, *Autobiography of a Working Woman* (London, 1912), pp. 100–2.
49. A.W. Humphrey, *International Socialism and the War* (London, 1915), p. 22 and Oscar Jaszi, *The Dissolution of the Habsburg Monarchy* (Chicago, 1929), p. 177.
50. Kolakowski, op. cit., p. 177.
51. Lorwin, op. cit., p. 77.
52. Wolfgang Abendroth, *A Short History of the European Working Class* (London, 1972), and Young, 'Elitism, Authoritarianism and Western Socialism', op. cit., pp. 68–71.
53. Carl Landauer, *European Socialism* (Berkeley, 1959), Vol. 2, pp. 318–23.
54. Walter Kendall, *The Revolutionary Movement in Britain, 1900–1921* (London, 1969), chapter two and Kirkup, op. cit., p. 339.
55. Paul Buhle, 'Marxism in the U.S.A.', *C.L.R. James: His Life and Work*, edited Paul Buhle (Chicago, 1981), p. 30.
56. David Montgomery, *Workers' Control in America* (Cambridge, 1979), pp. 91–112.
57. Victor Kiernan, *Marxism and Imperialism* (London, 1974), p. 6 and Julius Braunthal, *History of the International, 1914–1943* (London, 1967), Vol. 2, p. 319.
58. Julius Braunthal, *In Search of the Millennium* (London, 1945), p. 84.
59. Lorwin, op. cit., p. 89.
60. Kolaskowski, op. cit., p. 27.
61. Jaszi, op. cit., p. 163 and p. 178.
62. Tom Bottomore and Patrick Goode, *Austro-Marxism* (Oxford, 1978), pp. 2–3 and op. cit., p. 180.
63. In translating this important pamphlet from German into English, my friend, Barry McLoughin, University of Vienna, has helped me to understand the complex attitudes of Rosa Luxemburg towards nationality. I owe a debt to my friends in the University of Silesia, Katowice, who first told me about Rosa Luxemburg's writings on nationality and the rights of oppressed nationalities. As they remain members of the underground oppositional movement, Solidarity, I cannot acknowledge them by name.
64. *Daily People*, 2 January 1911.
65. Daniel De Leon, *Two Pages from Roman History* (New York, 1914), p. 86.
66. Daniel De Leon, *Socialism versus Anarchism* (New York, 1945), p. 41.
67. Georgy Plekhanov, *The Development of the Monist View of History* (Moscow, 1956), p. 278.
68. Braunthal, *In Search of the Millennium*, op. cit., p. 98.
69. F. Borkenau, *The Communist International* (London, 1938), p. 183.
70. George Lichtheim, *A Short History of Socialism* (London, 1964), p. 235.
71. Leon Trotsky, *The Living Thoughts of Karl Marx* (London, 1939), p. 16.
72. Stekloff, op. cit., p. 164.
73. Bertram D. Wolfe, *Marxism: 100 Years in the Life of a Doctrine* (London, 1967), p. 299.
74. Jaszi, op. cit., p. 21.
75. Henry De Man, *The Remaking of a Mind* (New York, 1919), p. 275.
76. Merle Fainsod, *International socialism and the World War* (Cambridge, Mass., 1935), p. 200.
77. Oscar Jaszi, *Revolution and Counter-Revolution in Hungary* (London, 1924), p. 144, p. 178 and p. 160.

78. Otto Bauer, *The Austrian Revolution* (London, 1925), p. 163, p. 173 and p. 175.
79. Adolf Sturmthal, *The Tragedy of European Labor* (New York, 1943), p. 42.
80. G.P. Gooch, *Germany* (London, 1925), p. 169; Maxwell H.H. Macartney, *Five Years of European Chaos* (London, 1923), p. 134; Braunthal, *History of the International*, op. cit., p. 131.
81. Heinrich Strobel, *The German Revolution and After* (London, N.D., probably 1923), p. 224, p. 74, p. 78 and p. 260.
82. A. Rossi, *The Rise of Italian Fascism* (London, 1922), p. 90.
83. George Seldes, *Sawdust Caesar, The Untold History of Mussolini and Fascism* (London, 1936), p. 211, p. 226 and p. 330.
84. Sturmthal, op. cit., p. 189.
85. Braunthal, *History of the International*, Vol. 2, op. cit., p. 390.
86. Macartney, The Social Revolution in Austria, op. cit., p. 120.
87. Georgi Dimitrov, 'Letter to the Austrian Workers', *Labour Monthly*, June 1934 and A. Max, 'The Legend of the Vienna Commune', *The New International*, July 1934.
88. M.S., 'Fatal Admissions', ibid., July 1934 and Otto Bauer, *Austrian Democracy under Fire* (London, 1934), p. 10 and p. 8.
89. Ibid., p. 44.
90. G.E.R. Gedye, *Fallen Bastions* (London, 1939), p. 152.
91. Max Eastman, *Stalin's Russia and the Crisis of Socialism* (London, 1940), p. 12.
92. Gedye, Fallen Bastions, op. cit., p. 52; Seldes, Sawdust Caesar, op. cit., p. 319; Denis Smyth, 'Reflex reaction: Germany and the onset of the Spanish Civil War', *Revolution and War in Spain, 1931–1939*, edited Paul Preston (London, 1984), p. 243.
93. Edward Conze, *Spain Today* (London, 1936), p. 111 and p. 119.

Chapter 2: H.M. Hyndman and Daniel De Leon: Socialist sinners

1. Raphael Samuel, 'Sources of Marxist History', *New Left Review*, No. 120, 1980, pp. 44–5.
2. Lewis S. Feuer, *Marx and the Intellectuals* (New York, 1969), p. 49.
3. Victor Serge and Natalia Sedova Trotsky, *The Life and Death of Trotsky* (London, 1973), pp. 2–3. For Trotsky's comments, see *The Case of Leon Trotsky: Report of Hearings on the Charges Made against Him in the Moscow Trials* (London, 1937), p. 437.
4. For example, Isaac Deutscher, *The Prophet Outcast* (Oxford, 1963), p. 326 and Irving Howe, *Trotsky* (Glasgow, 1978), pp. 146–7.
5. Stanley Pierson, 'Henry Mayers Hyndman', *Biographical Dictionary of Marxism* edited Robert A Gorman (Westport, Conn., 1986), p. 143.
6. W.J. Ghent, 'Daniel De Leon', *Dictionary of American Biography*, Vol. 5 (New York, 1970), p. 221.
7. Letter from a 'victimised committee member of the Railway Workers' Union, 10 October 1895. Socialist Labour Party Archives, Box 34, Folder 4. The State Historical Society of Wisconsin, Madison, the United States of America.
8. Ghent, op. cit., p. 223.
9. James D. Young, 'Daniel De Leon and Anglo-American Socialism', *Labor*

History, Vol. 17, No. 3, 1976 and 'Totalitarianism and the British Labour Movement before 1917', *Survey*, Vol. 90, No. 1, 1974.

10. Hal Draper, 'The Two Souls of Socialism', *International Socialism*, Winter 1962, p. 12.
11. H.W. Lee and E. Archbold, *Social-Democracy in Britain* (London, 1935), p. 130.
12. H.M. Hyndman, 'Trade Unions and Progess', *Justice*, 8 September 1900.
13. H.M. Hyndman, *The Record of an Adventurous Life* (London, 1911), p. 327.
14. H.M. Hyndman, *Further Reminiscences* (London, 1912), p. 293.
15. H.M. Hyndman, *The Evolution of Revolution* (London, 1920), p. 272 and p. 283.
16. Young, 'Totalitarianism and the British Labour Movement before 1917', op. cit., p. 137.
17. E.P. Thompson, 'A review of Chushichi Tsuzuki's biography of H.M. Hyndman', *Bulletin of the Society for the Study of Labour History*, No. 3, 1961, pp. 66–71.
18. Ibid., p. 67.
19. Quoted in A. Lozovsky, *Marx and the Trade Unions* (New York, 1935), p. 169.
20. Ernest Belford Bax, *Essays in Socialism Old and New* (London, 1906), p. 174 and Stuart Macintyre, *A Proletarian Science: Marxism in Britain, 1917–1933* (Cambridge, 1980), pp. 207–8.
21. Ernest Belford Bax, *The Religion of Socialism* (London, 1901), p. 174.
22. Thompson, op. cit., p. 68 and p. 70.
23. H.M. Hyndman, *The Economics of Socialism* (London, 1896), pp. 246–7.
24. J. Hunter Watts, 'Signs of the Times', *Justice*, 13 August 1889.
25. H. Quelch, 'Social Democracy and the Trade Unions', ibid., 22 May 1897.
26. Ibid., 11 March 1905.
27. Ibid., 23 March 1905.
28. 'In sum the socialist parties as they developed their institutions from the 1890s onwards could absorb much of the energy and much of the leisure time of the workers, who, for whatever reason, felt alone in a hostile world. This was undoubtedly one of their chief attractions but it may also have curtailed the revolutionary fervour of potentially radical workers. Busy in his separate socialist society the worker could to an extent ignore the larger environment'. Peter N. Stearns in Harvey Mitchell and Peter N. Stearns, *The European Labor Movement, the Working Classes and the Origins of Social Democracy 1890–1914* (Itasea, Illinois, 1971), p. 207. For collaboration of some of these points for a later period of European social democracy, see Joseph Buttinger, *In the Twilight of Socialism* (New York, 1953), pp. 533–5.
29. H. Pelling, *Origins of the Labour Part* (Oxford, 1966), p. 21.
30. Hyndman, The Record of an Adventurous Life, op. cit., p. 432.
31. See the comments by Irving Howe, 'Sweet and Sour Notes: On Workers and Intellectuals', *Dissent*, Winter, 1972, p. 265.
32. A.P. Hazell, 'Social Degradation of the Worker', *Justice*, 11 July 1885.
33. Eric Hobsbawn is in the SDF tradition when he says: 'It is not the working class itself which takes power and exercises hegemony, but the *working-class movement or party*, and (short of taking an anarchist view) it is difficult to see how it could be otherwise.' E.J. Hobsbawn, 'Class Consciousness in History', *Aspects of History and Class Consciousness*', edited Istvan Meszaros (London, 1971), p. 17. Emphasis in original.

34. 'Economic forms, I repeat, are ready. Intelligence and class discipline are lacking'. H.M. Hyndman, 'The Need for a British Republic', *Justice*, 5 April 1917.
35. Socialist League Archives, International Institute of Social History, Amsterdam.
36. Robert Tressall, *The Ragged Trousered Philanthropists* (Harmondsworth, 1941), p. 235.
37. In their sustained hostility to socialism-from-below. Sidney and Beatrice Webb were just as critical of working people's intelligence and capacity for struggle as the SDF. This comes out very sharply in the *Diaries of Beatrice Webb*.
38. 'The workers, generally, display the same cussedness in regard to every agitation that could be used by them to advance their interests. . . . They don't even care to do a little bleating'. A.P. Hazell, 'The Cussedness of Working Men', *Justice*, 21 April 188(?).
39. 'But the sad truth is that if we would make haste we must make haste slowly, and there is as great heroism in going on from day to day unceasingly, untiringly sapping and mining the citadel of capitalism till it totters to its fall, as in facing bayonets which protect the enemies' outworks.' J. Hunter Watts, 'Political Arena', ibid., 12 April 1890.
40. Herbert Burrows, 'Without Haste – Without Rest', ibid., 29 September 1888.
41. 'William Nairne (a stone mason who was the leader of the SDF in Glasgow) conveyed such an impression of integrity that he was taken to task by a Glasgow policeman, hailing, like Willie from the north country, as to why he, a respectable man, should consort with a lot of Fenians'. James Leatham, *Glasgow in the Limelight* (Turiff, N.D.), p. 78.
42. *Justice*, 28 December 1895.
43. 'The Cult of Abstractions', ibid., 4 January 1896.
44. Raymond Challinor, *The Origins of British Bolshevism* (London, 1977), pp. 9–10.
45. *Justice*, 21 September 1901.
46. Letter from John K. Ellam to Daniel De Leon, 19 April 1899. Box 36, Folder 3, Socialist Labour Party Archives, State Historical Society of Wisconsin.
47. Lee and Archbold, op. cit., p. 146.
48. Quoted in Chuchichi Tsuzuki, *H.M. Hyndman and British Socialism* (London, 1961), p. 151.
49. Ibid., p. 193.
50. Ibid., p. 190.
51. H. Collins, 'The Marxism of the Social Democratic Federation', *Essays in Labour History*, edited Asa Briggs and John Saville (London, 1971), p. 60.
52. 'Yet what is the greatest obstacle to the formation of a solid socialist party in this country? Precisely this very trade unionism, the erstwhile pioneer of working class emancipation'. E.B. Bax, 'Damn the Pioneer', *Justice*, 14 June 1898.
53. Even as late as 1924 the editor of *Justice* wrote: 'The propertyless wage earners constitute the majority of the nation, and they also experience the majority of the suffering and inconvenience that a huge strike undoubtedly causes'. Ibid., 27 March 1924.
54. *Falkirk Herald*, 18 January 1896.
55. *Minutes of the Aberdeen Trades Council*, 20 June 1883.
56. Murray Kaye, 'The Transformation of Glasgow', *Justice*, 6 June 1896.

57. Though this particular example came slightly after 1917, see the comments of F.J. Gould: 'The proletariat of Great Britain must meet the middle class, negotiate with the middle class, and firmly annex and absorb the middle class by means of middle class instruments; and the instruments are brains, education, discipline, astuteness, and an independent straight-forward spirit'. F.J. Gould, 'Shall We Be Bolsheviks?', *Justice*, 23 January 1919.
58. Ibid., 4 June 1898.
59. Andre Tridon, *The New Unionism* (New York, 1915), p. 148.
60. Quoted in Tsuzuki, op. cit., p. 236.
61. Daniel De Leon, *Two Pages from Roman History* (New York, 1968), p. 9.
62. L. Glen Seretan, 'The Personal Style and Political Methods of Daniel De Leon', *Labor History*, Vol. 14, No. 2, 1973 and James A. Stevenson, 'Letters to Daniel De Leon: The Intra-Party Constitutency for his policy of Strict Party Discipline, 1896–1906', ibid., Vol. 18, No. 3.
63. L. Glen Seretan, *Daniel De Leon: The Odyssey of an American Marxist* (Cambridge, Mass., 1979), pp. 168–70.
64. 'De Leon's flexibility is obvious in his IWW years'. Seretan, 'The Personal Style and Political Methods of Daniel De Leon', op. cit., p. 171.
65. Melvyn Dubofsky, *A History of the Industrial Workers of the World* (Chicago, 1969), pp. 131–3.
66. *Proceedings of the Industrial Workers of the World* (New York, 1905), p. 68.
67. Seretan, Daniel De Leon: The Odyssey of an American Marxist, op. cit., p. 56.
68. See any of the stenographica reports of De Leon's speeches or debates.
69. Since Leszek Kolakowski sees some of these attitudes in the writings of Antonio Gramsci, there is clearly a need for careful investigation of the extent to which Gramsci was influenced by De Leon's ideas. Leszek Kolakowski, *Main Currents of Marxism: The Breakdown* (Oxford, 1978), p. 150.
70. Leon Fink, 'Class Conflict in the Gilded Age: The Figure and the Phantom', *Radical History Review*, Vol. 3, No. 1, 1975, p. 61.
71. Seretan, Daniel De Leon: The Odyssey of an American Marxist, op. cit., pp. 22–81.
72. G.V. Plekhanov, *The Role of the Individual in History* (London, 1976), p. 15.
73. De Leon, Two Pages from Roman History, op. cit., p. 65.
74. Frank Budgen, *Myselves When Young* (Oxford, 1970), p. 86.
75. S.S. Prawer, *Karl Marx and World Literature* (Oxford, 1976), p. 315.
76. Daniel De Leon, *What Means This Strike*? (New York, 1972), p. 16.
77. Prawer, op. cit., p. 237.
78. De Leon, What Means This Strike? op. cit., p. 17.
79. De Leon, Two Pages from Roman History, op. cit., p. 102.
80. James A. Stevenson, *Daniel De Leon: The Relationship of the Socialist Labor Party and European Marxism, 1890–1914*, Ph.D. thesis, University of Wisconsin, Madison, America, 1977, p. 417.
81. De Leon, Two Pages from Roman History, op. cit., p. 100.
82. Stephen F. Cohen, *Bukarin and the Bolshevik Revolution* (London, 1974), p. 267.
83. Karl Kautsky, *The Social Revolution* (Chicago, 1902), pp. 100–1.
84. *The People*, 15 January 1899.
85. Stevenson, Daniel De Leon: The Relationship of the Socialist Labor Party and European Marxism, 1890–1914, op. cit., p. 409.
86. Budgen, op. cit., p. 89.

87. Stevenson, Daniel De Leon: The Relationship of the Socialist Labor Party and European Marxism, 1890–1914, op. cit., p. 411.
88. Daniel De Leon, *Socialism versus Anarchism* (New York, 1927), p. 34.
89. Ibid., p. 28.
90. Daniel De Leon, *Flashlights of the Amsterdam Congress* (New York, 1929), p. 165.
91. Ibid., p. 45.
92. De Leon, Two Pages from Roman History, op. cit., p. 105.
93. De Leon, Flashlights of the Amsterdam Congress, op. cit., p. 134.
94. *Daily People*, 15 June 1913.
95. De Leon, Flashlights of the Amsterdam Congress, op. cit., p. 97.
96. Ibid., p. 45.
97. Tattler (H.M. Hyndman), *Justice*, 30 June 1896 and Daniel De Leon, 'The American Flag', *Weekly People*, 4 July 1914.
98. Quoted in F.J. Gould, *H.M. Hyndman: Prophet of Socialism* (London, 1928), p. 34.
99. Daniel De Leon, 'Is It To Be', *Daily People*, 10 December 1905.
100. Tsuzuki, op. cit., p. 269.
101. Seretan, The Odyssey of an American Marxist, op. cit., p. 55.
102. *The Socialist*, June 1914.

Chapter 3: James Connolly and Karl Liebknecht: Socialist martyrs

1. *The Communist International in Lenin's Time*, edited John Riddell (New York, 1984), pp. 372–4 and Leon Trotsky, *Political Profiles* (London, 1972), p. 139.
2. Riddell, op. cit., pp. 372–9.
3. Trotsky, op. cit., p. 130.
4. H.M. Hyndman, 'Karl Liebknecht and Rosa Luxemburg', *Justice*, 30 January 1919.
5. Quoted in Frederick J. Gould, *Hyndman: Prophet of Socialism* (London, 1928), p. 213.
6. Bernard Ransom, *Connolly's Marxism* (London, 1980), p. 3.
7. Karl W. Meyer, *Karl Liebknecht: Man Without a Country* (Washington, D.C., 1957), p. 21.
8. Owen Dudley Edwards, *Mind of an Activist – James Connolly* (Dublin, 1971), p. 49 and Helmut Trotnow, *Karl Liebknecht: A Political Biography* (Hamden, Conn., 1984), pp. 10–11.
9. Isaac Deutscher, 'Introduction', *The Age of Permanent Revolution*, edited Isaac Deutscher and George Novack (New York, 1964), p. 15.
10. Austen Morgan, 'James Connolly', *Biographical Dictionary of Marxism*, edited Robert A. Gorman (Westport, Conn., 1986), p. 77.
11. Meyer, op. cit., p. 169.
12. Trotsky, Political Profiles, op. cit., p. 107.
13. C. Desmond Greaves, *The Life and Times of James Connolly* (New York, 1971), p. 41.
14. Carl Reeve and Ann Barton, *James Connolly and the United States: The Road to Easter 1916* (Atlantic Highlands, N.J., 1978), p. 8 and p. 231.
15. Greaves, op. cit., pp. 17–19.
16. *James Connolly Selected Writings*, edited P. Berresford Ellis (Harmondsworth 1973), pp. 9–10.
17. Ramsom, op. cit., p. 9.

18. James D. Young, 'The Irish Immigrants' Contribution to Scottish Socialism, 1880–1926', paper presented to the Eighth Lipman Seminar on Ireland, Ulster People's College, Belfast, 6 September 1986.
19. H.W. Lee and E. Archbold, *Social-Democracy in Britain* (London, 1935), p. 144.
20. 'The Death of John Leslie', *Justice*, 20 January 1921.
21. 'Mr. Chisholm Robertson', *Glasgow Observer*, 22 March 1930.
22. Ibid., 25 October 1885.
23. Quoted in Desmond Ryan, *Socialism and Nationalism: A Selection from the Writings of James Connolly* (Dublin, 1948), p. 7.
24. Reeve and Barton, op. cit., p. 14.
25. James Connolly to Henry Kuhn, 22 May 1896, Box 13, Folder 4, Socialist Labour Party Archives, MSS. 3A. State Historical Society of Wisconsin, Madison, USA.
26. John Maclean, 'Gleanings from the Scrap Book of a Navvy', *Forward*, 18 April 1911 and Harry McShanes and Joan Smith, *No Mean Fighter* (London, 1978), p. 36.
27. Interview with Harry McShane, 24 March 1986.
28. R. Samuel, 'Sources of Marxist History', *New Left Review*, No. 120, 1980.
29. Tom Bell, 'James Connolly: Some Reminiscences', *Labour Monthly*, April 1937 and Tom Bell, *Pioneering Days* (London, 1941), p. 51.
30. Greaves, op. cit., p. 86.
31. James D. Young, 'John Macleans's Place in Scottish History', *Bulletin of the Society for the Study of Labour History*, No. 39, 1979.
32. Oscar Williams, 'The Easter Rebellion', *Fourth International*, April 1943.
33. James Connolly to John Carstairs Matheson, 8 April 1903. National Library of Ireland, Dublin.
34. Reeve and Baron, op. cit., p. xi.
35. Quoted in Berresford Ellis, op. cit., p. 48.
36. Maurice Ahearn, 'The Irish Question', *The New International*, June 1936.
37. Albert Gates, 'James Connolly, Irish Rebel', ibid., June 1942.
38. 'Captain White, who was active throughout, suggested the arming of the workers. Connolly developed the idea and started the Citizen Army'. W.P. Ryan, *The Irish Labour Movement* (Dublin, 1919), p. 231.
39. Desmond Ryan, *James Connolly* (Dublin, 1924), p. 49.
40. Walter Weyl, 'The Man Liebknecht', in Karl Liebknecht, *The Future Belongs to the People* (London, 1918), p. 21.
41. *Karl Marx and Frederick Engels Through the Eyes of their Contemporaries* (Moscow, 1972), p. 61.
42. Trotnow, op. cit., pp. 17–18.
43. Meyer, op. cit., p. 21.
44. Ibid., p. 22.
45. Ibid., p. 18.
46. Trotnow, op. cit., p. 20.
47. Carl E. Schorske, *German Social Democracy, 1905–1917* (Harvard, 1955), p. 300.
48. Trotnow, op. cit., p. 16.
49. Meyer, op. cit., p. 21.
50. Trotnow, p. 72.
51. Ibid., pp. 34–5.
52. Ibid., p. 52.
53. Karl Liebknecht, *Militarism and Anti-Militarism* (Glasgow, 1917), pp. vi–vii.

54. Trotsky, Political Profiles, op.cit., p. 132.
55. Leon Trotsky, *In Defence and Marxism* (New York, 1973), p. 75.
56. Trotnow, op. cit., p. 208 and p. 212.
57. James Connolly, 'A Martyr for Conscience Sake', *Forward*, 22 August 1914.
58. Georges Haupt, *Socialism and the Great War: The Collapse of the Second International* (Oxford, 1972), pp. 170–1 and p. 153.
59. Julius Braunthal, *History of the International, 1914–1943* (London, 1967), p. 36.
60. Ryan, James Connolly, op. cit., p. 112.
61. *Irish Worker*, 15 August 1914.
62. Tom Bell, *British Communist Party: A Short History* (London, 1937), p. 32.
63. James Connolly, 'Revolutionary Unionism and War', *International Socialist Review*, March 1915.
64. Quoted in Reeve and Barton, op. cit., p. 234.
65. Ryan, James Connolly, op. cit., p. 126.
66. T.A. Jackson, *Ireland Her Own* (London, 1946), p. 390.
67. H.W. Lee and E. Archbold, *Social-Democracy in Britain* (London, 1935), p. 147.
68. W.P. Ryan, *The Irish Labour Movement* (Dublin, 1919), p. 241.
69. John Leslie, 'James Connolly: An Appreciation', *Justice*, 18 May 1916.
70. 'Liebknecht's Gauntlet to Junkerdom', *The Socialist*, January 1917. A different translation of the same letter had been published in another British socialist newspaper some months beforehand. See 'Karl Liebknecht Indicts the German Government', *Justice*, 19 October 1916.
71. Liebknecht, The Future Belongs to the People, op. cit., pp. 100–12.
72. Riddell, op. cit., p. 175.
73. Paul Frolich, *Rosa Luxemburg* (London, 1972), p. 224.
74. Trotnow, op. cit., p. 166.
75. Frolich, op. cit., p. 225.
76. Meyer, op. cit., p. 95.
77. Eric Waldman, *The Spartacist Uprising of 1919* (Milwaukee, 1958), p. 186.
78. Meyer, op. cit., pp. 171–2.
79. Braunthal, op. cit., p. 125.
80. For an assessment of Louis B. Boudin, see Theodore Draper, *The Roots of American Communism* (New York, 1957), pp. 57–60 and Louis L. Boudin, 'The Irish Tragedy', *New Review*, June 1916.
81. Arthur McManus, 'James Connolly: Socialist and Revolutionary', *The Socialist*, 17 April 1919.
82. Selma Sigerson, 'To the Irish Socialist', ibid., 27 February 1919.
83. Meyer, op. cit., p. 103.
84. William Paul, 'Karl Liebknecht: The Man and His Work', *The Socialist*, 1 May 1919.
85. Emile Burns, *Karl Liebknecht* (London, 1934), p. 31.
86. Meyer, op. cit., p. 103.

Chapter 4: Antonio Gramsci and Rosa Luxemburg: Individuality and socialist-humanists

1. *James Boswell's Life of Johnson*, edited J. Brady (New York, 1968), p. 297.
2. Thomas Carlyle, *Chartism* (London, 1860), p. 131.

3. Letter from Royden Harrison to the author, 24 January 1985.
4. Ellen M. Woods, *Mind and Politics. An Approach to the Meaning of Liberal and Socialist Individualism* (Berkeley, California, 1972), pp. 128–9.
5. Paul Frolich, *Rosa Luxemburg* (New York, 1972), p. 189.
6. *Comrade and Lover. Rosa Luxemburg's Letters to Leon Jogiches*, edited Elżbieta Ettinger (London, 1979), p. xv, p. 105, pp. 75–6 and p. 91.
7. Frolich, op. cit., p. 214.
8. In a penetrating commentary on individualism and individuality, Antonio Labriola said: 'We are to come to the point of confessing to ourselves that our individuality, to which we are all so closely attached through an obvious and genetic habit, is a pretty small thing in the complicated network of the social mechanisms, however great it may be, or appear, to us even if it is not such a mere evanescent nonetity as some hare-brained theosophists claim. . . . Therefore the privilege of heroes must be preserved in history, so that the dwarfs may not be deprived of the faith that they are to ride on their own shoulders and make themselves conspicuous'. Antonio Labriola, *Socialism and Philosophy* (Chicago, 1912), p. 8.
9. Giuseppe Fiori, *Antonio Gramsci Life of a Revolutionary* (London, 1974), p. 99.
10. Ibid., p. 107.
11. Carl Boggs, *Gramsci's Marxism* (London, 1976), p. 26; Alastair Davidson, *Antonio Gramsci: Towards an Intellectual Biography* (London, 1977), p. 90.
12. James Joll, *Gramsci* (Glasgow, 1977), p. 26.
13. Davidson, op. cit., p. 255.
14. Rosa Luxemburg, *The Janius Pamphlet* (London, 1964), p. 134.
15. Frolich, op. cit., p. 143.
16. Fiori, op. cit., p. 103.
17. For an interesting fictional account of the last phase of Luxemburg's life, see Alfred Döblin, *Karl and Rosa. November 1918: The German Revolution* (New York, 1983). *Antonio Gramsci: Selections from Cultural Writings*, edited David Forgacs and G. Nowell-Smith (London, 1985) is a rich source of material on Gramsci's attitudes to art, culture and education.
18. Stephen E. Bronner, *A Revolutionary of Our Time: Rosa Luxemburg* (London, 1981), p. 45.
19. *The Letters of Rosa Luxemburg* with an introduction by Stephen E. Bronner (Boulder, Colorado, 1978), p. 253.
20. Bronner, A Revolutionary of Our Time, op. cit., p. 113.
21. Frolich, op. cit., p. 76.
22. Bronner, A Revolutionary of Our Time, op. cit., p. 13.
23. The Letters of Rosa Luxemburg, op. cit., pp. 179–80.
24. John M. Cammett, *Antonio Gramsci and the Origins of Italian Communism* (Stanford, California, 1967), p. 7.
25. Joll, op. cit., p. 20.
26. Ibid., p. 18.
27. Fiori, op. cit., p. 94.
28. Lelio Basso, *Rosa Luxemburg: A Reappraisal* (London, 1975) p. 150.
29. The Letters of Rosa Luxemburg, op. cit., p. 173.
30. Fiori, op. cit., p. 48.
31. Davidson, op. cit., p. 191.
32. The Letters of Rosa Luxemburg, op. cit., p. 72.
33. Basso, op. cit., p. 145.
34. The Letters of Rosa Luxemburg, op. cit., p. 168.

35. Joll, op. cit., p. 88.
36. Rosa Luxemburg, *Letters from Prison*. Translated from the German by Eden and Cedar Paul (London, 1946), pp. 39–40.
37. Davidson, op. cit., p. 76.
38. Frolich, op. cit., p. 104.
39. The Letters of Rosa Luxemburg with an introduction by Bronner, op. cit., pp. 21–2.
40. E.H. Carr, *What Is History?* (London, 1972), p. 123.

Chapter 5: Jean Jaurés and Vladimir I. Lenin: The ambiguous saints

1. Daniel De Leon, *Flashlights of the Amsterdam Congress* (New York, 1929), p. 15 and *Daily People*, 12 June 1912.
2. Leon Trotsky, *Political Profiles* (London, 1972), pp. 38–9.
3. Clara Zetkin, *Reminiscences of Lenin* (New York, 1934), p. 7 and Maxim Gorky, *Days With Lenin* (London, N.D.), pp. 4–5 and p. 11.
4. Tamara Deutscher's introduction to *Lenin* by Isaac Deutscher (London, 1970), p. v.
5. J. Hampden Jackson, *Jean Jaurés* (London, 1943), p. 15.
6. Ibid., p. 7.
7. Bertram D. Wolfe, *Three Who Made A Revolution* (New York, 1948), p. 48.
8. Ibid., p. 42.
9. Jackson, op. cit., p. 158 and Stefan T. Possony, *Lenin: The Compulsive Revolutionary* (London, 1966), p. 453.
10. Jackson, op. cit., pp. 155–6 and Possony, op. cit., p. 454.
11. Jackson, op. cit., p. 117 and V.I. Lenin, *Selected Works* (London, 1941), Vol. 2, p. 405.
12. Wolfe, op. cit., p. 291.
13. N. Krupskaya, *Memories of Lenin* (London, 1942), p. 152.
14. Max Beer, *Fifty Years of International Socialism* (London, 1933), p. 159.
15. Gorky, op. cit., p. 34 and Beer, op. cit., p. 158.
16. Jackson, op. cit., p. 155.
17. Beer, op. cit., p. 145.
18. Jackson, op. cit., p. 158 and p. 31.
19. Krupskaya, op. cit., pp. 147–8.
20. Jackson, op. cit., p. 98.
21. Zetkin, op. cit., p. 44 and pp. 48–9.
22. Harvey Goldberg, *The Life of Jean Jaurés* (Madison, Wis., 1968), p. 92.
23. Ibid., p. 58.
24. Margaret Pease, *Jean Jaurés: Socialist and Humanitarian* (London, 1916), p. 29.
25. Goldberg, op. cit., p. 92 and Jackson, op. cit., p. 12.
26. Quoted in Jackson, op. cit., p. 34.
27. Gorky, op. cit., p. 50 and p. 52.
28. Ibid., p. 27.
29. Krupskaya, op. cit., p. 51 and p. 47.
30. Ibid., p. 141.
31. Goldberg, op. cit., p. 93.
32. Ibid., p. 489.

33. Matthew Josephson, *Zola and His Times* (London, 1929), p. 445 and p. 459.
34. Beer, op. cit., pp. 100–1.
35. Quoted in Jackson, op. cit., p. 75.
36. Val R. Lorwin, *The French Labor Movement* (Cambridge, Mass., 1954), p. 27.
37. Harold Weinstein, *Jean Jaurés: A Study of Patriotism in the French Socialist Movement* (New York, 1936), p. 49.
38. Jackson, op. cit., pp. 87–8.
39. Zetkin, op. cit., p. 14.
40. Pease, op. cit., p. 87.
41. Pease, op. cit., p. 85 and Jean Jaurés, *Internationalism and Peace* (London, 1903), p. 8.
42. Jean Jaurés, *Studies in Socialism* (London, 1906), p. 121 and p. 113.
43. Weinstein, op. cit., p. 79.
44. C.G. Coulton (Editor), *Jaurés on Democracy and Military Service* (London, 1916), *passim*.
45. Beer, op. cit., p. 130.
46. Emile Royer, *German Socialists and Belgium* (London, 1915), pp. 33–4.
47. G.D.H. Cole, *The Second International* (London, 1956), Vol. 2, p. 94.
48. Gorky, op. cit., p. 60; Goldberg, p. 80; and Wolfe, op. cit., p. 507.
49. Max Eastman, *Stalin's Russia and the Crisis of Socialism* (London, 1940), pp. 131–2.
50. Isaac Deutscher, *The Prophet Armed: Trotsky, 1879–1921* (London, 1954), p. 139.
51. Walter Laqueur, *The Fate of the Revolution: Interpretations of Soviet History* (London, 1967), p. 70.
52. Arthur Ransome, *Six Weeks in Russia in 1919* (Glasgow, 1920), p. viii.
53. M. Philips Price, *My Reminiscences of the Russian Revolution* (London, 1920), p. 377.
54. John Reed, *Ten Days That Shook The World* (New York, 1922), p. 377.
55. Ibid., pp. 303–4.
56. Nikolay Valentinov, *Encounters With Lenin* (London, 1968), pp. 48–9.
57. Leon Trotsky, *Lenin* (London, 1925), p. 223.
58. Quoted in Robert Payne, *Lenin* (London, 1964), p. 617.
59. Alfred Rosmer, *Moscow Under Lenin* (London, 1971), p. 100.
60. Anna Louise Strong, *The First Time in History* (London, 1924), p. 210.
61. Quoted in Edmund Wilson, *To the Finland Station* (London, 1974), p. 4.
62. Isaac Deutscher, *Lenin's Childhood* (London, 1970), p. 66.
63. Zetkin, op. cit., p. 45.
64. Price, op. cit., p. 7.
65. Rosmer, op. cit., p. 45.
66. Valentinov, op. cit., pp. 99–100.
67. Ransome, op. cit., pp. 78–9.
68. *Letters of Lenin*, edited Elizabeth Hill and Doris Mudie (London, 1937), p. 450.
69. Edward S. Mason, *The Paris Commune: An Episode in the History of the Socialist Movement* (New York, 1930), p. 251.
70. Lorwin, op. cit., p. 48.
71. Goldberg, p. 473.
72. Marcel Sembat, *Defeated Victory* (London, 1925), p. 61.
73. Payne, op. cit., p. 616.
74. Marcel Liebman, *Leninism Under Lenin* (London, 1973), p. 424.

Chapter 6: Joseph Stalin and Mao Tse-tung: The dictators

1. Raya Dunayevskaya, *Marxism and Freedom* (New York, 1958) and Ygael Gluckstein, *Mao's China* (London, 1957), pp. 314–15.
2. Royden Harrison, 'Marxism As Nineteenth-Century Critique And Twentieth-Century Ideology', Historical Association Lecture, 1980, p. 209 and p. 219.
3. Hal Draper, 'The Two Souls of Socialism', *International Socialism*, Winter 1962, pp. 12–20.
4. Max Eastman, 'Motive Patterns of Socialism', *The Modern Quarterly*, Fall 1939, p. 50.
5. Boris Souvarine, *Stalin: A Critical Survey of Bolshevism* (London, 1939), p. 104.
6. Leon Trotsky, *Stalin: An Appraisal of the Man and His Influence*. Edited and Translated from the Russian by Charles Malamuth (London, 1947), p. 15.
7. Souvarine, op. cit., p. 13.
8. Ibid., p. 34.
9. Ibid., p. 115.
10. Edgar Snow, *Red Star Over China* (London, 1937), p. 126.
11. Han Suyin, *The Morning Deluge: Mao Tse-tung and the Chinese Revolution* (London, 1972), p. 67, p. 72 and p. 98.
12. Stuart Schram, *Mao Tse-tung* (Hamondsworth, 1966), pp. 22–3.
13. Snow, op. cit., p. 153.
14. Souvarine, op. cit., p. 101 and p. 104.
15. Walter Held, 'Stalin in Reality and Legend', *The New International*, December 1935.
16. Leon Trotsky, *Workers' State, Thermidor and Bonapartism* (New York, 1933), p. 24.
17. Max Shachtman, 'Trotsky's Stalin: A Critical Evaluation', *The New International*, October 1946.
18. Isaac Deutscher, *The Unfinished Revolution: Russia, 1917–1967* (London, 1967), p. 86.
19. Suyin, op. cit., p. 113 and p. 81.
20. Ibid., p. 137.
21. Anna Louise Strong, *I Change Worlds* (London, 1935), p. 229.
22. Arthur Ransome, *The Chinese Puzzle* (London, 1927), pp. 36–7.
23. Anna Louise Strong, *China's Millions* (New York, 1928), p. 103.
24. Ransome, op. cit., p. 95.
25. Earl Browder, 'Wages and Conditions in China', *Labour Monthly*, September 1927.
26. C.L.R. James, *World Revolution, 1917–1936: The Rise and Fall of the Communist International* (London, 1937), pp. 242–5; Harold Isaacs, *The Tragedy of the Chinese Revolution* (London, 1938), pp. 66–7.
27. H. Owen Chapman, *The Chinese Revolution, 1926–27* (London, 1928), pp. 87, p. 91 and p. 251.
28. C.L.R. James, *At the Rendezvous of Victory* (London, 1984), pp. 60–2.
29. Jerome Ch'en, *Mao and the Chinese Revolution* (London, 1965), p. 84 and p. 113.
30. Ibid., pp. 166–8 and p. 189.
31. Quoted in Suyin, op. cit., p. 191.

32. Chen Ming Chu, 'The All-People's Front in China', *Labour Monthly*, December 1936.
33. Mary Saran, 'Problems of the Chinese Revolution', *Plebs*, June 1938.
34. Max Eastman, *Stalin's Russia and the Crisis of Socialism* (London, 1940), p. 21.
35. Souvarine, op. cit., p. 642 and p. 622.
36. Snow, op. cit., p. 161.
37. Ibid., p. 175.
38. Harold Isaacs, 'I Break with the Chinese Stalinists', *The New International*, September–October 1934 and Harold Isaacs, 'The Peasants War in China', ibid., January 1935.
39. Anna Louise Strong, *One-Fifth of Mankind* (New York, 1938), pp. 189–90.
40. Roger Howard, *Mao Tse-tung and the Chinese People* (London, 1977), pp. 182–7.
41. Rita Stone, 'Chiang Kai-Shek's China', *The New International*, March 1944.
42. Rita Stone, 'China under the Stalinists', ibid., April 1944.
43. Rita Stone, 'China under Japanese Domination', ibid., May 1944.
44. Li Fu-jen, 'China after World War II', *The Fourth International*, July 1946.
45. The Dean of Canterbury, 'China's Future', *Labour Monthly*, April 1944.
46. Chen Pai-ta, 'China's Destiny', ibid., June 1944.
47. V. Dedijer, *Tito Speaks* (London, 1953), p. 331.
48. Bertram D. Wolfe, *Marxism: 100 Years in the Life of a Doctrine* (London, 1967), pp. 316–18.
49. A.K. Wu, *China and the Soviet Union* (London, 1950), p. 73 and Gluckstein, Mao's China, op. cit., pp. 386–90.
50. Grace C. Lee, Pierre Chaulieu and J.R. Johnson (C.L.R. James), *Facing Reality* (Detroit, 1958), pp. 78–80.
51. 'Moshe Lewin', Henry Abelove, Betsy Blackmar, Peter Dimock and Jonathan Schneer, *Visions of History* (New York, 1983), p. 295.
52. James, At the Rendezvous of Victory, op. cit., p. 261.
53. Gluckstein, Mao's China, op. cit., p. 209.
54. Quoted in Gluckstein, Mao's China, op. cit., p. 292.
55. Karl Marx and Frederick Engels, *The German Ideology* (London, 1942), p. 69 and Georgy Plekhanov, *The Development of the Monist View of History* (Moscow, 1956), p. 277.
56. Marx and Engels, *Selected Correspondence*, (Moscow, 1955), p. 42.
57. Joseph Freeman, *An American Testament* (London, 1938), p. 402.
58. Harrison, op. cit., p. 217 and Ygael Gluckstein, *Stalin's Satellites in Europe* (London, 1952), *passim*.
59. Lewis Coser and Irving Howe, 'Authoritarians of the "Left"', *Voices of Dissent*, edited Irving Howe (New York, 1958), p. 96.
60. Deutscher, op. cit., p. 86.
61. Quoted in Gluckstein, Mao's China, op. cit., p. 379.
62. Ibid., p. 378 and p. 314.
63. 'Moshe Lewin', Visions of History, op. cit., p. 295.
64. Raya Dunayevskaya, *Philosophy and Revolution* (New York, 1973), pp. 168–75.
65. Harrison, op. cit., p. 218 and Michel Oksenbery, 'The Political Leader', in *Mao Tse-tung in the Scales of History*, edited Dick Wilson (Cambridge, 1976), pp. 114–16.

Chapter 7: Claude McKay and George Padmore: The black heretics

1. Eddie and Win Roux, *Rebel Pity* (London, 1970), p. 15.
2. Marxism and Geschichtswissenschaft, *International Conference of Historian of the Labour Movement, 1983*, edited Brigitte Galanda (Vienna, 1984), p. 524.
3. Julius Braunthal, *The History of the International, 1864–1914* (London, 1966), p. 319.
4. See, for example, F. Colebrook, 'Hobson's "The War in South Africa"', *Justice*, 24 March 1900.
5. Thomas Kirkup, *A Short History of Socialism* (London, 1913), p. 308.
6. Raya Dunayevskaya, *Rosa Luxemburg, Women's Liberation and Marx's Philosophy of Revolution* (New Jersey, 1982), p. 37.
7. Max Beer, 'The Lenin-Luxemburg Controversy', *Plebs*, May 1927.
8. James R. Giles, *Claude McKay* (Boston, 1976), p. 16.
9. James D. Young, Unpublished paper on 'Racism and the British Labour Movement: The Significance of the Race Riots of 1919' presented to the International Conference of Historians of the Labour Movement, Linz, Austria, 15 September 1984.
10. *The Passion of Claude McKay: Selected Poetry and Prose, 1912–1948*, edited with an introduction by Wayne F. Cooper (New York, 1973), pp. 13–15.
11. Lewis Grassic Gibbon and Hugh MacDiarmid, *Scottish Scene* (London, 1934), p. 123.
12. Hugh MacDiarmid, 'Lewis Grassic Gibbon', *Little Reviews Anthology*, edited Denys V. Baker (London, 1946), p. 189.
13. Claude McKay, 'How Black Sees Green and Red', *Liberator*, June 1921, pp. 20–22.
14. Antonio Gramsci, 'International Political Affairs', *L'Ordinine*, 7 June 1919. I owe this translated reference to Hamish Henderson, School of Scottish Studies, University of Edinburgh.
15. John Maclean, 'Notes', *The Vanguard*, November 1920.
16. Claude McKay, 'Socialism and the Negro', *Workers' Dreadnought*, 31 January 1920.
17. H.S. Ryde, *The Call*, 22 April 1920.
18. T.S. Ashcroft, *Plebs*, May 1920.
19. Claude McKay, *The Negroes in America*. Translated from the Russian by Robert J. Winter and edited by Alan L. McLeod (Port Washington, New York, 1979), pp. 8–9.
20. 'A Letter from Comrade Trotsky to Comrade McKay', *International Press Correspondence*, 13 March 1928.
21. Claude McKay, 'The Racial Question: The Racial Issue in the United States', ibid., 21 November 1922.
22. The Passion of Claude McKay, op. cit., p. 29.
23. Giles, op. cit., pp. 19–20.
24. The Passion of Claude McKay, op. cit., pp. 14–15.
25. Claude McKay, *Home to Harlem* (New York, 1928), p. 135.
26. Ras Makonnen, *Pan-Africanism From Within* (Oxford, 1973), edited Kenneth King, p. 103.
27. James R. Hooker, *Black Revolutionary: George Padmore's Path from Communism to Pan-Africanism* (London, 1967), pp. 19–20.
28. Ibid., p. 8.

29. Cedric J. Robinson, *Black Marxism: The Making of the Black Radical Tradition* (London, 1983), p. 306.
30. David Ivon Jones, 'Communism in South Africa', *Communist Review*, July 1921.
31. The Negro Worker, June 1934.
32. Peter Fryer, *Staying Power: The History of Black People in Britain* (London, 1984), p. 355.
33. C.L.R. James, *A Short History of Negro Revolt* (London, 1938), p. 71.
34. C.L.R. James, *At the Rendezvous of Victory* (London, 1984), p. 255.
35. Ferroccio Gambino, 'Only Connect', *C.L.R. James: His Life and Work*, edited Paul Buhle (London, 1986), p. 195 and p. 199.
36. Norman Leys, *Kenya*, (London, 1926), p. 350.
37. George Padmore, *The Life and Struggles of Negro Toilers* (London, 1931), p. 121.
38. *Daily Worker*, 9 October 1935.
39. *Abyssinia* (International Secretariat of the League against Imperialism (London, N.D., probably 1935), p. 19.
40. J.M. Kenyatta, 'Hands Off Abyssinia', *Labour Monthly*, September 1935.
41. Reginald Reynolds, *My Life and Crimes* (London, 1956), p. 116.
42. John La Guerre, Colonial Intellectuals in Politics: The British and French Experience, Ph.D. thesis, University of Manchester, 1971, p. 435.
43. Fenner Brockway, *Inside the Left* (London, 1942), pp. 326–7.
44. Jeremy Murray-Brown, *Kenyatta* (London, 1972), p. 199.
45. *New Leader*, 17 April 1936 and 5 June 1936.
46. Claude McKay, 'I Believe in the Social Revolution and the Triumph of Workers' Democracy', *Socialist Call*, 17 July 1937.
47. Claude McKay, 'Are the Popular Fronts Suppressing Colonial Independence?', *Crisis*, March 1938.
48. Reginald Bridgeman, 'Africa: A Confused Argument', *Labour Monthly*, September 1937.
49. George Padmore, *How Britain Rules Africa* (London, 1936), p. 395.
50. *The Anti-Slavery and Aborigines' Protection Society* (London, 1938), p. 13; C.L.R. James, 'Sir Stafford Cripps and "Trusteeship"', *International African Opinion*, September 1936.
51. Chris Jones, 'Why the Colonial Workers Oppose Conscription', *New Leader*, 9 June 1939; 'Conference of the African Races', ibid., 14 July 1939.
52. Ibid., 23 August 1941 and George Padmore, 'Imperialists Treat Blacks Like Nazis Treat 'Jews', ibid., 13 September 1941.
53. George Padmore, 'The Time is Now', ibid., 15 November 1941, and *Forward*, May 1942.
54. *New Leader*, 18 April 1942 and George Padmore, 'No Atlantic Charter for Colonies', 24 January 1942.
55. Nigel File and Chris Power, *Black Settlers in Britain, 1555–1958* (London, 1981), pp. 79–81 and Peter O. Esedebe, A History of the Pan-African Movement in Britain, 1900–1948, Ph.D. thesis, University of London, p. 154.
56. George Padmore, 'Chris Jones: Fighter for the Oppressed', *New Leader*, 22 September 1944.
57. Esedebe, op. cit., p. 238 and *League of Coloured Peoples News Letter*, August 1944.
59. Anopheles, 'Black Africa', *Left News*, June 1945 and P.S. Hellicar, 'Home Rule for Black Africa', ibid., August 1945.

60. Dr Kojo-ow Dzifa, 'The Case for African Freedom', *New Leader*, 14 July 1945 and Kojo-ow Dzifa (Gold Coast), 'The Political Psychology of Africans and Europeans', *Left News*, January 1946.
61. Peter Abrahams, 'Big Struggle Begins for African Freedom', *New Leader*, 20 October 1945.
62. Frank A. Ridley, 'Out of Africa', ibid., 15 June 1946 and Peter Abrahams, 'The Great Betrayal', ibid., 20 July 1946.
63. D.K. Fieldhouse, The Colonial Empires (London, 1965); Imanuel Geiss, *The Pan-African Movement* (London, 1974), pp. 403–5; George Padmore, *Pan-Africanism or Communism?* (London, 1956), p. 161.
64. V.G., 'So please put me down for one who would rather hear about "the revolt of the Black Man" or "The Coloured Peoples Struggle" or any other thing than the "Negro Question"', *Socialist Appeal*, 18 May 1940.
65. Peter Abrahams, 'The Colonial Cannot Live on Promises', *New Leader*, 20 April 1946; Murray-Brown, op. cit., p. 222; Margaret Busby, 'C.L.R. James: A Biographical Introduction', in At the Rendezvous of Victory, op. cit., pp. 208–11.
66. Giles, op. cit., p. 39.
67. The Passion of Claude McKay, op. cit., p. 41.
68. Geoffrey Bing, *Reap the Whirlwind: An Account of Kwame Nkrumah's Ghana from 1950 to 1966* (London, 1968), p. 95.
69. Padmore, Pan-Africanism or Communism?, op. cit., p. 300.
70. James, At the Rendezvous of Victory, op. cit., p. 260.
71. Hooker, op. cit., pp. 133–9.
72. Letter from Frank Maitland to the author, 7 July 1982.

Chapter 8: Clara Zetkin and Countess Markievicz: Socialist women

1. For example, Tony Cliff, *Class Struggles and Women's Liberation* (London, 1984), pp. 70–80 and Mike Milotte, *Communism in Modern Ireland* (Dublin, 1984), p. 49.
2. Karen Honeycutt, Clara Zetkin: A Left-Wing Socialist and Feminist in Wilhelmine Germany, Ph.D. thesis, Columbia University, 1975, pp. 26–8.
3. Ibid., pp. 25–34.
4. Ibid., pp. 50–7 and *The Comintern: Historical Hightlights*, edited M.M. Drachkovitch and B. Lanzitch (New York, 1966), p. 310.
5. *Prison Letters of Constance Markievicz. With a New Introduction by Amanda Sebestyen* (London, 1987), pp. 1–2.
6. Ibid., pp. 3–5 and p. xii.
7. Mari Jo Buhle, *Women and American Socialism, 1870–1920* (Chicago, 1981), p. xvii.
8. Shaw Desmond, *Labour: The Giant with the Feet of Clay* (London, 1921), p. 25.
9. Richard J. Evans, *The Feminists* (London, 1977), p. 177.
10. Marion A. Kaplan, *Jewish Feminist Movement in Germany* (Westport, Conn., 1979), p. 69.
11. David Kennedy, *Birth Control in America* (New Haven, 1970), pp. 21–2.
12. Honeycutt, op. cit., p. 464.
13. J. Strain, Feminism and Radicalism in the German Social Democratic

Movement, 1890–1914, Ph.D. thesis, University of California, Berkeley, 1964, pp. 236–40 and Evans, The Feminists, op. cit., p. 177.

14. Prison letters of Constance Markievicz, op. cit., p. xii.
15. Desmond Ryan, James Connolly: His Life Work and Writings (London, 1924), pp. 78–80.
16. W.R. Ryan, The Irish Labour Movement (Dublin, 1919), p. 225.
17. Philip S. Foner, 'Introduction', Clara Zetkin: Selected Writings, edited Philip S. Foner (New York, 1987), p. 39.
18. Ibid., p. 38.
19. Eric Waldman, The Spartacist Uprising of 1919 (Milwaukee, 1958), p. 44 and p. 101.
20. R.M. Fox, James Connolly: The Forerunners (Tralee, 1946), p. 173.
21. Ibid., p. 219 and 'In Memoriam James Connolly', The Plebs, June 1916, p. 117.
22. For conflicting accounts of the significance of the Easter rising, see T.A. Jackson, Ireland Her Own (London, 1946), pp. 378–81 and Frederick J. Gould, Hyndman, Prophet of Socialism (London, 1928), pp. 212–14.
23. Evans, The Feminists, op. cit., p. 182.
24. Emmet Larkin, James Larkin, 1876–1947: Irish Labour Leader (London, 1977), p. 256.
25. Prison Letters of Constance Markievicz, op. cit., pp. 85–9.
26. R.M. Fox, Rebel Irishwomen (Dublin, 1935), p. 32.
27. Quoted in Prison Letters of Constance Markievicz, op. cit., p. 101.
28. Sean O'Faolain, Constance Markievicz (London, 1934), p. 286.
29. Erich Eych, A History of the Weimar Republic (Harvard, 1969), p. 162.
30. Rosa Levine-Meyer, Inside German Communism (London, 1977), passim.
31. Ruth Fischer, Stalin and German Communism (Cambridge, Mass., 1948), p. 419.
32. Ibid., p. 608.
33. Foner, 'Introduction', Clara Zetkin: Selected Writings, op. cit., pp. 38–42.
34. Elizbieta Ettinger, Rosa Luxemburg: A Life (London, 1987), p. 226.
35. Alex de Jonge, The Weimar Chronicle (New York, 1978), p. 217.
36. Ettinger, op. cit., p. 101.
37. Fox, Rebel Irishwomen, op. cit., p. 34.
38. Milotte, Communism in Modern Ireland, op. cit., p. 47.

Chapter 9: Leon Trotsky and C.L.R. James: The socialist fugitives

1. James D. Young, 'A Polish Notebook and Western Socialism', Cencrastus, No. 15, 1984. 'There are Trotskyist influences all over the world. The idea of permanent revolution – of a fight that has always to be carried on against the tendency for societies to divide between privileged and unprivileged – has taken root and has often taken the place of an older and more optimistic Marxism'. Nicholas Mosley, The Assassination of Trotsky (London, 1972), p. 182.
2. C.L.R. James, At the Rendezvous of Victory (London, 1984), p. 204 and C.L.R. James Beyond a Boundary (London, 1963), p. 47.
3. Paul Buhle, C.L.R. James: His Life and Work (Chicago, 1981), p. 2 and

Margaret Busby, 'C.L.R. James: A Biographical Introduction', At the Rendezvous of Victory, op. cit., p. x.

4. Such Trotskyists as Abraham Leon agitated among German troops in occupied Europe during the Second World War. See Ernest Germain, 'A Biographical Sketch of Abraham Leon, in Abraham Leon, *The Jewish Question: A Marxist Interpretation* (Mexico, 1950).

5. James, Beyond a Boundary, op. cit., p. 29.

6. Leon Trotsky, *My Life* (New York, 1930), pp. 504–5.

7. Ibid., p. 167.

8. Ibid., p. 53 and Irving Howe, *Trotsky* (Glasgow, 1978), p. 10.

9. James, Beyond a Boundary, op. cit., pp. 38–9.

10. Victor Serge and Natalia Sedova Trotsky, *The Life and Death of Leon Trotsky* (London, 1973), p. 3.

11. Victor Serge, 'In Memory of Trotsky', *Free Expression*, August 1943.

12. Richard Small, 'The training of an intellectual, the making of a Marxist', C.L.R. James: His Life and Work, edited Paul Buhle, op. cit., pp. 16–17.

13. Margaret Busby, op. cit., p. vii and James, Beyond a Boundary, p. 149 and p. 122.

14. Bertram D. Wolfe, *Three Who Made A Revolution* (New York, 1948), p. 33.

15. Quoted in Mosley, op. cit., p. 180 and Gregory Rigsby, 'The Gospel According to St. James', C.L.R. James: His Life and Work, edited Paul Buhle, op. cit., p. 112.

16. J.R. Johnson (C.L.R. James), 'Trotsky's Place in History', *The New International*, July 1940 and C.L.R. James, *Notes on Dialectics* (London, 1980), especially pp. 30–68.

17. Wolfe, Three Who Made a Revolution, op. cit., p. 35 and Joel Carmichael, *Trotsky, An Appreciation of His Life* (London, 1975), p. 60.

18. Ibid., pp. 59–61.

19. Wolfe, Three Who Made a Revolution, op. cit., p. 36 and quoted in Mosley, op. cit., p. 178.

20. 'C.L.R. James', *Visions of History*, edited Henry Abelove, Betsy Blackmar, Peter Dimock and Jonathan Schneer (New York, 1983), p. 270.

21. C.L.R. James, *The Future in the Present* (London, 1977), p. 11.

22. Isaac Deutscher, *The Prophet Armed: Trotsky, 1879—1921* (London, 1954), p. 90.

23. Leon Trotsky, *Permanent Revolution* (London, 1962), p. 195.

24. Baruch Knei-Paz, *The Social and Political Thought of Leon Trotsky* (Oxford, 1978), p. 127.

25. Robert Wistrich, *Trotsky: Fate of a Revolutionary* (London, 1979), p. 63.

26. Ibid., pp. 65–6.

27. Ibid., p. 74.

28. Trotsky, My Life, op. cit., p. 245.

29. Isaac Deutscher, *The Prophet Unarmed: Trotsky, 1921–1929* (Oxford, 1959), p. 178.

30. Alice Ruhle-Gerstel, 'Memories of Leon Trotsky', *Encounter*, April 1982.

31. Julius Braunthal, *History of the International, 1914–1943* (London, 1967), p. 4.

32. Carmichael, op. cit., p. 185.

33. James, Trotsky's Place in History, op. cit., p. 165 and p. 159.

34. James D. Young, 'Marxism, Liberalism and the Process of Industrialisation', *Survey*, No. 70/71, 1969.

35. Walter Laqueur, *The Fate of the Revolution* (London, 1967), p. 33.
36. James, Beyond a Boundary, op. cit., pp. 25–6.
37. Small, op. cit., p. 18.
38. Ronald Segal, *The Tragedy of Leon Trotsky* (London, 1979), pp. 272–319 and Carmichael, op. cit., p. 305.
39. Arthur Rosenberg, *A History of Bolshevism* (London, 1934), p. 153.
40. *The New International*, July 1938.
41. Leon Trotsky, 'More on the Suppression of Kronstadt', ibid., August 1938. In an interesting and stimulating study of the Kronstadt revolt, Israel Getzler says that 'the veteran politicised Red sailor still predominated in Kronstadt at the end of 1920'. Israel Getzler, *Kronstadt, 1917–1921* (Cambridge, 1983), pp. 205–11.
42. Carmichael, op. cit., p. 449 and John G. Wright, 'Marxism and the Intellectuals', *The New International*, December 1935.
43. Eugene D. Genovese, *From Rebellion to Revolution: Afro-American Slave Revolts in the Making of the New World* (New York, 1981), p. 140.
44. Joseph Carter, 'History of the Communist International', *New International*, February 1938.
45. Earl R. Birne, 'Celine's Journey', *The New International*, July 1934.
46. Howe, op. cit., pp. 127–8.
47. Joseph Carter, 'A New Lenin Book', *The New International*, July 1938.
48. Francis Wyndham and David King, *Trotsky: A Documentary History* (Harmondsworth, 1972), p. 163.
49. Joseph Carter, 'Bureaucratic Collectivism', *The New International*, September, 1941.
50. Howe, op. cit., p. 51 and Deutscher, The Prophet Outcast, op. cit., pp. 438–40.
51. Leon Trotsky, 'The Iron Heel', *The New International*, April 1945.
52. Leon Trotsky, *Black Nationalism and Self-Determination* (New York, 1972), p. 17.
53. Fenner Brockway, *Inside the Left* (London, 1942), p. 326.
54. 'The Independent Labour Party Conference', *New Leader*, 22 April 1936.
55. J.R. Johnson (C.L.R. James), 'The Negro Question', *Socialist Appeal*, 25 August 1939.
56. Trotsky, Black Nationalism and Self-Determination, op. cit., p. 37.
57. Leon Trotsky, *In Defence of Marxism* (New York, 1942), p. 184 and p. 164.
58. G.F. Eckstein, (C.L.R. James), 'Ancestors of the Proletariat', *Fourth International*, September 1949.
59. Trotsky, In Defence of Marxism, op. cit., p. 8.
60. C.L.R. James, *At the Rendezvous of Victory* (London, 1984), pp. 33–4.
61. J.R. Johnson (C.L.R. James), 'Native Son and Revolution', *The New International*, May 1940.
62. C.L.R. James, *The Future in the Present* (London, 1980), p. 89.
63. Gabriel Kolko, *The Politics of War* (New York, 1968), p. 450.
64. Stanley Weir, 'Revolutionary Artist', in C.L.R. James: His Life and Work, edited Paul Buhle, op. cit., p. 88.
65. Quoted in G. Russell and Hugh Branan, *The Italian Revolution* (Glasgow, 1944), p. 28.
66. 'The 28th Anniversary of the Russian Revolution', *Fourth International*, November 1945.
67. Ernest Germain (Ernest Mandel), 'The First Phase of the European

Revolution', ibid., August 1946 and E.R. Frank (Michel Raptis), 'The Kremlin in Eastern Europe', ibid., November 1946.

68. E. Germain (Ernest Mandel), 'The True Testimony of Trotsky', ibid., August 1948 and Michel Pablo (Michel Raptis), 'World Trotskyism Rearms', ibid., November 1951.

69. G.F. Eckstein (C.L.R. James), 'Two Young American Writers', *Fourth International*, March 1950.

70. C.L.R. James, *Mariners, Renegades and Castaways* (New York, 1953), p. 136.

71. Grace C. Lee, Pierre Chaulieu and J.R. Johnson (C.L.R. James), *Facing Reality* (Detroit, 1958), p. 165.

72. C.L.R. James, *Nkrumah and the Ghana Revolution* (London, 1977), p. 15 and Lee, Chaulieu and Johnson, op. cit., p. 89.

73. E.P. Thompson, 'Time, Work-Discipline and Industrial Capitalism', *Past and Present*, No. 38, 1967 and James, Nkrumah and the Ghana Revolution, op. cit., p. 19.

Chapter 10: Leszek Kolakowski and Frantz Fanon: Totalitarian and colonial labyrinths

1. Leszek Kolakowski, *Main Currents of Marxism: The Breakdown* (Oxford, 1981), p. 372.

2. Peter Ceismar, *Fanon: A Biography* (New York, 1971), pp. 1–30.

3. C.L.R. James, *At the Rendezvous of Victory* (London, 1984), p. 231.

4. Max Eastman, 'Motive Patterns of Socialism', *The Modern Quarterly*, Fall 1939.

5. Raya Dunayevskaya, *Philosophy and Revolution* (New York, 1973), p. 315.

6. E.P. Thompson, 'Open Letter to Leszek Kolakowski', *Socialist Register 1973*, edited John Saville and Ralph Miliband (London, 1973).

7. Leszek Kolakowski, 'The Fate of Marxism in Western Europe', *Slavic Review*, June 1970.

8. Kolakowski, Main Current of Marxism: 'The Breakdown, op. cit., pp. 173–5.

9. Dunayevskaya, Philosophy and Marxism, op. cit., p. 248.

10. Kolakowski, Main Currents of Marxism: The Breakdown, op. cit., p. 171.

11. Ibid., p. 173.

12. C. Wright Mills, *The Causes of World War II* (New York, 1958), p. 128.

13. Power, Politics and People: The Collected Essays of C. Wright Mills, edited I. Horowitz (New York, 1967), p. 7.

14. Irving Howe, 'New Styles in "Leftism"', *Dissent*, Summer 1965, pp. 319–23.

15. Peter Worsley, 'Frantz Fanon and the 'Lupenproletariat''', *Socialist Register 1972*, edited John Saville and Ralph Miliband (London, 1972).

16. Kolakowski, Main Current of Marxism: The Breakdown, op. cit., p. 172.

17. Ibid., p. 523.

18. David Caute, *Fanon* (London, 1970), p. 8.

19. James, At the Rendezvous of Victory, op. cit., p. 235.

20. Basil Davidson, 'The African Prospect', *Socialist Register 1970*, edited John Saville and Ralph Miliband (London, 1970), p. 39.

21. Worsley, 'Frantz Fanon and the "Lupenproletariat"', op. cit., p. 198.

22. Caute, Fanon, op. cit., p. 15.

23. Worsley, 'Frantz Fanon and the "Lupenproletariat"', op. cit., p. 196.

24. Quoted in Caute, Fanon, op. cit., p. 48.
25. Worsley, 'Frantz Fanon and the "Lupenproletariat"', op. cit., p. 199.
26. Ibid., p. 197.
27. Ibid., p. 200.
28. G.R. Coulthard, *Race and Colour in Caribbean Literature* (Oxford, 1962), p. 45.
29. Howe, 'New Styles in "Leftism"', op. cit., p. 321.
30. Kolakowski, Main Currents of Marxism: The Breakdown, op. cit., pp. 489–91.
31. Frantz Fanon, *The Wretched of the Earth* (Harmondsworth, 1967), p. 62.
32. Thompson, 'Open Letter to Leszek Kolakowski', op. cit., pp. 20–5.
33. Leszek Kolakowski, 'Intellectuals, Hope and Heresy', *Encounter*, October 1971.
34. Leszek Kolakowski, 'Althusser's Marx', *Socialist Register 1971*, edited John Saville and Ralph Miliband (London, 1971).
35. Thompson, 'Open Letter to Leszek Kolakowski', op. cit., p. 66.
36. Ibid., p. 84 and p. 16.
37. Leszek Kolakowski, 'My Correct Views on Everything', *Socialist Register 1974*, edited John Saville and Ralph Miliband (London, 1974), p. 15.
38. Stanley Aronowitz, *The Crisis in Historical Materialism* (New York, 1981), p. 131.
39. Peter Worsley, *The Three Worlds* (London, 1984), p. 98.
40. James D. Young, *Making Trouble: Autobiographical Explorations and Socialism* (Glasgow, 1987), pp. 56–80.
41. Ernest Mandel, 'Introduction', Leon Trotsky, *The Struggle against Fascism in Germany* (Harmondsworth, 1975), p. xiv.
42. Ernest Mandel, *The Formation of the Economic Thought of Karl Marx* (London, 1977), p. 201.
43. J. Szezepanski, 'The Meaning of Life and the Meaning of Human Affairs', *Dialectics and Humanism*, Vol. III, No. 4, 1980.
44. James D. Young, 'Marxism, Liberalism and the Process of Industrialisation', *Survey*, No. 70/71, 1969.
45. Caute, Fanon, op. cit., p. 94.

Chapter 11: Contemporary Socialism: Tragedies and crises, 1939–86

1. Irving Howe, *Trotsky* (Glasgow, 1978), p. 166.
2. Isaac Deutscher, *The Non-Jewish Jew and Other Essays* (London, 1981), pp. 163–4.
3. Ignazio Silone, *The School for Dictators* (London, 1939), p. 235.
4. Boris Souvarine, 'Comments on the Massacre', *The Comintern: Historical Highlights*, edited M. Drachkovitch and B. Lanzitch (New York, 1966), p. 181.
5. Ernest Mandel, *The Meaning of the Second World War* (London, 1986), p. 34.
6. David A. Shannon, *The Socialist Party of America* (New York, 1955), p. 255.
7. *New York Times*, 31 July 1943.
8. Luisa Passerini, *Fascism in Popular Memory: The Cultural Experience of the Italian Working Class* (Cambridge, 1987), pp. 74–92.
9. 'Revealed: Italy's savage war crimes', *Observer*, 24 January 1988.
10. 'Stand by the Italian Revolution', leaflet in the author's possession.

11. Julius Braunthal, *In Search of the Millennium* (London, 1945), p. 97 and Harry Pollitt, *Answers to Questions* (London, 1945), *passim*.
12. Gabriel Kolko, *The Politics of War* (New York, 1970), p. 31.
13. J.F. Horrabin, '"Realism" and the Future of Europe', *Plebs*, April 1944: 'Manifesto on Italy', ibid., August 1944; Pierto Nenni, 'Socialist-Communist Unity in Italy', *Labour Monthly*, October 1944.
14. Quoted in Basil Davidson, *Special Operations Europe* (London, 1980), p. 17; Ian S. Wood, 'The resistable rise of Mussolini', *The Scotsman*, 30 July 1983; Mandel, op. cit., p. 40.
15. Ygael Gluckstein, *Stalin's Satellites in Europe* (London, 1952), p. 143; Preface by Adam Ciolkosz to *The Flaming Border* by Czeslaw Poznanski (London, 1944), pp. 8–12.
16. Adam Ciolkosz, *The Expropriation of a Socialist Party* (New York, 1946), p. 3, pp. 12–13; R. 'The Fate of Polish Socialism', *Foreign Affairs*. October 1949, p. 140.
17. Mandel, op. cit., p. 44 and p. 42.
18. Hamilton Fyfe, *Britain's Wartime Revolution* (London, 1944), p. 248; Davidson, op. cit., p. 154 and p. 158.
19. Maurice F. Neufeld, *Italy: School for Awakening Countries* (Westport, Conn, 1961), p. 469; Peter Novick, *The Resistance versus Vichy* (New York, 1968), p. 180.
20. Gabriel Kolko, *The Politics of War* (New York, 1970), p. 432.
21. Ibid., p. 438 and p. 450.
22. Mandel, op. cit., p. 158.
23. Ibid., p. 205 and M. Djilas, *Conversations with Stalin* (Harmondsworth, 1963), p. 90.
24. J.F. Horrabin, *The Future of International Socialism* (London, 1943), p. 17.
25. Cedric J. Robinson, *Black Marxism: The Making of the Black Radical Tradition* (London, 1983), p. 259.
26. E.P. Thompson, *The Poverty of Theory* (London, 1978), p. 103.
27. Gluckstein, op. cit., p. 173–82.
28. 'One of the great centres of the Left in Pittsburg from the I.W.W. days on had been the town of East Pittsburg . . . Today it is nothing but superhighways. The people themselves are gone'. 'David Montgomery', *Visions of History*, edited Henry Abelove, Betsy Blackmar and Peter Dimock (New York, 1981), p. 175.
29. Peter Fryer, *The Battle for Socialism* (London, 1959), pp. 79–98.
30. John L. Harper, *America and the Reconstruction of Italy, 1945–1948* (Cambridge, 1986), p. 161.
31. Hubert Ripka, *Czechoslovakia* (London, 1950), p. 291 and p. 270.
32. Chris Harman, *Class Struggles in Eastern Europe* (London, 1983), pp. 38–40.
33. Stefan Brandt, *The East German Rising* (London, 1955), p. 37, p. 30 and p. 64.
34. Raya Dunayevasaya, *Marxism and Freedom* (New York, 1958), p. 251.
35. Ivan Svitak, *Man and His World* (New York, 1968), p. 172.
36. C.L.R. James, *Mariners, Renegades and Castaways* (New York, 1953), p. 136.
37. Tamas Aczel and Tibor Meray, *The Revolt of the Mind* (London, 1960), p. 397 and p. 406.
38. Neal Asherson, *The Polish August: What Has Happened in Poland* (Harmondsworth, 1981), pp. 233–4.
39. Grace C. Lee, Pierre Chaulieu and J.R. Johnson (C.L.R. James), *Facing Reality* (Detroit, 1958), p. 15.

40. Bertram D. Wolfe, *Marxism: 100 Years in the Life of a Doctrine* (London, 1967), pp. 311–14.
41. James C. Durham, *Norman Thomas* (New York, 1956), p. 38.
42. Daniel Guerin, *Negroes on the March* (New York, 1974), p. 38.
43. Albert S. Lindemann, *A History of European Socialism* (Yale, 1985), pp. 340–2.
44. Julius Braunthal, *History of the International: World Socialism, 1943–1968* (London, 1980), p. 349 and 'Moshe Lewin', Visions of History, op. cit., p. 286.
45. Peter Fryer, *Hungarian Tragedy* (London, 1956), p. 7.
46. Braunthal, A History of the International: World Socialism, 1943–1968, op. cit., p. 491.
47. Ras Makonnen, *Pan-Africanism from Within* (Oxford, 1973), pp. 180–183 and George Lavan, 'The Gold Coast Revolution', *Fourth International*, vol. 16, no. 3, 1955.
48. F. Fejto, *Behind the Rape of Hungary* (New York, 1957), p. 328 and p. 331.
49. Lewis Coser and Irving Howe, 'Authoritarians of the "Left"', *Voices of Dissent*, edited Irving Howe (New York, 1958), pp. 88–100.
50. Ivan Svitak, 'The Czech Bureaucratic Collectivist Class', *New Politics*, Vol. XI, No. 2, 1974.
51. *Black Dwarf*, 1 June 1968.
52. David Caute, *Sixty-Eight: The Year of the Barricades* (London, 1988), pp. vii–ix.
53. Angelo Quattrocchi and Tom Nairn, *The Beginning of the End: France, May 1968* (London, 1968), p. 106.
54. J.R. Johnson (C.L.R. James), 'Native Son and Revolution', *The New International*, May 1940.
55. Michel Salomen, *Prague Notebook: Strangled Revolution* (Boston, 1971), p. 307.
56. Vladimir V. Kusin, *The Intellectual Origins of the Prague Spring* (Cambridge, 1971), p. 1.
57. Caute, op. cit., p. ix.
58. H.G. Gutman, 'Introduction' to *Working Lives*, edited by Marc S. Miller (New York, 1980), p. xvii.
59. See the critical discussion of the historiography of the authoritarian 'Left' in James D. Young, 'Nationalism, "Marxism" and Scottish History', *Journal of Contemporary History*, Vol. 20, No. 2, 1985.
60. Tariq Ali, *1968 and After* (London, 1978), pp. 89–90.
61. Neil McInnes, *The Communist Parties of Western Europe* (London, 1975), p. xi, and Amalia Fleming, 'The Romantic Revolt of the Greek Students and Its Bestial Repression', *New Politics*, Vol. XI, No. 1, 1974.
62. James D. Young, *Making Trouble: Autobiographical Explorations and Socialism* (Glasgow, 1987), pp. 112–14.
63. *Revolutionary Rehearsals*, edited Colin Barker (London, 1987), p. 80 and Miles D. Wolpin, 'Some Problems of the Left in Chile', *Socialist Register*, edited Ralph Miliband and John Saville (London, 1969).
64. Richard Clogg, *A Short History of Greece* (Cambridge, 1986), passim: Sheelagh M. Ellwood, *Spanish Fascism in the Franco Era* (London, 1987), passim; Hugo Gil Ferreira and Michael W. Marshall, *Portugal's Revolution Ten Years On* (Cambridge, 1986), *passim*.
65. Walter Laqueur, *Germany Today: A Personal Report* (London, 1985), p. 110.

66. 'Herbert G. Gutman', Visions of History, op. cit., p. 202.
67. Bill Resnick, 'The Right's Prospects', *Socialist Review*, Vol. II, No. 2, 1981.
68. Julius Jacobson, 'Socialism and the Third Camp', *New Politics*, Vol. 1, No. 1, 1986.
69. Joseph Buttinger, *The Twilight of Socialism* (New York, 1953), p. 549.

Index